PRACTICAL MARKETING RESEARCH

AN INTEGRATED GLOBAL PERSPECTIVE

Neil Bruce Holbert
The Chinese University of Hong Kong

Mark W. Speece
EastGate International, Hong Kong

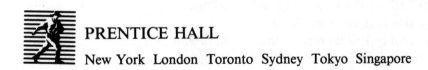

PRENTICE HALL

New York London Toronto Sydney Tokyo Singapore

First published 1993 by
Prentice Hall
Simon & Schuster (Asia) Pte Ltd
Alexandra Distripark
Block 4, #04-31
Pasir Panjang Road
Singapore 0511

Cover photograph: Superstock/APA Photo Agency

Printed in Singapore

1 2 3 4 5   97 96 95 94 93

ISBN 0-13-145954-6

Prentice-Hall International (UK) Limited, *London*
Prentice-Hall of Australia Pty. Limited, *Sydney*
Prentice-Hall Canada Inc., *Toronto*
Prentice-Hall Hispanoamericana, S.A., *Mexico*
Prentice-Hall of India Private Limited, *New Delhi*
Prentice-Hall of Japan, Inc., *Tokyo*
Editora Prentice-Hall do Brasil, Ltda., *Rio de Janeiro*
Prentice-Hall, Inc., *Englewood Cliffs, New Jersey*

Contents

Preface

Many texts have been written about marketing research with academic thoroughness and thoughtfulness. They explain in great detail what marketing research is, and what methods it uses to gather data and process it into information. Books have also been written about marketing research in action. Marketing research provides information so that marketers can come up with solutions to marketing problems that they may have. The two approaches to marketing research, academic and practical, share much, but they differ, too. As one of us has written:

> Academic and business research are sometimes so divergent, it is difficult to believe that they are addressing themselves to the same kind of tasks. The research practitioner, reading works in professional journals, might justifiably wonder what it is he's practicing. Similarly academics viewing the work of commercial researchers often wonder if the latter know (anything about research).... The academic tradition ... [is] characterized by system setting and model building. These are, of course, touchstones of the scientific method, but their use can become ... obsessive ...
>
> Marketing research in business aims first of all at *actionability* ... criterion measures ... action standards ... and the promise of implementability ... The business researcher is not a number gatherer, but ... a member of the marketing team ...
>
> The academic world and way and the business world and way need each other ... [Between them there are] more similarities than differences ... both ... have an overarching regard for objectivity and rationality, and this spirit unites them ...
>
> Each path ... can learn from the other: on the one side, increased interest in rigor, care, and historicity; on the other, increased interest in timeliness, directness, and actionability.[1]

It is in this unity of spirit that this book is conceived. The approach is "postmodern" in outlook. That is, it accepts and welcomes advances in technology (hardware and software), but does not make them a focus. Technology and technique are only the tools of marketing research, used to achieve better marketing usefulness. Marketing research is first and foremost about marketing and the information used in making marketing decisions.

Similarly, our approach accepts and welcomes the globalization of marketing research. But that does not become a focus either. The authors have lived and worked on five continents. They reject the implication that doing surveys anywhere other than in shopping malls in Omaha or Manchester or Sydney is somehow exotic. There are differences in application of such a people-oriented practice anywhere that cultures differ. But this is not exoticism.

The very differences, because they are in details of application, not basic principles, serve to show the universality of the marketing research process. Universally, marketing research aims to get pertinent information to input into the marketing decisions. Universally, marketing research follows the same process. Only the details of implementation differ to fit the specific situation. The "foreign" examples cited here are used to illustrate the universality and challenge of marketing research, not to showcase their strangeness.

We recognize that most readers will not become marketing researchers. Many will, however, commission and use research, and most will be *affected* by its findings: what it did, and maybe could have done better. It is to all such readers that we dedicate this book: to use it, to learn from it, to have fun with it. And, perhaps, to spark an interest in learning more about the world of marketing research and how marketing research can make for better marketing.

PRACTICAL MARKETING RESEARCH

PART I

What *Is* Marketing Research?

Part I explores the philosophy that underlies the very foundations of marketing research.

Chapter 1 underscores a theme running throughout the book: that marketing research is really founded on the "scientific spirit" of free inquiry. But marketing research has also moved beyond its foundations to find its place as an important business tool. Essentially, it has developed out of the rationalist tradition, looking at a problem, seeking how to attack it, and then assaying answers as they may fall out, without fear or favor. But it never loses sight of the fact that it is *marketing*, as well as *research*.

Chapter 2 then looks at the five interlocking, but often "warring", parts of research: as a business (and as a business tool); as art; as science; as integration-of-intelligence; and as a craft whose tools need to be mastered, but which must never master the researcher.

Marketing Research: Nature, Unity, Diversity, and Blend

There is no greater problem in marketing research than simply trying to understand what it is really all about. Marketing research has acquired a certain mystique which can obscure understanding of what it is and what it does. Views on marketing research sometimes even become quite silly. Some marketing researchers (not good ones) may believe that no decision should ever be made without precise, painstaking, complex analyses of mountains of data, reported in dry, statistical jargon, supported by masses of tables, graphs, and charts. Some marketing managers may believe that no decision can ever be helped by the irrelevant statistical treatises churned out (always months late) by scholarly researchers who have no understanding of real world marketing practice.

Such views (either kind) may be based on exposure to bad marketing research, but they show a complete lack of understanding about what marketing research really is. Once the mystique and silliness have been stripped away, it can be clearly seen that marketing research simply involves the *melding of facts and ideas to foster profitable marketing decisions*.

The American Marketing Association has wrestled with a definition too, like everyone else. The one they came up with is:

> [Marketing research is] the function which links the consumer, customer, and public to the marketer through information — information used to identify and define marketing opportunities and problems; generate, refine, and evaluate marketing actions; monitor marketing performance; and improve understanding of the marketing process. [It] specifies the information required to address these issues; designs the method for collecting information; manages and implements the data collection process; analyzes the results; and communicates the findings and their implications.[1]

This serves as a good starting point, and we will offer below a variation of our own that may be used very directly to follow the process.

The best way to illustrate a definition of marketing research is to show how it works in action. Throughout this book we will be looking at several examples of things that researchers grapple with, so that various stages of the marketing research process can be examined in their natural context: marketing management. Without close attention to *marketing*, marketing research can indeed become irrelevant nonsense.

So let's look at a first problem and see where marketing research fits in. We will take the viewpoint of the marketing manager. Should we consider marketing a home computer that is designed for people who neither like nor understand computers (to say nothing of mathematics or complex machines of any kind)? These kinds of people may be nervous around sophisticated machinery, afraid of advanced technology, terrified of higher mathematics.

We are convinced that there are many substantial things a home computer can do for people, whether they realize it or not. We would like to come out with one so simple that "even an adult" can use it. Even people with severe computerphobia will find it useful, practical, and even pleasurable.

Could such a product really sell and become a profitable addition to the product line? Or would introducing it just be another stab at a market that never really materialized, a waste of company resources? This is a difficult decision for the marketing manager. (It is also a *typical* decision that many have to face all the time.) What can marketing research do to help the marketing manager make the right decision? How can it help the marketing manager blend available technology together with an understanding of what people want, what they really need, (and *which* people want and need it)? Matching technology to market desires like this is the essence of coming up with successful products that fill real needs and become profitable to the company.

THE NATURE OF MARKETING RESEARCH

The marketing manager here is clearly not interested in numbers, formulas, statistics, or complex analyses. They will not help him solve the problem. For market research is not about numbers, formulas, statistics, or computers. It *is* about ideas and profits.

Of course, we may rely upon such things as statistics and models in conducting marketing research. But they are used only to help us grope with ideas and to assist in the decision-making process. It is absolutely essential to understand this. We can only proceed to look at what market research *really* is after we get away from the widespread, but terribly false, notion that marketing research is mainly about "number crunching".

And so to our problem of the essential nature of marketing research.

- Marketing research is an organized, objective, and universal approach to gathering marketing data. Often, but not necessarily, this data will be in the form of numbers. This information, when tabulated, analyzed, interpreted, and reported, can help the marketing manager — now or later — make better-informed and lower-risk marketing decisions. Thus, marketing research is about getting and using information to solve problems.

Let's look at each of the elements in our definition right now. They will all be discussed again later on, but it is essential that we understand the essence of these elements before we can even begin to understand how marketing research fits into the firm's marketing operations. Far too much poor marketing research is done because people doing it do not really understand what it is.

Organized.   There is a beginning, a middle, and an end to every research investigation. We must not jump into a project and immediately write a questionnaire, ask questions, and then try to figure out what we want to do with the data we come up with. It is tempting here to do just that: Do you own a computer? If not, why not? What would you like in a computer? What could you do better if you had a computer?

Of course, these things might be necessary at a later stage in the project, and we might very well end up asking just such questions. But it is hard to know exactly *what* will be necessary later if we are not organized in addressing the problem and deciding what to do.

Instead, the marketing researcher must follow a disciplined approach — a sequence of steps that will logically lead him into the correct methods to use (as in Chapters 3–9). And the key to the sequence is a firm understanding of why we are doing the project at all, what use it will be, and what decisions we can make (or make better) by *having* our findings, as opposed to *not* having them.

Objective.   Marketing research must never look for a specific answer, in order to please whoever asked us to do it, or for any other reason. We usually have a hypothesis ("hunch") before we start — either in quantitative terms, or just notions about how things may be. But our only goal is to find out whether that hunch is right or wrong (or neither or both). The market researcher cannot set out to "prove" the hunch.

Marketing researchers, and the marketing managers they are doing projects for, are as much "people" as anybody, and they have "feelings". But these feelings ("there's *got* to be a market for our simple home computer out there") must never get in the way of an objective, dispassionate, unbiased gathering and presentation of the information. There may well be a good market. But it may be that there is no market for home computers at all beyond their current uses: glorified typewriters or mini-video arcades. If the "correct" answer has already been determined before the research is done, there is absolutely no reason to do the research at all.

Universal.   Marketing research is done around the world, not only in developed nations, but also in developing and underdeveloped ones as well. It is done not only where national telephone probability samples are available to us, but also where roads to the nearest settlement may not be paved, or may not even exist. Obviously, different places will demand different approaches to sampling, different methods of data collection, different sensitivity to notions of privacy, and so forth.

Nevertheless, the principles of research investigation remain exactly the same in a First World or in a Fourth World country. Only the implementation of these principles must change to fit the situation. These principles, starting with the basic one that we are seeking input to help make better marketing decisions, are indeed universal, and override particulars of place. We must know where we are working and what the limits are, but we must never be drawn away from the basic goal of our quest: gaining information and ideas for marketing decisions.

This dichotomy between universal principles and specific implementation is exactly the same as in marketing management. Whether we peddle a new soft drink to poor people in a Fourth World country, market cosmetics in Newly Industrializing Countries to the newly affluent middle class, or sell home computers to highly educated people in the industrialized West, marketing principles remain unchanged. The product must satisfy some need, provide some benefit, or people will not buy it. Its cost must be consistent with the value they see in it. We must make people aware of the product and its advantages to them, and it must be distributed so that people can buy it conveniently. To figure out whether our product does all these things, we must penetrate the minds of customers to find out what they think of what we are offering.

In short, marketing research entails universal principles; but very particular implementation, depending on who we market to. To adjust the marketing mix to people in any particular market, the marketing manager must penetrate their minds, find out how they think and how they do things. This is what marketing research does.

Marketing data.   Marketing research is first of all about marketing, and only second-arily about research. Its entire purpose is to help marketing managers make decisions about marketing strategy or tactics. Thus, marketing research may share many ideas and methodologies with academic research (see, for example, Chapter 2), but it is not concerned with developing new theoretical principles or incremental ideas. The scientists and futurists in the company may have some useful things to say, but ultimately the marketing manager must sell computers to people. Selling computers is a *marketing* job, not a theoretical construct.

Of course, new principles or ideas may be generated from the very pragmatic work market researchers do, but we do not undertake research for this reason. Marketing research which is only "academic" or "interesting" is not likely to be something that a marketing manager wants or needs, because it is not likely to be very useful to him. Academic research is seldom concerned with the very specific problems which an individual marketing manager faces.

Finally, we should be very clear about *what* marketing data we are talking about: *any* data relevant to *any* marketing situation are marketing data. The marketing situation may be a *consumer goods* market, with familiar products such as soap, tooth-paste, breakfast cereals, or automobiles. It may be the market for *consumer services*, such as banking, airlines, or retailing. Marketing research is equally important in markets for *industrial goods and services*; such as supplying plastic tube packages to a toothpaste manufacturer, selling tires to one of the major automobile manufacturers, supplying airplanes to an airline, providing marketing research services to a bank that wants to understand its customers better.

Marketing situations can also include *governments*, which supply services to customers (taxpayers). Maybe the government wants to find out people's attitudes towards pollution, or what they think of current social issues such as family planning. Marketing situations even include *non-profit marketers*. What are people's attitudes towards giving blood, or toward supporting local cultural institutions? Marketing is going on in all of these situations, and in any other case where some person or organization supplies any product or service to someone else. Thus, marketing research can be profitably used in all of these cases to gather actionable marketing data which will help managers make their decisions.

Note also that marketing managers no longer (some of them never did) limit their interests to their domestic (home) market only. Korean exporters may well think that the most vital data of all is not what Koreans think, but how Americans view Korean products. For American companies, the key issue of the day might well be what Japanese consumers really want in the products they buy, and where US products can fit into these wants. In such international marketing research, there may even be a much wider definition of what exactly is marketing data. To Americans, understanding Japanese cultural values can be as critical as knowing what they think of specific products.

In the form of numbers.   Usually we do express our findings in terms of numbers. When we do "quantitative" research, indeed, the basic belief is that hundreds, or even thousands of interviews can be combined to produce the familiar tables and charts that we have come to think of as "research". These tables and charts help us make sense of patterns among such large numbers of respondents. The marketing manager may well end up with some numbers about attitudes toward computers in the home.

Yet in "qualitative" research, it's not *numbers* we are looking for. Rather, we desire *ideas*. These ideas can be derived from detailed discussions with small groups of people, or even from a series of in-depth interviews, each involving one person only. Such non-numeric findings can be the best (if not the only) way to research issues that are "soft", "fuzzy", "feely", and charged with emotion and overtones. We may well end up with numbers to analyze in our research on selling home computers to "computerphobes", but it may be very critical to explore the nebulous concept of "computerphobia" first.

Tabulated.   The marketing manager will not find useful hundreds or thousands of individual interviews in a quantitative study that have not been tabulated (literally "made into tables"). Nor will dozens of qualitative "interviews", such as those just mentioned, be particularly useful. Of course, the marketing manager can have each individual interview if he wishes, and actually some individuals may give quite detailed responses, quotes, etc., which can be very valuable as marketing strategies and tactics are developed.

But marketing managers are most often interested in *patterns* of data among groups of people — markets — rather than in how individuals respond. Usually only tabulated results are of interest, especially in dealing with quantitative information. It is this necessity for tabulations, in simple or complex forms, which has led to the mistaken idea that marketing research is about numbers, formulas, and computer analysis. The numbers, formulas, and computer analyses are tools and means to the ends of understanding markets. They are not the ends in themselves.

Analyzed.   As we will show in Chapter 8, the analysis of our data (whether in the form of numbers or not) should be thought out at the beginning of the project, before we start, and not after we gather our data. Once the problem is well defined, it is not difficult to determine what kind of data will shed light on it, and it is easy to anticipate how that data should be reported so that it will be clear.

This means we can draw up most of the tables we just mentioned *before* we ever actually gather any data. Many students and clients invariably ask: "How can you draw up the final tables before you have done the study?" We invariably answer: "How can you do the study before you have drawn up the final tables?" That is, the market researcher must know where he is going before he starts the journey. Of course, these initial tables are just a format; they do not have the actual numbers in them.

Once the data are in, it is a simple process of filling in the blanks in tables formatted beforehand. Of course, further ideas (and tables) may be developed when we get the print-outs and "let the numbers talk to us". But most of the final tables will be drawn up before we begin the survey itself. We should know what variables we will want to look at in identifying potential users of our home computers: variables such as age, sex, education, etc., combined with the desire to save time and effort in certain kinds of tasks, for example.

Interpreted.   Analysis does not, however, end once numbers fill up the spaces in the tables. A discussion of results involves much more than just presenting a table, or repeating a whole table full of numbers, or stating that a t-test resulted in a t-value of 2.47. Analysis includes talking about *patterns* in the data, about what the results *imply*. Even more, it is about making decisions based on what the data tells us about our marketing problem. When a marketing researcher says "I don't really know enough about the marketing background of this project to make recommendations", we say: "If that's true, then you should never have begun the project in the first place. You should know a mouse from a modem before you start research on computer markets, even though you may not be very technically inclined".

Certainly there must be a clear demarcation in the report between the *data* (these should be unobjectionable to everybody) and the *interpretation* of the data, which leads to recommendations. And certainly it is not necessary that the marketing manager agree with the researcher's interpretation or with his recommendations (Chapter 9). After all, it is the marketing manager's responsibility to make marketing decisions.

But the researcher is part of the marketing team, and he is the part with the most detailed knowledge about how the market views this situation. Providing complete information for marketing decisions necessarily includes interpretation and recommendations, and is a vital part of the job of any marketing researcher.

Reported. Finally, analysis involves presenting this discussion of data in plain language, which anyone, even if they know absolutely nothing about statistics or formulas, can understand. This is done both in written reports and in oral presentations, perhaps through several different versions of each kind of report. It does not matter how well the project is executed or how accurate and timely the information, it is completely worthless if it is not used. And it will not be used if the managers who hear the presentations and read the report do not understand what the researcher is saying.

Far too often, reporting is one of the weakest points in the ability of marketing researchers. Historically, the stereotypical researcher has been seen as a shy, inarticulate gatherer of facts who did not want to become involved in the rough-and-tumble of day-to-day marketing affairs. Unfortunately, too often the stereotype has been correct. In an age of shorter product life-cycles, shrinking margins, and leaner organizations, this simply will not do. The modern researcher must be well trained in communication skills, as well as research methodology and statistics.

Marketing manager and marketing decisions. The marketing mix is a vast and interwoven fabric. It consists of the *P*'s of *micromarketing*, those things that we call "controllable variables". We like to talk about a lot of *P*'s, not just the four *P*'s, but they are still the traditional domain of the marketing manager, like the *product* itself, its *premise* (concept) and *promise* as expressed in its *proposition* (i.e., product benefit issues), its *package* (including name and logo), and its *positioning*. Other traditional *P*'s include the *price*, *place* (channels of distribution and where the product can be bought), and *promotion* (advertising, public relations and publicity, personal selling, and sales promotion).

But there are also the *C*'s of *macromarketing*, the so-called "uncontrollable" variables (*change, competition, culture, challenge,* etc.), and the *M*'s (the executional elements, like the *market* target, the *message*, the *media*, the *money* (budget), etc.). All these (and more) must be considered by the marketing manager as he seeks to figure out where he has been, where he is, and where he wants to go. And it is the responsibility of the marketing researcher to be aware of all of these elements just as much as he must be aware of his own ever-changing craft (Chapter 2).

The researcher must be bilingual, able to speak the language of marketing management to the marketing manager, not the language of marketing research. Unless he can talk about marketing management comfortably, he will never be able to help the marketing manager make better decisions. Research input should not be a "crutch" or a "substitute" for the marketing manager's judgment, but it should play a large part in informing that judgment as it seeks to make marketing decisions.

DIVERSITY AND BLEND

Marketing research, as we have said, faces the same challenges and demands the same skills no matter where or how it is practiced. The basic concepts are exactly the same whether one is gathering data on packaged consumer products in the US, on attitudes toward use of hybrid seed in Sudan, or information to help sell home computers. Market research must translate understood marketing decision needs into projects. The projects (usually, but not always, involving questions — Chapters 6 and 7) must seek out the relevant and must generate answers that respond to those decision needs.

Further, marketing research seeks not only to answer questions, but also to question answers. It constantly raises new relevant issues that future research can address. It tests commonly held assumptions, and even explores "corporate *certainties*" that may turn out to be "corporate *myths*". Marketing research takes directly from "scientific method" the notion that research may have a clear beginning, but can have no clear end. Unlike religion, which offers "certainty without proof", research offers only "proof without certainty".

Even if we detect an unmet need for a home computer to do things we may discover are not being done now, we must open our minds to the possibility that new developments (hopefully by our company and not by the competition) could render our findings obsolete very soon. That should not happen, but it can happen, and does happen.

Beneath the unity of research approaches lurks diversity. The relevant skills necessary to ferret out potentially viable advertising themes (Chapter 15) may be very different from those necessary to find the most appropriate statistical methodology to express relationships between sets of "hard" data (Chapter 8). Indeed, the required skills of marketing research are almost endless. Researchers must not only know how to handle people (Chapter 2), but also how to come to grips with a variety of professional tasks.

It is common (and expected) that often individual researchers are not expert in one or more of these tasks, and it is common to call in specialists who can help out. Of course, such specialists can always be consulted, with the end of looking for helpful marketing insights, and not just for technical flourishes.

Beyond diversity even, there are basic elements in the nature of the research process that often appear to be (and are) contradictory to each other. The diverse set of skills required of marketing researchers come from a wide variety of disciplines and traditions, many of which are usually considered completely different in philosophy and approach. The nature of the research process is, in fact, five-fold, and may be thought of as an acronym: B-A-S-I-C.

B is the *Business* side of the industry — it is about selling goods or services at a profit. In some organizations such as government or non-profits, it is about providing goods or services in order to achieve some other objective.

A stands for the *Art* — the creativity that is a vital part of successful research.

S is the heritage from *Science* that is part and parcel of marketing research too: the discipline that derives from the use of Scientific Method.

I is about *Integrating intelligence*, which really is the heart of marketing research: gathering together a million strands that must be woven into a whole piece that is interpretable and useful.

C is the *Craft*, the tools that the researcher brings to the job of doing actionable research.

Each of these elements will be discussed in detail in Chapter 2. Here, we only need to note that these B-A-S-I-C ideas must be blended together seamlessly to move the research process along, and this blending itself requires skills in all five of the areas. Even deciding what is best within the scientific realm of methodology and technology entails art *and* craft. In other words, the researcher must perform a successful juggling act. He must avoid being run over by methodology or technology gone wild, but still must use them well, all the while keeping in mind that "numbers move mountains, but ideas move men".

Thus, our search (or rather, research) into the possibility of developing a major market for home computers will involve a blend of all the things this chapter has begun to set out. We need ideas combined with hard facts, with perhaps a little visionary thinking too. These ideas and facts emerge from the application of a multitude of skills and methodologies. The end result allows the marketing manager to see what *is* out there in the market and to imagine what *could* be there.

2

What's It *B-A-S-I-C*-ally All About?

As we saw in Chapter 1, marketing research is not made up of one single thing. Rather, it is made up of *five* diverse elements which must work together if the project is to succeed. The simplistic (even simple-minded) picture of marketing research as data collection and number crunching is dangerous to the health of the marketing research field and to the success of the marketing researcher. It is the notion of decision making for increased profitability that must dominate, and this can only come from a subtle blending of elements. That B-A-S-I-C-ally is what it's all about!

THE FIVE FINGERS

The five B-A-S-I-C marketing research elements do not always *want* to work together, but to make the marketing research project work, we must *make* them work together. They must *interweave*, that is, weave in and out of each other to form a pattern, as the individual threads would in a textile. Then the elements must *interlock*, hold together and keep marching in step rather than wildly going each their own way. And finally, there must be *synergy*. The whole must be greater than the sum of the parts, just as the five fingers on the hand form a useful thing (a hand) that is much more than just a pinky, ring finger, middle finger, index finger, and thumb all twiddling around by themselves. To put it another way, one plus one must equal more than two; at least three, but preferably five, ten, or some even larger number.

To repeat, the five B-A-S-I-C elements that combine to make up marketing research are:

- Business
- Art
- Science
- Integration-of-intelligence
- Craft

The *Business* side of research is not only the huge research industry itself, but, of course, the business of the client, who must sell goods or services at a profit. Marketing research helps insure that the organization makes what it can sell, rather than trying to sell what it decides to make. It focuses very clearly on *marketing*, which is what will make or break the client's business.

Research is also an *Art*, because so many parts of the research process call for judgment and interpretation. There are no hard and fast rules for many things. As an art, creativity and innovation are encouraged, and the researcher can make his voice heard and his "fingerprints" (or "signature") apparent.

Marketing research uses ideas borrowed from "scientific method", and thus is, in some sense, a *Science*. Not all research is art: some parts of the process require strict attention to (but not obsession with) proper approaches, proper methodologies. This is vital if the (quantitative) information gathered in a project is to be valid.

Research seeks to *Integrate intelligence* in a way that lets marketing managers see a lot in a little time and space to help them make profitable decisions. This timely gathering of data, integration of knowledge, and dissemination of marketing information is at the core of understanding the market. Marketing research is one of the key instruments through which the "marketing concept" is carried out.

As in most industries, marketing researchers must learn the tools of the trade. The *Craft* of the researcher is a diverse set of methodologies (tools) necessary for dealing with the wide variety of kinds of information and types of marketing situations that research must address. Let's look at each element in turn.

BUSINESS

Marketing research is a business in two very different, but related senses. It is a big business, a major industry of its own, employing large numbers of people and serving a whole range of clients: manufacturers, service companies, and governments. It also is a vital contributor to the business success of its clients, whose ultimate task is always to make money (and *stay* in business) by satisfying their markets.

The *marketing research business* consists of probably well over 1000 companies in the United States alone whose major service is providing marketing research to clients. Their total revenues amount to well over US$2 billion.[1] There are big marketing research companies, with thousands of employees, and there are small ones, with just one or two. There are specialists, who work only on the auto industry or the computer industry, and there are generalists, who do survey research projects on any topic. There are local, national, and even international companies. In fact, one-third of the total revenues of US marketing research companies is derived from work done outside of the US. On a worldwide basis, total marketing research expenditures for 1990 are estimated at US$6.7 billion.[2] These expenditures are broken down in Table 2.1.

Research is everywhere. One issue of a research company's newsletter a few years back contained a feature article on setting up a new national probability sample

Table 2.1. **Worldwide expenditure on marketing research.**[2]

		US$	%
EUROPE		3.1 bn	46 (European Community: 42)
France	0.7 bn		
UK	0.7 bn		
Germany	0.6 bn		
US		2.4 bn	36
JAPAN		0.4 bn	7
REST OF THE WORLD		0.8 bn	11
TOTAL		6.7 bn	100

in Malaysia: "... based on the detailed demographic characteristics of about 1000 mukims, that is subdistricts, [and] subdividing [them] to obtain second stage sampling units ... of kampungs [villages] in rural areas ..." Another article in that issue even talked about developing probability sampling methods in Papua New Guinea, including the capital, Port Moresby, the coastal areas, and the highlands.[3] A recent issue of another company's newsletter had a story about a seminar on opportunities for South Korea businessmen to research the China market. A second story was about marketing research in Indonesia on the dangers of dehydration, which led to corrective measures by health organizations in that country.[4]

Research may indeed be everywhere, and is more or less possible everywhere. Still,

> a researcher's life in some of the less developed countries ... is not always ... easy. In Indonesia ... research is arduous, says MBL's Jim Boyce. "The electricity system cannot meet demand and there is only a one in four chance of making a successful telephone call. We don't have primary statistics ... so the survey base is approximate. You have to be careful what you promise the client in terms of accuracy."[5]

Marketing Research for Business

There are an infinite number of ways to conduct marketing research, countless methodologies. A multitude of techniques for gathering data and for analyzing it are available to the researcher. But none of them mean anything unless they are put to the service of business. Marketers (once again) must make profits, and can only do this by satisfying their markets, whether they are dealing with established products that are doing well, established products that need to be revitalized, new products, or whatever else.

And satisfying markets requires understanding them. In trying to market our home computer for "computerphobes", the marketing manager will have to understand the vast majority of us who are not super-literate in computers. Business sense tells us that these "ordinary folks" are exactly the kinds of people we will have to listen to if we target this market segment. Marketers may have enough difficulty trying to get software jocks, hardware engineers, and other such technical types to descend from their technical clouds to think like "ordinary folks". They will have to pound some business sense into these technical product development people. Marketing managers should not also have to pound business sense into researchers, to convince them that *marketing* really does belong with *research* in marketing research.

All of the research applications and techniques we will discuss in this book, then, must work *toward a business end*. They must stimulate thinking which leads to decisions that will enhance profitability. How can *marketing* and *research* fit together to do this? Research can help make better decisions at any stage of the marketing process, from planning marketing strategies, to implementing the marketing plan, to monitoring and controlling the marketing process once it is implemented.

For example, just in planning marketing strategy, the manager may want information to:

- assess strengths
- expose weaknesses
- identify opportunities
- point out threats
- clarify problems
- challenge unsubstantiated preconceptions ("myths")
- look into the future in terms of ideas and numbers

Marketing research can get information on all of these things, in fact, on just about anything in the firm's external environment. (Of course, the cost of getting some information may be more than the marketing manager wants to pay, but that is a different issue.) This external orientation is essential. Marketing research is one of the major links between the business and its environment, and as such, is vital to successful application of the marketing concept. Without information about the environment flowing into the firm, it is difficult to have an environmental orientation. (The marketing concept is broader than just customer orientation, because more things out there than only customers can affect how we must market.)

Marketing research demonstrates by its very definition that the business *must* seek to look inward, outward, forward, backward, and every which way to gather news about what is going on, to build on old ideas, to discard useless ones, and to generally get its head out of the sand. It is hardly believable that:

> for years, U.S. automobile manufacturers failed to heed signs of changing consumer preferences and continued to regard foreign car companies as marginal competitors.[6]

Yet, it happened. And the failure to see what was going on all around them eventually cost these US companies billions of dollars in lost sales, as customers shifted to Japanese cars.

What went wrong? Maybe no marketing research at all was done. Maybe some was done, but clearly, if it was, the companies were not doing *good* marketing research. Maybe the research done gathered the wrong information. Perhaps researchers were unable to effectively communicate to management. Maybe too much pseudo-research was done. Possibly managers simply ignored the information coming in. This is all *bad* research.

Whatever went wrong, this sort of astonishing but well-documented occurrence only confirms how much research *can* do if it wills itself to do it, and then management *lets* it do it. Research can be used in *any* of the stages in developing profitable marketing.

Mission.   The company may wish to know if its very reason for being, its philosophical underpinning, is clear and believable, both to intended audiences outside and to people in the company itself. If such information is important, ongoing work in the area of corporate image is indicated. This type of research might include using both brainstorming and a constant (even obsessive) program of "environmental scanning" — both in the domestic and international spheres — to see what is going on and how it is changing in the world around us.

Scenario.   Scenarios or "what-ifs" should be included in every company's planning tools as creative workshops featuring free-flowing futurism, market modeling, simulations, and orderly forecasting (both heavily quantitative and heavily imaginative). Such methods are used to conjure up ideas about possible tomorrows and ideas on what we can do about them. It is here that we begin concept (idea) generation and testing, and work on the new products that flow from them.

Strategy.   What do we want to be and do, especially in the areas of long-term planning and proactive competitive moves? Broad-ranging market studies are especially germane here. Such studies might investigate what kinds of people buy our products, what kind do not, who buys competing products, which can all be used in making decisions on targeting specific segments.

Tactics.   Most of our efforts in marketing research take place at this stage: carrying out the projects and programs that have been sketched in and then fleshed out in the above three stages. Here we test product: which bundle of features is likely to be most successful. We determine what variation of packaging is most acceptable to consumers, what kinds of images brand names evoke, how memorable (or forgettable) a logo is. Advertising copy is tested, we determine who exactly responds to a coupon offer — are we gaining trial from new users, or are our old customers simply saving money on what they would buy anyway? What kinds of stores would people visit if they wanted the kind of product we offer? Do we have mainly price-sensitive (and brand disloyal) customers, or are they oriented toward quality or value? Marketing research can help enormously with any of the traditional four *P*'s of marketing tactics.

Monitoring and control.   Once we actually implement our marketing (i.e., we are actually selling the product), marketing research is used to keep track of how we are doing. We can measure whether we have achieved the brand awareness needed to build sales of a new product. We can determine whether store traffic increased during our big promotion. There is actually almost no end to how market research can be used to enhance our marketing efforts.

This book covers a wide variety of marketing situations that marketing research can address, and a wide variety of ways to do marketing research. The slant is always toward solving marketing questions toward the end of increasing profitability and assuring the company's permanence on the marketing scene.

Marketing research can, and must, serve the broad needs of the business by using its objective (dispassionate) approach with skill and enthusiasm, working with all the involved people in the organization. This is not always an easy task. Many of these people have strong interests in proving themselves right, and they will make every effort to discredit the finest research if it does not come up with answers that they would like to see. In other words, they would prefer pseudo-research. So part of doing good research, work which contributes to marketing profitability, depends not only on professional skills, but also on the researcher's courage in standing up for what he believes has to be done.

If he is a staff person (and most marketing research people are) in an organization where the corporate culture downplays analysis and sensitivity, and stresses toughness and directness, then the marketing researcher must himself become tough and direct. But he has to do this without sacrificing objectivity. At the very least, the researcher must acknowledge that he must learn the marketer's language in the quest for profits. The company is not in the research business; it is in the business of making money by satisfying the market.

Thus a good marketing researcher must learn to be a good businessman. Our home computers for "computerphobes" will not succeed if the marketing manager ignores the warnings that research has raised about (perhaps) limited potential, and about product ideas that lack real appeal. But if the manager does ignore the outcomes of his research, responsibility lies at least partially with the researcher. He has failed to convince the manager that he should listen to objective findings. Marketing will neither succeed if the researcher cares so much about fine-tuning the questionnaire that the data needed for the decision are available three weeks after the decision must be made. Marketing is poorly served if data are presented in such a bewildering, and needlessly technical way that nobody can understand, or even bothers to try to understand the data. The ability to manage people well, to organize time appropriately to meet deadlines, to communicate effectively are all marks of top managers. They are also the marks of top researchers.

Most of all, marketing tools and how they are used need to evolve. As a tool for business, marketing research will die if it does not constructively evolve, as all living things must. There is evidence that it *is* evolving. Citing a survey among marketing research directors, Ashcraft observed:

> that in a business environment of severe, sometimes global, competition, and mergers, and acquisitions, advice from researchers is needed to maintain a competitive edge, to evaluate and extend brand names, and to provide input on acquisition candidates.

We also found more marketing research director interaction with corporate CEOs, including participation in corporate strategy and planning. Many of the comments in the survey center around research changing from a support group function to being fully integrated into strategic planning. Respondents commented that top management relies on them more for consulting, particularly during troubled economic conditions. One research director put it quite well: he said he had moved from being an information source to being a decision source. These comments cut across industry and company size.[7]

ART

Marketing research as *art* requires creativity and innovation, which must be encouraged so long as they do not clash with the basic task of aiding decision making. A step-by-step scheme detailing exactly how to proceed, a "magic formula" telling one exactly what to do, does not exist for the *art* facet of research. The researcher who cannot come up with ideas about what to do in a situation which is *not* exactly like a hundred previously studied situations will not last long in this business.

Of course, creativity, here as elsewhere in business, is not something wild and undisciplined. Rather, it is something that the researcher should be thinking about all the time. The creative process goes something like the steps listed below.

Preparation. The researcher needs to always think about ways to get better information and about better ways to get information. Could we gain more depth of understanding if we changed the way we do the focus interviews? Could we reduce sampling error by adapting our random sampling method? Better ways of getting information would focus on how to do the research faster, or cheaper. Can we improve the *mechanistic* side with better control of interviewing, quicker data transmission, faster analysis techniques? How about improving the *humanistic* side? Should we find more research companies to work with to broaden our thinking? Maybe we should collaborate with fewer, different ones, to overcome the comfortable feeling of working only with long-term contractors whose ideas are becoming stale.

Saturation. The researcher needs to read everything, talk to everybody, and leave no source of new input unexplored. Researchers have to keep abreast of their profession, of current research trends and developments. They must also be knowledgeable about the products and industries on which they do most of their research. And they need to know about current marketing practices and advances in marketing if they are going to be *marketing* researchers. Basically, they should know everything about everything.

Incubation. The researcher needs to let things "stew" and "brew" and "slosh around" in the back of the mind, even as he attends to the everyday execution of the job of doing research. True creativity often involves leaps in understanding after we reach the limits of how far we can take ideas through consciously working them through. The leaps come when we put aside conscious consideration of the problem, and let it bounce around in the subconscious for a while.

Illumination.   The researcher needs to take advantage of that glorious moment of revelation when his untrammeled but controlled paths of thinking suggest a new solution. This moment of illumination never offers a final solution. It does, however, offer or lead the way to a new approach to his overall work or a breakthrough in how to design the project he is working on right now. Perhaps in the "computerphobe" market, where he is having trouble really understanding computerphobia, the new approach might involve putting a prototype computer in the respondent's home and letting the researcher live in the house for a while!

This might be a good way to see what could or could not be done with the computer, particularly if the respondent has never used a computer before. It would be quite clever if it worked, and certainly should not be dismissed out-of-hand just because this kind of anthropological approach had never been used before for this kind of marketing situation. The idea should be developed and then evaluated along with the other alternatives for getting the information.

Accommodation.   The new research idea should be evaluated the same way any other business decision should be evaluated: will it work at a cost that is in line with the benefits of doing it. It must be made to suit the context of our business set-up (accommodation); considering time feasibility, cost feasibility, and "fit" with the corporate culture. Handling people who may have to authorize implementation of our new thinking — accommodation to the organization — is surely another "art", one in which many researchers often do not do as well as they should.

Qualitative research (Chapters 4 and 6) is an area where the researcher's "art" especially comes into play. There are many diverse qualitative research techniques. But all are designed to explore, examine, and seek out relevant ideas, rather than to offer definitive answers (more the job of *quantitative* research). Definitive answers may require painstaking rigor, but ideas demand creativity.

Qualitative research techniques may involve a focus group of (perhaps) eight to ten people sitting around a table and exchanging views (sometimes quite heatedly) on relevant marketing issues while the researcher asks broad questions from his outline-guide. Or it can be a long in-depth interview that may use, in part, methods derived from psychoanalysis, such as inkblots and projective techniques. Projective methods ask people to tell us what they think other people would say, i.e., to "project" their thoughts onto others. They are often necessary for sensitive issues, or for situations where there are socially acceptable answers. "If it costs more to buy environmentally safe products, do you think your neighbors would buy them?" Many people might not like to say "no", even if they are thinking "I would rather accept some environmental damage than spend more money". But they could be more willing to say that their *neighbors* might say "no". Of course, the theory is that they are simply projecting their own thoughts onto others.

In this kind of research, there is no series of clear, clean, precise quantitative questions that can be asked, giving short, simple, one or few word answers. (At least if it is done correctly.) Rather, the questions must be subtle, imaginative, and creative in outlook. The answers to these questions will be lengthy, fuzzy, and lacking in precision. This is the area where the researcher, then, can really exercise his "art", and leave his "fingerprints" on the study, as he "sings" with his own "voice".

Finally, art also consists of selecting what issues to research at all — what issues may really be "levers" by which we can "pry open" a market? As Hodock notes:

> The Japanese are excelling, in part, because their marketing research brings them closer to the consumer. They bring a different philosophical approach to marketing research . . . [They] have a built-in motivation that we lack in listening to the customer's voice. Because their culture is so different from ours, they must work very hard to understand the European and American cultures . . .
>
> Mazda tested more than 150 potential tunings for the Miata's exhaust system to match the sound of the consumers' perceived idea of what a roadster should sound like. Would any American automobile manufacturer be so meticulous? Not likely. The sound of an exhaust system is presumably a trivial and unimportant detail. Would your marketing research have identified it as a need?
>
> What is an important research issue in the United States? Often, it is trivial, such as whether a bottle should have a white cap or a blue cap. What is an important research issue in the Japanese culture? Matching the sound of the Miata's exhaust system with the consumer's perception. Which research issue will give the customer an unexpected touch of quality that goes beyond the obvious? . . .
>
> When marketing research correctly interprets the voice of the consumer, it reaches out and touches life in a meaningful way. It's very exciting stuff. Managers find marketing research irresistible under this circumstance. Reflecting on the ability of research to reach out and touch life, a vice president of marketing commented at a recent meeting about a test market product, "This was a good research presentation because I don't remember any numbers, but I now understand why people are not buying our product." Aren't comments of this nature what it is all about?[8]

This too *is* surely what "art" is all about!

SCIENCE

In its quest for useful business information, marketing research follows a definite pattern as noted in Chapter 1. It *is* organized and it adheres to many of the basic notions that make science so powerful, perhaps the most powerful voice in the modern world. It seeks to examine dispassionately; to interpret; to classify; and to predict. Marketing research blends humanistic ("think") and mechanistic ("thing") elements together to look at every aspect of a problem. And it does this in a way that is both rigorous and reasoned *and* open to the joy of unexpected discovery.

Marketing research (the science) looks for *reliability*: will the same research, using the same instrument, produce similar results each time it is done, within the bounds of statistical probability? If not, it is difficult to be sure that the results are not entirely arbitrary, and of no use at all. For example, data from a poorly worded question that no one understands very well would be unreliable. People who answered would just be guessing. If they understood the question differently the next time we did the research, and guessed differently, results would be different. Certainly, we would not want to make decisions based on such data.

Research looks for *validity*: is it doing what the researcher says it is doing; measuring what it is supposed to measure? If not, it has no particular purpose, since it is not getting the marketing information the manager asked for. Valid research must conform to agreed-upon outside standards, it should converge with other accepted research findings, and it must make accurate predictions.

Suppose we invite shoppers into our mock-up store containing only a shelf with cognac brands, give them some money, and ask them to buy their favorite brand of cognac with the money. Can we predict brand share from such a laboratory experiment? Maybe not, since the situation may seem so artificial to consumers that they do not, in fact, act as they normally would. (Maybe they think, "Free money, I'll try that expensive one I can never afford.") Some sort of external check can help decide whether the experiment is *valid* or not. If it is not, there is certainly no point in continuing to use this research methodology which claims to predict market share. We could go into our test markets with our new brand, and find that the shares bear no resemblance whatever to predictions from the experiment.

Marketing research seeks *continuity*, building upon past research. It never accepts the notion that any answers are final and definite now and forever. External environments change and consumers' preferences may be shifting. Building on previous work can allow us to track that shift, and predict where it is going. Research methodologies advance and we develop ways to get more reliable, more valid data. Tracking improvements in our data, and in the decisions based on it, allows us to judge whether it is worthwhile to invest in acquiring new research technology. Marketing objectives change, so that we need to change exactly which information we get. Comparison of old data with new as we move up-market allows us to see, for example, whether quality conscious consumers really like our repositioned product as well as our old value-conscious customers did.

Research uses whatever *measurement approaches* it can that conform to scientific tenability, the simpler the better. Basic measurement techniques include the *pre-post* technique. This involves getting a measure before something is done, then doing something (introducing *and isolating* a variable), and then measuring again. We might measure product awareness, run a six-week advertising campaign, then measure product awareness again. Another measurement technique is the *test-control* technique. This technique involves comparing one group who got a certain stimulus with another that did not. We might compare sales in a retail store where prices were hiked with sales in another store which left prices alone. Such simple concepts are the keys to measurement.

Things often get very complicated, especially in poor research. But in good research, they usually do not *need* to be very complicated. Simplicity, clarity, and the ability to explain something to management should be the most important considerations. A good research professional should have the ability to find things that can be measured, that are *meaningful* to measure for marketing decision-making purposes, and then to measure and interpret them simply and without fear or favor.

Marketing research (the science) must be totally objective, dispassionate, and *honest*. It must not matter to us that what we want to happen does not happen. To a greater extent, it must not matter to us that what *others* want to happen does not happen. It is not difficult to manipulate the questionnaire, massage the data, and fudge the interpretation to get a very favorable view of how our brand is doing in the market, if that is what we would like to see. We might feel good reporting to the marketing manager on the product's fantastic performance. Certainly the manager will like the results, and can probably show them to his bosses for a raise. But the decisions made from such data, cooked to get what various people wanted, will be bad ones. Corporate profits will eventually suffer.

And so research uses these ideas, and others borrowed from the "scientific method". The rigor, the attention to detail, to proper procedure, and the honesty required all often perturb marketing managers, whose span of attention is typically quite limited (some say to about seventeen seconds at any one time), and whose real pressures (imposed from within, above, and without) make patience with perceived "niceties" very difficult indeed. Yet strong commitment to (but not obsession with) proper approaches is vital if the information gathered in a project is ultimately to be of use to the organization.

INTEGRATION-OF-INTELLIGENCE

Marketing opportunities (or threats) can come from two sources. On the supply side, technical advances on which the company is working and general advances in industry and the world lead to new products and new ways of manufacturing products or providing services. On the demand side, changing perceptions among consumers as their needs, wants, and aspirations change can lead them to demand new products. Unfortunately, products that the supply side comes up with do not always match the kinds of products that the demand side demands.

These two disparate sources of marketing development (and innovation) do not in any sense necessarily know each other, or have anything to do with each other. Indeed, it could be said that they are thoroughly at odds with each other. The company's R&D people (for example) are professional, rational, objective, devoted, and loyal (or like to think of themselves as such). Consumers in the market, on the other hand, tend to be unpredictable, whimsical, emotional, fickle, and disloyal (toward brands). But successful product and market development must be based upon both sources. Otherwise, any successes (there are some) simply occur by accident. Gernand put it quite well:

> Corning, Inc. uses two basic methodologies for identifying new markets for products the company might create . . . The first might be called . . . *inside-out* . . . you begin with the material or product and find the most appropriate applications and markets. In [the *outside-in*] method, you look at a broad area of activity to try to identify its future needs, and

then figure out whether your company has anything that might contribute to solving its problems.[9]

Even more than basing marketing development on both sources, separately, the approach most likely to succeed in the long-run bases development on integrating the two sources. It is marketing research's task to interface between, and to integrate, ideas coming from these two basic approaches to marketing — the *only* two approaches. The researcher must talk to the marketing people — people in brand management, R&D, sales, production — and to the market — customers. He must build on these talks to help initiate new successful marketing initiatives.

He must also talk to the marketing planners to make sure that their plans (reactive or proactive, strategic or tactical, thought-out or hysterical) make sense in light of the outside world and its realities, realities that can get lost in the heat of internal battles. The researcher, in sum, is an integrator of ideas more than anything else: ideas drawn not only from his own efforts and from the company's marketing management, but also from *competitors*. (More effort should probably be spent monitoring and learning from competitors, more perhaps, than learning even from our *own* company!)

So, the integrative task is very clear: gathering marketing intelligence, combating marketing "stupidity", sorting out facts and fancies, and in the final analysis, turning ideas into profits.

CRAFT

To do all of the countless things necessary in marketing research, the researcher needs tools, like any craftsman. These tools must guide him at all times if he is to answer questions, question answers, solve problems, deflate myths, and suggest new possibilities. These tools may be thought of as encompassing four different realms:

"Hardware".   Subject skills in the "hard" sciences, like statistics, economics, mathematics, computer science, and economic geography make up what we call "hardware". These skills, respectively, can help in analyzing and interpreting data, understanding the notions of choice and scarcity, modeling what is happening in markets, effectively and efficiently handling mountains of data where required, and getting a firmer grasp of sources of materials and their role as elements of Realpolitik.

"Software".   Subject skills from the "social" sciences are commonly referred to as "software". These "soft" subjects include things like language, which can help us understand better how to write questionnaires, or how people perceive messages. Sociology can show how people live together, or what the realities of power and authority are. Psychology helps the researcher understand what is really going on in people's minds and what motivates them to do what they do. Anthropology is especially important in our efforts to understand culture, that vital "glue" that makes one people different from another, and is inborn, learned, permanent, changeable, (and so difficult to grasp). History helps to remind us that nothing we seek to do or learn about is without roots. Futurism helps to remind us that we must study about what is *not* there as well as what *is*.

"Marketwear".   Further subject skills from the realm of business itself: marketing, research (of course), management, accounting, communications, and all the rest are also needed.

"Headware".   "Headware" are the "people" skills, necessary to work in the organization and cope with its problems (e.g., problems relating to bosses with huge egos, subordinates with low motivation, suppliers with great anxieties, and "significant others" both inside the organization and outside of it who are beset with enormous insecurities). These "people" realities that the researcher must cope with do not show up in books or in his job description. Yet they are pandemic, and must be faced. How the researcher handles them, using his whole bag of professional tricks — his experience, his ability to coax, threaten, and soothe — in the course of trying to develop empathy, serendipity and imagination, will quite likely spell his success or failure once the "hardware", "software", and "marketware" craft challenges have been mastered.

The craft (the necessary tools) of the researcher is constantly expanding, including newer and (sometimes) better ways to gather data and use it in reports. To what extent should the researcher take the trouble to learn the newer research methodologies and technologies? Ideally, he should utilize the best of new methodologies and technologies while maintaining his focus on the "humanistic" elements of his craft, a focus that tells him that *numbers* do not make marketing decisions, people do.

Craft means, then, as we said before, that marketing researchers should know everything about everything. By the time they have mastered existing methodologies and technologies, they will probably find that half of those tools have already changed. Thus researchers need to live with the fact that the learning process never stops.

A B-A-S-I-C APPROACH TO RESEARCH ON THE COMPUTERPHOBE MARKET

Is the "computerphobe" market viable? To work toward finding an answer to this question, to do research, we need business sense, creative ideas, scientific rigor, integrative skills, and knowledge of a thousand or so different fields. The B-A-S-I-C approach, then, presumes that there is a huge range of issues we need to consider as we explore this marketing possibility. The hard-nosed *business* part of the paradigm, the cost-benefit analysis (how much will this research cost and what can we hope to gain from it?) could well collide with the *art* part of the paradigm (my new way looks really neat . . . let's try it). It could also conflict with the *science* orientation of the research (after our preliminary work, we really cannot proceed until we form some very clear hypotheses).

The *integrative* function will help bring all these diverse parts together. By integrating the B-A-S-I-C elements we can work with the company to see what we can offer, *and* work with the market to see who they are, what they know, what they have done, and what they want. We are working to reconcile the possibly (probably) conflicting ideas of the various parts of our research, particularly elements like business, art, and science, which do not always all peacefully coexist with each other.

Once we think we have integrated things (theoretically), it will ultimately depend upon the *craft* of the researcher to integrate things in practice. To make things work like they are supposed to work, his skills at both the "humanistic" parts (such as problem definition and idea generation) and the "mechanistic" parts (such as sampling, computer tabulations, statistical testing) of research will be critical.

We may come up with some amazing ideas along the way, and this may lead to a profitable new business line. That would be good news. On the other hand, research may produce very negative news: no consumer interest, no foreseeable profitable market, in other words, we should not go ahead with the new product! But negative news is really good news, too. Forewarned, we can avoid substantial losses by scrapping the idea about a computerphobe market.

Of course, it will be up to the marketing management team to make the decision: go, no-go, revise, retreat, give up, etc. It is their jobs that are now at stake; it is their responsibility. The marketing researcher consulted with them before the project began and reached an agreement on the project's objectives, time, cost, etc. The marketing researcher has given them data, analysis, information, and has offered interpretations and recommendations.

Marketing managers (ideally) should not use these as a "crutch" or a "prescription", an excuse for actions they already want to take, or a formula for what they must do regardless of their own feelings. Marketing managers should factor the information into their decision-making process. If they do, and if the data can be used, then research has done all it can, should, and must do.

PART II

The Process of Marketing Research

Part II explores the stages that any marketing research study, big or small, must go through. These stages make use of "thing", techniques that are part of the craft; and "think", ideas and planning. They must be made to interweave into a seamless whole.

Chapter 3 discusses how we must uncover what the marketing problem really is. Until we figure that out, we surely should not start a research project. And Chapter 4 suggests that we *must not* start the research project until we have considered the *final deliverable product* (the "backward" approach). So before we begin the research process we must know where we are going, why, and what we will end up with when we are done.

Chapters 5, 6, and 7 deal with how we actually get our data: working out issues of sampling, technique, questionnaire, or non-question-asking methods. Whether the data we gather is any good depends directly on the issues touched in these chapters.

Chapter 8 discusses how to go about analyzing data to turn them into information. This is at the heart of the craft part of research. Technology and technique are treated, but (again) as a "servant", and not as "master" of research.

Chapter 9 takes us down the road through the interpretation stage of research (what in the world does it all mean), to the active use of the research results by the marketer. A relevant, marketing-oriented report is essential in any marketing research project.

3

Identifying the Problem and Planning the Research

One of the hardest things to get novice researchers to do is to slow down and think about what they should be doing before they start doing it. To many people not very familiar with research, or not very good at it, research means collecting data — only collecting data. Certainly, research must include data collection, and the vast majority of the entire research process is devoted to collecting data in some form or another and then analyzing it. But the very first steps of the whole process, possibly the most important steps, focus on figuring out why we are doing the research in the first place, and what we are trying to find out.

PROBLEM IDENTIFICATION

Figure 3.1 summarizes some of the typical steps in most marketing research projects. Most of the steps listed in some way involve collecting, analyzing, or presenting data, in other words, getting data and turning it into information. But the very first step of the process requires us to determine what the problem really is, and what kind of information we need in order to address this problem. If the marketing researcher does not get this first step right, the rest of the project is likely to be a waste of time, effort and money. If we are not going to get the marketing information needed by the marketing manager to address the marketing problem, we might as well save ourselves a lot of time and effort and just spend the project money on a nice vacation for the marketing department.

The very critical first step in any marketing research project is about marketing, not about research. The researcher absolutely must understand the marketing problem. This necessarily involves close communication with the marketing manager. What decisions does the marketing manager have to make? What kind of situation does he face? Does the company have any particular strengths or any constraints that could affect these decisions? The researcher must temporarily forget about research and think about marketing actions and the competitive environment.

- Define the problem
- Define information needs
- Set priorities on information
- Develop a research plan and budget
- Pilot/exploratory research — qualitative
- Large scale survey — quantitative
- Research design — determine how to get information
- Instrument design — make the tool for getting the information
- Testing the instrument
- Collect data
- Analyze and interpret data
- Write up report/prepare presentation
- Oral and written presentation

Figure 3.1. Typical steps in the market research process.

Perhaps the marketing manager must develop a pricing strategy for a new product. Some companies are very good at production and can achieve cost leadership for the product category. Marketers in this position have a wide range of options. They may decide to pursue a penetration pricing strategy, with low margins but aiming for high volume, if that is appropriate to the product and the target market. They may decide to pursue a prestige pricing strategy, targeting quality conscious customers, gaining high margins, but assuming lower volume. Other companies cannot achieve very low production costs relative to competitors, and they have fewer options. It is difficult to compete on price if production costs are high.

Maybe the marketing manager must decide whether to put more money into the advertising budget. Usually, to be effective, advertising must rise above the general noise level of all advertising. This implies a certain commitment of resources to make sure that the quality of the advertising is good and that it appears sufficiently often. Does more money for advertising imply less for other kinds of promotion? Sales promotion is usually more effective in boosting short-term sales, so what exactly are the marketing manager's objectives?

Many distribution managers must determine whether to expand the company's warehouse facilities in a particular location. Should this location be developed into the hub of a network of warehouses? Do the current facilities have sufficient capacity to stock all products in enough volume to meet routine and/or unexpected orders in any situation? These kinds of warehousing issues directly influence the company's ability to provide top quality service to customers on their orders.

The marketing researcher must work closely with the marketing manager to understand such marketing problems, what kinds of marketing actions must be taken, what kinds of options are available, and what constraints may restrict action. No research project is likely to be worth the money, time, or effort unless marketing management takes place during the first stage of the process. Later, the marketing researcher must turn these marketing problems into research problems (Table 3.1).

Table 3.1. Examples of problems.

Marketing problems	Marketing research problems
What pricing strategy is needed for a new product?	Determine price sensitivity Determine competitive response
Should the print advertising budget be increased?	Evaluate advertising effectiveness Compare with alternatives
Should warehouse facilities be expanded?	Evaluate customer satisfaction Estimate future demand

A market-based (as opposed to cost-based) pricing strategy for a new product would require knowing something about price sensitivity. This can become a research problem — the task at hand is to determine the price sensitivity of various market segments. Presumably, if our target customers are mostly concerned about product quality or good service, rather than price, then competing on price is not a very good plan. On the other hand, some segments are very price conscious, and low prices are necessary if they are to be attracted to the product. Perhaps it is also important to attempt to predict the competitive response when the new product is priced at a particular level. Price wars are not easy to win if the competitor has ample resources and a lower cost structure.

Before deciding how much to spend on advertising next year, the marketing manager should know something about advertising effectiveness, how many people are seeing the current advertising, and what they think of it. If people who see the advertising generally develop favorable attitudes toward the product and eventually buy it, but not many actually see the advertising, then more money might be the solution. But spending more money would certainly be a waste if people are seeing the advertising but the correct message is not getting through. Then the solution would entail developing better copy, not spending more money. To determine the proper budget allocation between advertising and other areas of promotion, comparison of effectiveness between alternatives may be needed. Would spending more on advertising boost sales more than spending the money on in-store demonstrations?

The decision to extend warehouse facilities may hinge upon customer satisfaction with delivery. If customers are perfectly satisfied, the distribution system may be operating quite adequately, and there may be no real need to expand facilities. If they are not satisfied, perhaps because stockouts often cause delays in shipment, insufficient warehouse capacity could be one of the causes. The distribution manager would also need to consider future demand. Current capacity problems may disappear if the longer term trend is toward a drop in demand. This could happen if some of our products are nearing the end of their product life-cycle, or if the economy is moving into a recession.

Of course, the marketing research problems touched upon here are only a few examples of the kinds of research problems that arise from such marketing management issues. Many more could be developed. *Developed*, though, is the key word; they are developed through discussion with the marketing manager. They are not simply listed casually by the researcher. The researcher and the marketing manager must agree on the marketing research problems before the project can proceed further.

DEVELOPING INFORMATION NEEDS

Secondary Data

Once the problem is thoroughly digested, in both its marketing management and marketing research forms, information needs must be defined. Very simply, this means figuring out what we need to know in order to address the problems that we have just defined, that is, what information is needed to help the marketing manager make a decision. The best way to approach this task is to make a list of all the kinds of information we would like to have in this situation. The list must be specific, that is, information on age, income, and occupation, not demographics; recall of the current advertising message, not media influence. If our information needs are defined too broadly, there is no real way to gauge how useful our list will be. We may spend a lot of time later gathering information that turns out not to be relevant to the decision.

Any information we would like to have which is relevant to the problem should go onto this list. Of course, it is not likely that we can get all the information listed, because most research projects face limited budgets. But we will worry about the budget a little bit later. For now, any information we might want should be on the list. That way, it can be systematically evaluated along with all of the other pieces of information to determine how important it is to the decision. Money should be spent fleshing out the most critical information. We do not want to find out at a later stage that we spent a lot of time, effort, and money, but did not provide some information needed by the marketing manager, simply because we were in too big a hurry to thoroughly analyze what information was needed.

When developing the list of information needs, we should also think about how and where the information may be obtained. But this how and where will be considered in the context of budget development, so that the researcher and marketing manager can weigh the importance of the information relative to how much it will cost to get it. How and where is not used to screen out certain information from our list. The task now is simply to set out for examination all information which may potentially be useful in addressing the marketing problem, along with where and how we are likely to find that information. Then it can be sifted and evaluated to determine how easy or difficult it will be to get it, how much it will cost, and whether the cost is worthwhile.

That said, what kinds of things should go into the list of information needs? What kind of information is available? Where does it come from? Often, certain kinds of information may be available through published sources. It can be obtained easily by going to the library, ordering it from the appropriate government office, perhaps buying it from a syndicated research firm. Where the information may be obtained is not the key question here. It is more important at this point in time to ask ourselves what kind of data we can anticipate may have been gathered by someone already, so that this project will not have to gather it all over again. Much of the information that can be obtained from secondary sources falls into five broad categories.

International marketing managers must evaluate the risk of operating in any market. Risk assessment requires data on political, legal, and financial aspects of the market environment. Managers need to assess political stability in specific country markets. They must be able to estimate the likelihood of various kinds of government intervention into business activities, ranging from new regulation to expropriation. They must understand the legal requirements of operating in markets, from possible restrictions on forms of foreign ownership to product and packaging regulations. Financial risk assessment may require information on inflation rates, foreign exchange fluctuations, or restrictions on capital flows.

Marketing managers must estimate how difficult and how costly it will be to keep in touch with operations and to implement marketing strategies. Analyzing these issues requires data on physical infrastructure, such as communication and transportation. Operating in a country with an extensive phone/fax network, a good postal system, good roads, railroads, air transport, and seaports is much different from marketing where such infrastructure is not very well developed. Planning marketing strategies may also require information on institutional infrastructure, such as the retail structure or mass media. For example, market access for foreign products may be facilitated if retailing is dominated by department stores and/or large chains. It is often difficult to gain placement in small independent stores at the end of long, complex channels.

Any marketing manager should know about risk and infrastructure in any market where he operates. These are basic environmental variables. Managers concerned wholly with their own domestic market, though, may not formally investigate some of these issues. They may take some things for granted unless they actually move into new markets in other countries, where environments are unfamiliar. But all managers, even those who market products only in their own domestic markets, must pay explicit attention to the other three categories. They are at the heart of marketing, whether it is international marketing or marketing in a single country.

Good marketing managers must understand the competition and competitive environment. On a broad industry level, some of the issues that must be understood might include industry structure, type of firms in the industry, ease of entry and exit, scale of economies, or technological innovation. Some industries are dominated by a few giants. Successful marketing in a concentrated industry structure is much different from that in industries where there are many small competitors and no giants.

An example of different types of firms might be IBM and AT&T in the computer industry. IBM, for which computers constitute a major part of sales, certainly has different commitment and strategies from AT&T, where computers have been a relatively very small part of the business. Not every company could afford to enter industries like petrochemicals, with huge capital requirements. Entry into an industry like apparel may be easier for more companies.

Exit may also be easy or difficult. AT&T, for example, produced a fairly good PC in the mid 1980s, but was not particularly successful at marketing it. Exit was difficult, though, because customers might question AT&T's long-term reliability as a communications equipment supplier if AT&T refused to provide support services for those AT&T computers that those same customers bought. Economies of scale are an advantage in industries where the products involved are basically commodities, but may hold no advantage in markets or market niches where customers are less concerned with price than with product quality and product features. Technological innovation can change the nature of competition in industries rapidly. In Hong Kong, Newly Industrializing Country companies must now rapidly develop capabilities to manufacture TVs with NICAM. Otherwise, they will lose their market share to Japanese companies which have had these capabilities for years, but were just waiting for the right time to introduce NICAM to the Hong Kong market.

At a micro-level, marketing managers must also keep track of important individual competitors. Who are the key competitors? What kind of strategies do they use? What are their relative strengths and weaknesses? Information about these things and much more, especially about marketing strategies, is essential. The marketing manager can develop his own marketing strategy to effectively counter or preempt competitors if he knows a lot about them. Not knowing anything about competitors simply gives competitors a substantial advantage if they know something about you.

To assess market potential and develop marketing strategies, data on buyers or customers in the market are also needed. In consumer markets, this usually includes data on the population, such as demographics, spending patterns, product ownership, and cultural values. Sales potential of high-quality imported Western food products, for example, might be estimated by knowing something about the income distributions, foreign travel, and geographic concentration of high-income families with some exposure to Western material culture. Hong Kong Chinese who are likely to eat a US steak have often spent some time in the West, where they became familiar with Western foods and cooking styles. They tend to have high incomes, and are usually clustered in certain areas of the territory.

When assessing industrial markets, managers may need to know many of the same things just discussed above in relation to competitors. What are the customers' industries like? Information on the industrial structure, the technological level of companies of various sizes, access to capital among such companies, and commitment to the industry, can all tell a considerable amount about what kinds of products a customer may purchase or what the key purchase criteria will be.

The fifth main category of information often available through secondary sources is data on specific products. Estimating market potential and formulating marketing strategies may require data on the production and consumption of our product, complementary products, or substitute products. Such data on many industrial products and many consumer durables are often available, though consumption data may need to be purchased.

We can start our search for general information on most countries in the statistical yearbooks or other publications from the United Nations, World Bank, International Monetary Fund, OECD, or other international organizations. Such sources may cover a wide variety of topics, including country macroeconomic and financial data, production and trade statistics, data on the labor force, demographic information, and even ownership of some products (such as automobiles, TVs, and telephones) which are often used to indicate relative levels of prosperity or development.

When working within a specific country, it is also important to remember that most national governments also publish a wealth of information. The US Department of Commerce, for example, publishes a wide variety of reports on market conditions in individual countries. The purpose is to provide information to US companies that may be interested in exporting to these countries. Other countries also provide such services to their nationals, and equivalent departments or ministries publish similar reports. Of course, national governments also publish extensive statistics on their own countries. Non-governmental organizations and private companies also publish many excellent sources of data.

These are only very few examples of the extensive amount of secondary data that are available. Further ideas on how to approach research based on secondary data are presented in Chapter 6. But here, it should be stated that it is often more important to contact people and organizations than it is to plunge immediately into easily available statistical sources. Where secondary data must be gathered, the researcher should very early on seek the assistance of a competent reference librarian in a major library.

Relevant government offices, at the national, state or provincial, and local levels should be consulted to find out what government data are available. Relevant trade organizations should also be contacted as they are responsible for keeping up with the sort of secondary information we may find useful, particularly information about their industries. At this stage, these people can help sharpen the focus of the information that goes onto our list. Contacting these organizations at this stage of our research will save us considerable time later, by providing us with the directions to specific, relevant sources of information.

Primary Data

When using secondary data, researchers must keep in mind that only rarely will secondary data directly address the key marketing or marketing research problems. The data published in secondary sources were not gathered specifically with these problems in mind. Some secondary data, however, will certainly be useful. For a general overview of markets, if that is all that is needed, secondary data will sometimes be sufficient. But they can rarely lead to a deep, detailed understanding of markets and the consumers or companies that make up markets. The researcher should use relevant secondary data whenever they are available, but should not assume that secondary data are likely to answer all, or even most, of the research questions.

So, researchers should count themselves lucky for any information that is already gathered and available. Many things will not be available. This may be the case because no one has seen the need to gather such information before (usual scenario), or because data were gathered by a competitor and is proprietary (less usual scenario). Whatever the reason, if the researcher wants information which is not already available, he will have to gather it himself (or direct its gathering) by some method.

One fairly common way information can be gathered is through observation, just watching what happens in a given situation. One can watch customers in a store to see which aisles they go down most often, which levels of the shelf they usually look at, whether they stop to examine the end-of-aisle display. It is easy to tell if retailers properly display point-of-purchase materials, for example, by simply visiting stores and making observations. The interaction between customers and sales people can be observed to see what issues customers are most concerned about, or to see what areas require better sales training. Market place price data are easy to obtain simply by visiting various stores and recording prices.

Observation does not necessarily have to be done by people. For example, the grocery store optical scanner that records prices at the check-out counter is actually observing exactly which products are sold at the store. If these observations are recorded (and scanner systems usually can record), they can be analyzed to gain a very thorough understanding of purchase patterns. There are also a wide variety of machines that can measure, usually in a laboratory setting, people's physiological response to various stimuli, such as seeing an ad. Emotional reactions can be judged through measuring body chemistry, eye movements can be tracked to see what part of the ad people look at first, or to determine how long it takes them to focus on the key visual part of the ad.

Two essential points need to be borne in mind about the limits of observation as a research tool. It produces information on current behavior, actions, or physical situations, and it is usually a fairly passive way of obtaining information. The "current" aspect of observation means that behavior patterns measured can be of quite short duration. Keeping the research team in the field for weeks or months to see if the behavior persists is not a very practical alternative. Further, information that cannot readily be culled from observations or which is overlooked by the researcher will simply remain unavailable. Other methodologies (e.g., surveys, interviews) will need to be used to get at this less observable information.

Computers can also be used to simulate a market situation, based on models that the researcher builds which set out patterns of behavior. In this case, relationships are posited, and then hypothetical numbers (or numbers gathered from surveys) entered to see what ultimate effect (usually brand share) might result if things really did go on in the market the way it has been modeled. Checks should be built into the model so that some aspects of it can be compared with the real world. Sometimes the model must be refined. When the model is made to work fairly well, the numbers can be played with in all sorts of ways, so that various scenarios (what-ifs) can be tested.

Many kinds of information are not available from secondary sources, and cannot be obtained simply by observation, measuring physiological reactions, or building computer models. This kind of information is typically in people's heads, and can only be obtained by asking people questions. Marketing researchers may be able to determine brand shares in various geographic areas from scanner data. They can look up demographics in the government census publications and correlate them with store locations. But they cannot normally tell simply by looking at people why they buy the different brands, what attitudes they have toward them, or how they became aware of product benefits. The only way to get at this kind of information is to ask questions.

Typical Survey Information

Satisfaction of people's *needs and wants* is the foundation of marketing. But to satisfy needs and wants, marketers must know what those needs and wants are. If the project is set up well, it may be easy to observe what kinds of products people buy, where they shop, and how much they pay. However, there may be a wide variety of needs and wants underpinning very similar kinds of behavior, such as product purchases. Discovering how different people buy things for different reasons is the essence of segmentation. A simple example can show this: when people buy automobiles, is their basic need transportation?

For many people, transportation would indeed be the basic need. But there are other ways to satisfy this need. In Hong Kong, for example, it is easy to take the Mass Transit Railroad (MTR). Many colleagues who live outside of the main urban area own cars which they never drive into town. They drive them to the train station, park, and ride the MTR. To these people, convenience is likely a more basic need than transportation in the decision to buy a car. They do not have to walk, wait for a bus, or call a taxi to get to the station. In Hong Kong, one also can observe a large number of luxury car brands on the road such as Rolls Royce, Jaguar, and Mercedes Benz. Prestige may well be a major consideration to people who buy these cars when they decide what brand to buy.

Attitudes are a sort of predisposition to act focused on some object or idea. Attitudes are sometimes thought to be the foundation for product decisions. Of course, predisposition may not always lead to actual action, such as purchase, but favorable attitudes are much more likely to than unfavorable ones. Generally, to measure attitudes, we need information on several components. Knowledge, what people know about a product, for example, is important. Attitudes depend on how much people know or believe they know. Often, this aspect of attitude can be directly assessed through some kind of awareness question.

In addition to knowledge, attitudes consist of some feeling about the object or idea, the product. People like or dislike the product. The intensity of feeling also varies; they strongly like the product, or they moderately dislike it. We may need to know both about the feeling itself and its intensity. People who strongly like a brand are likely to be brand loyal, and difficult targets for a new product launch. People who mildly like it probably think it meets their needs as well as anything, but not as well as what they would ideally want. They may be good prospects if the new product matches their needs better.

An *image* is a kind of mental "picture" of something. Images usually consist of many components. Images of products are based on how people perceive various aspects, or attributes of the product. For example, consumers might construct an image of a computer based on how they perceive such things as accuracy, speed, ease of use, size of memory, durability, reliability, warranty, and many other things. Of course, different people have different ideas about these attributes, and there is no guarantee that a particular individual's image will be accurate in any objective sense.

Fully measuring an image is likely to prove impossible, because the image will consist of innumerable components, some of which we may not even discover. But generally a core set of components can be identified which account for most of how people form their images about products, and measuring this core set is sufficient. These most relevant attributes must be determined through pilot interviews with typical respondents, rather than set in advance by the researcher or client.

Information on the *decision-making* process is another very common goal of survey research. Here, the researcher would attempt to determine how respondents come to a purchase decision. Information sources used by the consumer would be one key aspect that would show something about the process. Consumers may base decisions on information obtained through personal experience, from contacts with friends, relatives, or colleagues, or from some media source. The influence of media can be measured in a number of ways which assess varying levels of impact. For example, it is relatively easy to determine simple exposure to various messages. Measuring how much attention people gave to a particular message is more difficult, and establishing that the message actually had some impact on the purchase decision is even harder.

Another aspect of decision making is the criteria that people use in evaluation. This aspect of decision making is related to image, in that here we are concerned with the importance of the various attributes that make up the image. However, even though the image may consist of many attributes, most people use only a few key attributes when they make a product decision. Pinpointing those few key attributes is often one very important task of survey research. It may also be important to find out whether respondents will actively look for information on these key criteria before making a decision. For many low-involvement products, the decision is simply not important enough for people to spend time gaining more information, even though they may not know much about the key attributes of the product they are deciding to buy.

Behavior is often measured by survey research. Of course, current behavior can be determined, usually more effectively, by observation. But now, when we are doing the project, it is too late to measure behavior that happened last week or last month. And it is too early to see what people will do next week or next month. Generally, information needs for behavior should be specified in terms of the "question words:" who, what, when, where, why, how (often). Who chose the product, who shopped for it, who will decide when to buy another one? What brand, style, size, model was purchased? When do people purchase products, what time of day do they prefer to eat, which days of the week do they go to the grocery store? How soon do they intend to buy another product of this kind? Going through questions like this one can build quite a complete list of behavioral information useful in developing marketing actions.

Information on past behavior is usually more or less true, though not always precise. Future behavior, though, has not actually happened yet. After the survey, people can still change their minds. Actually, often changing minds is not as big a problem as the simple fact that intentions may never get carried out for some reason. Perhaps something will come up and the consumer will never actually go out to a Western restaurant for dinner next week, even though they have every intention of doing so at the time they are asked. In individual cases, intentions do not always correspond very well to actual behavior. The information must be used very carefully if it is applied to individuals. Fortunately, in the aggregate, intentions are usually more accurate indicators. The responses of those who never do what they intended to do are balanced by those who do carry out what they had not previously thought of doing.

Nearly every survey research project will gather *demographic* data. This is not usually because, as some novice researchers seem to think, extensive demographic information is useful in itself. In a market research survey, a huge demographics section in the questionnaire asking for all sorts of detailed information often betrays the lack of experience of the researcher. There must be some use for those demographics other than just reporting on them in the final report. People do not often choose to buy a certain automobile because they happen to be in a certain income category, hold a particular job, or are of a certain age. We do not need market research simply to gather demographic information. Census data are much more extensive and much more complete.

Why are demographics always on market research questionnaires, then? One important reason is for sample validation. The demographic characteristics of the sample can be compared to the initial definition of the target population for the research. At the beginning of the project, the marketing manager and the researcher decided who they wanted to get information from. Demographics help show how well the survey did at getting information from those people.

Another equally important reason is for information association. It is difficult to look at someone and tell easily whether they want a car for basic transportation, convenience, or prestige. It is difficult to determine without asking what their attitude toward a Toyota is, or what kind of image they have of a Jaguar. The only people for whom we know these things, then, are those that have been asked in the survey. But if patterns of needs, attitudes, images, and so forth can be associated with particular demographic characteristics, then it is possible to "look" at someone and have a good idea about how they might view automobiles.

INFORMATION NEEDS, PRIORITIES, AND REALITIES

Returning to the research problem about determining price sensitivity, we can use these different information categories as a guide in developing a list of information needs that will help in the new product pricing decision. Understanding price sensitivity for a new product will require asking consumers some questions. There is no sales record from which to get volume sales at various prices so that an elasticity can be computed. Figure 3.2 lists several examples of the kinds of information one might want from consumers that would help measure price sensitivity.

Price sensitivity could well be a function of which particular need a product will satisfy. For example, people who want an automobile for basic transportation are much more likely to be concerned about how much a car costs than people to whom prestige is a major consideration. The specific things people know about the product relate to the knowledge part of attitude. Often, views toward a product, be they positive or negative, become stronger as people acquire more knowledge, and these views will affect how much people think the product is worth.

Image is behind the issue of how people view substitute products. If the product image people hold of a substitute is close to that of their ideal, it will be hard to get them to switch to the new product. If it is not so close, proper positioning of the new product close to people's ideal would make it easy to build sales. Finding out what key product attributes are used in decision making, combined with measuring how our product does on those attributes (product image again) can give a good indication of how much people will pay. If convenience is a key factor to the career woman in choosing prepared food, she is likely to be willing to pay more for foods that truly are convenient. Housewives may have plenty of time for food preparation and be totally unwilling to pay extra for convenience. To tap this convenience factor though, our food product must rate highly on convenience.

- What kind of need does buying the product satisfy?
- What specific things do people know about the product?
- How do people view substitute products?
- What are the key product attributes used in decision making?
- How does our product rate on those attributes?
- What overall value does our product have for people?
- How much are they willing to pay to obtain that value?
- Can we correlate these things with demographics?

Figure 3.2. Possible information needs for new-product pricing.

Any product manager should have an idea about how customers value products, and how their perceptions of value translate into the money that they will pay to obtain that value. It is not enough to know that a product does well on all kinds of things like image. To set prices, the manager must know how all of the favorable attitudes or good image translate into cold cash. People might well like to have more prestige, have favorable attitudes toward Jaguar, believe that Jaguar closely matches their ideal on prestige and other important attributes, consider prestige when buying a car, and so forth. Nevertheless, they may still buy a Toyota rather than a Jaguar. They simply place much less value on all of these things than the actual price of a Jaguar.

Once these kinds of information have been written down, the researcher and the marketing manager must evaluate each piece of information on the list and assign a priority to it. It would be nice if data on everything in the information list could be gathered. Unfortunately, most projects have limited budgets that will not allow for gathering huge amounts of information. This may simply be because not much funding has been allocated to research in the first place, or it may be because the decision itself does not justify a large budget. If the new product is being launched to fill out the product line, but no one expects it to achieve more than a few hundred thousand dollars in sales, it certainly makes no sense at all to spend a hundred thousand dollars on research. Certainly, better marketing decisions could be made if the money were spent, but in this case, even uninformed, terrible decisions may be less costly than a large research project.

It is also important to recall the distinction between *data* and *information*, since the researcher may have to gather a lot of data to get a little bit of information. On most projects, much of the budget is spent on gathering data, which only become information when some of the money is spent on properly analyzing it. The project may ask thousands of people only a single question, what is the main reason they buy an automobile. Then there will be lots of data (thousands of numbers), but they only translate into one piece of information: basic needs of the market. The questionnaire may contain questions on ten product attributes that are important to image. There will be even more data (tens of thousands of numbers), which still all reduce to one piece of information: image.

Even big research budgets are unlikely to cover the cost of getting all possible information relevant to the problem, and small budgets may not even get most of it. Prioritizing is essential. Which pieces of information on the list are absolutely necessary for making the decision? In our new product pricing example, maybe knowing about value and willingness to pay fall into this absolutely necessary top priority category. Sometimes the marketing manager needs to know things for improving decisions, but could go ahead and make the decision with some degree of confidence even if the information was not available. This is a second priority level. Perhaps knowing how people view substitute products falls into this category.

Usually, the majority of information in these top two categories is likely to require primary research. Only a company with the same marketing problem is likely to have ever gathered these specific data, and if they did, they are unlikely to share them with a competitor. But often much information in the third priority category can be found in secondary sources. This information would be interesting and useful, kind of nice-to-know, but perhaps not so directly critical to the decision at hand. In our example, what people specifically know about the product might fall into this category. Often, industry background information is also of this priority. It is useful to have, but rarely worth the cost of getting through primary research. Anything that is not obviously in one of these top three categories can be classified as "everything else". Research money should not be wasted on gathering any information at all that falls in the "everything else" category.

Note here that we, the researchers, have set the priorities in the above discussion. In an actual project, we would have to make sure that the marketing manager verified these priorities, and change how we ranked each piece of information if the manager had different priorities. But even after the manager and the researcher have agreed on priorities, it is important to probe a little bit further to see if the information is truly important to the manager's decision. We might arbitrarily set several values spanning the range of possible results for a piece of information, then ask the manager in turn what the decision would be if the result is each of these values.

For example, the researcher might ask the manager: "Suppose 90 percent of the respondents in the survey said they were willing to pay between HK$200 and 250 for the new product. How would you price it?" We could get an answer and then ask the question several more times: "What if sixty percent are willing to pay between HK$200 and 250?", then thirty percent, then maybe: "What if no one is willing to pay as much as HK$200 to 250?" If this information is really important to the manager's decision, his answer must change as we go through the possibilities. If he says "HK$220" every time we ask, clearly, the information has no impact on the decision. If it has no impact on the decision, it cannot really be important at all, and there is no point in spending money to get it.

Unfortunately, far too much money is spent gathering exactly this kind of information. Sometimes, it is only a particular piece of information that is like this. Then it can be assigned to the "everything else" category, and eliminated from the list of information that will be gathered. The situation is much worse if managers have already decided what to do, regardless of the research results. They may insist that all of the information is top priority, but they will not use any of it at all in making their decision.

Pseudo-research of this sort is really for the purpose of covering tracks, "engineering" consent, justifying decisions already made, giving the appearance that the decision was based on careful analysis of market information. Pseudo-research, though, is really no different from simply throwing the money away. It contributes nothing toward better marketing. There is no real purpose for doing it, except perhaps for job security if the researcher is so junior in the firm that he cannot afford to point out the folly of wasting money on worthless things.

PLANNING THE PROJECT

Given that information priorities have been figured out, a budget must be drawn up. It is critical in developing a budget not to think of money first. Instead, figure out where and how data will be obtained, who will perform each task to get data, analyze them, and write up the report, and how long each task will take. Then the money questions are easy. (Figuring out these things requires a preliminary idea about the research methodology, which is the topic of the next chapter.) Table 3.2 illustrates the spreadsheet for a simple budget on a small survey project. The costs developed here are for the case where the researcher is working as an outside consultant. Projects done internally by a research department may be budgeted somewhat differently, but still, the principles of figuring out the budget remain similar. Simply multiply the pay rate of each person involved in the project by how long they will spend on the project.

Table 3.2.   Sample budget for a simple survey project.

Activity	Estimated hours by personnel			Cost by activity
	Field assistants	Research assistants	Principal researcher	(HK$)
Secondary data analysis		20	15	19,000
Questionnaire development			5	5,000
Consumer interviews (500 @ 5 interviews/hour)	100			5,000
Data input		10		2,000
Trade interviews (50 @ 1 interview/hour)		25	25	30,000
Analysis and write-up			40	40,000
Hourly rate by personnel (HK$)	50	200	1,000	
Cost by type of personnel (HK$)	5,000	11,000	85,000	101,000

Costs are in Hong Kong dollars at prevailing rates for experienced undergraduate interveiwers, experienced graduate research assistants, and faculty consultants.

The project involved a consumer survey with a very short phone interview and in-depth interviews with retail managers.

One thing to note, which often surprises people inexperienced with performing survey research, is that only a relatively small proportion of the budget is a true variable cost with respect to sample size. Often clients who balk at the cost of a project ask the researcher to cut sample size to reduce costs. Things do not work that way. Consulting secondary sources takes the same amount of time regardless of whether two hundred or two thousand people are questioned. The questionnaire must be developed, tested, and (maybe) translated and back-translated, regardless of sample size. (Tracking surveys, where most of the tasks involved in setting up the project have already been done, are one partial exception. Then, data are gathered with a questionnaire that has already been used previously.)

The data must be analyzed. Doing statistics on two thousand respondents does take longer than doing them on two hundred, but in the age of computers, it will only take seconds and fractions of seconds longer, not hours and days. Interaction with the client, writing up the report, and so forth, do not depend on how big the sample is. Only the actual process of asking questions itself, supervising the survey field team, and data entry actually vary in time depending on how many respondents are in the sample. And these tasks are not usually performed by the more highly paid consultants or analysts. In other words, a high proportion of any research project is fixed costs with respect to sample size. Asking fewer people will not reduce the cost of the project very quickly.

Costs are not fixed, though, with respect to information. They can be reduced by cutting back on how much information is generated by the project. The time spent pursuing data from secondary sources can be reduced, so that anything that takes a long time to dig out is disregarded. Fewer questions can be asked on the questionnaire, so that it takes less time to administer and enter into the computer. It also takes less time to analyze, since there are fewer statistics to run. The analysis can be less thorough, so that the data is not turned into as much information. We can give up doing a lot of cross-tabs so that we understand the top ten purchase criteria among different income categories, various job categories, and for each educational level. Instead, we might settle for information only on the top three purchase criteria by income category only.

What about changing the methodology instead of throwing out information? This is really much the same thing. Different methodologies are able to generate different kinds and different amounts of information. For example, we could save money on interviewers by doing a mail survey, but no one would answer it if it contained as many questions as a personal interview questionnaire, so it must be much shorter. Unfortunately, spending less money mostly means getting less information. Here is where priorities come in. When faced with a smaller budget than required to get all of the information left on our list, lower priority information should be sacrificed first. Sometimes, so much must information must be thrown out that there is not much point in doing the project. Usually, though, a rigorous approach to developing and prioritizing information needs, along with a creative approach to research design, will insure that even a meager budget will allow for some critical information to be obtained.

Timing is another critical aspect. Some researchers, especially academics who rarely have to face a real deadline, often insist on such painstaking attention to rigor and detail that a project can take forever. The marketing manager who must make a product launch decision for the Christmas shopping season does not have forever. To him, information of outstanding quality delivered six months from now is entirely worthless. But slightly less reliable, lower quality information could be very useful if the manager gets it ten weeks from now. In other words, research projects are subject to time budgets as well as financial budgets. The tradeoffs in adjusting to time budgets are much the same as in adjusting to money budgets.

4

The Two Roads and the "Backward" Approach

Some of the most difficult and critical moments in marketing research are those we have just discussed. Research serves little purpose unless researchers first correctly identify the problem that needs to be addressed and grapple with how to address the problem in ways that will help marketing managers make better decisions. Now we are past that stage, though: we have consulted with the marketing manager, picked his brain to draw out of him what is really needed, and thought about the situation. We now understand the problem, at least as best as it is likely to be understood. The project seems interesting, important, and feasible. We are ready to get moving.

Now we are tempted to go steaming ahead — to be "busy" — to "do a project". Naturally, we think about things like: How do we go about getting the answer? What techniques should we use? What questions should we ask people? What sample size should we choose? How shall we analyze the findings?

This is the *wrong* way to proceed. All of these are excellent things to ask, *but definitely not now*. At this stage of the research process these are precisely the *wrong* things to ask, the *wrong* things to do. The essence of marketing research is very easily and very commonly lost at this point in such a welter of attention to detail, to things, to doing something. The researcher loses sight of the reasons for doing research and the real purpose of the project. Reason is left behind in a flurry of frenzied activity to move the project forward.

Those following this path may hope that such "busy work" will pass for credible marketing research. Or they may just assume that it is real research. And sadly, this "busy work" often does pass for credible work, at least for a time. The far too common late discovery that the research done has turned out useless information fully attests to the fact that one can nearly get away with this folly. By the end of the project, however, someone must actually try to use the results to make a decision.

Ultimately someone will find out that though the researcher has "done a project" he has made no contribution to the marketing decision-making process. The research has, at best, turned out to be an aimless and nameless, and — if the researcher is lucky — blameless exercise. If the researcher is not lucky, the project will turn into yet another example of why his research should not be taken seriously by the company or by the agency, why it should be ignored or even abandoned.

This sad but common outcome need never occur. One need only have a grasp of the logic of research to avoid such an aimless, nameless project. At this early stage, we must imagine the end of the project, the presentation, what will be said to whom, and what decisions will be based on our results. We must think about this end-point, and then work backwards to see how to get to that end. An appreciation of this "backward approach" is essential to successful marketing research.

An appreciation of the "two roads" we can travel to get to the end is also critical. The researcher must negotiate the right road at the right time; either the "soft" road of ideas, imagination and insight, or the "hard" road of numbers, formulas, and calculations. We will now explore these "two roads" and the "backward approach", looking at the senior citizen market, dogs and their owners, and children and candy bars.

THE TWO ROADS

The first thing the logic of the survey analysis process demands is that the researcher recognize at the beginning that there *are* two roads. The roads are mutually exclusive and complementary at the same time. They are mutually exclusive because they cannot (must not) be done at the same time, mistaking one for another and back again. But they are also complementary in that one typically builds upon the results of the other. Our trek down the second road is made substantially easier and more rational by our trek down the first road.

These roads go by different names and have many components, but broadly speaking, the *first* road is the *qualitative* road, and the *second* the *quantitative* road. The qualitative road usually involves asking questions of small groups or small numbers of individuals. The quantitative road, as its name suggests, involves numbers, formulas, computers, print-outs, and firm number-based decisions. This means larger numbers of respondents.

In broadest terms, though, it is useful to conceive of qualitative research as involving any and all activities except the big, number-oriented quantitative study. Qualitative research, thus, may *also* emcompass secondary research, internal database research, and anything that can help cast light on our problem, short of that big "quant" study. Nevertheless, if we think of qualitative and quantitative research in terms of survey research, as is usually done, their basic natures can be dichotomized as in Table 4.1.

A detailed look at the contrasting pairs of words in this table will help in understanding the nature of "qualitative" versus "quantitative" research. The pairs of words we have chosen are by nature arbitrary, although they are drawn from long and often painful practice. But the message is crystal clear: there is an overriding need

Table 4.1. The two roads.

QUALITATIVE emphasizes	QUANTITATIVE emphasizes
"Soft"	"Hard"
Hidden	Obvious
Diagnostic	Evaluative
Humanistic	Mechanistic
Art	Science
Strategy	Tactics
"Pre"-action	"Re"-action
Personal	Massive

for patience if we are to understand what is really at issue. We should not rush into a judgment based on half-baked and half-cocked ideas.

"Soft" vs. "Hard"

The very concept of "soft" research is itself "soft"; it is difficult to pin down into a precise definition. It implies a search for the right way to go. It involves discussing still unformed topics in great detail with a few people (representative respondents from our target population). We cannot even call these topics "questions" yet, but later we can turn these discussions into questions to ask people. Soft research includes spelling out what we do know and groping toward an understanding of what we need to know but do not know. We must put this information and lack of information together into some clearer shape once we have added further input to it.

"Hard" research is easier to grasp, since it is what the inexperienced researcher immediately wants to do. The concept "hard" suggests that we know exactly what we need to know, how much of it we already know, and exactly how to get what we do not yet have. The important decisions left before proceeding with this research are mainly *how many* and *who*, i.e., sample size and target population. Hard research seeks numbers for the researcher to analyze, and marketing actions await only their gathering. Unfortunately, if we jump to hard research too soon, we are usually left with the unanswered question: *why?*

Let's take an example. Suppose that a company sells foods and beverages, and the marketing people perceive that the *senior market* is growing. The marketing question will come up: should the company enter the senior-citizen market with a line of products, entailing both food and drinks of all sorts, that are aimed at senior-citizen needs? This might mean products that are low in calories, low in cholesterol, low in fat, high in protein, high in fiber, salt-free, packaged in small portions, and so on. It is a bold thought, and at this time it is indeed only a thought, a vision.

The marketing manager may have the gut feeling that this market has been isolated, patronized, ignored, and would respond favorably to such products. What about a separate line exclusively featuring senior models in the advertising and promotion? How about focusing our advertising non-exclusively on the senior media? In earnestly seeking out these people, should the promotional message face the fact of "senior-hood" (i.e., old age) squarely, or skirt around it?

The marketer and the researcher know that these seniors are of all types — men and women (more women, demographics tell us), married and otherwise, younger olders and older olders, financially comfortable and financially insecure, healthy and not so healthy, and so forth. But not much is known about the exact breakdown of seniors into these different types, or about how seniors regard and respond to marketing efforts even if something is known about who fits into which type. The challenge is working out a program to research these issues.

The first step in attempting to respond to this breathtaking assignment must be to *step back* and gasp at the enormity of it. In other words, it is absolutely essential to appreciate the *scope* of a problem like this. Only then can we begin to see what insights we can develop as research professionals. And the first insight must be that it is too soon to specify methodology or technique. First, one must step back and logically examine the problem. In so doing, the first answers will be found.

The researcher must first develop an understanding of the problem; only then does it make sense to put some numbers to it all. The "developing understanding" part is "soft" research. It is a painstaking exploration of what the issues are and how intelligence can be applied to those issues. The "numbers" part is "hard" research: a no-nonsense set of studies that asks specific questions to get at "how many", and "in what way" answers. This "hard" research is very important, but it cannot come first. There is no need for numbers before one understands what is going on. Indeed, at this point they would only get in the way of developing a marketing understanding: ideas that lead to decisions that enhance profitability.

The "soft" and "hard" parts of research are never contradictory nor competitive. Typically, in massive projects, researchers develop ideas during the "soft" part of research, and hammer them home during the "hard" part. Put another way, during the soft part the researcher makes sure he identifies all the key issues, learns the consumer's language and jargon, and generates hypotheses (hunches) to test during the hard part.

So soft answers are very likely to be ideas, reactions to ideas, or maybe even a few hesitant numbers that begin to suggest a course of attack. They are hints and glimmers. As such, generally soft answers should not be used as bases on which to make decisions. The hard data later on will provide the base: from the foundation that the soft work has done, research moves on to big samples, numbers and techniques, to see if the ideas, reactions to ideas, and hunches are correct or not.

The techniques in this stage would typically revolve around some kind of in-depth interview with *small groups* of seniors, with *individual* seniors, or perhaps with both in one order or the other. In the interview, the researcher would chat about the kinds of problems that seniors face (things, people, health, etc.), how they cope with the problems, which products satisfy them, which do not, and why. These discussions help the researcher develop the questions that need to be studied. The researcher cannot assume that he already knows all the questions. After all, marketers must be consumer oriented, and let consumers tell them what is important. Deciding for them what is important is not a very smart way to do marketing.

That is the soft part. The hard part then would consist of putting big numbers to our thoughts. At this point, it is mostly a process of counting heads. How many, that is, what proportion of the population of seniors share these views we have uncovered in the soft part of our work? Who wants what? What segments emerge? From this hard research conclusions can be drawn, and form the basis on which marketing decisions can be made. The soft and hard roads to research have many facets and nuances, but looked at broadly, they provide a very effective means of explaining the qualitative versus quantitative research issue.

Other Dichotomies

Hidden/Obvious.   The qualitative phase is exploratory. The researcher must explore the issues, get at what is hidden, not only from him, but maybe from the seniors themselves. Often to address such issues, researchers must try to delve into the seniors' conscious (and even unconscious), to get associations that they themselves may not be aware of. While this process must not be made painful for them, sometimes candor can only come by presenting stimuli of all sorts (pictures of the old, the nature of loneliness, the real meaning of health for them, etc.) and challenging their rationalizations.

After all, the ideas, values, fears, needs, and wants that come out of this process must have real substance. They cannot simply be inconsequential ideas or beliefs to which consumers have no commitment whatever. Otherwise, we would be measuring nothing at all when we go on to measure things in the quantitative part of the research project. The new products that will come out as a result of the research (if the decision is to come out with anything) must address real needs and wants that spring from the depths of the consumer if they are ultimately to succeed. Far too many new products fail simply because they do not really address anything of any consequence to anyone.

The paths in the realm of qualitative research are well known, yet lead to endless — and sometimes hidden — possibilities. These paths include depth interviews (drawn from psychoanalytical psychology), group sessions (not unlike "support groups" in the broader society), game playing, psychodrama, and so forth. The appraisal of such research remains very personal in the final analysis. The evaluation of results is based upon experience, "feel", and general groping. Nothing is obvious, nothing is predetermined. Here we are dealing with words and thoughts and ideas, rather than numbers.

Once the qualitative research has done whatever possible to get at the ungettable, then the quantitative phase will seek to find out if anybody really cares about what we are about to do, and, if so, who, and how many. The "quant" trail is different from what has been done in the qualitative phase. The methods here — personal interviews, telephone surveys, mail surveys, diary surveys, etc. — have been well traveled and the possibilities are obvious. Techniques for sampling, questionnaire construction, analysis, and presentation have been developed over the decades, and are available for all to peruse and use. While new technology constantly offers new possibilities, and while imagination is still valued, the use of computer programs, algorithms, and packages of all sorts help in sorting out what is what to make the road less tortuous.

If the researcher has thought things out well early on, in the planning phase and in the qualitative explorations, the quant phase can be relatively untroubled, assuming that he does not eschew serendipity all along the way. Most importantly, here results are mostly based on numbers, and numbers do offer the very solidity that ideas never can. This does not make them superior to ideas; the ideas of the qualitative phase and the numbers of the quantitative phase are, of course, complementary. But numbers do make what we do more obvious, and they certainly make decisions based on research results more obvious.

Diagnostic/Evaluative. This dichotomy turns up over and over in research, and in this context it is very clear. In the qualitative phase the focus is on understanding why something works (or does not work), what is right (or wrong) with it. This is the "what is going on" phase of research. Marketers must diagnose, find out what is going on, first. The diagnosis will then lead to a course of action (treatment, so to speak). In other words, the marketer then formulates marketing decisions, what to do about this situation that has been uncovered.

The quantitative research then provides information to evaluate the viability of such treatment. Knowing about how many people in the population think a certain way, how strongly they hold attitudes, and so forth, allows the marketer to judge the probable outcome of a marketing decision. After this evaluation, the treatment is applied, that is, the marketing decision is implemented (or not implemented).

For example, the marketer might want to examine (diagnose) in the qualitative phase why various existing advertising campaigns, and maybe also several potential campaigns, appeal or do not appeal to seniors. While the marketer may have his own ideas about this, they are his own ideas, not the ideas of the seniors, the target customers. The best way to diagnose what is going on among seniors with these ads is to ask them. This requires detailed discussions with seniors to really get at such things as what images the campaigns evoke, or how credible they really believe the campaigns are.

These discussions help the marketer to decide on possible changes in the campaign, or on entirely new campaigns altogether. Then later on in the quantitative phase he can evaluate the campaigns relative to alternatives and competition by using big samples and getting hard data. The diagnostic emphasis enables us to see both strengths and weaknesses in the whole and in the parts, and helps us to possibly recombine good things from different places. It avoids the often brutal, premature, and devastating "keep it or kill it" thinking that pervades much quantitative work: work that is too often simplistic and destructive.

Humanistic/Mechanistic.   In the qualitative phase, the researcher uses whatever approaches he can think of to attack the problem. Maybe he will read books about seniors before starting (he should), and articles in the professional press (sociology, gerontology, social work, etc.), and the popular press too. There may be a wealth of knowledge about seniors, some of which could be relevant to the problem the project is going to address.

He may turn to various disciplines for models, for organizing concepts on which to hang his early thinking as he begins to develop his understanding of the problem. Maybe he will look to sociology (people living together — and apart — in extended, distended, and pretended families); to psychology (Freudian, post-Freudian, experimental); anthropology (emphasizing the culture of the old); or economics (spending patterns, savings rates). There is a wealth of knowledge about how to organize knowledge about human beings. Marketing is, after, all, an applied social science. The theoretical structures of the social sciences may well be relevant to the project.

We should take all those *humanistic* approaches that might improve our understanding of the problem. This phase is also humanistic in the sense that it may be highly creative, as noted below. In the course of undertaking humanistic approaches, the researcher will seek to isolate key variables, try out alternative themes on small numbers of people, play with the words (and the music) as he goes along, seek out relevant segments, and so forth.

After these stages have been mastered, and the researcher has developed an understanding of the problem, he must move into a *mechanistic* mode. At this stage there is less flexibility in how to do things. Once the researcher starts thinking about numbers, formulas, and computers, about sampling and sample size, and about statistical analysis, structure is imposed. There are still choices to be made in how to proceed, but the choices follow from the nature of the problem. There is less room left for exploring, testing various paths, developing an understanding.

Art/Science.   Qualitative work is as much art (Chapter 2) as anything else. Of course, the researcher seeks out what went on before and builds on it. After all, there may be considerable relevant knowledge and experience that he can tap into. But the voice followed here, to a great extent, is the researcher's own; it is a personal voice, his own song, which perhaps draws on the vision of seniors he has known, loved, and lost. Creativity is especially important at this stage. Indeed, often the greatest contributions come at this stage from a new, personal way of viewing the problem.

But when the project moves into the quantitative stage, then the work must stand on its own and be judged by associates, clients, and successors by the canons of scientific method (such as reliability, validity, etc.) that were introduced in Chapter 2. There is not much room for creativity here. The scientific method lays out how things should be done, and it also lays out the means by which the work can be painstakingly evaluated. Creativity is critical in qualitative work, but rigor and precision take over in quantitative work.

Strategy/Tactics. This dichotomy is far too often misunderstood by many researchers. In the qualitative phase, few limits are placed on what issues to look at, what questions to discuss, and what methodologies to use. The research should explore the widest possible range of issues, it should be wide in scope. This is critical in looking at strategic issues; marketers have to know what is going on pretty well before committing the company to a course of action with long-term implications.

For example, in developing a promotional strategy for the senior product line, the marketer must know how seniors think. The researcher needs to explore the broad questions that will be translated into the promotional message: what are their views regarding youth (becoming young again) or old age (its irreversibility); about independence, dependence, and interdependence; about needs or whims. These are the broad strategic issues that must be addressed before the marketer can go on with the research.

Once these depths have been plumbed, then (yes, *only then*) can the marketing manager proceed to the tasks (tactics) of designing packages (will they be frivolous or serious?); choosing names (*Again? Tomorrow? Great Gray Way? Me?*); shaping promotional messages. Only then can the research project go on to the quantitative task of evaluating the probable effectiveness of the tactics. Logic demands that we consider strategy (in the qualitative phase) before tactics (in the quantitative). If we do this, we will not put Descartes before the horse!

Pre-action/Re-action.   The marketing manager and marketing researcher must look into the senior market extensively (an expensive undertaking) in order to give themselves adequate time to explore (almost another synonym for qualitative work), to test, to back, to fill, to modify, to do things "our way" and in "our time". This "pre-action" (or "proactive" approach) is typically associated with qualitative work.

While quantitative work is not always a *re*-action to competitive threats and overpowering forces which become too vast to ignore, it frequently comes down to just that. At its best, quantitative work reacts, if not to sudden and unanticipated nastiness on the outside, at least to findings in the qualitative (pre-active) phase. It proceeds from there.

Personal/Massive.   This final dichotomy can be used to sum up the basic nature of the qualitative and quantitative roads. The logic of a study — of an issue like the analysis of the senior market — must take into account two widely different notions. The qualitative phase must emphasize the personal — the one customer who will sit in front of the TV set, read the advertisement, eat the food products, and take the drinks. The researcher must truly understand that one customer, with a lifetime of memories behind, realities at hand, and uncertainties to face. This is the heart of small-group or individual research, the humanistic approach, the art.

This stage simply cannot be ignored. The qualitative work uncovers information that helps the researcher learn what individual seniors want and what they do not want. It shows what they like to eat and drink, what they do not like, and what they would like to have available for consumption. It uncovers how these likes, wants, and needs may differ with different kinds of people, that is, segments. This depth of knowledge about individual consumers is essential. In the final analysis the marketing manager must influence and appeal to masses of people one by one. That influence and appeal is not likely to be very effective if he does not understand even one individual out of those masses.

Yet at some point, the researcher and the marketer must also face the fact that one individual person is not a market. Rather, millions of people are. *Marketers must appeal to one, but they must sell to many*. The qualitative work leads the way to the quantitative work that will put those "hard" numbers on all of our in-depth knowledge. We need to know how many think like this particular senior we have come to know, and how many are like that other one with different wants. Between the "one" and the "all" lie the "segments" that marketers must inevitably sort out to succeed.

The *trick*, the logical imperative, is to see where the emphasis of the research task should lie at various stages of the research process. "Soft" or "hard", "art" or "science", there is a time and place for each facet or road in the research process. These facets must be skillfully blended together in the correct order. Until the researcher fully understands that research must encompass both of these facets, he has no business starting any research at all.

A Heresy

Heresy is a word one does not hear much today, but in times past it was very important, a matter of life and death. Heresy is disagreement with established belief (usually religious belief) that threatens (or seems to threaten) the very establishment itself. In times past, one could get burned at the stake for heresy. What does heresy have to do with marketing research?

After laying down "the law" about the nature of the two roads and the necessity of utilizing *both* approaches, we must inject just one final note. Occasionally, (and we do mean *occasionally*, not *usually*, not *often*), one is permitted, even encouraged, to break that law. That is heresy to many. To say we can break the law at all is heresy to purists who think that the whole purpose of research is to rigidly uphold some standard of rigor. These people would refuse to do any project that cannot be done full scale. To them, the research itself is the important thing, not the marketing that research should be supporting.

At the other extreme, our statement is also heresy because we *strongly* stress the *occasionally* part. Tight budgets, limited time, or simply the assertion that research can find out all it needs in either the qualitative or the quantitative parts alone are far too often covers for sloppy, poorly thought-out work. These people forget that the need for marketing to remain in control of marketing research does not automatically make the data obtained in research good. Good data comes from good research, but bad research can easily yield useless data. Worse, bad research sometimes even results in bad data. If it is simply useless, at least it will not be used and will not influence the marketing decision. But if the data are misleading, they may be used and lead to disastrous marketing decisions.

So when can one break the law of the two roads? As stressed again and again, marketing research is all about decisions seeking to enhance profitability based on ideas drawn from research. The ideas part of this mostly comes from the qualitative road, so sometimes the qualitative road alone is sufficient. Marketers do, in fact, make marketing decisions (and often very major ones) based only upon qualitative data: a few focus groups, a few in-depth interviews. Sometimes, this is just bad practice, and the marketer may pretend he has gotten quantitative data, although a few of this and a few of that in no sense constitutes real quantitative research as any reputable researcher would conceive of it. But sometimes doing only qualitative work is perfectly well suited to the situation.

How can one recognize such situations? The feeling among marketers or marketing researchers is that for screening out poor ideas, for polishing up good ones, and in general for handling things where "touchy-feely" considerations are key, a few voices, carefully heard and insightfully handled, are enough. For example, pragmatically speaking, suppose the researcher could take the advertising agency creative team to group sessions. And further suppose that the team could create new ads on the spot after hearing panelists voice their opinions, revise the ads on the spot after getting further feedback from the panelists, and continue on with the process until everyone agreed that the ad was very effective. Then maybe one need only travel the "soft" road.

Of course, this situation is unlikely in real life, but it can be stretched out, so that ads are tested on another group later, and so forth. But even then, it would be impossible to stop at qualitative research if the marketer needed to have estimates of audiences or segment sizes and proportions. How many people in the marketing territory think the ad was terrific, like those six people in the focus group? How many thought it was awful, like the other two? Such estimates cannot be obtained from qualitative work. So qualitative work should only be used alone if the marketer already has very good knowledge of issues like how many, and what proportions. Often, this knowledge will have come from previous research.

It is wrong to want to stop the research after the qualitative work alone has been completed simply because there is not sufficient time, money, or patience for a quantitative testing-out of the ideas propounded in the groups to be done. But research was not created to force marketers to follow tenets and theories as if they were handed down from on high. It was created so that marketers could make decisions based on input beyond their egos and their guesses. In such circumstances, when "feel" is what it is all about, qualitative research can be — and sometimes even *should* be — used without quantitative follow-up. This is particularly true if the alternative is no research at all, with nothing but egos, guesses, and dreams to guide the decisions.

After all, marketers were not created for marketing research; marketing research was created for marketers. Competent marketers will know something about their markets already. Researchers must have some trust in that. Adherence by the researcher to the marketing concept dictates that professional use of qualitative findings — even alone — to help guide decisions is justified where gut feeling tells the marketer it is safe to do so.

THE "BACKWARD" APPROACH

The qualitative phase, as the reader may have perceived, is more or less a free-form phase. As long as the research follows from a basic rationale, is examined and reexamined as the project progresses, and builds on itself, nothing is prescribed and nothing is proscribed. The quantitative phase is a different matter entirely. Here the logical course of action is quite clearly spelled out. And the process may seem backward at first glance. But backward it is not.

It is rather like a palindrome ("Madam I'm Adam"), that runs the same both forward or backward, and inexorably proceeds to where it most surely must end. What seems backward is, rather, forward, and straightforward at that. The logic of quantitative research requires the researcher to see the end first, and, like that palindrome, to work inexorably backward to a point where he can start. The logical sequence begins, then, at the end, and moves backward in time. It roughly follows the following sequence:

- The "boards"
- Question areas
- Dummies
- Criterion measures and action standards
- Questionnaire

The "boards". Researchers should clearly understand this step of the research process. It is one of the most important things in the research process, because if this is done poorly, the best research in the world is most likely to end up ignored and unused.

At the end of a study, the researcher will stand in front of the client, the marketing manager, or whoever asked him to do the study. He will have about ten large "boards" that can be put up on an easel. (With modern technology, sometimes the "boards" are really slides, or overheads.) Each of these boards will have several facts on it; findings, numbers, whatever. Each one must address a key issue that the project set out to investigate, and as such, will correspond closely with the set of information needs that were identified at the very beginning of the project. Sometimes, in fact, this collection of "boards" may constitute the basis for the whole written report.

The first board will have the most important findings, the second the next most important, etc., so that if the audience's attention runs out early (or whatever), they will get the message from what you have shown. Suppose the research team has just finished a project on *marketing pet food for dogs*. The first two boards might look something like the example set forth in Figure 4.1. Think of these boards as providing the grist for the mill. They give the data for decision making on whatever marketing decisions (on product, package, advertising, etc.) must be made. Or they provide new knowledge to help formulate the next step in the learning process. To most of the audience at the final presentation of research results, they are the end result of all the work done in the project. Only a few people will ever read the entire report thoroughly. A few more may read the executive summary.

But the marketing people's initial gut feelings about how to decide usually come from seeing the presentation, and reading the boards. Moreover, decisions about whether the research is any good or not are mostly made here. "Good" research is not really good, no matter how well it is executed technically, unless it is presented well enough that it is actually used. If people completely ignore it, it is *bad* research. It would have been better to save the money it cost.

So pay attention to these boards. Work out at the very beginning of the quantitative phase what the boards will look like. The words that should appear on them are mostly the ideas that have been developed in the qualitative phase, so it should be easy to take care of this aspect of the boards. On the other hand, the numbers that appear on them are the whole point of the quantitative part of research. It is much better to grapple with the purpose of this technically demanding quantitative stuff before we even start the research process rather than midway or mostly as we conduct the survey.

- Most Dog Owners (87%) Don't Regard Dogs as "ANIMALS" but as PEOPLE.
- Examples: a substitute child
  a trusty friend
  a working partner

Dog Owners' Images of Their Dogs		
Child	40%	87%
Friend	31%	
Partner	9%	
General Family Member	7%	
Just a Dog	10%	
No clear image	3%	

Figure 4.1. Examples of the "boards".

Does it matter if these particular boards never actually get used, or even if there is never a formal presentation? Of course not. It is quite common that as the detailed data come in, the researcher will see that he has to shift some of his thinking a little bit. In that case, new versions of the boards would be drawn up. It also happens sometimes that no formal presentation is made — the report is simply sent in. In that case, the boards simply serve as a guide to important topics that need to be covered somewhere in the report — usually in the executive summary, as well as in more detail in the main body.

The vital thing is to draw up these boards at the beginning stage of quantitative work, taking advantage of the full range of creative thinking and understanding about the real nature of the issue being researched. This exercise provides some discipline to the process — it obligates the researcher to highlight in the questionnaire and to pinpoint in the analyses those issues/facts that the user of the research really needs to know about. Drawing up these boards (without the numbers, of course, and maybe with unnamed categories: image-group A, image-group B, etc., for child, friend, etc.), and showing them to the marketing manager before the quantitative survey is started provides the first logic check.

It tells the researcher whether he really understands what the marketing manager had in mind when this problem emerged as the focus of a study. The boards are a visual representation of what the study is all about — why it is really being done. The marketing manager should recognize in them potential answers to the most pressing problems he needs to address in making particular marketing decisions.

But if the boards do not speak to the marketing manager's concerns, then it is time to stop. The demanding chain of quantitative survey logic surely cannot start with such a blatant flaw. If the user is not satisfied with what the researcher thinks he will find out, the researcher must pause to think more carefully about what the project is about.

If the researcher has not grasped what the marketer wants, stopping the research process immediately to give the project more thought is simply a prudent act of self-preservation. It might save, say, ten weeks of needless effort, US$100,000 of expenses and two careers. The researcher should not proceed further with the project until he really understands what the marketing manager wants, or until he finally concedes that nothing that the research could dig up would really be of much use to the marketing manager.

Question areas.   The working backward aspect of the process now should begin to unfold pretty clearly. In order to produce those boards, the researcher will have to ask questions about certain things. He might ask, for example, the following questions:

- How many people are there in the family?
- How many dogs?
- What kind of dogs are they?
- How big are they?

- Where do they sleep?
- What association do certain types of dogs conjure up?

Note that these are not yet "questions". They are the "areas" to be explored. It is more important at this point to know what the survey must ask about than it is to know the exact way of phrasing the questions. In fact, getting bogged down in the details of how to phrase questions can too easily distract our attention away from what it is the questionnaire should be asking. These "question areas" will later be transformed into the questions of the questionnaire, but only after several further steps have been taken.

Dummies. By now, the essence of the quantitative survey should have become pretty clear from drawing up the boards and listing the question areas. The next step is to produce the final tables that will be included in your report. These tables, called *dummies* or *dummy tables* or *shells*, will have everything in them except the numbers. They will correspond to question areas, though not necessarily on a one-to-one basis. Sometimes it may take more than one table to address a particular question area. They should be drafted now and shown to the marketing manager. The researcher should tell the marketing manager: "These are the tables you will be getting — no more and no less than these. Once they are filled in with the data we will generate, will they help give you the information you need?"

These dummy tables provide yet another logic check. The answer to the researcher's question may be "yes", in which case he can move ahead with some assurance. But if the answer is "no" or "well . . .", then there must be a serious discussion of just what tables would be necessary, and what analyses are required to do the job. If there is a lack of communication, this is one of the last chances the researcher has to correct things. At this stage, there is time to review the question areas, even the boards, before the project goes any further. If he proceeds another few steps to the stage when interviewers are out in the field asking consumers questions, efforts to correct things will prove increasingly expensive and the budget will dwindle rapidly.

Drawing up these dummies really constitutes an important part of the analysis. It is critical to sort out how to organize data, what is important and what is not. Logically, this must be done now, not later, after the questionnaires have come back. The researcher should not waste time and effort getting data that no one wants or needs. An even more unpardonable sin in research would be not to ask something that the marketing manager really needed to know. Without dummies, one cannot really be sure. It is better, surely, to be safe than sorry.

What does a dummy look like? Table 4.2 is an example. Looking at such a dummy — and the groups that must be analyzed — may suggest that some proposed sample sizes will be too small for certain types of analyses. For example, not many households with heads in the 25–34 or the 55-and-over age brackets may have teenaged family members. This may lead to a decision to increase the sample size in that cell (oversampling to achieve higher counts), or to combine groups, etc. So these

Table 4.2.   Example of a dummy table.

	Table XX: Usage of Specified Brands by Age of Household Head and Presence of Teenagers in Family.											
	Age of household head											
	25–34			35–44			45–54			55 and over		
Use Brand	Total %	With teens %	No teens %	Total %	With teens %	No teens %	Total %	With teens %	No teens %	Total %	With teens %	No teens %
A												
B												
C												
D												
.												
.												
.												

dummies enable the researcher and the marketing manager to see the results (without the numbers) in the way in which they will actually be presented in the report.

Criterion measures and actions standards.   These are two final items to consider in the quantitative chain of logic before the researcher can actually move on to drafting a questionnaire. *Criterion measures* are those things that the marketing manager *most* wants to know about, those pieces of information that will be instrumental in allowing him to make the decision or advancing his understanding and grasp on the marketing situation. The researcher should get a list of these information needs and work out a priority ranking for them with the marketing manager.

For example, suppose in a product test the *reactions of children to the chewiness of a candy bar* matters the most in the decision on formulation of the product. It is important for the researcher to know this. It may lead to putting questions about chewiness to the children very early in the interview, (before they are worn out, have talked themselves out, and are tired of the whole thing). It may require an extensive series of probing questions on issues such as: What did you think of when you bit into this candy bar? What kinds of things did it feel like? etc.

Only by determining right at the beginning how relatively important things are can the researcher determine the best structure of the questionnaire. How much time and space should a specific topic get? One cannot ask everything, though some people try. Where should the topic come, at the beginning, in the middle, at the end, after a difficult question, after an easy question? How deeply should the interviewer go into the topic? How deeply should we analyze the topic? These are really unanswerable questions if nothing is known about the marketing manager's criterion measures.

Action standards should also be discussed with the marketing manager at this point. They concern what he will do if the data comes back showing certain things. Suppose the researcher and the manager have agreed upon the criterion measures. It is entirely proper to ask: "OK, what if we get 80 percent or more people answering "yes" on this one — what action are you likely to take? Suppose we get 50 percent, what would you do? Suppose 20 percent?"

It may well be difficult to elicit answers about some of the criterion measures. Trying to get answers may even spur some opposition or hostility from the marketing manager ("I can't really think about it till I see the results"). Nevertheless, it is vital to explore action standards now. If it turns out that the decision would not be affected by *whatever* level is found on this measure, then the researcher should begin to suspect that this measure is no criterion at all.

If it really does not matter very much after all, then perhaps something else should be emphasized in the questionnaire. Or perhaps it even points to the fact that the researcher does not yet understand enough the marketing implications that will result from the survey. This is the last logic check before the questionnaire is drafted and taken to the field. It is almost the last chance to confirm that the research is on track before it is too late. Only when all these steps have been taken in the chain of logic for the quantitative phase is it time to write the questionnaire (Chapter 7), or seek answers without questions (Chapter 6), or some combination.

Research Design

Research design is about *how* to get what we have just decided we need to get. It is a very important step, but there is no point in developing a research design until we know what we want to know, and the marketing manager agrees that we know. Otherwise, the project design may well be wonderful, but the information collected will mostly be irrelevant, of little use to anyone. The objectives of the research, the information needs, and behind those, the marketing problems of the marketing manager must guide the development of the research design.

Research design has several levels. In a broad sense, it is about a philosophy of how to approach the problems of finding out about things. There are the marketing problems and the research problems to consider. But the problem of how to do the research well is also critical if we are to address those marketing and research problems. Do we need to grope around a little bit more to really understand this marketing situation? We certainly do not want to prepare a lengthy questionnaire and interview five hundred respondents until we are pretty sure that the questions on that questionnaire are relevant to our marketing/research problem *and* to the people who will have to answer the questionnaire. *Exploratory research* may be necessary.

Once the researcher has a good grasp of the situation, he is ready to get involved in more extensive (but less intensive) forms of data collection. If the marketing manager mainly needs to get a "picture" of what the market is like currently, *descriptive research* is probably appropriate. What is the awareness level of our new product? Sometimes the marketing manager needs some "proof" that some marketing action actually works before going ahead to implement or continue implementing it. Does all that expensive advertising really increase sales? Such a problem may require *causal research*.

EXPLORATORY RESEARCH

Is it important to really understand the consumer or the situation in greater depth before we can even write up a questionnaire? There are many cases where this might be necessary, and usually some kind of qualitative exploratory (or pilot) research is needed. Sometimes the problem is just not very well defined. The marketing manager may not really know what is wrong — what he says is the problem may really be a symptom. For example, suppose sales are far below projections at the new store. The store manager might ask the researcher to find out why sales are so poor. On the surface, this seems like a legitimate problem to research, but when the researcher gets down to thinking about information needs, the list could get huge, because he does not really know the problem at all.

Simply looking at the standard four *P*'s of marketing, we can identify four entirely different types of problems that may be behind the symptom of poor sales. Poor sales might be related to a problem of *promotion*. Maybe people are simply unaware of the existence of the store, or they are unaware of what the store carries. If people are not shopping because they do not know about the store, then the research project must be oriented toward information needs such as awareness, source of awareness, what they actually know about the store if they have heard of it, where people look for information about stores when they plan their shopping, and so forth. Solving promotion problems requires knowing about how consumers get and use information.

Maybe consumers know about the store, but do not like the *product* assortment, or are unhappy with the quality of the products in the store. This is a different problem, and it requires a different research project. Information is needed on such things as attitudes toward products, criteria in choosing products, what products people expect to find and buy together (complementary products), and product and brand preferences. Product problems must focus on what people think about things.

The problem could be *price*-related. Consumers may think prices are too high at the store. Alternatively, they may think prices are too low. Most potential customers in the vicinity of the store could be very quality conscious and might just not believe that products at these prices could have the quality that they demand. Research on this kind of problem should focus on quality/price tradeoffs among consumers.

Place or location of the store could be wrong. The store may not be located in an area convenient for parking. Most of the store's customers may be from dual income families, and cannot shop during the store's 9 to 5 hours. Where and when people travel to shop would be addressed to solve this problem. The scope of the research can be narrowed considerably if the researcher can develop through exploratory research a better idea of exactly what the marketing problem is. If it is mainly a problem relating to place, there is not much point collecting a lot of information about promotion.

Related to this, exploratory research can be used to establish research priorities. Suppose that place was the key problem, but that awareness was low among certain consumer segments. Further, maybe most people walk, and do not drive. They do not usually go far to shop at this kind of store and only buy small, easy to carry, amounts of product at any one time. Most customers are from dual income families. Knowing these things helps us define priorities. We need to consider a lot of questions about place, focusing on things like store hours and convenience from people's daytime workplace. Not so much is needed about what people think of parking availability. We would want to include some questions addressing consumer information sources. We do not need much at all on pricing or product issues.

Maybe the researcher (and the marketing manager) need more knowledge and familiarity with the problem, the situation, and/or the respondents. For example, before we do a survey for the marketing manager of an American meat packing company on attitudes toward beef among Chinese consumers, we may want to really look into Chinese consumers' minds. What are all the little details about what they think of eating beef, what role does it play in their lives, what makes them choose beef rather than another meat, what makes them choose beef from the US rather than from the People's Republic of China (PRC)? Answers to these kinds of questions would all tell a good marketing manager much more about how to market in Hong Kong or Singapore than data from standard questions such as how much beef people eat (100–200 grams/week, 200–300, etc.), correlated with age or income level.

Why would he need to know these kinds of things? For example, a very large proportion of Singapore Chinese do not eat beef at all because of their Buddhist religion. Hong Kong Chinese, although most are also Buddhist, mostly do eat beef. A large proportion of the Singapore market is excluded from the potential market for reasons that have nothing to do with age, but in Hong Kong, just age and income might be more useful.

Many business people in these cities specifically order US beef when entertaining business colleagues with a Western meal in a restaurant. But they buy PRC beef when cooking Chinese meals at home. US beef has more prestige, and is appropriate on a social occasion such as entertaining important people. It is also higher quality than PRC beef, and necessary for a Western meal to taste good. These people are also quite aware that US beef would be higher quality in Chinese cooking. The problem is *not that they are unwilling* to pay for quality. They are willing, and do pay, daily. But *they do not think it is important* to have high quality beef in a Chinese style dish.

It is not difficult to ask five hundred people straightforward questions about such issues *if we know about them*. But we are unlikely to know about them if we do not take the time to understand the situation and the people that we are going to ask. Certainly a fresh *guilo* (Westerner) is unlikely to think of such issues unless he has had considerable experience studying food consumption among Chinese. Even a Hong Kong Chinese researcher might not think to ask about the strength of religion in Singapore.

The exploratory research may be used to develop hypotheses about the situation. Once the researcher is more familiar with the Chinese consumer of beef, he may begin to get the idea that maybe younger people in Singapore are becoming less concerned with religion, and so eat more beef. Maybe Hong Kong people who work in foreign firms, have more contacts with Westerners, have foreign experience, and like to project a Westernized image. They buy more US beef. Hypotheses are just ideas about what we think is going on, and these ideas are hypotheses. The researcher can include questions in the questionnaire that will tell him, when the data are collected and analyzed, whether his ideas have any validity.

Exploratory research can be used to clarify concepts. People who spend a lot of money on US beef are probably quality conscious. But what exactly is quality to the Chinese consumer who buys beef? Is it freshness, taste, texture, juiciness, size of the cut, cleanliness, nutritional value? The same answer to a question like: "how important is quality to you?" can mean many different things. The consumer who shops in the low-priced wet market, where the meat is so fresh that the steer was probably walking around yesterday, thinks freshness is a very important attribute. To her, quality means freshness, so she answers "very important". The customer who shops at the high-priced Japanese supermarket says "very important" because she thinks hygiene and taste are more critical than anything else.

Fuzzy concepts result in fuzzy information. Sometimes fuzzy information can be worse than no information at all. The researcher may not recognize that it is fuzzy and think he knows a lot when he actually has learned very little. In this beef example, nearly everyone in the sample might well answer that quality is very important. But since quality means different things to different people, this really tells very little about the Hong Kong market.

The reader who is paying attention to details should be thinking by now that these examples of exploratory research do not all fall in proper sequence as set out in our list of steps in the research process (see Figure 3.1). We have placed exploratory research on the list in sequence in which it commonly is undertaken, but there are often needs for it to be carried out during any of the early stages of the research process. Any time the researcher is not very clear about exactly how to proceed because he does not know enough about the marketing situation or the survey respondents, there is room for exploratory research. Fuzziness is expected, indeed, is the rule, in these early stages. Exploratory research enables us to deal with it. The fuzziness must be cleared up before we get to later quantitative stages of the research process. There is no way to deal with it in methodologies which require rigor and precision.

Exploratory research is the "ideas" part of research that we have stressed so much in the beginning chapters. It develops, clarifies, and prioritizes ideas. This means that qualitative methods are very often the most appropriate. But exploratory research also uses a wide variety of other methods, such as review of secondary data. An experience survey, talking to people within the industry about what they know, is also common. As mentioned many times, when dealing with ideas, we can use about any method we want that gets us the information needed to work with those ideas.

DESCRIPTIVE RESEARCH

As the name implies, the purpose of descriptive research is to describe. We are no longer developing ideas, clearing up fuzzy concepts, and trying to learn something about the situation. Now, we think we understand what is going on. We need to describe the matter at hand with more precision, in more quantitative terms. Qualitatively, we may say: "Younger people in Singapore are less concerned with religion and eat more beef." The marketing manager may well want to know more. How many younger people are less concerned with religion? All of them? Half of them? One-tenth of them? How much less concerned? Most of them say religion is not important at all? Half of them say religion is somewhat important? How much beef do they eat? One steak a month, or do they visit a Western restaurant twice a week to eat beef cooked Western style?

For many, perhaps most, marketing decisions, qualitative information is not enough. The difference between 60 percent eating beef once a week and 30 percent may well be the difference between profit or loss if the company decides to set up a sales office to go after the Singapore market. We have the ideas now, the understanding of different viewpoints, trends. It is time for some numbers to verify that what we think we now know is actually true.

One common focus of descriptive research is to describe characteristics of certain groups. The groups may be people, consumers. The marketing manager could ask for a profile of the meat consumption patterns of Singaporeans aged 25 to 35 with incomes above S$1500 per month. The groups may be based on product usage: what is the demographic profile of those in Singapore who buy US beef more than once a month? The groups may be large and broadly defined, as in a project that simply wants to determine consumption in Hong Kong of beef from different countries. Hong Kong is a group of nearly six million. The groups may be small and narrowly defined. How much Kobe (Japanese) beef does the community of Japanese expatriates in Hong Kong consume?

Another common use of descriptive research is to estimate the proportion of people in the population who are something or do something. What proportion of Hong Kong Chinese are Westernized, as evidenced by their food consumption patterns? What proportion of Hong Kong Chinese buy US beef more than once a month, where doing something is buying a specific product. Of course, some of the most common proportions that marketing managers want to know are things like market share, brand awareness, proportion of samples that result in trial, and proportion of repurchases after trial.

These two objectives may not seem very different at first glance, but understanding the difference between them is critical to developing a descriptive research project where either of these two objectives is important. Unfortunately, sometimes both objectives cannot be accommodated at once. The methodologies needed to accurately describe groups may differ from those required to accurately estimate proportions. We may have to decide which objective is most important and sacrifice accuracy on the less important one.

For example, if we want to estimate country preference in Hong Kong for US, Australian, and New Zealand beef, a random sample is the best way to proceed. A well-executed random sample (of sufficient sample size) will reflect the proportions of the population quite well. If 30 percent in Hong Kong prefer Australian, then approximately 30 percent of the sample will prefer Australian, give or take a few percent due to sampling error.

If we want to compare how Japanese in Hong Kong view US beef with how Chinese view Australian beef, a purely random sample is a poor methodology. Less than half of 1 percent of the Hong Kong population is Japanese. Even in a sample of 1000, we are likely to get fewer than 5 Japanese, but well over 950 Chinese. No comparison is possible, because with fewer than five responses, we really have very little idea at all what Japanese think. We need something like a quota or a stratified random sample. Then we can determine that we want, say, at least 100 Japanese so that we can do accurate statistics on their responses. But this sampling method cannot be an accurate representation of population proportions, so it is more difficult to estimate preference shares very well.

A third common use of descriptive data is to make predictions. Because 30 percent of the population is highly quality conscious and thinks taste and tenderness are very important in choosing beef, then up to 30 percent of the market is potential customers for US beef. Of course, this prediction might only come true assuming that US beef is marketed effectively. More importantly, this is really kind of a vague "prediction" anyway, what might happen (potential) rather than what will happen (forecasting). Maybe the researcher could be more precise about certain segments: 10 percent of Hong Kong Chinese have some substantial foreign experience. Our survey data show that these 10 percent consume a certain amount of US beef each year. Government statistics show the increase in foreign experience (immigration, return, foreign travel, etc.), so we can project how many Westernized Chinese there will be next year and project beef sales.

The questionnaire could be set up to look at specific levels of advertising awareness and purchase experience. A quota sampling methodology could specifically aim to get a certain number of people who recall seeing the advertising three times, or five times, or ten times, or remember only one point or three different points of the message. Different levels of exposure or of recall could be correlated with the purchasing rate. The researcher could predict what the purchase rate would be if enough were spent to raise advertising exposure and recall to a certain level.

These kinds of prediction are made from descriptive research all the time. Technically, without knowing causes of behavior (causal research), such predictions are suspect. They are based on associations which may or may not have something to do with each other. Westernization may well be a cause of higher beef consumption, but it may not be, too. We would need to conduct causal research to be more sure. Perhaps the cause of more beef consumption is rising incomes. As people's incomes rise, they are able to afford more travel, so foreign experience is up at the same time that beef consumption is up. The increases are associated with each other, but Westernization and beef consumption are not directly related.

The survey may show that high advertising awareness is associated with higher sales. This is probably true, but descriptive research cannot prove it. Suppose the product is a snack food. People who watch a lot of TV eat a lot of snack food, and they also see a lot of commercials. There is nothing wrong with making predictions based on descriptive research, provided one is aware of the limitations of those predictions. Finding an association in descriptive research, and projecting that association into the future, does not in any sense "prove" that one thing causes another. At best, it gives the manager a clue. Use predictions based on descriptive research, certainly, but use them with caution.

Forecasting is another kind of prediction, which is usually (not always) based on descriptive research undertaken out of secondary sources, not survey work. Time series forecasting is based on fitting a statistical or mathematical model to past data (a time series) and projecting past patterns into the future. For example, we applied a diffusion model to forecast that fax line installations in Hong Kong for the current generation of fax machines would decline in the early 1990s (Figure 5.1; faxes are not becoming less popular, but the new generation of fax machines does not depend on a dedicated line). This kind of prediction requires that data be available over time. For faxes, the data "describes", with a number, the level of installations each month over the past several years.

Conceptually, there is really not much difference between this kind of prediction and those based on survey data. The forecast is still based on a correlation between two variables (installations and time period). The forecast simply projects the past pattern into the future, i.e., it assumes the patterns seen in the past and now will continue to hold. They might hold, if market conditions do not change. But if Westernized Chinese decide that Scottish Angus beef is even better than US beef, TV viewers are bombarded with even more advertisements by a competitor, or satellite technology eliminates the need for faxes, market conditions will change, and predictions of any type based on projecting patterns and associations into the future may not work well.

If the researcher knows in advance that survey data will be needed for use in forecasting or simply for tracking, then a consistent program can be set up to period-ically gather the same data from people. This is often done in panels, a fixed sample, in which the same people are periodically asked the same questions. The reason for this is that repeated measures sampling reduces sample variation, since individual variation is controlled. For example, if one finds a ten percent increase in reported awareness, one is fairly certain that ten percent is a good estimate for increased awareness. The same people have been asked, and we know whatever sampling error there is in this sample has been held constant.

The other way of estimating increased awareness would require one sample at first, then a new, different sample later. This is commonly done also. Statistically, it is not as accurate, because the sampling error in the two samples may well differ in both

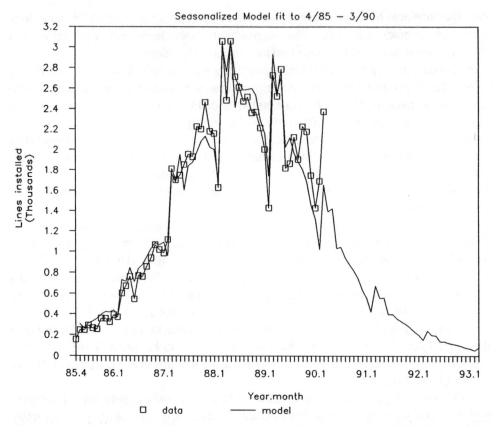

Figure 5.1. Fax line installations in Hong Kong: Observations vs. diffusion model.

magnitude and direction. For example, what if the first sample had a few more people who do not watch much TV, and a few less who watch a lot. And then the second sample had a slight shift toward heavy TV watchers. As we will see in Chapter 8, this is certainly possible. But in terms of the advertising awareness, it is difficult to say that awareness increased ten percent between the times of the two samples. Some of the apparent increase may simply be that people who watch more TV see more advertisements, and there are more of these people in the second sample.

If panel samples are statistically better, why are they not used all the time? Researchers should not be ignorant of statistical issues. One main reason is cost. In a panel, the project must keep track of each respondent over time, which requires a lot of (costly) administration. Sometimes increased accuracy in the data is simply not worth the increased cost. Another reason is that answering our questionnaire over and over in a panel may in fact influence respondents' answers. Did awareness really increase because more respondents saw the advertising on TV and remembered some of what it said? Maybe they recalled the questions about the advertising in previous questionnaires, and paid more attention than usual. Higher awareness among the panel might not really represent increased awareness among the population. Even worse, maybe they are simply aware of the brand because they recall it from the questionnaire, and they do not recall the commercial at all.

These kinds of tradeoffs exist everywhere throughout research. We have seen them in previous chapters, and they will show up in later ones. At every stage, the needs to control cost, maintain statistical rigor, get more information, and reduce bias from numerous sources must all be balanced by the researcher. At every stage, he must think about the impact on the overall validity and usefulness of research results if one thing is sacrificed to improve another.

CAUSAL RESEARCH

Making predictions based upon projecting past and present patterns into the future can be risky, whether it is done from a single survey or from time series data. Sometimes it is important to have more assurance that one thing indeed causes another, and not just happens to show up at the same time. Does more advertising really cause more sales, or does it just look that way because the company tends to spend more on advertising during periods of economic growth, when sales also tend to go up? Causal research can provide a more rigorous test of causality.

The first thing to realize about causal research is that we can never "prove" one thing causes another. We can only provide strong evidence that it does, but there is always a chance that we could be wrong. To provide that strong evidence, the researcher generally needs to demonstrate several things. The thing caused and the thing causing it should vary together consistently. If advertising causes higher sales, then sales revenue should go up when advertising expenditure increases. This can be a statistical relationship: sales tend to go up, on the average, when expenditure increases. There may be a few times when it does not work, but it usually does. However, if we find that when expenditure increases, advertising may go up or may go down, and neither one is more likely than the other, it would be hard to see any causality.

The order in which things happen is not arbitrary. The cause must precede the effect or end result, i.e., increased advertising must come first if it causes increased sales. A situation where increased sales came first, and the advertising budget was increased later, would not demonstrate that more advertising contributes to more sales. (In fact, in many companies, it does seem like sales cause advertising. When sales go up during an economic boom, they spend more, when sales decline in a recession, they spend less. Not the marketing way of doing things, but common nonetheless.)

Finally, to demonstrate causality, it is critical that the researcher be able to eliminate any other possible explanation for the patterns in which cause and effect vary together. We have already seen some examples of alternative explanations above. These examples illustrate why descriptive research might not be a reliable tool for making predictions (or showing causality). Westernization might cause higher beef consumption, but it might not. Higher income could lead to both more Westernization and to more beef consumption, so that both rise together. High advertising awareness might cause higher sales, but it might not. People who watch a lot of TV eat a lot of snack food, and they also see a lot of commercials. Awareness and sales of snack foods would both be higher for these people.

To deal with these important issues in determining causality, researchers usually use some kind of experimental methodology. By controlling other variables, particularly the ones associated with the alternative explanation, and varying only the variable(s) associated with the "cause-and-effect" relationship observed we can check whether the "causative" variables do what they are supposed to do. So, fix how much TV people watch, vary advertising exposure, and see what happens to sales of snack food. This controlled aspect makes most causal research relatively expensive, because tight control is not easy (or cheap).

DATA COLLECTION

For descriptive research, survey methods are probably the single most common approach used in marketing research. And since descriptive research is probably more common than any other kind of formal marketing research, survey methods have tended to dominate research designs. Surveys are even used in exploratory and causal research. This does not mean that survey research is always the best method. For many situations, it is not. It does not mean that other methods cannot work better. In some situations, they do. Chapter 6 discusses many data collection techniques other than survey methods. All of them are valid in marketing research. Any of them may well be the most appropriate method for some specific problem.

Nevertheless, because survey research is so much more common than any other single method, marketing researchers and users of research must be familiar with it. And in doing survey research, one of the first issues to come up is how to collect the survey data. Modifications of techniques, as well as modern technology, may have blurred distinctions somewhat, but there are still basically three choices: mail, telephone, and personal interviews.

Deciding which of these three methods to use is not as simple a matter as it may seem. There are numerous advantages and disadvantages associated with each one. Each method is capable of obtaining different qualities and quantities of data from respondents, each has different levels and types of bias associated with it, each takes different amounts of time, money, and interviewing skill to carry out. The researcher must carefully match the method with the objectives of the research, the population and sample, the form and content of questions, and the research budget, to name only a few of the most important considerations.

Personal interviews bring the interviewer face-to-face with the respondent, allowing for the most complete interaction. In many situations, this interaction is essential. For example, if we want to measure recognition of a brand of cereal, we may want to actually show the product. Reaction to a proposed advertising layout and copy can only be measured if people see the ad. There are many of these kinds of questions that require showing respondents something. We may even want the respondent to handle the product, or taste the cereal. Of course, we could put a picture in a mail questionnaire, but then we cannot control the precise time at which the respondent sees such pictures. We may need to ask questions about general attitudes toward breakfast cereal before we ask about specific brands. The general answers must not be biased by the fact that people think the specific brand we show tastes like soggy cardboard.

Often interaction is needed because the questionnaire is complex and requires explanation. If we have a difficult scale, for example, it is often easiest to show people how to understand it. Explaining a fixed sum scale (Chapter 7) over the telephone is not so easy. Explaining a difficult branching pattern (if yes, go to 14, if no, go to 18) is much easier in person, especially if the interviewer can simply follow the branch so that the respondent never even has to think about it. Complex things in a mail questionnaire, explained or not, usually simply discourage response.

Interaction is also needed to encourage response, especially if the questionnaire is long. Some degree of personal relationship is established in face-to-face interviews. Granted, this relationship is tenuous, but it is still stronger than the relationship that can be established over the phone. No relationship at all is established by mail. This tenuous relationship makes people somewhat more willing to spend time talking to the interviewer. In Hong Kong, for example, people do not generally like to give information or spend time giving information. But personal interview survey response rates are higher, and the length of the interview can be longer (even up to half an hour for some particularly long questionnaires).

Data quality is often better, also. People are more inclined to give truthful answers (on most, not all) questions if they are talking to someone face-to-face. Usually, this is not because people are prone to lying, but simply because they do not think the topic in the question is very important. The criteria people use to choose a breakfast cereal, or the specific brand they choose, are really not very vital issues to most people. They may tend to answer whatever comes to mind first without really thinking about the question. Sometimes we want this top-of-mind kind of answer, but other times, we want more thought. People are more likely to think if they are talking to a real person, because they feel some small obligation to cooperate.

Some questions people are not as likely to answer truthfully in personal interviews. These include questions where there may be socially desirable answers, or that are embarrassing or sensitive in some way. In those cases, people are more likely to answer truthfully if they believe they will remain anonymous. They certainly will not believe that their answers will remain anonymous if they are standing right in front of an interviewer when responding. Even if they trust that their identity will not be recorded or revealed, they have to tell the interviewer, a stranger, and the interviewer knows what they said.

For example, we once did a survey on student sexual activity on campus for the Student Health Center. The Center wanted to determine what kinds of medical services and counseling should be offered. Obviously, most students are unlikely to talk freely or answer honestly about such issues if an interviewer asks them such questions. Surveys conducted in Hong Kong to assess the level of confidence as 1997 approaches might pose similar — though less extreme — difficulties. The socially desirable answer to most people is that Hong Kong will be fine, everything will work out, and that they plan to stay and help Hong Kong build its future. This is what people may say to an interviewer. If they answer a mail survey knowing that no one at all will ever know what they said, they may be more willing to admit that they have a foreign passport, have sent their money abroad, or have registered their company offshore.

In many cases, questions must be asked of respondents at a specific location. For example, determining how brand choices for cereals are made may be best accomplished at the time and place where the cereal is purchased. In other words, interviewing shoppers at the store immediately after they have actually made the choices is likely to get the most accurate data. Determining what people think of the cereal when they eat it might require interviews at home around breakfast time. In many cases, personal interviews are the best way to guarantee that the interview takes place in a specific place at a specific time. Phone calls might be able to handle the in-home situation, but store interviews would have to be personal.

Personal interviewing can be hard on the budget, both in terms of time and money. It requires more time to administer the questionnaire, it requires more field supervision, it requires generally high interviewing skills levels, so interviewers must either be trained well or already be experienced (and costly). It can be a slow process, especially when compared with telephone surveys. This means that for a given budget, fewer respondents can usually be surveyed through personal interviews than through telephone or mail surveys. The researcher may have to decide whether he needs more data from fewer people, or less data from more people.

Some sampling methodologies are impractical, also, mainly because of these budget constraints. Pure random sampling, for example, would result in a list of respondents all over Hong Kong. Interviewing time and cost would be multiplied by the large amount of time spent traveling around to reach all of the respondents. Other sampling methodologies are quite well suited. Geographic cluster sampling is ideally suited to personal interviewing designs, as are various convenience methods.

Personal interviewing can potentially introduce some kinds of bias attributable to the interviewer. The sample may tend toward people who the interviewer thinks look like someone he would like to talk to, especially if convenience sampling is used. The answers may tend one way because the interviewer implies by tone of voice or facial expression what he thinks is a proper response. Provided the researcher is aware of their potential, these bias issues can be minimized through proper training and control.

Telephone interviews allow voice interaction with respondents, but not visual contact. (Technology may eventually change this.) Not much in the way of demonstrations or showing can be done, unless the interviews are combined with some other method. For example, the survey could call to determine responses to a free sample that was distributed door-to-door that day. Phone interviews do allow explanation of difficult questions or scales. But the ability to explain things on the phone is not as great as in person, where the interviewer can judge from the respondent's facial expression whether everything is understood or show how to read the scale. Branching can easily be followed in phone interviews; in fact, the respondent should never know there is a branch at all.

Phone interviews must be shorter, less complex than personal interviews. In Hong Kong, where one can sometimes get away with up to 20 to 30 minutes in a personal interview, people will rarely talk on the phone for more than about 10 to 15 minutes. So we cannot get as much data from any one respondent. Nor is the quality likely to be as good, especially on any questions which touch upon difficult topics or involve difficult scales. But telephone interviewing is cheaper, so a given budget can cover a bigger sample if a bigger one is needed. The advantages are especially apparent if the survey population is widely dispersed geographically. With telephone interviewing, the project is not paying for the time field workers spend in tracking down the respondents.

Response rates are generally relatively high for phone interviewing, though not as good as with personal interviews. The voice contact does establish some kind of minimal relationship, which encourages people to answer. For those topics that fall in the category of somewhat sensitive, phone interviews can even get higher response rates than personal interviews, because respondents feel somewhat more anonymous. For *very* sensitive topics, they are still unlikely to answer, and some form of mail survey will be required.

Phone interviewing is very effective at controlling the timing of the interview. Respondents can be called in mid-morning and asked how they liked what they ate for breakfast, before they have had lunch and are thinking about that meal. They can be called in the evening to see whether they were watching the evening news when the commercial was run, and what they recall about the commercial if they were watching the news. When conducting telephone interviews, however, one cannot control the time that respondents will be present. Calls made in mid-morning will tend to be answered by housewives. Yet, it may be more important to get working women because they like the time-saving convenience of breakfast cereal. Researchers must judge the suitability of telephone interviewing in terms of who will be on the phone line when the calls are made.

Phone interview methods require that the survey population actually has telephones. This is obvious, but sometimes overlooked by those who have operated only in an industrial country. In a developed place like Hong Kong or Singapore, most of the people and businesses one would be interested in surveying do have telephones. In many cities throughout the developing world, though, this might not be true. There, phone interviewing might only be valid for surveys of upper-income consumers. Telephone surveys would not work at all in rural areas. In rural Sudan, where we conducted a survey once, there is often not even any electricity.

Even in developed countries, the researcher must consider whether the type of people least likely to have a phone (low-income people, people who have recently moved) are important to the survey or not. To survey attitudes toward breakfast cereal in Hong Kong, perhaps the focus should be on middle- to upper-income people. Lower-income, less Westernized people are unlikely to be potential customers anyway. Some of them may not have phones, but understanding their views on cereal may not be so important. But a survey on preferences in rice packaging could hardly afford to leave these people out.

Telephone interviewing also usually requires lists of the survey population so that sampling can be carried out. In most Chinese cities, for example, such lists are not available, so developing a telephone sample is very difficult. Of course, random digit dialing may work even better than lists in some cases. This is popular in industrialized countries where there are lots of telephones available to most of the population, and lots of telephone numbers. It is not so practical in a place where the vast majority of the randomly dialed numbers are not actually assigned.

Mail surveys are self-administered by respondents. Whether the survey truly actually goes out by mail is not really the relevant issue. It may be left on respondents' doors, handed to them, or left for them to pick up. The essence is the same. There is no interview, so there is no control over the response process by anyone on the research team. Respondents complete mail surveys on their own, at their own convenience, and return them at their own discretion.

Because of the lack of control, there can be several potentially very serious problems with mail surveys. The most serious is non-response bias and self-selection. Since respondents decide for themselves whether to respond, many of them do not. Response rates are rarely very high; in fact, a response rate of over 30 percent would be very unlikely in most cases. In surveys we have done in Hong Kong, response rates are more typically around ten percent. This means that to achieve a specific sample size, the researcher may have to send out ten times as many questionnaires as responses needed in the sample. Sample size is the number of people actually *in* the sample (returns), not the number of people we might have liked to be in it (mailings).

But a low response rate is not, in itself, the reason that mail surveys can have problems. If 10 percent of every kind of person receiving the questionnaire answer, there would be no problem. Ten percent of the people who love breakfast cereal and eat it every day answer, 10 percent who hate it answer, and 10 percent of those who really do not have much of an opinion about it at all answer. Ten percent of the busy people who rush off in a hurry every morning, and 10 percent of those with lots of time to waste answer. We can get accurate results. If we want more precision, we can simply increase the mailing, so that 10 percent of 2000 people answer, instead of 10 percent of 1000.

The real problem is that this 10 percent is not constant across all kinds of people. People with little interest in the topic tend not to answer at all, while those with strong interest answer more frequently. People who really love cereal, think it is great for the family's nutrition, are likely to answer. People who really hate it, think all the pre-sweetened sugary stuff is destroying children's health, are likely to answer. The vast majority of people in the middle, who probably just do not think about breakfast cereal very much, may have little interest in the topic. They are not likely to answer. This is made even worse because among any of these groups, busy people are less likely to answer than those who are not very busy.

Before deciding on any kind of mail survey method, the researcher must consider the impact of these issues upon the goals of the research. If the main purpose of the project is to find out if there are any strong views toward breakfast cereals, mail surveys may work. Mostly strong views come back in them. If the goal is to find out the general view in Hong Kong about eating cereal for breakfast, a mail survey will not work. The general views are less likely to be reflected.

Given that the researcher has decided that these non-response issues are not serious in a particular survey, mail has certain advantages. For certain kinds of sensitive information, people are more likely to answer by self-administered questionnaires than if asked directly. Then, the possible problems of bias may be less important than the problem of not getting any data at all. For example, the survey noted above on student sexual activity was administered by handing out questionnaires to every dormitory room and instructing students to fill out the questionnaire in private and mail it to the Student Health Clinic. The fact that students knew the sponsor (the clinic) was highly credible and that they would remain completely anonymous resulted in a fairly good response rate.

Mail surveys are relatively easy on the financial budget, though they can take a long time to complete. There is no field staff to train, send out, and supervise, so costs are lowered. The fact that there is no interviewer also eliminates any potential interviewer bias. For a given budget, a much larger sample can usually be collected than with interviewing methods, even allowing for non-response. Since interviewers are not traveling, and there are no long-distance costs, mail surveys are often well suited for covering wide geographical areas.

But no interviewer also means no control, as mentioned above, so there are also disadvantages. No one can explain to the respondent how to interpret the question, how to understand the scale, how to follow the branching. No one can control the order in which the questions are read, or the exact time that the respondent looks at any picture which may be included. No one can make sure that the respondent completes the questionnaire at a specific place or at a specific time. Many respondents read over the whole questionnaire before deciding to answer. Many take the questionnaire home, or to the office, to some place other than where it was received. Some answer immediately, some put it off until days or weeks later.

This lack of control can potentially lower data quality. But good researchers should anticipate these problems and construct a questionnaire to minimize them. For mail surveys, this almost always means constructing a short and simple questionnaire. Mail surveys can collect less data per respondent, the questions cannot make people think as much, the choices cannot be as complex as with interviewing. The longer the questionnaire gets, the more difficult the questions are, the lower the response rate and the more serious the self-selection bias become. The best mail surveys, in terms of getting accurate data without much bias, can generally ask no more than about five minutes worth of relatively simple questions.

True mail surveys (those with actual mailings) require lists that match the research population. If accurate lists are not available, samples obtained from mailings would be biased even without self-selection. Self administered question-naires also require literate respondents. Even in industrialized countries, this may be a problem if certain groups are included in the sample. In the US, for example, some sources estimate that as much as twenty percent of the work force is functionally illiterate. Developing countries certainly have varying degrees of illiteracy.

Mail surveys also require time. It takes a certain number of days for question-naires to reach respondents once they are mailed. Once they are sent back, it takes that time again. But most of the time it takes to receive responses to the survey mailings is due to the fact that people do not always answer the questionnaire right away. They put it at the bottom of the "to do" pile to get to at the end of the day, the end of the week, or maybe the next week. Survey questionnaires can come trickling in weeks after the mailing. A follow-up mailing to remind people to return completed question-naires if they have not already done so can trigger off another wave of returns. The researcher just has to set some cutoff time beyond which returns will be ignored.

SAMPLING PROCEDURES

Once the best way to gather the data has been determined through carefully consid-ering the respective advantages and disadvantages of personal or phone interviews and mail questionnaires, the researcher must decide how to take the sample, who gets in it, and how many. For the how, there are two basic choices: probability (random) or non-probability. Each is appropriate to different kinds of problems and situations. To understand why it is important to distinguish the two choices, we need to know something about sampling error.

Whenever we are dealing with samples rather than whole populations, we have sampling error. Only part of the population is actually being measured. The respon-dents in the sample *may* be representative of the population, and it is the task of sampling methodology to insure that they *will* be representative. Even if the sample is representative, though, not everyone answers the same way. There is some distri-bution to the way the population feels or the way the population acts. For example, people do not all spend the same amount on soft drinks in a week. Some spend more, some less. There is some mean spending figure for the population.

Because of sampling error, any specific sample mean is unlikely to exactly equal the true (but unknown) population mean. Suppose that two samples actually do come from the same population. One sample could just happen to get a few more high-spending people, but a few less low-spending ones. The sample statistics will come out slightly different from the true population statistics. Another sample might just happen to get a few less high spenders, and a few more who spend less. Again, the sample mean will not exactly match the true (unknown) population mean.

Table 5.1 illustrates this. It shows 20 samples drawn from the same population. In this case we have chosen a population for which we know the true mean and standard deviation, so that the point could be illustrated. None of the sample means is exactly equal to the population mean of ten. If we were unaware of sampling error, we might even believe (incorrectly) that sample 1 and sample 2 actually came from different populations. Such sampling error occurs not only for means, but whenever we want any statistics from the sample. For example, Table 5.2 shows cross-tab tables constructed from ten samples out of the same population. None of them are exactly alike, and none are exactly like a table that would occur if there were no such thing as sampling error.

Table 5.1.   Illustration of sampling error in means.

Twenty samples of 45 observations each drawn from a population distributed normally with mean = 10 and standard deviation = 5.

Sample	Mean	Standard deviation	Sample	Mean	Standard deviation
1	10.732	5.403	11	10.323	6.146
2	9.740	5.237	12	10.142	6.182
3	9.190	4.989	13	9.448	4.295
4	9.384	5.153	14	8.475	6.525
5	10.297	4.903	15	9.914	5.269
6	10.335	4.407	16	9.960	4.840
7	10.001	5.446	17	10.402	4.532
8	8.692	4.474	18	10.316	4.471
9	10.391	4.527	19	9.531	4.299
10	10.218	5.068	20	9.565	4.966

Measures of this sample of samples:

	Means	Standard deviations
Mean	9.853	5.057
Minimum	8.475	4.295
Maximum	10.732	6.525

To get an idea about how big a problem sampling error is, we need to know the standard error of the estimate. When the parameter estimate is a mean, the standard error of the sample mean is simply the population standard deviation divided by the square root of the sample size (Box 5.1). Note, then, that sampling error depends on how variable the population is, *and* on how big the sample is. Also note that strictly speaking, computation of the sampling error in any sample is only legitimate when

Table 5.2. Illustration of sampling error in cross-tabs tables.

In a population where rows and columns are not related, and
 rows are distributed   1 (50%) 2 (30%) 3 (20%) and
 columns are distributed 1 (20%) 2 (40%) 3 (40%);
without sampling error, the distribution of 100 observations would theoretically look like:

ROW

COL	1	2	3	ALL
1	10	20	20	50
2	6	12	12	30
3	4	8	8	20
ALL	20	40	40	100

Here are 10 samples of 100 drawn from that population:

	1	2	3	ALL			1	2	3	ALL
1	9	22	24	55		1	11	20	25	56
2	7	9	11	27		2	4	11	14	29
3	3	8	7	18		3	3	6	6	15
ALL	19	39	42	100		ALL	18	37	45	100
	1	2	3	ALL			1	2	3	ALL
1	6	15	31	52		1	9	27	19	55
2	4	14	14	32		2	4	11	15	30
3	2	7	7	16		3	4	3	8	15
ALL	12	36	52	100		ALL	17	41	42	100
	1	2	3	ALL			1	2	3	ALL
1	8	18	21	47		1	16	17	22	55
2	3	12	17	32		2	4	12	13	29
3	3	8	10	21		3	3	4	9	16
ALL	14	38	48	100		ALL	23	33	44	100
	1	2	3	ALL			1	2	3	ALL
1	8	29	18	55		1	10	18	23	51
2	7	12	9	28		2	4	11	15	30
3	1	11	5	17		3	4	7	8	19
ALL	16	52	32	100		ALL	18	36	46	100
	1	2	3	ALL			1	2	3	ALL
1	7	24	17	48		1	13	24	22	59
2	6	15	10	31		2	2	9	13	24
3	2	8	11	21		3	5	7	5	17
ALL	15	47	38	100		ALL	20	40	40	100

the sample results from some random method. If the sample is not random, we can do the computations on sampling error, and most researchers do actually do them. But there is simply no way of knowing whether those computations are accurate. They are not statistically valid.

BOX 5.1. STANDARD ERRORS AND CONFIDENCE INTERVALS

Computing standard errors of parameter estimates obtained from samples is important in deciding how much trust we should place in those estimates. From those standard errors, confidence intervals can be computed. For example, $S_{\bar{x}}$, the standard error for the sample mean, can be computed as:

$$S_{\bar{x}} = \frac{\sigma_x}{\sqrt{n}},$$

where

σ_x = the standard deviation of the population,
n = sample size.

Of course, if we actually knew the standard deviation of the population, we would undoubtedly know the mean of the population, and would not have to estimate it. In most real cases, σ_x is not known, and must be estimated by the sample standard deviation, S_x. Then

$$S_{\bar{x}} = \frac{S_x}{\sqrt{n}}.$$

The standard error of the sample mean is used in computing a confidence interval around the sample mean:

$$\bar{X} \pm Z S_{\bar{x}}.$$

Z here is the value of the standard normal distribution at a specified confidence level. The manager chooses the confidence level based on the amount of risk he is willing to take that we may be wrong in deciding what we know about what the population mean is. For example, at a 90 percent confidence level, $Z = 1.645$. (For small samples, we would use a t value, not a Z value; cf. Chapter 8.)
We interpret this confidence interval with the help of the equation

$$\bar{X} - Z S_{\bar{x}} \leq \mu \leq \bar{X} + Z S_{\bar{x}}.$$

where μ is the population mean which we want to estimate. This says that we can be 90 percent sure (confident) that the true population mean lies somewhere inside the confidence interval.

For example, suppose we took a sample of 100 and found mean spending per year ($\overline{X}$) was US$275, and the sample standard deviation (S_x) was US$85. The manager has specified a 90 percent confidence level, so that $Z = 1.645$. (Technically, we should use a t value, but t values approach Z values when sample size gets large. For $n = 100$, the difference only appears in the second decimal digit.) The confidence interval looks like:

$$275 \pm 1.645 \times \frac{85}{\sqrt{100}}, \quad \text{or} \quad 275 \pm 13.98.$$

Rounding the $\pm$ part to 14, we come up with an interval ranging from 261 to 289. We can say that we are 90 percent sure that the true mean of spending in the population is somewhere between US$261 and 289.

Suppose the manager wants to be more sure about things. With this example, there is still a 10 percent chance that we are wrong, that the true population mean does not really lie somewhere between 261 and 289. What happens if we want to be 95 percent sure? Then $Z = 1.96$, and the interval is ± 16.66. In other words, the confidence interval gets wider (258.3 to 291.7). More certainty that the true mean is in the interval means less precision about exactly where it is.

Normally, changing confidence levels is not a valid way to do things, anyway. How much risk the manager is willing to take that he does not know what the true mean is should not depend on what he wants to find out. So confidence level should be set before hand, and adhered to. If we want to increase precision without changing risk (confidence level), the only way to do it is to change the sample size. Since the half-width of the confidence interval depends on $1/\sqrt{n}$, a larger n means a smaller confidence interval. Unfortunately, we can see that doubling the precision (cutting the confidence interval in half) will take four times as large a sample, and thus, four times as much of the variable cost associated with sampling.

Calculations for confidence intervals on proportions are similar to those for means, except that the expression for standard error of the estimate is different:

$$S_p = \sqrt{\frac{p(1-p)}{n}}.$$

Then, the confidence interval around the proportion, p, is written as

$$p \pm Z S_p.$$

Suppose that 25 percent of the sample of 100 prefers brand A. Then, the 90 percent confidence interval looks like:

$$0.25 \pm 1.645 \sqrt{\frac{0.25\,(1-0.25)}{100}} \quad \text{or} \quad 0.25 \pm 0.07.$$

The issues of reliability and validity, which were mentioned in Chapter 2, are also closely tied in with sampling. Recall that reliability is the ability to get the same results every time the same research is done. Partly this is connected with sampling error, since high sampling error is one thing that would cause low reliability. Low reliability translates into large confidence intervals. Reliability, to the extent that it depends upon variance in the population, can be improved by larger samples. (But there are also other causes of low reliability.)

Validity is the degree to which the research actually measures what it is supposed to measure. In other words, how can this sample of 200 represent the population of Hong Kong, which is near to six million? The proper answer to (an uninformed) question like this is that validity (representativeness) is really not related to sample size at all. But it is closely related to how the sample is taken. To be confident that a sample is representative, it should be random. Non-random samples *may* be perfectly representative, but one cannot be certain.

Random samples, technically, probability samples, are taken in very precise, well-defined ways. Random does *not* mean arbitrary. It does mean that every person (or element) in the population has a known probability of being included in the sample. It also means that people are actually chosen by some objective method which allows no scope for the personal choices of researcher or field-workers. Accurate calculation of sampling error requires that these probabilities be known and not distorted by personal whim.

Simple random samples are the simplest form of probability sampling. In simple random samples the probability of getting into the sample for every element in the population is equal. Usually, to draw a simple random sample a list of the population is required. For example, to get a simple random sample of 100 students out of the student population of 8000 on a campus we could use a random number generator to get four digit random numbers (since 8000 is a four digit number). Say the first random number is 1018. Then the 1018th person on the list of students would be included in the sample. The next random number is 7365, so the 7365th student on the list is included. This is repeated 100 times.

With this method, each of the 8000 students would have a probability of exactly 1/8000 of being included. This method does work well if the list is computerized, but it is quite cumbersome for a hard-copy list. Then we might want Nth name sampling. Take N/n, where N is population size and n is sample size. Here, N/n is 80. Generate a random number between 1 and 80. Suppose it came out to be 32. Then the 32nd person on the list is in the sample, and every 80th person after that, including 112, 192, and so forth. Now, after we choose the place to start on the list, everyone else is fixed. But the probability before we start defining the sample that anyone will get in it is 1/80, equal for everyone.

Stratified random sampling is used when we need to divide the population into separate groups during sampling in order to get sufficient data in one or more of the groups. For example, if we want to compare spending on soft drinks between faculty members and students on the campus, a simple random sample is not a very good approach. There may be 400 faculty members in the school of 8000 students. Since the proportion of faculty in the population is 400/8400, not quite 5 percent, a simple random sample of 200 would expect to get about 190 students and 10 faculty members. Ten is not a big enough sample of faculty members on which to do any trustworthy analysis about them (reliability is low).

But a stratified sample would set numbers of students (one stratum) and faculty (the second stratum) in advance, perhaps 60 faculty members and 140 students. Then, we would have to work from two lists, for faculty members and for students. We would draw a simple random sample of 60 faculty members from the faculty list; everyone on it would have an equal 1/400 chance of being chosen. Likewise, a simple random sample of 140 students would be drawn. Stratified samples are typically taken to increase reliability. This example improves reliability for one group (faculty) by getting a bigger sample size for that group. In order to actually carry out stratified sampling, though, we must be able to identify membership in the strata in advance, and we must be able to random sample from each stratum independently.

Cluster sampling also involves dividing the population into a (large) number of subsets. But the purpose here is not to sample from each subset. In fact, cluster sampling is usually only useful if there are many subsets, because a random sample of subsets is chosen. In one-stage cluster sampling, all people in the selected subsets would be surveyed. In two-stage cluster sampling, only a sample of people would be taken within each selected subset. One example of when cluster sampling is typically used is in dividing up the research population geographically. We may get a list of all of the housing estates in Hong Kong, randomly choose 20 housing estates, and interview ten randomly chosen people in each one.

Compare this method with getting a simple random sample of 200 from the Hong Kong population. Travel time would be quite large if we had to go all over Hong Kong, since the field interviewers would have to make about 200 trips to reach everyone. With the cluster method, there would be 20 trips, then ten interviews in the same general location. Cluster sampling is often used to cut field costs in personal interviewing. For example, travel costs for two personal interviews can differ greatly depending on whether the two respondents are far apart (not in the same cluster) or close together. But mailing cost is unlikely to depend on whether the two respondents are close, so cluster sampling would not be of much advantage to a mail survey.

Area sampling is distinguished by some as a separate method, though we consider it one form of cluster sampling. We might take a map of Hong Kong urban population areas, draw a grid on it, number the cells in the grid, and randomly choose 20 of those cells. One-stage area sampling would gather data on everyone within the chosen cells. Two-stage area sampling would randomly choose people within the cells. Conceptually, this is pretty much the same method we just described for cluster sampling above. Area sampling is often necessary when no lists exist of the population.

Generally, cluster (or area) sampling is only valid (representative) if the population is divided into many clusters, and our sample contains many of these clusters.

Using 20 housing estates is much better than just using 4, because we can never be sure that any particular housing estate will be very representative of Hong Kong. We may happen to get a high-income area, or maybe a low-income estate. Over many housing estates, this problem will tend to balance out, but over few, it may not.

Convenience samples are one major form of non-probability sampling. They are distinguished by the fact that people get into the sample depending on where they happen to be at the time that the sample is taken. For example, a convenience sample of Singapore shoppers could be taken by going to Plaza Singapura and approaching people as they entered the shopping mall. Clearly, this is not a random sample. Not everyone in the Singapore population has an equal chance of being in this sample. People who did not go shopping the day the sample was taken, people who shopped at some other place, all have zero probability of getting in. People who do shop at Plaza Singapura have some non-zero, but unknown probability.

Because convenience samples were not drawn by random methods, they may not have very high reliability or validity. They do not necessarily have to be poor on these, but we simply do not know for sure. We have no real idea of precision in our estimates, because statistically, we cannot know the sampling error without knowing the probabilities of getting into the sample. We can do the computations, of course, and many people do report confidence intervals from non-probability samples. But one should never trust confidence intervals very much if the data is not from some form of random sample. Similarly, we should always be aware that we cannot guarantee that the sample is representative.

This is not to say that convenience samples are bad. In fact, they are very commonly used, and they may well be quite reliable and quite valid. There are many good reasons for gathering them, not the least of which is that they can be quite convenient and easy to gather. And there is nothing wrong with the fact that they are convenient and easy, provided the methodology matches with the objectives of the research. There are a great many research problems where we do not really need precise estimates of population parameters. There are techniques for implementing convenience sampling that serve to reduce any problems of bias or representativeness.

When doing store intercept interviews, locations for the intercepts should be worked out in consultation with the marketing manager. Specific stores could be chosen randomly from a list of all stores, or judgmentally to include key stores in various income or occupation areas. For interviewing respondents, we would need to specify, for example, that after arriving at the store the field worker approach the first person to exit the store. After the interview was over, the next, or the second, person to exit the store should be approached. Whether it is the first, second, or some other number is not important. But the number should be fixed, so the field interviewer does not have any choice in the matter. Personal choices in who to choose to interview almost always introduce bias.

Convenience samples are quite often necessary when there are no lists and there is no clear geographic area which would allow area sampling. Of course, a shopping mall or a store is a specific location, but the respondents are not tied to it, they are coming from somewhere else. Convenience sampling, especially intercept interviewing, is also common when we need to get answers at a specific place, like at a store where the respondent has just finished the shopping we want to ask about.

Quota samples are a form of convenience sample which are the non-probability counterpart of stratified samples. Quota samples rather than stratified samples are gathered where we cannot determine beforehand who belongs in each group. There are no lists showing membership, so the only way to find out is to ask. Then we set up quotas. Say we want to compare attitudes toward soft drinks by what brand people prefer. Proportions are not important here, so we do not want a purely random sample. We want to make sure that there are enough respondents for each major brand to do some statistics on attitude, so we need to specify that we want, say 40 respondents for each major brand. We cannot randomly sample from a list of Coke drinkers, a list of Pepsi drinkers, 7-Up drinkers, and so forth.

So we set a quota of 40 respondents for each brand when interviewing. Once we have obtained responses from 40 people who drink Coke mostly, we screen other Coke drinkers out at the beginning of interviews. Once we have 40 Pepsi drinkers, similarly we do not accept more Pepsi drinkers. This is not a probability method. Even if we started with a random sample, by applying quotas, we no longer know the probability that people in the different groups appear in the sample, because we do not know the proportions in which the groups occur in the population.

Judgment samples are so named because the researcher uses his own judgment when deciding who to put into the sample. This is not the same as allowing the field worker to decide on the spur of the moment who to talk to. Rather, the researcher spends considerable time, in close consultation with the marketing manager, deciding which respondents are representative of the people he needs information from. In exploratory research, which is usually qualitative, judgment samples are often used. They are also sometimes used in descriptive research, especially in research on industrial markets rather than consumer markets.

Consider, for example, a survey of plastics manufacturers about attitudes toward installing industrial robots. The researcher must take into account that a few large manufacturers may account for the majority of production, and thus, would account for the majority of purchases of industrial robots. A purely random sample of a population which included hundreds of small manufacturers may well miss those few large plastics manufacturers. The researcher would want to use his own judgement to make sure that the large manufacturers, who represent most of the potential purchasing power, are included in the sample. It would not be left to chance.

In any kind of sampling method, the researcher needs to carefully distinguish who exactly we mean by respondent. In technical terms, this means defining the sampling unit. Is it a business, a household, or an individual? If it is not an individual, then the researcher must decide who within the unit (business, household) he wants to talk to. (With mail surveys, there is little control over this.) Who is likely to have the information needed, the general manager, the shop floor supervisor, the chief engineer, husband, wife? Sometimes, in dealing with organizations, it is necessary to get responses from several different individuals within a single sampling unit. Chief engineers have much different ideas about key purchase criteria than purchasing managers.

SAMPLE SIZE

Finally, after deciding how to get respondents and who to get, the researcher must decide how many to get. Determining sample size is a very important issue. In a qualitative sense, there are a number of guidelines for this, which depend on survey objectives and methods. Generally, any time the marketing manager needs very precise estimates of values, large samples are needed. If he needs to know very accurately the mean number of soft drinks that citizens in different cities drink each week, perhaps because stocking decisions will be made from this data, more people will have to be surveyed. Management situations where the research sponsor would need high confidence in estimates would arise when the decisions which will be based on the survey are very costly. Building a new computerized warehouse system is expensive, and the manager would certainly want to make sure that the systems accurately match demand in various cities.

Everything else being equal, smaller samples give less precision. But in many cases, a rough idea is sufficient. Perhaps the marketing manager simply wants an overview of spending patterns across a number of cities, to identify particularly high or low volume ones. Then gathering very large samples on each city would be a waste of time and money. If the decisions are smaller in nature, the benefits of higher precision may not be worth the cost of getting high precision. For example, the manager may want to implement a relatively low-cost, low-key intermittent promotional campaign to gradually raise sales in low-volume cities. High-cost research to support a low-cost decision does not make sense.

Large samples are needed if the individual questions on the questionnaire are the main interest. The manager wants to know the quantity of soft drinks people buy, how much they spend, which brand they choose, where in the city they make their purchase, when they make their purchase, what the key purchase criteria are, and so forth. In short, the manager wants to look at each question individually. But if the main issue is the patterns among the variables (the relationships) then sample size usually does not have to be as large. The manager needs to relate spending to brand, spending and brand to awareness, and so forth, and then all of these things to demographics such as age and family income, so that he can build up a profile of who does what with regard to soft drinks. Often, this would not require as large a sample as the case where the precise estimates of each variable is important.

Building profiles based on relationships, though, usually requires more data from each respondent, which is an issue that already came up in looking at survey methods. Any situation calling for lots of data from each respondent usually means that fewer people can be surveyed, especially if budgets are limited. The other case would be where the researcher wants only a little bit of information from each respondent, but needs lots of respondents. As noted above, lots of data from fewer people is usually associated with interviews. Personal interviews allow for more data than telephone surveys, but each interview costs more, so telephone surveys can get more people at a given cost. Mail surveys are ideally suited for very large samples, but the amount of information that can be obtained from them is quite limited.

Whenever statistics are computed, a certain minimum number of observations are needed if the results are to be trusted much at all. With too few data points, sampling error can be potentially large. One rough rule of thumb commonly cited is that about 30 observations are needed to obtain moderately reliable statistics. But the rule of thumb may have to be adjusted upwards if the population has high variance. How large the sampling error might be depends on this population variance. If people have widely varying spending on soft drinks, then it will take a larger sample to accurately estimate the mean spending for the city. If most of them spend similar amounts, it will take a smaller number of respondents to make the same estimate. In the extreme case, if everyone in the whole city spends exactly the same amount, then average spending could be estimated with a very small sample: one single respondent.

We will return to this issue of variability in the population later, because it is also important in figuring out quantitatively how big the sample should be. Suppose now, though, that we know the population variance is relatively low, so that a smaller sample is sufficient. If we want to look at spending in different groups, then we will need that minimum number of observations *in each group*, not just in the total sample. Estimating soft drink spending by age and income across five age categories and five income levels would take a 5 × 5 table. But even if we just use the rough rule of thumb mentioned above, total sample size is not 30, but 30 in each of the 25 cells in the 5 × 5 table, or 750.

Of course, in practice, the researcher might decide to eliminate some of the table cells, because it would be very difficult to find respondents to fit some of them. For example, the survey team might have to search for a long time to fill a quota of 30 people in the 11–20 age category with incomes over US$40,000. Even eliminating some unlikely cell combinations could still leave a relatively large sample, though. The researcher still has to make tradeoffs in deciding how important large samples are. The final qualitative issue that must be mentioned here is simply matching sample size to budget, time, and resources available to get the sample. In doing this, keep in mind the difference between the fixed and variable costs in the project.

Sometimes it is important to know more exactly than can be determined by these qualitative considerations how big the sample should be. Usually, this would be the case when the manager is mainly interested in precise estimates of single variables. Part of the precision would be the confidence interval, the plus-minus around the estimate. To compute the sample size, the manager must specify the half-width of the confidence interval, the plus-minus. He must also set a confidence level, i.e., the level of risk he is willing to take that the specified confidence interval actually does contain the true population value that we are trying to estimate.

Once we know how big the confidence interval can be, it is a simple matter to calculate sample size. The mechanics for the calculation are shown in Box 5.2. Conceptually, it is important to note that we always have to balance precision with cost. We can always increase precision simply by getting a larger sample. Unfortunately, though, precision only increases with the square root of sample size. In other words, the costs of getting the sample go up much faster than accuracy. In the example shown, cutting a confidence interval in half, from ± 10 to ± 5, required increasing sample size by four times, from 196 to 782.

BOX 5.2. SAMPLE SIZE

If the manager can state the precision he wants in terms of the size of the confidence interval, that can be used to compute sample size. We know that a confidence interval around a sample mean looks like:

$$\mu = \overline{X} \pm Z S_{\overline{x}},$$

where

μ = population mean, which we want to estimate,
$\overline{X}$ = sample mean,
Z = value of the standard normal distribution at a specified confidence level,
$S_{\overline{x}}$ = standard error of the sample mean.

We also know that the standard error of the sample mean looks like:

$$S_{\overline{x}} = \frac{S_x}{\sqrt{n}},$$

where S_x is the standard deviation of the sample and n is the sample size. Suppose the manager can state that he wants the half-width of the confidence interval to be H. Then

$$H = Z \frac{S_x}{\sqrt{n}},$$

and we can solve for n:

$$n = \left(Z \frac{S_x}{H} \right)^2.$$

For example, suppose the manager would like to have a confidence interval of ± 10 in estimating soft drink spending. He wants a 90 percent confidence level, and we estimate the standard deviation to be about $85.

Then

$$n = \left(\frac{1.645 \times 85}{10}\right)^2 = 195.5 \simeq 196.$$

A sample size of 196 will give a confidence interval of ± 10. Suppose the manager wants a confidence interval of ± 5. Then

$$n = \left(\frac{1.645 \times 85}{5}\right)^2 \simeq 782.$$

Confidence intervals around proportions are similarly written:

$$\pi = p \pm Z S_p,$$

where

π = the population proportion, which we want to estimate,

p = the sample proportion,

Z = value of the standard normal distribution at a specified confidence level,

S_p = standard error of the proportion, and

$$S_p = \sqrt{\frac{p(1-p)}{n}}.$$

Suppose we estimate that the proportion of people choosing brand A is about 25 percent, and the manager wants a confidence interval of ± 4 percent at 90 percent confidence. We compute n the same way:

$$n = \frac{Z^2 p(1-p)}{H^2} = \frac{1.645^2 \times 0.25 \,(1-0.25)}{0.04^2} = 317.$$

A confidence interval of ± 2 percent would require a sample size of

$$n = \frac{1.645^2 \times 0.25 \,(1-0.25)}{0.02^2} = 1268.5 \simeq 1269.$$

Simply studying the equations might indicate that determining sample size is much easier (if one likes equations) than it is in actual practice. First of all, if the standard deviation of the sample is known, that means that the sample has already been taken. But the researcher needs to figure out how big the sample should be before it is gathered. So the standard deviation used in that equation is usually an educated guess. Sometimes an idea about variance can be obtained from the exploratory research, or from a test of the questionnaire. Sometimes, research may proceed with a provisional sample size. After some data has been gathered, sample standard deviation can be computed, used in the equation, and a final sample size set.

The researcher (and marketing manager) must also decide which question is going to determine sample size. The question about monthly spending on soft drinks has one value for its standard deviation. The question about attitude toward the sweetness, rated on a seven-point scale, has another value. Each has precision set by a different number. Applying the equation to these two questions is likely to result in two different sample sizes.

Finally, if the analysis is going to be by groups, rather than on the population as a whole, the researcher must determine sample sizes for each group. What precision is necessary for teenagers and what is needed for people aged 40 to 50? The researcher must figure out a guesstimate for standard deviation, and balance the importance of different questions across all of the important groups.

6

Answers Without Questions

It cannot be emphasized too strongly or too often that marketing research is *not about* numbers, formulas, computers and computer software, and such things. Of course we *do* use quantitative research often, indeed most frequently, asking exactly the same questions to large numbers of people, using questionnaires (Chapter 7), and analyzing the "data" to turn them into useful "information" (Chapter 8). There is, in fact, almost always a quantitative phase to *all* the kinds of studies that marketing researchers do (Chapters 10–18).

The heart of the research process is, after all, looking into the consumer's mind to see what is there by using *our* ideas to learn *their* ideas, which we then use to generate still *more* ideas. So we ask questions. We have to.

We know many things about questions. For example, we know that people try to sound smart, or knowledgeable, or modern, or all of these and many more things when they answer. After all, they have their self-images, their egos, their "face" to protect.

And we know that they will tend to say nice (or at worst, neutral) things about what we ask, rather than nasty, negative things. This is because they feel that they should be polite, and that (in spite of our careful protestations) nice things are what the interviewer wants to hear. (Maybe he will lose his job if he brings back negative answers. After all, in times past they did execute messengers who brought bad news!)

We also know that the answer to a question is a function of the question itself: how the question is asked, where it is located in the questionnaire, etc. And we know that even on questions about actual behavior, answers can be distorted by faulty memory and a telescoping of time.

We do have techniques that can help alleviate some of these inevitable problems associated with quantitative (large-scale question-asking) research. The techniques may not be perfect, but we still do have to go on doing quantitative research.

But there are *other ways* to gather valuable marketing data too, to *prepare the way for* quantitative research, to *complement* it, to *supplement* it, and sometimes to *obviate the need for it* at all.

In fact, when the researcher is approached to do a survey (that is, a quantitative survey), the best idea of all is that his first response should be to "just say no". He should find out first whether the data already exist, or whether non-question-answering work can — and should — be done first, or even instead of the quantitative survey.

SECONDARY RESEARCH

Secondary research, ironically, comes *before* "primary" research, or research that develops data for the "first time". Secondary research consists of two different parts: the *external* and *internal* parts.

First, secondary research can be gathered *externally* from books, articles, government sources, even competitors' literature, etc. (so-called "desk" research). Every country, state, province, city, etc., has its own statistical agencies which gather enormous amounts of data through surveys (and even censuses). This data is usually published in books, articles, reports, or put on data tapes, disks, etc. The researcher just needs to go to the library and ask for much of this data.

Even more is available if the researcher takes the time to locate individuals in government, trade associations, etc., who know a lot. The purpose of many of these individuals' jobs is to provide information to the public. Many of these individuals are just waiting for somebody to ask them questions. Even much "competitive intelligence" on other companies, incidentally, is readily available from companies' annual reports, publicly filed financial information, testimony before government bodies, articles, etc. The researcher just has to go after it!

So if the researcher were (say) working on a study of trade barriers for a client (maybe leading to a quantitative study down the road), where might he look for information on *non-tariff* barriers, all those things that keep goods from entering foreign nations *other than* tariffs?

Table 6.1 suggests the range of sources that one could go to (and *must* go to) before even contemplating one single "primary" interview, whether that interview be qualitative or quantitative, with manufacturers, importers, government bodies, or anyone else.[1]

But secondary data by no means consists only of external sources. *Internally*, the company or client in all likelihood has mountains of information, much of which can help develop the issue further. This internal information can be things like memos and reports. There are also data to be retrieved from computers: databases of all types, some of which may have been turned into reports, some not. Here, one must work with the EDP (Electronic Data Processing) group. Sometimes the researcher must get them to understand that their vast array of data is not just there to be

Table 6.1.   Source of information on non-tariff barriers.

State or local

Small business exporters (international business directories)
Commercial banks (international divisions)
State department of commerce
Export development councils
Export management companies
Export trading companies
Colleges and universities (international business programmes)

Federal government

US Department of Commerce
US International Trade Administration
US Small Business Administration
US Department of State
Export-Import Bank
Office of US Trade Representatives

Other US sources

World Trade Center
Industry trade associations
Foreign Credit Insurance Association
Foreign embassies or consulates

Overseas sources

State trade development offices
US Foreign Commercial Service
US embassies or consulate
US Chamber of Commerce
Importers' associations
Foreign banks
Consulting firms (marketing, accounting, management, etc.)
Trade fairs
Foreign government agencies (e.g., JETRO in JAPAN, Hong Kong Trade Development
    Council in Hong Kong)
Import brokers, agents
Foreign trading companies

---

gathered and stored, but also to be *used* (in often creative unforeseen ways) to solve more and more, newer and newer, and even old and older marketing needs.

And beyond written sources are the *people* in the organization: the so-called "corporate mind". These are people who were involved in similar successful (or unsuccessful) marketing exercises before, and who — usually with relatively little persuasion — will gladly tell researchers about their experiences in the earlier work. They can say a lot about why they were successful (*their* doing, of course) or unsuccessful (*not* their doing!).

It is a fact that the contemporary multinational corporation is essentially an "empire", directed from the center. But the outer reaches do *not* always get the information from the center or other parts of the empire. This is often because they do not know the information exists, or, even more often, because they don't *want* to know. (The latter is the infamous "NIH" syndrome: if it's "Not Invented Here", then it can't possibly matter.) Gentle persuasion can often help marketing people to retrieve a lot of this stuff too.

Of course, secondary research should not just mean gathering data from printed matter, computers, or on-line services. Like any other research, it should be a stimulus for further thinking, not just a dull, gray way to gather numbers. It can be exciting and integrative (remember "Integration-of-Intelligence" in Chapter 2), working with other forms of research and taken out of this very dull gray isolation.

> You can look at what you have, identify gaps, and attempt to fill them with other secondary or primary research efforts. . . The trick is in interpreting the stated facts to glean information and in using primary interviews (with experts identified in the article, for example) to flesh out the findings.[2]

No doubt when we start work on our home computer project, we will want to do a lot of secondary work. What is the state of the home computer market in the developed countries? What brands do people buy? What do they use home computers for, do they like them, what *don't* they like about them? A whole host of questions like this may be answerable through secondary research.

It is hard to believe that one would begin research on something like the home computer project *without* such secondary research. Yet too often this happens.

QUALITATIVE RESEARCH

We have already explained the "quant" road in great detail (Chapter 4), and noted that while quantitative research is "hard", "definitive", "scientific", and all that, the "qual" road or qualitative research is "soft", "suggestive", and more "art" than anything else. In qualitative research, each interview leads (hopefully) to a better *next* interview. We do not want to (and *will not*) add numbers together. Rather, we must expand our minds on the basis of what is — and *is not* — being said in these interviews. It involves "think" rather than "thing", and is "lateral" rather than "literal".

In this broad realm of qualitative research, we gather the consumer's "lingo" (his range of words used to describe a brand, a category, a company, a feeling, etc.). We make sure we have focused on all the relevant issues so that our quantitative survey questionnaire will truly be a valid and useful instrument. And (if we are going to do it), we build hypotheses to be tested in the "quant" phase to follow. There are many fashionable words today to describe what kinds of projects are best handled (and maybe exclusively handled) by qualitative research: "high-touch" (as opposed to "high-tech") or "touchy-feely", or whatever. The bottom line is that if we need tonality, timbre, shades, hints, subtleties, and *ideas*, then obviously "qualitative research" is what should be conducted.

We may stop at qualitative research (Chapter 4) or go on to quantitative surveys, also. Remember that the best marketing research builds on itself. Every project should answer questions, question answers, and raise new issues that need to be studied.

Remember finally that when we talk here of "non-question-asking" techniques, we mean the kinds of questions — Yes/No, Rating, Ranking, Scaled Opinion, etc. — that are the heart of quantitative surveys. *Of course* we ask questions in qualitative research (plenty of them, especially to ourselves), but the questions are "soft", not "hard": tentative, groping, and gray rather than black-and-white. They are "subjunctive" ("maybe") rather than "indicative" ("for sure").

Perhaps one of the most trenchant summaries of the qualitative — quantitative issues comes from Goodyear. She reminds us that what matters is not asking or not-asking questions; nor whether the research is qualitative or quantitative, or the area where they overlap. What matters is not *what*, but *why*. As she notes:

> When do you use one type of research rather than another? One guideline is to consider what kind of information is required at the end of the exercise . . .
>
> Advertising-led markets — spirits, cigarettes and beers, for example — where added values form the basis of brand discrimination, may call for a more qualitative approach than understanding more need-driven markets, such as washing powders or deodorants. It is not just the nature of the problem that will determine the choice of research but also, in part, the product category.
>
> In theory, at least, the distinction between qualitative and quantitative, and why you use each, is clear enough: they are complementary and in many instances should be used together or at least sequentially in order to gain a full understanding of a problem . . .
>
> All the signs suggest that "Q2" research — the new synthesis of the two disciplines — will be a successful development because it provides a welcome alternative to some of the poor qualitative research that has been on sale and is another step in the process of discrimination that signifies a maturing industry.
>
> The real Age of Reason will arrive, however, when more than just a few people realize that qualitative, quantitative and Q2 research are only as good as the brain behind them.[3]

OTHER NON-QUESTION-ASKING TECHNIQUES

Observation can involve *just watching*. We can learn a lot from just watching.

> The use of systematic observation as a research tool is prevalent among sociologists, anthropologists, and ethnologists. Whether we are observing children in a nursery school, a street corner gang, the courting habits of the Canada goose, or a consumer following the recipe instructions on a package, we are describing behavior.
>
> The practicality of systematic observation is readily apparent. One research used 200 hours of videotape recording of diaper changing at a day care center to help with redesign of disposable diapers.
>
> A large food retailer tested a new slot-type shelf arrangement for canned goods by observing shoppers as they used the new shelves.
>
> Toy manufacturers regularly put children in one-way mirrored rooms to watch how they play with product prototypes.[4]

Indeed, cultural anthropologists *live* in the societies they are trying to understand. The researcher whom we have talked about is sent off to "live with" the consumer who is trying out our new home computer. They become part of that culture, "observing" it, but, like the Star Trek crew, are bound to try not to be judgmental or to try to change that culture.

In addition to watching children *play* (above), we may wish to learn if they *play a role* in the store in selecting the brand of breakfast cereal mother buys when they go shopping with her. Put your interviewers into the store, let them pretend to be ordinary shoppers and view the cereal section all day long (in teams, probably, so that store management doesn't get wise and blow our cover), and see! Make notes (in little notebooks, probably, with pre-printed instructions and grids) as to what happened when mother came with kid or kids in tow: how many brands were considered, which was selected, what was the child's behavior, etc.

So observation could mean taking any valid marketing issue, and seeing what really happens. Many kinds of things can be studied. Do shoppers note and act upon large signs indicating special sales at special prices? How many customers come to a store and don't buy? How many passengers at airports fuss and scream at the check-in counter?

Observation by just watching can help. Such studies cannot give the researcher the *why's*, but they will give him some *what's*, some tentative numbers, and a lot of things to think about as the research project develops. Maybe, the research will even finish right there.

"Mystery shopper".   Observation can be more than just watching, too. As a variant, the researcher can send in a "mystery shopper". This technique is typically employed when we really need to know at the retail level what is going on at the "moment of truth" when the customer meets the sales people. We might send in an interviewer, for example, who will ask to open a new account at a bank. Or the interviewer might ask the retail salesperson for a recommendation on a certain product category (say skin creams, cough medicines, etc.), and so forth.

This interviewer will ask questions, but not as an interviewer! He will act like a shopper, asking questions that a shopper would ask, allow the situation to play itself out as it would happen (in fact, *is happening*) at the real-life level. Then, he will write a report based on the encounter.

The "mystery shopper" technique must be handled carefully. Like any observational work, a carefully considered panel of stores, banks, etc., must be used to get representativeness. The hours and days must be chosen to give a complete, rather than merely anecdotal, picture. This is probably not properly a "quant" job. But it could be a "non-question-asking 'quant'" job if the researcher needs to do big numbers of "mystery shopper" encounters — say at least 50. However, whether qualitative or quantitative, mystery shopper observational research should not merely provide the researcher with "war stories" unconnected by any organizing idea developed before the interviewer was sent in.

Of course, in the "mystery shopper" realm, names of specific employees should *never* be given back to management. That would turn research into rather under-handed, even unethical, employee evaluation. This is not the function of marketing research!

More active observation. And yet observation can involve even more, and researchers could carry it out, or, at least set it up. We have already mentioned gathering competitive information through the use of secondary data. But how about gathering it through observation, like a "mystery shopper", but with different, although still legal and legitimate ends in mind? Take the following case, for example:

> One Sunday morning in the summer of 1986, six Marriott employees on a secret intelli-gence mission checked into a cheap hotel outside of Atlanta. Inside their $30-a-night rooms, decorated with red shag rugs and purple velour curtains, the team went into their routine. One called the front desk saying that his shoelace had broken — could someone get him a new one? Another carefully noted the brands of soap, shampoo, and towels. A third took off his suit jacket, lay down on the bed, and began moaning and writhing and knocking the headboard against the wall while a colleague in the next room listened for the muffled cries of feigned ecstasy and calmly jotted down that this type of wall wasn't at all soundproof.
>
> For six months this intelligence team had traveled the country, gathering information on the players in the economy hotel business, a market Marriott strongly wished to enter. Armed with detailed data about potential rivals' strengths and weaknesses, Marriott budgeted $500 million for a new hotel chain it felt would beat the competition in every respect, from soap to service to soundproof rooms. Fairfield Inn, launched last fall, has an occupancy rate ten percentage points higher than the rest of the industry.
>
> When it comes to competitive intelligence, the art of legally spying on rivals, Marriott is one of America's few stars. While practically all US managers would agree they want to know about the competition, few have assigned subordinates to intelligence gathering or designated that goal a high priority in the organization. That situation is changing.[5]

James Bond stuff? Maybe. But isn't it research too?

PSYCHOPHYSICAL METHODS

Psychophysical methods are another area in which we gather useful marketing-oriented data without asking quantitative-type questions. Frequently, such research is conducted without any questions at all. Or, we may ask questions but be uninter-ested in the verbal answers. It is the psychophysical response that we want to measure. For example, we might have to ask for respondents' perceptions of the ad they see, to get them to consider the ad. But we want to record physical reactions, not answers. Psychophysical responses translate what we see and record in the *mind* into *physical* changes (hence, psychophysical) in the body. Psychophysical measures might record increased pulse rate, the flick of the eye, salivation, or any kind of physiological response.

Specific techniques here might include the *light box*, in which the researcher would typically set up a display with a product. The box starts out dark, and the amount of light illuminating the product is progressively increased until the respondent says he has seen the product, or the specific feature, which the researcher was interested in. The *tachistoscope* ("T-scope") would operate similarly, except that the light now would go on for increasing periods of time (say $\frac{1}{50}$ of a second, then $\frac{1}{25}$, $\frac{1}{10}$, $\frac{1}{2}$, etc.), until, again, the respondent has seen whatever is of interest to the researcher.

One can well imagine many uses and variations for such psychophysical work, like investigating package changes, variations in displays, visual copy in ads, etc. As always, one should not do psychophysical work (or *any* work) blindly, without reason, just because it has always been done this way or that way. We must always ask ourselves questions about the realism of the laboratory situation relative to, for example, actual consumer viewing in the store. We must also always carefully think out such matters as research design, sample selection, etc.

Other psychophysical procedures include *basal skin reaction*. Viewers are exposed to a commercial, for example, and in addition to asking questions (or *instead* of such questions), we get a measure of the "sweating" or "excitation" elicited by the stimulus. This can be useful if it is related to subsequent buying behavior ("predictive validity", as mentioned in Chapter 2), or it can be just a "trendy game". As always, nothing should be done without asking why we are doing it, and whether it measures what it is supposed to be measuring.

Also in the psychophysical area one finds *eye-movement* procedures, which are usually used in connection with package or advertising testing. Here the respondent is asked to place his head in a comfortable viewing apparatus, while packages (or slides, or whatever) are displayed. The respondent is asked to read the package or the ad, and then move on to the next one. We may tell the respondent that we will be asking some questions later about what he saw. But what we are really interested in is the measurement by various incredibly sensitive devices of the movement of the eye as it reads over the material displayed. We can determine what people actually looked at or did not look at.

We can answer many questions from this. Notably: if the respondent does not remember a certain element in the package or advertisement, like a key promise or ingredient or the name itself, was it because he saw it and forgot it (lack of salience), *or* because he never looked at it, never saw it at all? Perhaps the brand name or the key product benefit promised were so embedded in a lot of other elements that nobody even noticed them. This is an entirely different problem from people seeing and then forgetting them. As we learn more, we can go back again and again (though we usually lack the patience required for multiple iterations) to play and replay the testing method, moving elements around, changing the focus, until respondents see the elements we want them to see.

Like other techniques that involve high-technology elements, eye movement has been, over the years, vigorously championed by modernists and denounced by traditionalists. The reality, of course, is that it is valuable insofar as it can play a part in a well-thought-out total research program, giving actionable answers to meaningful questions. If it is just an interesting "toy", such research is not valuable at all.

DIARY STUDIES

Often, people can report their shopping behavior accurately to interviewers in survey research. Just as often they can't. To try to capture more accurately the real buying behavior of real people over time, the researcher can set up diary studies. As the name suggests, the method involves getting a person in the household (typically the housewife) to record (on a form the researcher gives her) every purchase made by the respondent. The diary can cover one or more selected categories, and various lengths of time. When the time period is over, the researcher collects this data — having typically given the respondent some reward for recording it all — and processes it along with diaries from thousands of others.

Typical data for each item bought might include:

- brand (very specifically — name *and* type!)
- quantity
- price
- size
- place of purchase
- on sale or not
- used promotional items or not (money-off coupons, etc.)
- if yes, which items
- who is the user (if different from purchaser)

Almost anything the researcher wants to know about product purchase and use can be recorded. It should be obvious that such data is invaluable (even unduplicable) for getting measures of loyalty, price-consciousness, deal-consciousness, etc. It surely is better than testing memory.

Diary data are not perfect, of course. Nothing is. Research, like politics, is the art of the possible. The respondent may forget to record things, or even mis-record them. If the instructions are broader than just individual purchases, and call for the inclusion of records of purchase made by *all* members of the family, some members will inevitably fail to report everything. Still, with a huge computer-based program to analyze patterns of purchase, the researcher may well learn about customers (and non-customers!) better with diaries than with any other method, especially when the data are combined with demographic information about the diarists and their households.

There are high-tech versions of diary research. Respondents may be given a "magic wand" to scan the bar codes of everything bought. Then, the researcher just collects the "wands" and prints out what has been bought, when, and how much. Alternatively, the respondent may be given an identification card to take to the store, and the store clerks can record the identification and all of the purchases via scanners, keeping the records on tape or disk. The researcher would enlist a "panel" of all stores within a given distance of the respondent's home to keep such records.

A further refinement of diary research comes in what is often called "single source" research. Here, the researcher tries, for example, to match up the respondent's viewing of television programs and commercials with what, when, and how much the respondent buys. Purchase data can be related to data on television viewing, which can be obtained by using meters installed in television sets belonging to the same respondents (or even by another diary).

But in all of these methods, the techniques, as we point out again and again, are not the key issues. The key issues are what marketing data managers need and (in this case) whether that data can be obtained in a "real", "non-question-asking", way.

The five elements of our B-A-S-I-C idea (Chapter 2) all come into play here very clearly. The "craft" lies in the ability to best utilize the techniques and technology ("science") available from our suppliers, and to put this in the service of our "business" needs. The "art" lies in finding the best ways to execute this all for *this* brand in *this* company at *this* time, and to "integrate the intelligence" gained from the research towards increased profitability.

EXPERIMENTS

Although the word "experiment" is not always used, researchers frequently do many experiments in their research to ascertain the effect of a stimulus. (Academics and scientists often use the same mind-set and approaches to experimental research as used by commercial research practitioners in trying to find out something. But the traditional terminology of the two former groups is seldom heard in meetings of commercial research practitioners.)

An experiment of some sort is a common method of causal research, which is used when the manager needs to know with some certainty if some stimulus causes some response. The stimulus might be a product feature, advertisement copy, or a price. The response might be purchase behavior, attitude, and so forth. For example, in standard commercial research practice, the researcher may want to know at the "Concept" stage (Chapter 10) whether a *round* or a *triangular* shape is better for the final product offering. A simple experiment might be appropriate. In the experiment, the variable of interest (the shape) is effectively "isolated". This means that only this one element is changed from treatment to treatment. Everything else is kept the same. Then, any change in response from treatment to treatment is due to that one element.

Thus, the researcher could show, for example, one ad with a *round* product and another with a *triangular* product. The round one would be shown to the first respondent, the triangular one to the second, the round to the third, the triangular to the fourth, and so on. Everything else in the ad (color, headline, body copy, etc.) remains unchanged. Then answers to a likelihood-to-buy question could be summed up for all the *round* products, and for all the *triangular* products shown, to see which elicited the most favorable responses. If a following "why do you say that" question were also asked, there would be even stronger evidence that the shape of the product accounted for the more favorable response. The researcher gains information this way without having to ask *directly*: "Which did you like better: the round or the triangular product?"

In a case like this, the marketing manager may decide to use such an experiment to aid in product design. Or he may decide that such a question is just too abstract and meaningless to ask at this stage, because (among other things) it turns the respondent into a product design and packaging expert, something which he does *not* want to do. At any rate, he will have gained some insights by conducting an experiment, whether it is actually called an experiment or not.

The case just discussed is actually an example of a laboratory experiment. In marketing research, a laboratory is not (necessarily) some place with advanced scientific equipment where complex tests are carried out on the physical properties of some element. Rather, it is any artificial setting, where the researcher can control all of the variables (advertisement copy, color, what the respondent can see or hear in the background as he views the advertisement, etc.). In other words, the laboratory is some place that is not the real world.

Marketing researchers also do experiments outside the laboratory, in the real world. Then, they are rarely actually called experiments. Usually, they are called something like "test markets". Selling a Big Mac at one price in one store and at another price in another store in a different part of town to see whether the response differs is an experiment. But it is not so tightly controlled. Suppose people buy more Big Macs where the price was lower. Was that because they are price conscious, or was it because there was a rapid transit delay in the neighborhood, so that everyone was hungrier by the time they got to the store?

SIMULATION

In place of, or supplementary to, doing test markets (Chapter 18), the researcher can do another kind of non-question-asking research: simulation. As the name suggests, simulation is not the "real thing". It "simulates" (or mimics) what is believed to be the process by which the "real thing" operates. By modeling the process, the researcher can change inputs into the process to forecast what that "real thing" will result in.

If a test market is used to substitute for the "real thing" of national distribution (and to try to predict what it may show), then, in a way, simulation is used to substitute for the test market; perhaps, now, we are two steps away from the "real thing".

For example, simulation might involve putting into the computer large amounts of data from different studies on awareness, trial, repeat purchase, image, etc. Then, using algorithms (a model) that are constantly being reviewed, the researcher can attempt to predict ultimate brand share. Such algorithms can be "canned", i.e., already written and available commercially (like ASSESSOR), or new ones can be created for the specific situation.

These exercises in simulation can be complicated (like most canned programs), or simple. A very simple simulation might be something like setting up simple displays (on a plain shelf or even in a simulated "store") and introducing a new brand in the midst of them. After showing advertisements (say) for some current brands *and* the new one, respondents could be asked to choose one to try — or to choose a first *and* second selection. So far, this is an experiment, and much simulation data can come from experiments.

The simulation part is the model into which the data is entered. A very simple model might just convert stated brand preference into actual brand purchase by computing proportions. If 80 percent of people who say they prefer brand A actually buy brand A, the model might be: Purchase = $0.8 \times$ Preference. The researcher can find out which brand of the existing products people actually buy, figure an average conversion proportion, and predict brand share for the new product.

7

Questions and Answers

Chapter 6 discusses a number of data collection methods which do not involve actually asking anyone questions, or at least are not primarily aimed at asking. But, as we saw in Chapter 3, there are many kinds of information that cannot be obtained without asking someone about something. The asking can be *qualitative*, open-ended, and unstructured, or *quantitative*, close-ended, and substantially structured. Asking questions for qualitative research is very different from asking them in the quantitative phase of survey research. The two sorts of questions require very different types of questionnaire development, and very different kinds of interviewing skills.

QUALITATIVE QUESTIONING

The most common use of qualitative questioning, and the areas for which it is usually most well suited, is exploratory research. This is the phase of the process where the researcher must develop ideas. Recall some of the characteristics of qualitative research from Chapter 4. It is soft, with no hard and fast answers. We must not tell the respondents the answers by, for example, providing a multiple choice list of responses. They must tell us. What they really think may be hidden, so we will have to draw it out of them. Qualitative research is humanistic: people relations are very important. It is art, requiring creativity. The whole process of qualitative interviewing can be very fuzzy. People who are not comfortable dealing with such fuzziness do not make good qualitative researchers, and they do not make good qualitative interviewers.

The key to qualitative questioning is the *apparent* lack of structure on the surface. Of course, qualitative interviews should have a sort of *underlying structure*. But this underlying structure spells out adherence to a basic theme, to a set of relevant topics, and is *not* a list of specific pre-designed questions with set answers. Therefore, there is really no such thing as a qualitative "questionnaire". The researcher should, of course, have a carefully thought out list of topics to discuss in the interviews. But the interviewers should be sufficiently well trained that they will deviate from the list, skip some things on the list, ask additional things not on it, as the situation demands. *The underlying structure is the guide, not the piece of paper with the list.* Flexibility is essential.

An interview on airline travel, for example, may have a list that includes topics related to customers' concerns for safety. Suppose it becomes apparent in the course of the interview that a respondent does not think safety is an issue in choosing airlines. Then instead of continuing through the list of safety topics, it would be much better to shift to a discussion of why safety is not important to this person. Perhaps we will find out that the respondent thinks all major airlines are basically the same in terms of safety. He believes that the infrequent accidents are mainly due to chance, not to any deficiency by a particular airline. The marketing manager may learn that there is no point in worrying about whether to stress aircraft age, maintenance records, or safety inspections in the advertising message. Respondents like this one are not going to pay much attention to any kind of safety message.

The interviewer must be good at encouraging respondents to go beyond just what is asked from the list of topics. If we already knew everything about the marketing problem, and understood the research problem perfectly, there would be little need for qualitative research. We could proceed directly to confirming (or not confirming) the things we know with a quantitative survey. If we do not know everything, and we rarely do, someone must tell us or we will never know. In qualitative interviews, the list of topics are mostly things we already know something about. The respondents are the someones who can tell us something we do *not* already know. But if we force them to talk only about the list, we will not learn about what we do not know.

For example, take research for an export trade association aimed at determining which of its promotional activities foreign retailers thought were most effective. The association provided cooperative promotional support to the retailers for the generic promotion of products from the home country. Qualitative interviews covered various activities, such as in-store demonstrations, point-of-purchase displays, and consumer advertising. During interviews, most retailers said that they were perfectly happy with the promotions the organization supported. But during the course of the interviews it became evident that they did not like the paperwork required when they received the support. (This was *not* one of the topics on the original list.) They were so irritated that they were thinking of terminating their cooperative arrangement with the export trade association to focus on doing promotions with another country's export association. Sticking to the prepared list of topics would not have allowed the discovery of this important issue.

This sort of flexible, semi-structured approach is basic to all qualitative techniques which involve questioning. Most involve in-depth interviewing of some sort, either on an individual basis or in groups. Specialized techniques include protocols and projective techniques. **Projective techniques** aim at getting respondents to discuss what they believe *others* think about an issue. Of course, the hope is that they are really indicating their *own* thoughts. The interviewer may show a scene, such as someone shopping, or using a product, and ask what the person in the picture is thinking. A picture of a traveler talking to a clerk at an airline counter could be used to foster discussion about attitudes toward customer service.

Projective techniques are often used when topics are somewhat sensitive. For example, in Hong Kong, the return to China in 1997 is a sensitive issue to some. Many people are uneasy about their future, but they do not like to talk about it openly. In a survey on business confidence, the question "How confident are *you* in Hong Kong's future" can get very different answers from "How confident are *your colleagues* in Hong Kong's future". Many of the same people who say that they are very confident and plan to stay in Hong Kong also want their foreign passports (just in case). They will say that their colleagues are worried and are also getting foreign passports.

Protocols essentially place respondents in some situation and then ask them to "think out loud" as they go through the process of deciding what to do. In marketing research, the situation is often a purchase decision. Respondents may be brought into the laboratory or accompanied to actual shopping situations. Technically, protocols can be pure observation, and need not even have an interviewer. Respondents can carry a tape recorder and simply talk to it as they shop. In practice, the technique usually works better when an interviewer is present. Many people basically feel silly talking to themselves, and are more comfortable and willing to talk if they are talking to someone. The role of the interviewer in this technique is minimal. He must not guide the thought process at all, but must only encourage the respondent to keep talking about how he is thinking.

The majority of in-depth interviewing, though, probably involves more direct discussions with people about how they feel, what they do, and so forth. **Individual interviews** usually require the interviewer to be somewhat more active than with the two special techniques. Human relations are critical in getting people to discuss the list of topics. The interviewer must encourage respondents to really bring out their thoughts, not just give one- or two-word answers. Probing for more detail is critical. An ability and willingness to follow up on what the respondent says and guide the discussion into areas not even on the list of topics is important.

Focus group interviews are conducted in a group setting. Usually there are about eight to twelve respondents and an interviewer who acts as a moderator. Groups that are too small tend to be dominated by one or two respondents. If the group is too large, people easily get bored waiting for a chance to talk. Usually, groups work best if the people in them have similar backgrounds. The focus of discussion should remain on the issues important to the researcher, and not on any disagreements or misunderstandings that can come up between people of widely varying background. Diversity is achieved by holding several focus groups. Focus group research on microwave foods might include one group of career women, one of housewives, and one of men.

Focus groups have become quite popular because they have a number of attractive advantages. There is a certain synergy in a group, which may be able to develop deeper insight into the topic than individuals alone could. There can be snowballing, in which comments from one person lead to other comments from others, and issues come up which may never surface in individual interviews. People often feel more inclined to talk when they are with other people who are discussing the same things, and when they see some of their own concerns being brought out. Answers may be more realistic. No one has to grope for an artificial answer to something they may not know much about. Someone else in the group will probably have something to say, and others can wait until they have something to contribute before they have to talk.

These advantages do point out one of the shortcomings of focus groups, and indicate a guideline for when they might best be used. In focus groups, people's opinions are formed and expressed in a social context, through developing consensus or through debate. In other words, people are paying attention to other people. Many attitudes are formed this way, and many product decisions are made this way. But people also arrive at some attitudes and product decisions without much reference to others. In choosing whether to conduct individual in-depth interviews or focus groups, researchers must consider whether the issues involved are ones where people are likely to be concerned about what others think.

Novice researchers might think that qualitative questioning must be easy because it does not involve carefully crafted questionnaires, painstakingly developed questions, or precise scaling. It is not easy at all. Good qualitative interviewers are rare. Quantitative survey work is certainly difficult, too, but not as much at the interviewer level. With proper training, most moderately competent people can do a good job on quantitative interviewing. Most of the need for high levels of skill to make quantitative questioning succeed is in questionnaire construction. The next sections focus on some of the key issues in developing questionnaires.

SCALING

Answers that result from any question may reflect what the respondent really thinks about an issue. Indeed, the task of questionnaire construction is to make sure that answers do reflect respondents' feelings as much as possible. But answers also depend on how questions are asked, and an important part of how they are asked is tied up with the scale used in the question. Scales determine the form of quantitative data that will be obtained from the question.

These forms, *data levels*, are more properly discussed in detail in Chapter 8, because they are really statistical issues. Readers who have never heard of data levels should read those sections in Chapter 8 now. Here, we present only a very brief review of data levels to show how they fit into scaling.

Quantitative data are not all alike in terms of their quality or the amount of information that they carry. Some carry very little information at all. The numbers themselves are entirely arbitrary, and simply show membership in some qualitative category. Some numbers carry a great deal of information. They allow the analyst to determine that one thing is greater or less than another, they show how much more or less, and allow for comparisons that can be stated in ratios.

Arbitrary numbers showing only memberships in categories are called *nominal data*. A question about marital status might have answers like: married, single, divorced. But computers are not very good at dealing with words, so when the answers are put into the computer, they go in as numbers: 1 = married, 2 = single, 3 = divorced. These numbers mean absolutely nothing beyond the identification of category, and the categories have no particular order. In fact, answers could be coded: 1 = single, 2 = divorced, 3 = married, and nothing has changed at all in terms of the information available in the computer.

Categorical data which has order is called *ordinal data*. The questionnaire might ask about monthly household income, and the answers would most likely be in categories, perhaps: HK$0–9999, 10,000–19,999, 20,000–29,999, above 30,000. Computers still cannot deal with categories, even though the categories are ranges of numbers, so one number is assigned to each category, 1 = 0–9999, 2 = 10,000–19,999, and so forth. Here the categories do have order. With nominal data, we could not say that the category "married" was more or less, better or worse, bigger or smaller than the category "single". But we can say that the category "10,000–19,000" is smaller than the category "20,000–29,000".

If one person answered "10,000–19,999" and another said "0–9999", we would know that the first made more money than the second, but we would not know how much more. With *interval data*, the numbers do not represent categories, but rather specific points on a scale. Distance between the points is known, we know how far apart things are. A very good example of interval data is temperature. We know how far apart 20 degrees is from 25 degrees. There are no very good examples of truly interval data from survey research, but researchers do treat many scales as interval. (They are really pseudo-interval scales, as we note below.)

Interval scales are not anchored by a fixed zero point, so the analyst cannot talk about ratios like "twice as much", or "half as much". *Ratio data* do allow ratios to be taken. If we ask about age and get number of years for an answer (rather than requiring respondents to check an age category), we have ratio data. Someone who is 25 years old is half as old as someone who is 50. Age (in numbers) has a natural zero point.

In this list of data levels, the data get "better", in the sense that they contain more information as we move down the list. Ordinal data have more information than nominal data. Interval data contain more information than ordinal data, and so forth. Whenever possible, any researcher would like to have more information rather than less. And it is possible to ask about almost anything in a way which gets any one of these four data levels as an answer.

For example, suppose we are investigating soft drink preferences: what do people like. To make the example simple, we will assume only four brands: Coke, Pepsi, 7-Up, and Sprite. We might ask:

(1)   Do you like Coke? _____ yes   _____ no.

This question gets nominal data. To analyze answers, a number must be assigned to the two categories "yes" and "no". The numbers are arbitrary, and do not signify any order.

There is some basic information in this question useful to investigating soft drink preferences, but not much. It gives no clue to the respondent's liking of other brands, for instance. We can fix it by asking a "check list" form of question such as:

(2)   Please check all the soft drinks that you like (may choose more than 1)

_____ Coke _____ Pepsi
_____ 7-Up _____ Sprite

But this still gets nominal data. It is really a series of yes-no questions, do you like Coke, do you like Pepsi, and so on. Checking implies yes, not checking implies no.

We could ask the question to get ordinal data:

(3)   Please rank the following soft drinks according to how much you like them. (1 = like most, 2 = like second most, etc.)

_____ Coke _____ Pepsi
_____ 7-Up _____ Sprite

Now, we have information to compare liking of one brand to another. If someone answers Pepsi = 1, Sprite = 2, we know that they like Pepsi more than Sprite. We have no real idea how much more, though. Maybe a lot more, maybe only a little.

The question could be phrased in a way to get (pseudo) interval data:

(4)   Please rate how much you like the following soft drinks.

	like very much					dislike very much
Coke	1	2	3	4	5	6 7
Pepsi	1	2	3	4	5	6 7
7-Up	1	2	3	4	5	6 7
Sprite	1	2	3	4	5	6 7

Now we can get a better idea of how far apart brands are in liking.

A ratio data question on soft drink preference might look something like:

(5) Please think of your ideal soft drink. Please assign a percentage from 0 to 100 to each soft drink according to how much you like it relative to your ideal.

| _____ Coke | _____ Pepsi |
| _____ 7-Up | _____ Sprite |

This question gives the most information of the five. We get a measure of whether the respondent likes a brand, whether he likes the brand more or less than another one, and how much more.

If we can ask anything to get any of the different levels of data, should we not always try to get the best possible data on every question? No. Unfortunately, such a choice is not without its tradeoffs. Note that as the questions get better and better data, they also get more and more difficult to figure out. They require more thinking. More people are going to answer the questions wrong or not answer at all because they do not understand them or want to think hard. We have used versions of the scale in question (5) above on a survey of marketing research students at the end of the semester. Even many of them get it wrong, and they have studied question construction and scales in the class.

When writing questions and choosing scales, the researcher is safest to assume that most people will be unable to figure out very complicated questions. This is *not at all* because respondents are stupid. They are not. But the researcher should *never* overestimate how interested respondents will be in his questionnaire. Most respondents are not interested, most are in a hurry to finish the answers, and few of them will devote a great deal of thought to answering questions. Simple questions are best, and most simple questions have simple scales that get less, rather than more, information. Even with simple scales, or if scales do not seem hard to the researcher, clear instructions should be given whenever respondents are asked to answer a question.

Save the complex scales, the questions that require some thought to figure out, for only a few of the most important information needs. Most people, because they naturally like to be cooperative, will answer a few tough questions. They will not answer many. They may seem to be answering, but after more than a few difficult questions that respondents had to think about, many respondents have really shifted their thoughts to something else. Their answers are simply designed to get the interview over with quickly, and no longer reflect what the respondents really think.

That said, we should look at some of the most common scales used in survey research. But we should not read about the scales with the aim of memorizing them all and fitting every question to one of them. The scales discussed here simply illustrate the diversity of ways that answers can be structured to get different kinds of data. In any specific situation, one of them might be useful and appropriate. If it is, use it. If none of them seems to fit well, look for others, or even make one up. It is much more important to make the questions and scales fit the situation than it is to make the questionnaire conform to the examples in some textbook.

COMMON SCALES

Multiple choice scales are probably the most common type of scale used on marketing research surveys. One of the simplest multiple choice scales is one that asks only for "yes" or "no", as in question (1) above: Do you like Coke? Unless the survey focuses very directly on only one single product, concept, or idea, though, this kind of question is not very useful. Most brand managers would want to know, for example, how liking for their brand compares with liking for key competing brands. So the question may need to ask about several products or categories, not about just one (Coke).

When there are several categories, there are two main ways to ask. More than one answer can be allowed, as in this question to manufacturers in Hong Kong:

(6)   Please check each application that you use your PC for (may choose more than 1):

_____ word processing	_____ accounting
_____ customer service	_____ inventory control
_____ CAD/CAM	_____ process control
_____ communications	_____ decision support systems
_____ local area network	_____ mainframe terminal

This shows whether respondents use the PC for anything on the list, but it does not distinguish which application they undertake most. Of course, we get a sort of "most common" measure by looking at which answer had the highest proportion. But it is certainly possible that all manufacturers use their PCs for word processing, so all would check that. Word processing may not be the main use for any of them. Some could use PCs mainly for CAD/CAM, some mainly for process control, some mainly for mainframe terminals, and so forth. In other words, if different manufacturers have different main uses, a "choose more than 1" checklist may not tell us much about the main use.

We could ask the respondents:

(7)   Please check the application that you use *most* on your PCs.

The checklist would be the same as in question (6), but now respondents would only check one answer. This will solve the problem of figuring out the most common use at the individual manufacturer level, so that manufacturers could be grouped by their key applications. But note that when some information was gained (most used at the individual level), some information was also lost (other applications which are used, but not as often).

Whether the question is asked one way or the other depends on the objectives of the research. Question (6) might be good for a software company investigating the overall market for different applications. They may need to decide where to focus development efforts in their efforts to penetrate mass markets. A software developer pursuing a market niche strategy might be more interested in question (7). Question

(7) might also be better for a PC salesforce, so they have some idea of how to position their products when they call on different types of customers.

Multiple choice scales should have a limited number of choices. For personal interviews and mail surveys, maybe eight to ten categories should be the maximum. With phone interviews, there must be fewer choices. (This is true of all scales.) Each category should be distinct, so that respondents are not confused about which category their answer belongs in. The categories should cover at least about 90 percent of the answers that any respondent is likely to give. Of course, there are always going to be a few respondents who have some PC application that is very uncommon. For those cases, we may want to add an "other" category.

The choices should not try to cover every possible answer, or the list could become very long. If those 90 percent of all answers cannot be covered in a short list, the question needs to be asked differently. Maybe even an open-ended question is more appropriate, although *most* open-ended questions on survey questionnaires reflect lack of preparation by the researcher, not real need. The researcher should have a good idea about the kinds of answers that will come up from the exploratory research. If he does not know how people are likely to answer, he is *not* ready to write this question yet.

Likert scales are used to get at peoples's attitudes by asking them to agree or disagree with statements about something. They are also sometimes called summated ratings scales because they are almost always used on a series of questions about the same object. Total scores over the series can be computed to give an overall rating toward the object. For example, suppose a tourism promotion board in Alaska wanted to know the attitudes of people outside the state toward Alaska. A list of several key aspects that attract tourists could be drawn up and formed into statements with which respondents could agree or disagree:

Alaska has beautiful scenery.

Strongly Diasgree	Disagree	Neutral	Agree	Strongly Agree
1	2	3	4	5

The rivers and sea in Alaska are often polluted.

Strongly Disagree	Disagree	Neutral	Agree	Strongly Agree
5	4			

Alaska has very clean air.

Strongly Disagree	Disagree	Neutral	Agree	Strongly Agree
1				5

Travel in Alaska is quite difficult.

Strongly Disagree	Disagree	Neutral	Agree	Strongly Agree

Hotel facilities in Alaska are good.

Strongly Disagree	Disagree	Neutral	Agree	Strongly Agree

Of course, there may well be a longer list, but this will serve as an example. Note first that negative statements are interspersed with positive ones. When the answers are entered into the computer, positive statements might be coded:

Strongly Disagree	Disagree	Neutral	Agree	Strongly Agree
1	2	3	4	5

while negative statements would have a reversed scale:

Strongly Disagree	Disagree	Neutral	Agree	Strongly Agree
5	4	3	2	1

People who have favorable attitudes toward Alaska will presumably agree with positive statements, which will get a high score. They will disagree with negative statements, but this represents a positive attitude, and gets a high score also. The opposite will occur if a respondent has unfavorable attitudes. People who just have a tendency to agree or to disagree may not express their true attitudes at all. These people would come out near the neutral position in the summated scale if positive and negative items are properly balanced.

To use Likert scales, the researcher must be able to develop a list of statements that represent a diverse range of things about the issue or object toward which he is trying to measure attitudes. The scale generally is not as effective in measuring overall attitude toward something (Alaska) if it covers only a narrow range of things. If we only asked about scenery in Alaska, for example, most people would likely agree that it was beautiful. But some of those people might think that the coastal waters are still polluted (they are not) because of the oil spill in 1989. They might think Alaska is too primitive to have good hotels and transportation (it does have many good hotels and many excellent roads). Measuring only one aspect might give a false idea of overall attitude.

Horizontal numeric scales are a multi-purpose general form of scale. In construction, they are not very different from Likert scales. One key distinction, though, is that the numbers in the scale are usually what the respondent chooses, not category labels. In the case of Alaska tourism research, a few questions might look like the following:

How important is it to you to have convenient public campsites available in places where you choose to vacation?

	very important				not at all important
	1	2	3	4	5

How satisfied were you with the campsite facilities the last time you stayed at a campsite?

	extremely satisfied				extremely dissatisfied
	1	2	3	4	5

What do you think the quality of most public campsites is like in Alaska?

	excellent				terrible
	1	2	3	4	5

The form of the Likert scale discussed above gets ordinal data from the respondents. "Strongly disagree" is more extreme than simply "disagree", but there is no way to tell how much more extreme an answer it is. (See the discussion of ordinal data in Chapter 8.) People have their own conscious idea of how much a specific category is if they are told the category, but how far each category is from each other cannot be determined from those questions.

The horizontal numerical scales shown here gain (pseudo) interval data. Only the end categories are supplied. We hope respondents see "3" and assume it is halfway between the end-points. They see "4" and assume it is halfway between "3" and "terrible", for example. In other words, respondents construct their own interval scales in their heads, with equal distances between the points on the scale.

Both the Likert and horizontal numerical scales discussed have had five categories, with a midpoint. Why five, why not four, or six, or seven, or any other number of points? Here five is used simply for illustration (though it is standard for Likert scales). Generally, scales should have enough points to distinguish strong from weak feelings about something. People who "strongly agree" that travel in Alaska is difficult may be difficult to persuade. But advertising could show people who just "agree" that their preconceptions are wrong. Scales should not have too many points, though, because people are not good at making very fine distinctions. Most scales are from four to seven points.

Whether a scale should be even or odd depends mainly on the situation. An odd scale allows a neutral point. We want this neutral point whenever some people are likely to truly be neutral. But sometimes people answer "neutral" or "3" because they simply do not want to bother thinking about what they really think. If that could be a problem, then an even scale forces them to get off the fence and show what they think. It takes some thought beforehand to decide whether the situation warrants even or odd scales. Some information on the issue should be available from the exploratory (pilot) research. More should become available when the questionnaire is tested.

Semantic differential scales are similar to Likert scales and usually are used to measure attitudes or images. Several questions focus on a single concept by getting respondents to rate whether they think the concept matches one or the other paired bipolar adjectives describing the concept. The resulting pattern across questions is of most interest. These scales usually do not have numbers in them, but rather consist of delineated blanks as shown here.

Please think of the service you have received in Hong Kong restaurants. How would you describe the waiters/waitresses in those restaurants?

courteous | | | | | | | | discourteous

fast | | | | | | | | slow

competent | | | | | | | | incompetent

Semantic differential scales require a set of two bipolar adjectives. It is not always easy to find appropriate opposite adjectives. The **Stapel scale** avoids this problem by simply asking how well a single adjective fits the concept. For example:

Please think of the service you have received in Hong Kong restaurants. How well do the following words describe the waiters/waitresses in those restaurants?

| Not at all | | | | | | Perfectly |
| 1 | 2 | 3 | 4 | 5 | 6 | 7 |

courteous __

fast __

competent __

For both of these scales, researchers also often ask respondents to rate an "ideal" on all of these adjectives, also, for comparison with ratings of the concept itself. Because there are no labeled interior categories, semantic differential and Stapel scales can be treated as yielding (pseudo) interval data. Both are shown here as seven point scales simply because they are commonly used with seven points.

Verbal frequency scales are quite similar to Likert scales in many respects, but are used to measure actions, not attitudes. To discover the behavior of tourists on vacation, the tourism board may ask things such as:

Please indicate how often you do the following things when you take a vacation. Write the number corresponding to the frequency next to each activity.

1 = always   2 = often   3 = sometimes   4 = seldom   5 = never

_____ Stay in organized campsites.
_____ Explore an area away from the road in an off-road vehicle.
_____ Go on a nature walk or hike.
_____ Hunt and/or fish.

Again, only a few activities are listed here to keep the example simple. Scores on these questions may be added up, though individual questions can be analyzed also. Note though, that generally the list should be focused on a specific kind of general actions. This list would identify the type of tourists who like the outdoor activities which Alaska can provide. The summated scores should not be very useful if the statements mixed actions likely to be done by very different types of people. Adding a question to this list about how often people stay in five-star hotels may be useful, but it should not be added in as part of this specific list.

A more general case than the verbal frequency scale is the **ordinal scale**. They are basically multiple choice categories that divide up an inherently numerical scale into sections. This would be done in cases where respondents are unlikely to know or be able to recall the exact numbers. For example, in a survey on breakfast cereals, one of the questions might be:

What time of day do you usually first eat during the week?

    _____ First thing after getting up in the morning
    _____ A little while after getting up
    _____ Mid-morning
    _____ Late morning
    _____ Noon
    _____ A little after noon

Time of day is inherently numerical, but respondents may have difficulty specifying something like "8:10 am" or "10:15 am". They probably will have some idea of when they eat relative to their daily routine. This kind of scale is useful if the researcher needs relative measures, but is not too concerned about establishing the exact place on the scale. In other words, mid-morning is sufficient, whether it is 10:15 or 10:30 is not important. Similarly, the verbal frequency scale shown above is a substitute for numbers, since respondents are unlikely to remember that on 80 percent of vacations they stay in campsites. Both verbal frequency and ordinal scales get ordinal data, of course.

Forced ranking scales are used when it is important to know order. The scale is often used to determine preference, such as for brands, or to gauge importance, perhaps of decision criteria.

Please rank the following foods according to your preference for eating at breakfast. (1 = prefer most, 2 = prefer second most, etc.)

    _____ congee   _____ bread
    _____ noodles   _____ cereals
    _____ rice   _____ eggs

Please rank the following criteria according to how important they are to you when you choose a campsite. (1 = most important, 2 = second most important, etc.)

    _____ clean

_____ easily accessible from the main road
_____ facilities
_____ camping cost

There cannot be too many things to rank or the task of ranking gets to be difficult for respondents. Certainly, more than ten things in a list is too many for most surveys; no more than six to eight is better. For phone interviews, people will forget the first thing on the list by the time they hear the last one if there are more than about five in the list. With a larger list, it may be better to have only a partial ranking, as in "Please rank the top three criteria". Often, it is not particularly important to know the fourth, fifth preferences or criteria, and so on. People are only likely to buy their top few preferred brands, or choose based on a few criteria most important to them.

Recall that this scale is ordinal. Users of marketing research should note, though, that forced ranking scales are more commonly (mis)treated as interval data than almost any other form of ordinal scale. One often sees reports that state something like "the most preferred food at breakfast was noodles, with a mean ranking of 1.5". Technically, the means of ordinal data are meaningless, so if such statements come up, treat them with caution.

Forced rankings are just one form of **comparative scale**, which can take several other forms as well. Paired comparisons pose a series of questions asking the respondent to choose between two things only. For example:

For each of the following pairs, please check the one you most prefer to eat at breakfast.

_____ congee	_____ noodles
_____ noodles	_____ rice
_____ congee	_____ noodles
_____ rice	_____ cereals
_____ congee	_____ noodles
_____ cereals	_____ eggs
_____ congee	_____ rice
_____ eggs	_____ cereals
_____ cereals	_____ rice
_____ eggs	_____ eggs

It is clear that if there are very many choices, the set of pairs can become huge. Paired comparisons scales must therefore be used with only a small number of choices, except for some very specialized data analysis techniques (conjoint analysis). Generally, except for those specific techniques, we see little advantage to paired comparison rather than a forced ranking list.

Another form of comparative scale asks respondents to directly compare some aspect of the product to the same aspect of another product. It is usually appropriate when there is one standard to be compared against one or a few other things. It is not very suitable if there are many pairs to be compared, as above.

Compared with other states where you have vacationed, how do you find the scenery in Alaska? Alaskan scenery is

much more beautiful		about the same		much less beautiful
1	2	3	4	5

By leaving off the category labels on "2" and "4", this scale can be treated as yielding (pseudo) interval data.

Fixed sum scales require the respondent to allocate some fixed number among the alternatives in proportion to how he prefers or does something. The numbers expressed can be percents, which should add to 100. For example:

Please indicate the percentage of time that you eat each of the following breakfasts. (The total for all choices should add up to 100 percent.)

_____ congee	_____ bread
_____ noodles	_____ cereals
_____ rice	_____ eggs
_____ other	

The fixed sum that the numbers add up to can be any other number that respondents have to allocate. We might want people to think of actual recent action rather than just generally. For example:

Of the last ten times you have used your PC, how often did you use it mainly for each of the following? (The total for all choices should add up to 10.)

_____ word processing	_____ accounting
_____ customer service	_____ inventory control
_____ CAD/CAM	_____ process control
_____ communications	_____ decision support systems
_____ local area network	_____ mainframe terminal

Constant sum scales, as they are also called, yield ratio data. They also have the advantage that they force people to think about alternatives. They cannot simply say everything is important, or that they eat everything. The main disadvantage is this required thinking. The scale is more difficult for people to answer.

MEASURING SURVEY TOPICS

Scales, of course, are only part of the total question. We also need to combine content and form with each individual question or group of questions as the questionnaire is developed. General guidelines can be outlined for measuring some of the main types of information which survey research typically gathers. Read these guidelines as a clue on how to get started in developing the questions, not as a rigid prescription on what must be done. Sometimes another method or another scale may get at information needs more effectively. If so, it is completely irrelevant that a particular way of asking things is usually done or a specific scale is usually used.

In measuring **needs and wants**, it is usually important to get some sort of comparative measure, so one of the comparative scales may be used. Otherwise, people tend to say that they need or want lots of things. For automobiles, they may respond that transportation, convenience, and prestige are all very important. Projective methods are often useful also, since people may not like to admit a particular need of their own if it does not seem very socially desirable. Many people who buy a car primarily for prestige may not be willing to admit directly that prestige is the main thing they want. They may rationalize that they really need the car for transportation.

Thoroughly measuring **attitudes** requires getting information on the several attitude components. Knowledge about the product (awareness) should be measured first. Once other questions about the product appear in the questionnaire, respondents will have gained some knowledge of it, even if they had not heard of it before. *Unaided* questions usually get at top-of-mind awareness best; so the question might be something like: "Please name the brands of chocolate that come to mind first."

Unaided awareness questions can potentially underestimate actual awareness of all but the strongest brands. Consumers may actually have heard of several other brands, but the brands do not come to mind readily. For this reason, unaided awareness is often most appropriate for low-involvement products where consumers are not likely to spend much time in evaluation before making a purchase decision. Knowledge which is not readily recalled is not very likely to lead to strong favorable attitudes and ultimately to product purchase.

Sometimes we do want *aided* awareness, and we might ask: "Have you heard of Cadbury chocolate?" Some people who had heard of it may not be able to recall the brand in an unaided question, but would now recognize it. This is often more appropriate if consumers would spend time gathering information. During their information search and product evaluation, they are likely to run across something that will jog their memories so that they recall, and consider, the brand. Unfortunately, some who had never heard of Cadbury chocolate before have just now heard of it in the question, and they will also answer yes. So aided awareness questions can overestimate knowledge of the brand.

If measuring proportions of the population which have awareness is an important issue, using both an unaided and an aided awareness question can give a more accurate idea. Another way to check aided awareness questions is to follow up with one or a few questions that ask about specific attributes of the brand. If people do not know anything about package size, color of the label, what kind of ad appeared, and so forth, perhaps they do not really have any knowledge of the brand at all. Similarly, the extent of the respondent's knowledge can be assessed by checking how many questions about objective attributes of the product can be correctly answered.

The "feelings" part of attitudes about the product can easily be measured by rating scales such as the Likert scale or some version of the horizontal numerical scale. These types of scale would ask respondents to indicate whether they think the product is good or bad, whether they are favorable toward it or unfavorable, whether they agree or disagree with some statement about the product, or something similar. Sometimes, relative feelings are important, so we might want to measure whether the respondent thinks our brand is better or worse than another brand.

In addition to the **direction** of feelings, their **intensity** may also be important. It is usually somewhat more difficult to accurately measure intensity than direction. Scales with wider spread get at some of the intensity issue. Rather than asking whether respondents like, dislike, or are indifferent toward a product, the scale can go from strongly like to strongly dislike. If intensity is a critical issue, we could also develop a better idea about it by asking separate questions about how strongly they feel about what they have said about the product, what would cause them to change their view, and so forth.

Such scales must always be evenly balanced, so that respondents do have the same opportunity to answer "bad" as well as "good". Inexperienced researchers sometimes use unbalanced scales out of ignorance, but unbalanced scales are also often one tell-tale mark of "pseudo-research". It is not difficult to show through "objective" research that, for example, there is overwhelming support for a political candidate if there are several possible levels of "like" on the scale, a neutral point, and only one possible "dislike" answer. Such a scale will invariably show that people "like" the candidate to some degree, regardless of what true feelings are in the population.

On the other hand, we need to be aware of a "yea-saying" tendency in marketing research. That is, people tend to say "nice" things about products, ads, or whatever we are asking about, because they think the interviewer wants these answers so that he can report good news. To get around this, we sometimes very deliberately overbalance the positive side (like extremely, like very much, like somewhat, like a little, etc.), and give just one or two negative choices. Here, a low answer on the positive side (like a little) can be clearly taken as a negative, or at best, a warning.

Images typically have a number of relevant attributes, and are very commonly measured with semantic differential or Stapel scales, though other scales are used also. The attribute list must be chosen by reference to what typical respondents think is relevant, not by what the marketing manager or researcher may think appropriate. This is learned from pilot surveys. Attributes should appear in random order when they appear in the set of questions in the questionnaire.

Usually an image of one specific product is not very useful. Rather, the image of interest must be compared with the image of something else, such as an ideal product, or key competing brands. Finding out that customers think waiters in the client's restaurant in Hong Kong are slightly discourteous, only moderately fast, or halfway between competent/incompetent, is only good or bad depending on how diners in Hong Kong feel about ideal service and about service in competing restaurants. The somewhat mediocre profile of the restaurant's waiters given here may well be good if people think the waiters next door are downright rude, slow, and thoroughly incompetent.

Questions on the *decision-making process* need to get information regarding information sources, including experience, social influence, and media. **Media exposure**, especially, is often measured by some sort of checklist. **Attention** can also be measured this way, by listing a number of points that people may have seen in an advertisement. The points should include things that were not actually in the advertisement at all, to test whether people just want to seem knowledgeable and check some things, or actually do recall points.

Criteria used in evaluation are often measured with some sort of horizontal numeric scale, forced ranking, or some other sort of comparison scale. Generally, the list of criteria should correspond closely to the set of attributes (which may be) measured as part of images. But while people may have a fairly complex image of products, situations, or services, made up of many attributes, they usually make decisions by considering only a few of the most important attributes. In that case, partial rankings may be sufficient, such as ranking the top three. This makes the response task easier, and it gets most of the information that would be needed anyway.

Measuring **behavior** is usually easier if actions can be expressed in terms of times per some specific time period. "How often did you eat out in the last two weeks" (a specific two weeks) is much better than "How often do you normally eat out in a two week period" (a general, vague two weeks). People recall specific and recent behavior much better than general behavior or something that happened long ago. Verbal frequency or fixed sum scales are more common for behavior questions than questions which ask specifically how many times people did something. Which to use depends on how likely people are to remember the specific number of times they go about doing a given thing. It also depends on the objectives of the research. To find out if people generally like to eat out, a verbal frequency scale ("often") may be sufficient. To measure market potential for a restaurant, it is more important to know how many times.

CONSTRUCTING INDIVIDUAL QUESTIONS

Scales are only part of the whole question. The way the individual questions themselves are asked also matters. But the very first issue that must be considered in constructing an individual question is whether the question should be asked at all. Go back to the list of information needs, go back to the dummy tables, and review what the marketing manager wants to find out. Any question that does not directly address those information needs should not be composed in the first place. If there is no need for the data, there is no point to marvelous wording and excellent scaling. Only if the question passes this relevance test is there any need to think about how to make it a good one.

Focus is very important, and the only way to achieve it is to keep the list of information needs closely at hand. For example, if the marketing manager is interested in brand preference, a question on computer brands might be asked: "Which brand of PC do you like best?" But if the manager is mainly interested in purchase intention, the question should be: "Which brand of PC are you most likely to buy?" These two questions are asking for different kinds of information, since preference and purchase intention are not always the same thing. Perhaps the respondent really prefers an IBM, but would actually buy a clone brand because it does not cost as much. Even for a relatively simple product, preference and purchase intention may be different. Some people may like regular coke best, but they buy diet coke because they are concerned about health.

This issue of focus can come up anywhere. If the sales manager is surveying customers so that product support calls (maintenance on the photocopy machine) can be scheduled more efficiently, "What time do you usually eat lunch?" is not exactly what office workers should be asked. The real interest is in: "What time does your office close for lunch?" Respondents may eat lunch from 1 pm, but actually leave the office at 12:45 pm. More importantly, the real issue is whether anyone will be in the office when the sales person arrives. Some offices designate a person to stay and keep the office open, even though the respondent himself may go out to lunch. Some offices close. Always make sure that the question directly addresses exactly what the manager needs to know.

Focus also concerns making things very clear. "How important is it that PCs have a hard disk and two floppy disk drives?" This is not a very focused question. Important to whom? The question should state clearly its guiding criteria, or some respondents will think, "Disk drives are important to me". Others think, "Disk drives are important to the analysts who work for me." Still others think, "I don't care much about all those disk drives, but the computer salespeople seem to think they are very important."

Suppose the "to you" is added to the question: "How important is it to you that PCs have a hard disk and two floppy disk drives?" What does "not important" mean within the context of this question? It might mean the respondent does not think disk drives are important. It might mean they do not think a hard disk is important. Maybe floppy drives are not important. The question is not focused on one piece of information. It is trying to get information about two different features of the PC at the same time. If the interest is in the importance of the individual features, the question must be broken up into two questions. If we need to know whether people want the whole set of disk drives at once, the question needs to be more specific at saying this.

Focus also concerns eliciting specific rather than general sorts of answers. This is especially important for behavior questions. "What percentage of times do you buy the following brands of floppy disk for your computer?" is rather vague. Respondents must generalize about their behavior. They must decide on a time frame (in the past several years, or just since I bought the new laptop a few months ago). "The last five times you bought disks, how many times did you buy each brand?" There is no need to generalize to answer this, and there is no need to figure out what time frame is appropriate.

Questions should be *short and simple*. Always use words that are simple and easy for *everyone* to understand, whether or not they have a degree in marketing research, linguistics, or anything at all. "With what frequency have you experienced calamity with your computer?" is a very poor way to say "How often have you had a serious problem with your computer?" The purpose of the questionnaire is to gather information, not to impress respondents with our vast vocabulary and sophistication. But, of course, we also need to use the exact "technical" terms the respondents use if we are doing interviews in a specialized field. If the sample will be doctors, questions may need to talk about "carcinoma" and not "cancer".

Keep grammar simple, also. If the sentence is too long, if it has several clauses or qualifying phrases, see if it can be broken into two or more sentences. Questions that are not very short or simple sometimes do not get information that is as good or as complete as we would like. "Please tell us how many computers you have, whether they are PCs, laptops, main frames, what brands they are, and what software applications you mainly use on each one." Someone might answer: "Two, laptop and PC, IBM and Zenith, word processing and statistics." This is a complete answer to the question as asked.

If the manager needs to associate applications with type and brand, though, the answer is not so good. Maybe the IBM is a laptop, maybe the Zenith is. Maybe the person uses both applications on both computers, maybe he uses only one application on each, maybe he uses both applications on one and one application on the other. Break up the question. "How many computers do you have?" "What type (laptop, PC, mainframe) and brand is each one?" "What software applications do you use on each one?"

Avoid leading the respondent. The way questions are asked can imply what answer people are supposed to give. Sometimes leading questions occur because of simple inexperience. Often they are a sure sign of "pseudo-research". Suppose the objective is to find out what people think about the role of advertising in their society. "Don't you think advertising forces people to buy things they don't really need?" implies that *we* think the respondent *should* think it does. The sentence construction should be more neutral. The word "forces" is quite strong, implying that people should feel strongly. This question would provide good ammunition for the anti-advertising lobby, but it would not provide good data on how people really think.

A more neutral way to ask might be: "Does advertising influence people to buy things they don't really need?" An even more neutral way to phrase this might be: "Some people think that advertising influences people to buy things they don't really need. Some people don't believe this. What do *you* think?" This does not reveal what we personally think about advertising, and it does not force respondents to take a strong stand in their answer. The scale can be constructed to show strength of feeling if that is important. (Yes, very much; yes, somewhat, no, not much; no, not at all.) This question will still support the anti- advertising lobby if people truly have bad feelings about advertising. But the question now allows for the possibility that people do not think advertising is influencing people against their wills.

There is more than one way to "load" a question. "Do you think the government should ban advertising during Saturday morning cartoons in order to protect children?" It is not very easy for someone to answer "no", implying "I don't think we should protect children". A more neutral question might be: "Does protecting children require a ban on advertising during Saturday morning cartoons?" Here, "no" does not imply that protecting children is unimportant, but rather that a ban on advertising will not help to protect them.

People tend to want to cooperate. The mere fact that they are answering the questionnaire shows this tendency. Avoid giving them a chance to cooperate through answering what they think we want to hear by making sure the question does not imply anything about what we think. People tend to want to fit in to what is socially desirable. Questions containing socially desirable issues (protecting children) must be carefully structured. Strong words (force) can call up strong feelings, even about things which respondents do not normally view strongly. The strength of feeling should be measured in the scale, which allows for both positive and negative attitudes, not in the question itself.

ORGANIZING THE QUESTIONNAIRE

After insuring that each individual question efficiently gets precisely the required information without influencing how people answer, the questions must be organized. Questionnaires have a structure similar in many ways to a report. There must be an *introduction*. Typically this is quite short, no more than a few sentences long and precedes the first question. The interviewer should state his name, affiliation, and the purpose of the survey. If it is not obvious (as in an intercept interview), he should state how respondents were chosen and whether respondents will remain anonymous. Specify how long the interview will take, and then go on to the first question.

> "Good morning. I am T.C. Chan from Holbert-Speece Marketing Research. We are conducting a survey on what people think of computers, which will take up only a few minutes of your time. (If a phone interview: Your phone number was chosen randomly from the phone book.) Your answers will be completely confidential and you will remain anonymous. So first, Do you own a computer?"

The introduction is short and simple. (Just like individual questions. The more things that are short and simple, the better in survey research.) Note that the interviewer's affiliation is the research company, not the client. Generally, the client should remain anonymous to the respondent, to avoid problems of bias. Sometimes respondents like the company, and answer very favorably even if they do not much like the particular product involved in the research. Sometimes they are irritated at the company and answer unfavorably, even though they may like the product.

Also note that the introduction moves directly to a first question. *There is no explicitly stated opportunity for a respondent to back out, refuse to answer.* (We should not ask: "Can we take a few minutes of your time?") Certainly, people can and do refuse to participate, but there is no need to encourage them not to answer by giving them an easy way to quit right at the beginning. Asking a question quickly implies that we expect them to cooperate, and people tend to want to cooperate. This initial question should be easy to answer without thinking, so people do just answer it before they have had a chance to think of whether they want to spend a few minutes on the survey. The more involved they get, the less likely they are to back out. Of course, some people will still decide they do not want to answer, and they should never be pressured or forced to continue against their will.

After the short, but very important, introduction comes the *body* of the questionnaire, where the real information needs are addressed. This part must move from the general information we are seeking to the specific. For example, questions on general attitudes toward computers should come first, then later any questions about what people think of specific brands. Once IBM or Zenith have been mentioned in the questionnaire, respondents will no longer be thinking about what they think of computers in general. They will be thinking about what they think of IBM computers, or Zenith computers.

The questionnaire should flow smoothly from one issue to the next. Questions should be grouped into coherent topics, so that the issue being discussed fits in and makes sense to respondents. The topics must not jump from awareness of a specific brand, to what feature is important on computers, to what people would pay for different kinds of computers, back to how people became aware. Once the respondent gets into this confusing sequence, he is no longer thinking about "how much would I pay", or "where did I first learn about that brand". Rather, he is thinking "I thought we were talking about cost. Why are they asking me if I saw advertising? Am I missing something here?"

A good guide to structuring the questions into groups is the original list of information needs (or "question areas"). In general, these information needs usually focus on one of the general types of information discussed in Chapter 3. Questions about attitudes should come together, questions about behavior would be placed in a separate section, and so forth. Which come first depends on the research objectives and priorities. To get an accurate view of images about computers in general, these image questions should come before a section on behavior (what people buy, why they buy that, etc.) But maybe the marketing manager is considering offering samples (try this terminal for a month, buy it if you like it, ship it back if you don't). Image questions should come after behavior questions so that image answers are influenced by people's actual experience.

Sometimes certain questions or topics are not applicable to some of the respondents. For example, if they do not own a computer, respondents cannot say what brand they bought, what store they got it at, and so forth. Branching (if yes, go to 25; if no, go to 30) can be used to make sure that respondents are in the right section of the questionnaire. However, none but the most simple branching ("skip patterns") should ever be used in mail surveys. There is no interviewer around to make sure that the branch is correctly followed. With mail surveys, it is usually best if no branching at all is used.

Complex branching is usually bad. It confuses respondents, interviewers, analysts, and anyone else who must make sense of what is on the questionnaire. Unfortunately, complex branching is not so uncommon. Often it betrays sloppy thinking about how to structure the questionnaire, laziness in figuring out the best way to ask the question, and even a poor grasp of the research objectives. Much branching can be eliminated by more careful thinking about what the manager needs to know and about how to get it.

In a survey on purchase of computers by direct mail, for example, one section of the questionnaire might ask people who *have* bought a computer or computer supplies through the mail to answer a section about reasons for buying. Another section might ask people who have *not* bought through the mail to answer questions about why they do *not* like to buy by this method. We want to know what the reasons for buying were among the buyers, and what the reasons for not buying were among the non-buyers. A lot of branching would be necessary to make sure that the proper people answer the proper section. But this construction does not allow comparison between buyers and non-buyers, because they are each answering a different set of questions. Rather than one section on reasons for buying, and another on reasons for not buying, it is more efficient to make a single section on decision criteria for buying through the mail. Questions would include both positive issues (e.g., convenience, better price, etc.) and negative ones (e.g. one cannot see or try product first, no local maintenance, etc.). Both buyers and non-buyers would answer. Instead of finding out only what buyers say about the convenience of mail order, we can compare what buyers and non-buyers say about it. Instead of finding out only what non-buyers think of not being able to actually see and touch the product before buying, we can see if this is a potential problem with buyers, also.

The *demographics section* is the final part of most questionnaires. Demographics are usually boring to most people. They have been asked about their age, income, education, etc., hundreds of times. Worse, some demographics questions fall into the sensitive issues category. Many people do not like talking about their income, for example. Others do not like to tell their age. They think these things are no one else's business. We do not want to bore or irritate people right at the beginning of the interview. They might decide to terminate after only a couple of questions if they decide the whole questionnaire is going to be this way.

Even if they do not terminate, irritated people may give biased answers to later questions. (I don't like this, so I'm going to answer negatively to whatever they ask.) When the demographics section is last, people may still get bored or irritated, but they have already answered most of the questions. Usually, they will just answer the final few. Even if they do not, we gained most of the information we needed from them.

Use *instructions* generously. Nothing at all should be left for the respondent (or the interviewer, for that matter) to decide except for what their own answer is. They should not be interpreting questions, they should not be determining how to read the scale, they should not be deciding where to go for the next question. Any branching should be plainly stated, any scales should be clearly explained. (For example, respondents often mix up rating and ranking scales.) Never overestimate how well people will understand things. If there is any way to do something wrong on the questionnaire, some of them will do it wrong. They are not stupid, but they are simply not very involved in the task of answering a (to them) boring, time-consuming questionnaire.

Pretesting is essential. No matter how carefully the questions, scales, and overall questionnaire are crafted, there is always a chance that something will remain to confuse or mislead people. Try it out on a small sample of respondents who are representative of the target population. Considerable insight can be gained by simply going through the interview as it would be conducted in the real survey. As we conduct the interview, we see where the obvious problems will be. Respondents have to ask what we are talking about, and may misunderstand some of the questions. Even more insight is gained if there is a follow-up in-depth discussion of exactly how the respondents viewed each question and the answers to each question.

8

Analysis: Philosophy and Basic Techniques

Once all the quantitative data have been collected and coded, they must be analyzed if they are to be of any use to anyone. But what is data analysis anyway? Many people who don't know much about data analysis believe that it is running the computer and printing out a lot of statistics. We stressed in the very beginning that marketing research is not numbers, statistics, and computers. We stress here that neither is data analysis these things. Numbers, statistics, and computers are simply tools that we use in one part of data analysis.

The data analysis stage of the research process is itself a process. The key steps are:

1. Determine what kind of data is available.
2. Decide what needs to be discussed in order to tell what the data show.
3. Choose techniques to best get information on specific parts of what has to be discussed.
4. Put the numbers into the techniques (equations) and grind out the results.
5. Figure out what the results mean, what kind of patterns can be seen, what kind of statistical decisions should be made.
6. Write about the results to explain what is going on to someone who doesn't like numbers and has never heard of statistics.

Clearly, we started talking about some of this long before we got to this chapter. The researcher must start thinking about data analysis long before actually having to apply methodologies to crunch out the numbers from data gathered in the survey. Data analysis is built around information needs, the dummy tables, and everything else that was painstakingly developed before the survey data were ever collected. In other words, the *plan of analysis* (what will be done to show the data and see what they mean) *must be decided well before any data collection begins.* It is far to late to begin thinking about what kind of analysis should be done once the data are in.

DATA LEVELS

In a well-organized research project, the first step of the analysis process will have been addressed at least by the time the questionnaire was being drafted. This first problem is determining what kind of data is (or will be) available to work with. Not all quantitative data are alike in terms of their quality or the amount of information that they carry. And different types of data must be analyzed with different kinds of statistical techniques.

Computers are not very smart — they mostly only have good memories and know how to manipulate numbers, so if we want to analyze data with the computer, data must be entered in numbers. But numbers mean different things. Some numbers come naturally in collecting data. Some are completely arbitrary, and depend entirely on the whim of the researcher, not on any intrinsic characteristics of the data that have been collected. Let's look at the numbers associated with four kinds of data, often called "data levels".

Nominal data. Numbers on this kind of data are completely arbitrary. They stand for categories of things that are not inherently quantifiable. For example, think of student numbers. Suppose one student has the Student Number 8436276. Another has Student Number 8093743. The first student's number is bigger than the second's. But these numbers do not signify that the first student is smarter, gets better grades, is taller, or anything else. The number has simply been arbitrarily assigned to identify the student; it has no meaning at all beyond *identification*.

In marketing research, of course, one would rarely collect nominal data for quantitative analysis that are completely different for every respondent and leave it at that, since marketers are interested in markets, not individuals. But very often one collects data and assigns arbitrary numbers to categories of things. For example, in a project on foreign firms in Hong Kong, one might gather information on whether companies were Taiwanese, PRC Chinese, American, British, Japanese, German, or others. Computers don't want to hear about "Chinese", "American", and so forth, so each category must be assigned a *number* when the data are coded.

Consider the hypothetical data in Table 8.1. Code numbers are assigned to the categories simply to identify what nationality a firm is. In the left hand table, a "6" indicates a German company. There also happens to be six German companies in this sample. But the right hand table has a different coding scheme. There, a "2" means a German company. Which coding scheme is better? It makes absolutely no difference at all. The numbers coded into the computer simply identify nationality; they have no other meaning. The information content of the two tables is exactly the same. There are still six German companies, regardless of what code we happen to give them.

Because the numbers coded to this data have no meaning, the results of most statistical techniques applied to those numbers have no meaning either. Suppose, for example, one took the mean of nationality for this sample of 71 observations in Table 8.1. On the left hand side, the mean would come out 4.31. But on the right hand side, it is 3.69. The frequency of companies of each nationality is exactly the

Table 8.1.   Two coding schemes for nationality.

Nationality	Code	Frequency	Nationality	Code	Frequency
Taiwan Chinese	1	5	Taiwan Chinese	7	5
PRC Chinese	2	8	PRC Chinese	6	8
American	3	11	American	5	11
British	4	15	British	4	15
Japanese	5	13	Japanese	3	13
German	6	6	German	2	6
Other	7	13	Other	1	13

same in the two tables, so clearly something is wrong if we are getting different answers. What is wrong is trying to take a mean of nominal data in the first place. *Such statistics have absolutely no meaning.*

With nominal data, about the only kind of statistical analysis that makes sense is some method that simply counts how many observations are in each category. At the simplest level, for one single variable, frequencies do this. Sometimes people only report mode, which simply means the category with the greatest frequency, but we prefer a more complete discussion of all the key categories.

Ordinal data.   Data which are categorical, but for which the categories have some particular order, are called ordinal. For example, suppose the researcher has asked responding companies in Hong Kong to rank the level of after-sales service for Japanese, American, British, and Hong Kong companies. We can assign numbers to the categories best, second best, third best, and last, as noted in Figure 8.1. As with nominal data, the numbers we assign to the categories are arbitrary.

But with ordinal data, more information is contained in these numbers than simply identification of categories. *The categories themselves have order.* Best is better than second best, second best is better than third best, and so on. If a respondent answers that Japanese companies have the best after-sales service, it indicates that the respondent thinks Japanese companies are better than the others on this criterion.

The problem is that we do not know how far apart best is from second best, how far third best is from last, and so forth. No distance between categories has been fixed. Perhaps the respondent thinks Japanese firms perform best on after-sales service, but American firms are pretty close, then British firms are also pretty close after that. Hong Kong firms are very poor. This situation is shown in the first scale in Figure 8.1.

Or suppose the respondent believes that Japanese firms are best and no one else comes close. American firms are rated second, British third, and Hong Kong last, but they are all close together and all provide much worse after-sales service than the Japanese companies. Then the last scale in Figure 8.1 is appropriate. *In fact, with ordinal data, we simply do not know what the scale looks like.* It could also be one of the two center scales in Figure 8.1, or it could be an infinite number of other possibilities.

Order listed by respondent	Code	Alternate Code
Japanese	1	4
American	2	3
British	3	2
Hong Kong	4	1

A few possible relative scales:

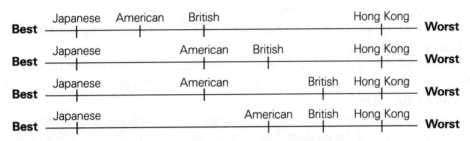

Figure 8.1. **Coding schemes for ranking.**

All we know is the order, because all we have asked people to do is to *rank* items — first, second, third, etc. — and not to *rate* them!

Ordinal scales are very commonly used in survey research. With ordinal data, strictly speaking, medians and percentiles are valid statistics, and again, mode is also sometimes used. But although these are technically correct, in practice these measures often do not really describe the kinds of ordinal data distributions we get in marketing research very well. We prefer a discussion of frequencies in most cases.

Interval data.   With interval data, the problem of scale is not present. We know how far apart things are. A very good example of interval data is temperature. A temperature reading of 30°C is warmer than a reading of 15°C. This kind of data has order. But we also have a fixed scale: 30 is exactly fifteen degrees from 15. If we have intermediate readings, 20°, say, then we know exactly how close it is to both 15 and 30.

Interval data, though, have no anchor, no natural zero point. This means we cannot talk about ratios like twice, half, etc. We cannot say that 15°C is half as warm as 30°C. This is clear if we simply change the scales of our data. Expressing the Celsius temperatures in Farenheit, we get 59°F and 86°F. Certainly, it no longer even looks like 86° is twice as warm as 59°. The zero point of the Celsius scale is not the same as the zero point in Farenheit, or, in other words, the scales are not "anchored".

These kinds of scale are also very common in survey research. They can be analyzed with familiar statistics like mean and standard deviation. But because of their lack of an anchor point (no natural zero), they cannot measure absolutes. They are only useful for comparing with other scales constructed exactly alike. So, for example, absolute satisfaction with the service levels of Japanese firms could not be measured with an interval scale, but identical interval scales could be used to compare satisfaction with Japanese and American firms.

Ratio data.   Ratios can be taken with ratio data. We can talk about things like twice as much, half as much. Money is a very good example of this kind of data. US$80 is certainly more than US$40, and we know that it is exactly US$40 more. An intermediate value like US$55 is exactly fixed at US$15 more than 40, and US$25 less than 80. Now, there is also a logical zero point. Zero money remains zero money no matter how we choose the scale, i.e., no matter what currency we change it into. Now we can say that US$40 is half as much as US$80. It stays half as much even if we change scales: US$80 equals HK$624, and US$40 is HK$312. In Hong Kong dollars, 312 is still half as much as 624.

This kind of data also lets us measure absolutes. If we know the net income of a Hong Kong firm, that number contains useful information, even if we do not have data on another firm for comparison.

Means and standard deviations are common ways to talk about ratio data distributions, just as with interval data. It should be noted, though, that statistics valid for any particular data level remain for "better" data also. For example, mode is sometimes used for nominal data, so mode is also valid for ordinal, interval, and ratio data. Whether it would actually be used depends on whether it can add clarity to the discussion.

BASIC DATA ANALYSIS TECHNIQUES

The dummy tables can form the focus of the analysis. But the discussion in the actual final report must be somewhat broader than simply a discussion of the dummy tables. For example, take the dummy table presented in Chapter 4 (Figure 4.1). Before reading an analysis of a complex table on brand preference by age of household head by presence of teenagers, most managers will want some kind of overview of brand preference alone, and of age distribution of heads of household. If they have this overview first, then understanding the details of a more complex table becomes easier. Draw them into the complex nature of the research gently; do not smack them over the head with it right at the beginning.

So one key to good data analysis is to start with the general, then work toward the more specific things the dummy tables show. Start with simple methods first, then progress to a more complex discussion. Sometimes, simple descriptive statistics (means, percentages, cross-tab tables, etc.) will suffice. In such cases, the credibility of the research report will be greatly diminished if too much complexity is used. Managers do not like to puzzle over obscure, difficult-to-understand methodologies or complex, five-way tables of everything by everything else when simple, clear description is all that is needed. Use as much sophistication as necessary, but no more, to discover the important patterns which answer the research questions.

To illustrate this part of the data analysis process, consider the following example of a simple soft drink survey. This particular data set is simulated, generated for the purpose of demonstrating some of the key issues of basic data analysis. The data consists of several pieces of information on demographics and on consumption, as summarized in Table 8.2. Suppose the client has asked for a basic idea of how consumption of soft drinks relates to certain demographic characteristics.

Table 8.2.   Simulated data set.

Variable	Description (Coding)
ID	Identification number
JOB	Employment category 1 = upper management, professional 2 = white collar 3 = blue collar, clerical 4 = unskilled, unemployed
COLLEGE	Education 1 = college 0 = no college
INCOME	Annual family income (US$)
SPEND	Average annual spending on soft drinks (US$)
TYPE	Type of soft drink preferred 1 = sparkling waters 2 = fruit flavored 3 = colas
SPEND2	Average annual spending on beer (US$)

The data from the 237 observations collected look like this:

ID	JOB	COLLEGE	INCOME	SPEND	TYPE	SPEND2
1	2	0	20428	191	3	241
2	3	0	13788	604	2	683
3	3	0	19117	700	3	664
4	3	0	14419	390	3	376
.	.	.	.	.	.	.
.	.	.	.	.	.	.
.	.	.	.	.	.	.
237	4	0	8035	393	3	476

The data say that respondent no. 1 (ID = 1) is a white collar worker (JOB = 2), had no college education (COLLEGE = 0), had an annual family income of US$20,428 (INCOME), spent an average of US$191 on soft drinks annually (SPEND), preferred colas (TYPE = 3), and spent an average of US$241 on beer annually (SPEND2).

The first point to note is that this is exactly the kind of rather vague problem statement that researchers often start with in marketing research. Managers rarely give detailed instructions such as: "Get me a cross-tab of job by preference, then do a regression of spending on income." If they do, it can be helpful in guiding the analysis if it appears pertinent to what the research seems to be about. Sometimes it can also be troublesome if the instructions are based on habit, misguidedness, or confusion; i.e., fascination with the methodology rather than with the information that is supposed to come out of the methodology. But generally, managers are not interested in the techniques or methodologies used to address the problem. Rather, they usually want to know in general terms about consumption and demographics.

It is the analyst's job to turn the often vague managerial statement of problem into something to work with. In a real project, of course, this is what the researcher must do throughout the project, but especially in the "backward" approach discussed in Chapter 4. Start by thinking about what information will be available. Here, it has already been gathered. In this particular data set, there are three pieces of information on *demographics* — job category, educational level, and income. There are two variables about *consumption* — what people consume (*preference*), and how much they consume (*spending*).

The data types were set during the backward approach and in the questionnaire design. In this case, two of the demographic variables come as *nominal* data. There are four categories of job, identified by a number from 1 to 4, and there are two categories of education, identified by 0 and 1. The third demographic variable is *ratio* data; income is in dollars. Similarly, one consumption variable, the type of soft drink preferred, is nominal, and the other, spending, is ratio.

To discuss thoroughly how consumption relates to demographics, the analyst will need to talk about several things. First, just so that users of the analysis have some idea of who were in the sample, there should be a description of the demographic variables. Managers always want to know sample characteristics. There should also be a discussion of the overall consumption patterns, so that readers of the report have an overview before they have to start making sense of a lot of detail. These points can be accomplished by discussions of one variable at a time, which is about the simplest thing that can be done.

For nominal and ordinal data, such descriptions are just basic frequencies. (Technically, with ordinal data it is also valid to talk about medians. But in practice, medians rarely show much about the nature of the data with most scales commonly used in consumer research.) Frequencies are just counts, telling how many observations fall in each category. They are usually reported in tables, but sometimes it is useful to present such frequencies in graphic form, such as bar charts or pie charts, especially in presentations.

Frequencies are usually turned into percentages for reporting purposes, because counts are specific to the sample. Percentages are generalizable to populations, keeping in mind that because of sampling error the percentage in the population will not exactly match that in the sample. After all, we do not really care about the sample at all, except for what it tells us about the population it is supposed to represent. (From Figure 8.2, would you be comfortable telling the marketing manager that there are 76 blue collar workers in the city where this sample was taken? It makes more sense to say that 32 percent of the people [76/237] are blue collar.)

Value label	Value	Frequency	Percent	Valid percent	Cumulative percent
Upper management	1.00	45	19.0	19.0	19.0
White collar	2.00	62	26.2	26.2	45.1
Blue collar	3.00	76	32.1	32.1	77.2
Unskilled	4.00	54	22.8	22.8	100.0
	TOTAL	237	100.0	100.0	

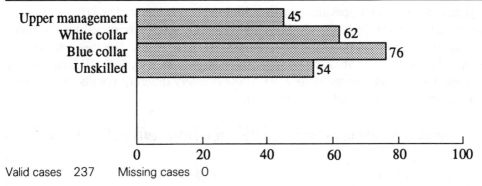

Valid cases   237   Missing cases   0

Figure 8.2.   Example of frequencies on a single nominal variable: JOB (job classification).

Most statistical programs also report "valid percent". This means that percentages are calculated by excluding missing data. If someone did not answer the question, the category they belong in is unknown, so they are not included when figuring out what proportion of the sample falls in different categories. Cumulative percent is the percentage that falls into all categories from the top of the table down to the category in question. Cumulative percents do not really mean anything with nominal data, where the categorization is completely arbitrary. But it is sometimes useful with ordinal data. For example, suppose 22, 30, and 26 percent of the sample fall into the income categories US$0–10,000, 10,001–20,000, 20,001–30,000, respectively. The cumulative percent at the 20,001–30,000 category would be 78 percent, which shows that 78 percent of the sample make US$30,000 or less.

In the soft drink survey example, when talking about job category by itself about all that can be done is to discuss frequencies — it is a categorical variable. For example, we might say:

> Nearly one-third of the respondents in the sample of 237 were blue collar workers (Figure 8.2). White collar workers constituted the next largest group, followed by unskilled. Upper management people, at 19 percent, were the smallest category.

Note here that *discussion* of Figure 8.2 is not simply repeating the numbers in the table. If the reader wants to know all the numbers, he can refer to Figure 8.2 in the appendix. It is easier to deal with lots of numbers in table form, anyway, not by reading about them. The discussion states where the table can be found. *The discussion should not focus on the numbers, but should talk about the patterns in the data.*

Only a few numbers need to be brought in to show the scale of the patterns being described. The overview of educational level and preference for soft drink type can be handled the same way, with frequencies, since they are both nominal variables.

Income and spending are both ratio, so to talk about them, the analyst will need to describe the location, dispersion, and shape of their distributions. There are many measures of location and dispersion, and which ones should be used depend on the nature of the distribution that is being described. The familiar mean and standard deviation are only appropriate if the distribution is fairly symmetric. This is because mean and standard deviation are both highly sensitive to extreme values. Consider the distribution consisting of the five numbers: 2, 5, 7, 8, 11. The mean is 6.6, the standard deviation is 3.36. Now consider the distribution 2, 5, 7, 8, 21. The mean is 8.6, and the standard deviation is 7.30. These are very different results, but the two distributions are not actually very different.

BOX 8.1. SOME MEASURES OF LOCATION AND DISPERSION

VALUE	SORTED VALUE	
75.5	28.4	
75.9	28.8	
53.0	32.6	
50.6	38.5	
52.6	43.6	First quartile
52.4	44.4	$Q1 = 44.0$
43.6	47.1	
28.8	48.5	
50.0	48.7	
47.1	50.0	Median
28.4	50.2	50.1
74.9	50.6	
48.7	52.4	
61.1	52.6	
65.3	53.0	Third quartile
50.2	61.1	$Q3 = 57.05$
48.5	65.3	
44.4	74.9	
38.5	75.5	
32.6	75.9	

$$\overline{X} = \sum_{i=1}^{20} \frac{X_i}{n} = 51.105 \qquad \text{Median } Q2 = 50.1$$

$$\hat{s} = \left(\sum_{i=1}^{20} \frac{(X_i - \overline{X})^2}{n-1} \right)^{1/2} = 14.014 \qquad \begin{array}{c} \text{Interquartile range} \\ Q3 - Q1 = 13.05 \end{array}$$

$$\textit{Range} = \text{maximum} - \text{minimum} = 47.5$$

Extreme values can come from errors (in coding, keying in data, etc.). In that case, not much can be done, unless the error can be identified and corrected. But most extreme values probably simply come from the tails of distributions. There are always a few people in any population who are very different than most of the rest, and sometimes those different people will turn up in the sample. If the distribution is symmetric, it does not matter, because extreme values on one side of the distribution will tend to be canceled by those on the other side. In that case, means are not displaced and standard deviations are OK, although the estimate of standard deviation may be slightly too large.

But if the distribution is skewed, as in the simple five-number distribution above, the mean is pulled up toward the long tail of the distribution, away from the center of the distribution. Suppose the distribution was 2, 5, 7, 8, 51. The mean would be 14.6, which is larger than four-fifths of the data in this distribution. Clearly, the mean is not a very good estimate of the center of the data when the distribution is skewed. But the median, or middle value, is. The median in all three of these simple five-number distributions is 7. It is not affected by extreme values in skewed distributions, it stays at the middle of the distribution. Once again, a healthy dose of *common sense* should be used (as in so much of marketing research) before blindly deciding to report means (or any other statistic).

For measures of dispersion in skewed distributions, one would usually want to talk about some percentile. The first quartile (25th percentile) and the third quartile (75th percentile) are commonly used. (Note that the median is the second quartile — the 50th percentile.) Percentiles, except for those at the extremes (1st, 2nd, or 98th, 99th percentiles, etc.), are not sensitive to a few extreme values.

How does one decide in a specific case whether to describe a distribution with means and standard deviations or medians and percentiles? There are some formal statistical measures and tests that can help determine symmetry, but they are mostly more trouble than they are worth for most practical applications, especially since few people except for statisticians are familiar with them. Look at the distribution. Use judgment to decide if it looks sort of symmetric or not. Compare the mean and the median. In a symmetric distribution, they will be the same. Of course, because of sampling error, one rarely finds a sample distribution that is exactly symmetric, or one where mean and median are exactly equal. So use judgment — that "healthy dose of common sense" mentioned above. Even in the mechanistic science of the quantitative phase, one *cannot* just turn everything over to the computer and stop thinking.

Consider Figure 8.3, for example. Here is what we might write about it:

The income distribution was skewed toward heavier representation at lower incomes. One-fourth the sample had incomes of US$12,600 or less. Median income was just under US$18,500, and fewer than one-quarter made more than US$28,000, although the range of the sample extended to US$75,000 (Figure 8.3).

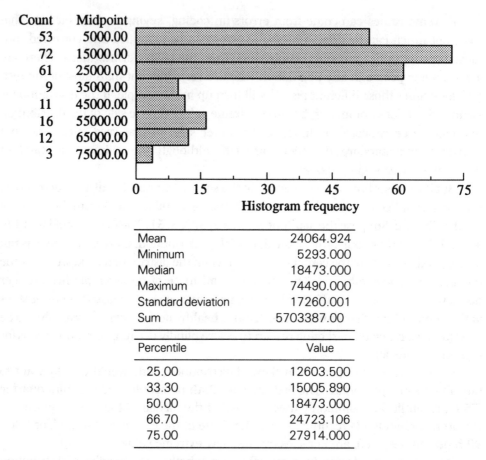

Count	Midpoint
53	5000.00
72	15000.00
61	25000.00
9	35000.00
11	45000.00
16	55000.00
12	65000.00
3	75000.00

Histogram frequency

Mean	24064.924
Minimum	5293.000
Median	18473.000
Maximum	74490.000
Standard deviation	17260.001
Sum	5703387.00

Percentile	Value
25.00	12603.500
33.30	15005.890
50.00	18473.000
66.70	24723.106
75.00	27914.000

Figure 8.3. Example of a ratio data distribution: INCOME (annual income in US dollars).

Note that this particular discussion does not talk about means and standard deviations. Reference to Figure 8.3 shows clearly that this distribution is not very close to being symmetric, so mean and standard deviation would not give very good measures of location and dispersion. (In fact, about two-thirds of the incomes are less than the mean.) The discussion mentions *shape* (skew) and which way the distribution is skewed. *Location* is given by median, and *dispersion* is indicated by mentioning a few benchmark numbers representing the quartiles. The numbers are not exact. People are used to thinking in terms of rounded numbers, and readers do not really learn more about the basic pattern by reading that the median was really 18,473 and the third quartile was really 27,914. If they want to know exact numbers, the discussion told them where to find them: in Figure 8.3.

Discussion of the other ratio variable, spending, would be similar. In this example, the only difference would be that the spending distribution actually turned out to be fairly symmetric, so that the discussion would focus on mean and standard deviation to describe it. But the topics are still shape, location, and dispersion, to describe patterns, not lots of specific details.

ANALYZING RELATIONSHIPS AMONG VARIABLES: CATEGORICAL DATA

After this overview, the analyst can begin looking at more than one variable at a time, at relationships among variables. But which relationships, which variables together? Novice analysts typically abandon intelligent thought at this stage and start mechanically cranking out every possible combination of every variable with every other one. What should take minutes at the computer turns into hours. Pages of computer print-out turn into huge piles. Hours spent in analysis of output turn into days. And most of the hours, piles, and days are completely worthless.

Most of the relevant relationships should already have been set out in the dummy tables. If it is not in a dummy table, a particular relationship is probably not important enough to spend much time and effort on. Of course, after the data is all in, occasionally the researcher realizes (through "letting the numbers talk to him") that some additional relationship can shed light on the problem. That is fine. But the point is: there must be thought and reason behind changing what the manager and researcher agreed was important before the survey started. Thought and reason will find a few additional things, but most of the endless combinations of variables will probably not be relevant to the *marketing* issues at hand.

The problem statement for this example suggests that the correct approach would be to start looking at relationships between the consumption variables and the demographic variables. *This is not a sociological study*, so lots of detailed analysis of how various demographic variables relate to each other would not be appropriate. To begin with, the simplest relationship to look at is between two variables, for example, between preference and job. The two variables TYPE and JOB are both categorical, so cross-tabs is a technique that would work well. Cross-tab tables are simply two-dimensional frequencies tables. Rather than just counting up how many people fall into the upper management job category, for example, the people in this category are divided into subcategories according to which type of soft drink they prefer.

The first thing to look at is whether there is really any relationship between job and preference to analyze. If the chi-square statistic was not significant, that would indicate there was no relationship to discuss, and the analyst would stop there. She would say: "The data from our sample does not show any relationship between job type and soft drink preference" (Table 8.3). That would be all there is to say about it. There would be nothing to learn from the table that could not be learned from looking at the job type by itself and preference by itself. If the reader wanted to confirm this, he could check Table 8.3.

How is this chi-square statistic used to make this decision on whether there is a relationship to discuss? First, set up a null hypothesis: "there is no relationship

Table 8.3. Example of cross-tab table: JOB (job classification) by TYPE (preferred type of soft drink).

Type JOB	Count Row pct Col pct	Sparkling water 1.00	Fruit flavors 2.00	Colas 3.00	Row Total
Upper management	1.00	17 37.8 56.7	20 44.4 27.8	8 17.8 5.9	45 19.0
White collar	2.00	10 16.1 33.3	25 40.3 34.7	27 43.5 20.0	62 26.2
Blue collar	3.00	2 2.6 6.7	19 25.0 26.4	55 72.4 40.7	76 32.1
Unskilled	4.00	1 1.9 3.3	8 14.8 11.1	45 83.3 33.3	54 22.8
	Column total	30 12.7	72 30.4	135 57.0	237 100.0

Chi-square	DF	Significance	Minimum EF	Cells with EF < 5
67.86540	6	0.0000	5.696	None

Number of missing observations = 0.

between the column variable and the row variable." If this is really true, it is easy to figure out what the distribution of counts in the cells of the cross-tab table should be. In our example, 26.2 percent of the sample is white collar. Table 8.3 shows that 30.4 percent of the sample drink fruit-flavored sodas. If job has nothing to do with soft drink preference, then white collar preferences should have the same distribution as preferences in the population as a whole. In numbers, this means that 30.4 percent of white collar should prefer fruit flavor, and this would be $0.304 \times 0.262 = 0.080$, or 8 percent of the sample. The sample is 237 people, so one would expect 18.88, about 19 people to turn up in the sample who were both white collar and preferred fruit flavors.

In fact, there were 25 in this sample. More than expected, so maybe our null hypothesis is wrong — it should be rejected. But sampling error makes things more complicated. Even if the null hypothesis is true, and job and preference are not related in the population, it is not very likely that any specific sample will show exactly the distribution that would be theoretically expected. Table 5.2 in Chapter 5 illustrates this problem. At the top is the theoretical distribution of 100 observations from a population where the variables represented in the rows and columns are not related at all and have certain independent distributions. The rest of the table shows ten actual samples from that population. None of the sample tables looks exactly like the theoretical distribution.

Is the sample distribution only a little different from the theoretical distribution, so that the null hypothesis (no relationship) is probably true? Or is the sample distribution so different that it is unlikely the null hypothesis could be true? Chi-square shows this. It adds up the scaled squared deviations within each cell of the table (the difference between what is expected and what is actually observed, scaled by how big the expected count was). Suppose now that the sample really does match exactly what is expected. Then there will be no deviations, and when they are squared and summed up, they will still be zero. So a chi-square of zero would indicate that the null hypothesis is correct.

BOX 8.2. THE CHI-SQUARE STATISTIC

The actual sample of 100

	1	2	3	All
1	5	10	5	20
2	5	15	10	30
3	8	14	28	50
ALL	18	39	43	100

Expected cell percentages

	1	2	3	ALL
1	0.036	0.078	0.086	0.200
2	0.054	0.117	0.129	0.300
3	0.090	0.195	0.215	0.500
ALL	0.180	0.390	0.430	1.000

Expected cell counts in a sample of 100

	1	2	3	ALL
1	3.6	7.8	8.6	20.0
2	5.4	11.7	12.9	30.0
3	9.0	19.5	21.5	50.0
ALL	18.0	39.0	43.0	100.0

The chi-square statistic is computed:

$$\chi^2 = \sum_{i=1}^{9} \frac{(O_i - E_i)^2}{E_i}$$

where

O_i = observed value in cell i

E_i = expected value in cell i, and

DF = (number of rows $-$ 1) × (number of columns $-$ 1)

The computations are:

$$\chi^2 = \frac{(5-3.6)^2}{3.6} + \frac{(10-7.8)^2}{7.8} + \frac{(5-8.6)^2}{8.6} + \frac{(5-5.4)^2}{5.4} + \frac{(15-11.7)^2}{11.7}$$

$$+ \frac{(10-12.9)^2}{12.9} + \frac{(8-9.0)^2}{9.0} + \frac{(14-19.5)^2}{19.5} + \frac{(28-21.5)^2}{21.5} = 7.912$$

DF $= (3-1) \times (3-1) = 4$

From Table B.3 in Appendix B, $\chi^2_{4,.95} = 9.49$.

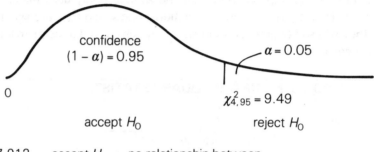

$\chi^2 = 7.912 \Rightarrow$ accept $H_0 \Rightarrow$ no relationship between
row and column variables

Because of sampling error, the tables will always come out a little bit different from what is expected under the null hypothesis, even if the null hypothesis is true. (Check Table 5.2 again.) But not too different, so chi-square will be small. If the null hypothesis is wrong, then the sample table would not look much like the expected table at all, and the chi-square would be big. So there is the decision criterion: simply compute the chi-square, check if it is small (accept H_0) or large (reject H_0). The chi-square distribution looks like that in Box 8.2. There will be a particular value of chi-square (called the decision value) that is the cutoff point for what is small enough that H_0 is probably true, but beyond which H_0 is probably false.

This decision value depends on the situation, in particular, on the dimensions of the table and on the amount of risk one wants to take that the decision we make about H_0 is wrong. Bigger tables have more values to compare and sum, so that the exact shape of the distribution is different. To determine the decision value for a specific distribution, the degrees of freedom must be computed. For tables, this is simply (number of rows – 1) × (number of columns – 1).

Amount of acceptable risk is specified by a confidence level (or the related alpha level). Because of sampling error, even if H_0 is true, we would occasionally expect to find a really large chi-square statistic, beyond the decision value. Alpha tells how often "occasionally" is, for example, 5 percent of the time ($\alpha = 0.05$; confidence $= 0.95$). Strictly speaking, the manager determines this, not the analyst. But often managers may not know much about statistics, so analysts must draw out from them some idea of how risk averse they are, and try to match a confidence level to a rather vague specification.

In the jobs vs. preference example, the chi-square statistic is actually "significant" (statistics jargon), indicating that there is some relationship between job and preference (managerial language). The statistic can be trusted, as can be seen from the number of cells with expected frequency (EF) less than 5. There are none in this case. If there were too many, then the chi-square statistic, whatever it tells us, would not be reliable. This is because the sample size in those individual cells would be too small to give reliable statistics. But this is not a problem here. Chi-square indicates, reliably, that it makes sense to talk about job vs. preference.

That is all the chi-square indicates; it says nothing about the nature of the relationship. To see that, the patterns in the table itself must be analyzed. There are two ways to approach a cross-tab table. One can talk about how columns are broken down by rows, or how rows are dispersed across columns. What soft drinks do different jobs prefer? This is a row percent question, which we might write up this way:

Upper management people mostly prefer sparkling water and fruit flavors, with fruit flavors only slightly ahead at 44 percent (Table 8.3). White collar workers prefer fruit flavor and colas almost equally, between 40 to 44 percent each. Both blue collar and unskilled workers show a very strong preference for colas, 72 percent for blue collar, and 83 percent for unskilled. Almost no one in either of these two groups prefers sparkling waters.

What sort of customers do the soft drink types get? This is a column percent question, and here is how we might say it:

The majority of sparkling water drinkers (57 percent) are upper management people, and most of the rest are white collar. Fruit flavors drinkers are more evenly spread across job categories. Slightly more than a third are white collar, and a little more than a quarter each are upper management and blue collar. Cola drinkers are concentrated among blue collar (41 percent) and unskilled (33 percent) workers, with white collar workers accounting for most of the rest.

Again, *there are not too many numbers here.* The *patterns* are what count in the discussion, and only a few numbers are brought in to show the scale of the pattern under discussion. If someone wants to know each and every one of the 24 row and column percents in Table 8.3, the reference shows them where to look. Again, the numbers are percentages, not actual counts. Percentages are generalizable to the population, counts are specific to the sample only.

Testing *differences in proportions* can also be important in some situations. Strictly speaking, before we report to the manager that, for example, the proportion of unskilled workers who drink colas is greater than for blue collar workers, we should do a test. Box 8.3 illustrates how to do it. We use the standard normal distribution (z-distribution) for this test, which assumes large samples. The z-score is computed, and compared to the decision value. The mechanics of a z-test are quite similar to those of the more common t-test, so a more complete discussion of setting up hypothesis and performing these differences tests can be found in the next section.

BOX 8.3. DIFFERENCE IN PROPORTIONS TEST

From Table 8.3, suppose we wanted to check whether the proportion of unskilled workers drinking cola is different from the proportion for blue collar workers. Certainly it looks that way, since 83 percent of unskilled, and only 72 percent of blue workers do. But sampling error could make the proportions in a sample different when they are actually the same in the population. There is a simple test for this, if we are dealing with large enough samples. Generally, a rule of thumb to insure that the test be reliable is that we need $np \geq 10$, and $n(1 - p) \geq 10$ for each group, where n is the number of observations, and p is the proportion we are testing.

Then, to test the null hypothesis H_0: $\pi_1 = \pi_2$, or $(\pi_1 - \pi_2) = 0$, we use a z-test:

$$z = \frac{(p_1 - p_2) - (\pi_1 - \pi_2)}{\sqrt{pq \left(\frac{1}{n_1} + \frac{1}{n_2} \right)}},$$

where

π_1 and π_2 are the population portions (of cola drinkers) in the two groups,
p_1 and p_2 are the sample proportions,
n_1 and n_2 are the sample sizes,
p is the pooled proportion, and
$q = (1 - p)$.

Since in this case $(\pi_1 - \pi_2) = 0$ if H_0 is true, this can just be written:

$$z = \frac{(p_1 - p_2)}{\sqrt{pq \left(\frac{1}{n_1} + \frac{1}{n_2} \right)}}.$$

The pooled proportion, p, is just the weighted average of the proportions in the two samples:

$$p = \frac{p_1 n_1 + p_2 n_2}{n_1 + n_2}.$$

Let's compute z for this case.

$$p = \frac{0.724(76) + 0.833(54)}{76 + 54} = 0.769,$$

$$q = (1 - 0.769) = 0.231,$$

and

$$z = \frac{(0.724 - 0.833)}{\sqrt{0.769(0.231) \left(\frac{1}{76} + \frac{1}{54} \right)}} = -1.45.$$

Since the decision value $z_{90} = 1.645$ (and -1.645), our data support H_0 (see the figure). In managerial language, this means we cannot strictly show with our data that unskilled workers choose colas more often than do blue collar workers. Bear in mind, though, that proportions tests, even more than most of the other tests we have discussed, rarely show anything for relatively small sample sizes. These are relatively small, in fact for unskilled workers, $n(1-p) = 8.96$, which means we have violated the rule of thumb about large enough samples.

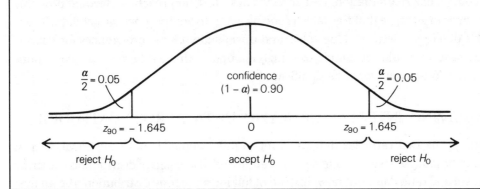

Note here that even though the difference in proportions we tested was fairly large (over 10 percent), the difference turned out to be not significant at a 90 percent confidence level. The difference in proportions test is quite conservative, i.e., it takes very large differences, or very large sample sizes, to actually show differences when they exist. Estimates of proportions in a sample are notoriously unreliable, as can be seen by referring again to Table 5.2. The true proportion of row 1 respondents was 0.50, but the proportions of row 1 in the ten samples ranged from 0.47 to 0.59.

This illustrates another issue in the application of statistics. *We must continue to think and use good judgment.* Our test does not show any significant difference between proportions of blue collar and proportions of unskilled workers who prefer colas. But in the description above, we (implicitly) report a difference by stating two separate numbers. In this case, we have applied our "gut feeling" to the situation, based on long practice in statistical application and intimate knowledge of this market. This leads us to believe that the pattern we report in these numbers is real, even though we cannot formally support this particular detail with this particular test. (If we were critically concerned with formal statistical support, there are several other less common non-parametric tests we could try, though they would offer less direct support.)

Be *very* careful about ignoring statistical tests, either by not performing them at all, or, as here, by not paying attention to the result. Often "gut feelings" can be completely wrong. We would not rely on this gut feeling alone. But in this case, we do have the chi-square test to demonstrate that there is pattern within the table overall. We can recognize by visual inspection a pretty clear, *consistent, and logical* pattern in the magnitudes of the proportions. The only problem is that the sample is too small, especially when divided among the different cells of a 4×3 table, to statistically support all the minor details of the pattern.

Therefore, we decided not to change the discussion above about what kind of soft drinks different jobs prefer, even though our proportions test could not support one detail of the pattern we see. We might simply add a note that because of small sample size, not all the details we think we see can be supported with a formal statistical test. (Of course, in a real situation, we use the "backward" approach, and would probably recognize in advance that this table is one we want to analyze once we get data. Then, if this difference between blue collar and unskilled workers' preferences for colas is important, we could set sample sizes high enough so that a difference in proportions of about 10 percent would be significant.)

ANALYZING INTERVAL OR RATIO DATA ACROSS CATEGORIES

If one of the two variables that we want to put together is not categorical, then it cannot be analyzed with frequencies. Location and dispersion of distributions describe interval and ratio data. But now, instead of talking about one distribution, the analyst must talk about several and compare them. These several distributions come from talking about the interval/ratio data in category 1, category 2, and so on, of the nominal/ordinal data we are relating it to. In practice, analysts usually focus only on location (means), unless it is important to know something about how much people differ within each specific category (dispersion).

For example, suppose we want to know how much people with different jobs spend on soft drinks. This question relates ratio data (SPEND) to nominal data (JOB). We can start to answer it by looking at the mean spending in each of the four categories of jobs. Table 8.4 *seems* to show that blue collar workers spend more than other types of workers, followed by upper management, unskilled, and white collar workers. But hold on! We have only started to answer the question. How do we know that blue collar workers in the population really spend more than upper management people? Can we say that upper management people in the population spend more

Table 8.4.   Example of means of a ratio variable across categories.
Summaries of SPEND (average annual spending on soft drinks in US dollars) by levels of JOB (job classification).

Variable	Value	Label	Mean	SD	Cases
For entire population			343.7384	148.9034	237
JOB	1.00	Upper management	266.4222	85.5420	45
JOB	2.00	White collar	256.7258	88.0529	62
JOB	3.00	Blue collar	522.0526	81.8046	76
JOB	4.00	Unskilled	257.1111	84.1931	54

Total cases = 237.

than unskilled workers? All we have to go on is a sample of the populations of blue collar, upper management, and unskilled workers. What about sampling error?

Because of sampling error, any specific sample mean is unlikely to exactly equal the population mean. Suppose that two groups really spend exactly the same amounts (i.e., they come from the same population). A sample could just happen to get a few more high-spending upper management people, but a few more low-spending white collar workers. Then the sample means would come out different, and this could lead us to incorrectly decide that these two jobs have different spending patterns in the population. Refer again to Table 5.1, which illustrates this. None of the 20 sample means is exactly equal to the population mean of 10, even though all 20 samples are from the same population. Simply relying on sample means might lead us to decide (incorrectly) that some samples actually came from different populations.

A formal statistical test is needed to address this problem. To set up a difference in means test, hypotheses must be defined about what the true situation looks like. Either the two groups come from populations having the same mean (i.e., we are dealing with a single population; H_0), or the two groups are from two populations which have different means (H_a). (Technically, this is called a two-tail t-test; see Box 8.4.) To decide which of these two situations is true, all we have is a sample from each population. Even if H_0 is true, Table 5.1 shows that the two sample means will probably be unequal. But they are likely to be close to each other. If H_a is true, the sample means are likely to be farther apart.

BOX 8.4. SETTING UP A HYPOTHESIS AND PERFORMING A t-TEST

The exact statement of the null hypothesis (H_0) depends on exactly what the manager wants to know. For example, suppose she asks: "Is spending by upper level managers different from spending by white collar workers?" This question can be answered "no", which in mathematical notation looks like:

$$\mu_1 = \mu_2, \quad \text{or} \quad (\mu_1 - \mu_2) = 0,$$

or it can be answered "yes", which looks like:

$$\mu_1 \neq \mu_2, \quad \text{or} \quad (\mu_1 - \mu_2) \neq 0,$$

where μ stands for population (not sample) mean. The way the question was stated, it makes absolutely no difference whether $\mu_1 < \mu_2$ or $\mu_1 > \mu_2$. Either way, the answer is still yes. This is called a two-tail test, because the H_0 can be wrong in either direction away from $\mu_1 = \mu_2$.

Suppose the question had been stated as: Do upper management people spend more than white collar workers? Then, mathematically, the "yes" answer looks like:

$$\mu_1 > \mu_2, \quad \text{or} \quad (\mu_1 - \mu_2) > 0 ,$$

and "no" is written as:

$$\mu_1 \leq \mu_2, \quad \text{or} \quad (\mu_1 - \mu_2) \leq 0 ,$$

Here, it does not matter whether $\mu_1 = \mu_2$ or $\mu_1 < \mu_2$. Either way, the answer is still no, upper management people do not spend more. This is called a one-tail test — H_0 can be wrong in only one direction.

The null hypothesis is the equation which contains the equal sign. To test something, we must have a fixed number to check. At the equal sign, we can test whether $(\mu_1 - \mu_2) = 0$. But we have no fixed number for, e.g., $\mu_1 > \mu_2$. Do we mean $(\mu_1 - \mu_2) = 5$, or 15, or what exactly? So the set of hypotheses for the two questions above look like:

QUESTION 1   QUESTION 2

$H_0: \quad (\mu_1 - \mu_2) = 0 ,$ $H_0: \quad (\mu_1 - \mu_2) \leq 0 ,$
$H_a: \quad (\mu_1 - \mu_2) \neq 0 .$ $H_a: \quad (\mu_1 - \mu_2) > 0 .$

Our question in this section was: how do we know that upper management and white collar spending do not really come from the same population, but just look different because of sampling error? This is the two-tail form of the problem, i.e., question 1 above. If H_0 is true, then the population distributions of upper management and white collar spending overlap and have the same mean. If H_0 is false, i.e., H_a is true, then our samples of upper management and white collar spending come from separate population distributions (check the diagram below). Unfortunately, we cannot observe the populations of upper management or white collar spending directly. All we can do is look at samples from these populations, and we have to use information from these samples to judge which of these two situations is most likely to be true.

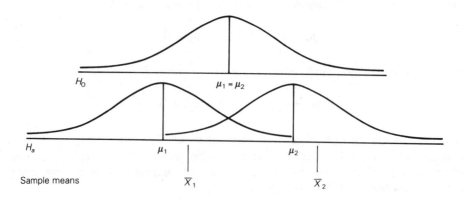

To make the decision about which is probably true, we use the t-distribution.

The quantity

$$\frac{(\overline{X}_1 - \overline{X}_2) - (\mu_1 - \mu_2)}{s_{(\overline{x}_1 - \overline{x}_2)}}$$

is distributed as a t-distribution. (In this equation, $\overline{X}_1$ and $\overline{X}_2$ are the two sample means being compared, and $s_{(\overline{x}_1 - \overline{x}_2)}$ is the standard deviation of the difference in sample means, $(\overline{X}_1 - \overline{X}_2)$. Since $(\mu_1 - \mu_2) = 0$ if the null hypothesis, H_0, is correct, we can write this as:

$$t = \frac{(\overline{X}_1 - \overline{X}_2)}{s_{(\overline{x}_1 - \overline{x}_2)}}$$

How to compute $s_{(\overline{x}_1 - \overline{x}_2)}$ depends on whether we can assume the population variances are equal. If they are

$$s_{(\overline{x}_1 - \overline{x}_2)} = \left(\frac{s_{x_1}^2 (n_1 - 1) + s_{x_2}^2 (n_2 - 1)}{n_1 + n_2 - 2} \right)^{1/2} \left(\frac{1}{n_1} + \frac{1}{n_2} \right)^{1/2}$$

is the formula for computing the pooled variance case. If they are not, then

$$s_{(\overline{x}_1 - \overline{x}_2)} = \left(\frac{s_{x_1}^2 + s_{x_2}^2}{n_1 + n_2 - 2} \right)^{1/2}$$

is used. There are formal tests which can be performed on the two sample variances $s_{x_1}^2$ and $s_{x_2}^2$ for checking whether the population variances σ_1^2 and σ_2^2 are equal. But in practice, usually it is sufficient just to judge this simply by looking at the sample variances (or standard deviations). If they are pretty close, that is good enough to use the pooled variance equation.

Although it looks more difficult, the pooled variance form is slightly more likely to confirm a real difference when one exists. However, only rarely in borderline cases would a decision differ depending on which version was used. In any case, the computer does the computation, anyway, and most statistical packages print out the t-value from both versions of the equation.

Let's actually compute a t-value and then illustrate how to interpret it. Take the data on spending by upper management and white collar people in Table 8.4.

	UPPER MANAGEMENT	WHITE COLLAR
$\overline{X}$	266.4222	256.7258
s_x	85.542	88.053
n	45	62

Visual inspection of the sample standard deviations indicates that they are close enough to use the pooled variance form of the equation. So

$$t = \frac{(266.4222 - 256.7258)}{\left(\dfrac{85.542^2(45-1) + 88.053^2(62-1)}{45+62-2}\right)^{1/2}\left(\dfrac{1}{45}+\dfrac{1}{62}\right)^{1/2}}$$

$$= \frac{9.6964}{17.0395} = 0.569$$

From Table B.2 in Appendix B, $t_{105,90} \simeq 1.65$.

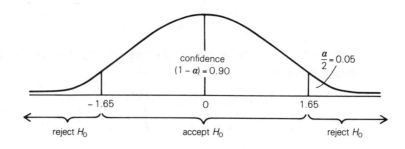

$t = 0.569 < t_{105,90} \simeq 1.65 \Rightarrow$ accept $H_0 \Rightarrow$ there is no difference in spending levels by upper management or white collar workers.

How close is "close enough" to decide to accept H_0, and how far apart is necessary for rejecting H_0 and accepting H_a? Usually, we determine this with a t-test, which measures the probability that these two means actually came from the same population. It does this by computing a t-statistic, as illustrated in Box 8.4. The difference in the two sample means, divided by the standard deviation of that difference, results in a number which is distributed in a t-distribution.

Suppose that H_0 is true and that there is absolutely no sampling error. Then the difference in the two means will be exactly zero, and the t-statistic will be zero, the center of the t-distribution. The farther apart the sample means are, relative to the variability of the samples, the bigger the t-statistic becomes and the more likely H_0 is false. Just like with the chi-square test, a decision value sets the point on the t-distribution where "close enough" ends. Decision values for the t-distribution differ depending on degrees of freedom and confidence level. In a difference of means test with pooled variance, degrees of freedom are $(n_1 - 1) + (n_2 - 1)$, where n_1 and n_2 are the sample sizes of the two groups being compared.

Table 8.5 contains two t-tests on the results from Table 8.4. Results of the first test indicate that the levels of spending on soft drinks by upper management and white collar people are not significantly different. Therefore, the analyst *cannot* report to the marketing manager that there is any order in spending levels among upper management, white collar, and unskilled workers. (We did do the rest of the t-tests.)

Table 8.5.   Examples of *t*-tests

Independent samples of JOB (employment category)
Group 1:   JOB EQ 1.00   Group 2:   JOB EQ 2.00
t-test for: SPEND (average annual spending on soft drinks in US dollars)

	Number of cases	Mean	Standard deviation	Standard error
Group 1	45	266.4222	85.542	12.752
Group 2	62	256.7258	88.053	11.183

F-value 1.06, 2-tail probability 0.849

	Pooled variance estimate	Separate variance estimate
t-value	0.57	0.57
Degrees of freedom	105	96.52
2-tail probability	0.571	0.569

Independent samples of JOB (employment category)
Group 1:   JOB EQ 1.00   Group 2:   JOB EQ 3.00
t-test for SPEND (average annual spending on soft drinks in US dollars)

	Number of cases	Mean	Standard deviation	Standard error
Group 1	45	266.4222	85.542	12.752
Group 2	76	522.0526	81.805	9.384

F-value 1.09, 2-tail probability 0.722

	Pooled variance estimate	Separate variance estimate
t-value	– 16.33	– 16.15
Degrees of freedom	119	89.21
2-tail probability	0.000	0.000

The data only show similar spending levels, without real differences among these three groups. On the other hand, the second *t*-test indicates that blue collar workers do spend more than upper management. (Keep in mind that there is always the small probability [α] that we are wrong in saying this.)

A complete description of spending by job type would look something like:

Blue collar workers spend over HK$520 annually on soft drinks. Everyone else, regardless of their job type, spends about half the level of blue collar workers (Tables 8.4, 8.5).

Note here that we do not report all the separate numbers for upper management, white collar, and unskilled workers. First of all, the discussion is on *pattern*, not numbers. Numbers can be found in the appropriate tables. Only one figure is needed to show the magnitude of the pattern. Secondly, reporting separate means for these three jobs would mislead the reader into thinking that the means are all different. We just showed with *t*-tests that they are not.

Another form of the *t*-test is called a *paired-sample t-test*. This form of the test is used when the two samples being compared are not independent. Usually, this means that two measurements have been taken on the same respondent. Our data set includes how much people spend on beer. To compare beer spending with spending on soft drinks the data on soft drinks should not be considered separately from the data on beer. Maybe some people just spend a lot on drinks. They would tend to have high spending levels for soft drinks and for beer. Other people may drink water all the time, and not spend much on either. A paired-sample test accounts for the fact that the variability found in soft drink spending and in beer spending is due to variability among individuals. This variability should be counted only once because these two sets of spending data are from the same people.

To do a *t*-test in a case like this, we want to measure, for each individual, the difference in spending on soft drinks and beer. Each difference is computed by subtracting beer spending from soft drink spending. (We could do it the other way around.) Then we work with this difference, not the two original spending levels, so that individual variability is accounted for only once. Now, we want to check the null hypothesis, H_0, which says that the mean of these differences is equal to zero.

The question of whether people spend similarly on soft drinks and beer can be discussed very briefly as follows:

On average, people spend over HK$40 more on beer compared to soft drinks. However, spending patterns are quite variable, and not everyone spends more on beer (Table 8.6).

We know beer spending is higher on average because the *t*-test is significant. We also have a measure of how much larger. (Do not just say "soft drink spending and beer spending are different". The manager will always want to know how they are different.) We know the spending patterns are variable because the standard deviation of the difference in spending is quite large compared to the magnitude of the difference.

Table 8.6.   Example of a paired sample *t*-test

Paired samples *t*-test: SPEND (average annual spending on soft drinks) and SPEND2 (average annual spending on beer in US dollars)

Variable	Number of cases	Mean	Standard deviation	Standard error
SPEND	237	343.7384	148.903	9.672
SPEND2	237	386.3924	162.464	10.553

Difference (Mean)	− 42.6540	*t*-value	− 13.79
Standard deviation	47.624	Degrees of freedom	236
Standard error	3.093	2-tail probability	0.000

CORRELATION

Correlation analysis examines association (co-relation) among two or more interval or ratio data variables. (This is the commonly used product-moment correlation. Rank correlation, used on ordinal data, is not discussed here.) A correlation coefficient (r) shows how much and in what direction two variables move together. For example, suppose we think that people who spend a lot on soft drinks must also spend a lot on beer. Both of these are ratio data in our data set (Table 8.2), so we can check whether this is true with correlation analysis.

Suppose two variables move together all the time. When one increases, the other always increases, and by an amount exactly proportional to the first. The correlation between the two variables would be exactly 1. Correlation can also be negative; when one variable increases, the other decreases. Perfect negative correlation ($r = -1$) would mean that the variable always decreases in the same proportion. But if the two variables have absolutely nothing to do with each other, the fact that one increased tells us absolutely nothing about what the other one did, the correlation would be zero.

Of course, perfect correlation ($r = 1$ or $r = -1$) is quite rare in real world social science. Every time we increase advertising by 15 percent, we do not always get a 5 percent increase in sales. It may be only 3 percent, it may be as much as 6 percent, occasionally there may be no increase at all. But if sales tend to increase when we spend more on advertising, then the two are positively correlated ($r > 0$). If sales tend to decrease with more advertising (we hope not), the two would be negatively correlated ($r < 0$). If we have ratio data on sales and on advertising spending, we can compute the correlation coefficient and determine whether and how strongly sales and advertising expenditure are associated.

Unfortunately, though, because of sampling error, even if two variables are completely unrelated, we would be unlikely to get exactly $r = 0$. So if we find a positive correlation between beer and soft drink spending, we must consider the possibility that it only seems positive because of sampling error. This should make one think of statistical tests, and indeed, a t-test can be used to decide whether a non-zero correlation actually shows anything or not.

Table 8.7 shows the output of a correlation computation. This "correlation matrix" is symmetric, so that the upper right value (0.9569) is the same as the lower left value. (In other words, the correlation of beer spending with soft drink spending is exactly the same as the correlation of soft drink spending with beer spending. For this reason, many statistical programs only print half the matrix.) The correlation of a variable with itself is, by definition, exactly 1 (every time beer spending changes by one dollar, beer spending has changed by exactly one dollar).

The correlation between soft drink spending and beer spending here is positive, as we thought, and quite strong. The P-value shows that the coefficient ($r = 0.95$) is unlikely to be the result of sampling error. Recall that this P-value is the area left in the tail of the t-distribution at the point where the computed t-statistic falls. We have

Table 8.7.   Example of correlation

		SPEND	SPEND2
	Correlation coefficient	1.0000	0.9569
SPEND	No. of cases	237	237
	2-tailed significance		P = 0.000
	Correlation coefficient	0.9569	1.0000
SPEND2	No. of cases	237	237
	2-tailed significance	P = 0.000	

Recall from Table 8.3 that SPEND is spending on soft drinks, and SPEND2 is spending on beer.

not bothered to actually compute a t-value, because the P-value tells us all we need to know: the null hypothesis (H_0: $r = 0$) is false. When there is no area left in the tails of the distribution (to the decimal points reported), we certainly must be farther out the tail of the distribution than the place where there would be 10 or 5 percent left (90 or 95 percent confidence levels).

9

Presenting the Results

The *presentation* of the research results is one of the two most important parts of the whole research process. Before starting the actual research, we said that *defining the problem and developing information needs* were critical. They are obviously the *other* vital part of the research process. If the researcher does not know what he is working on and what information he needs to obtain to work on it, it is impossible to carry out a good project. At the end of the research comes the presentation — a no less important task.

Between the initial stages of the research process, with its stress on *problem definition and information needs*, and the last stage, i.e., the *presentation*, everything else is technique. It must be done well, certainly. But doing it well will not save a poorly defined project, because we would merely be doing a good job at getting information which is of no use to the marketing manager. Similarly, the most competently executed research project cannot be saved if the presentation is poor. Managers do not give credibility to material that is presented badly. They do not pay attention. *They do not use it.* And if it is not used by marketing managers to help in their marketing decisions, it is bad research, a waste of time, effort, and money.

THE REPORT

There are a number of specific things which must appear in most marketing research reports. We will discuss such things below, but do not think that our discussion is the only model for the "correct" way to write a marketing research report. The correct way is the way the client wants it. If they want something different from our outline, it does little good later to point out to them that you read about how to write a report in some book. Use the discussion as a guide, not as a rigid model.

We are going to start by talking about the *body* of the written report itself. In the written report, there are many things that precede the body in the ordering of pages. But these things are written after the report has been written, so we will follow the order of doing things, not the order of organizing the report. One of the first things to do in writing a report, though, is not to write, but to find out who is going to read it. The report must be oriented toward the reader.

There may even be more than one level of reader, maybe the brand manager *and* the marketing vice-president. Maybe even different versions of the report are needed, with more fine detail in one, and more about strategic implications in the other. Whoever the reader is for however many versions, the objective of the report is simply to give that reader the information he needs.

The body of the report starts out with an **introduction**. This should contain first a discussion of the problem which the research addresses. Do not assume that everyone knows why the research was done. While the researcher and the marketing manager who has worked with the researcher know why the research was done, others may not know. This introductory explanation can be relatively short, consisting of only a few sentences, if the problem is easily defined. It may be long if the problem is complex.

Sometimes background information must be included, depending on whom the report is written for. If it is an internal document, background can be kept to a minimum. The researcher should assume that company employees do not need to be told a great deal about their company's operations. Cover only the background specific to the problem. If the report is going to be distributed externally, more background may be needed. For example, if the marketing manager must submit a market analysis report to the banker to gain financing for a major campaign, the banker may need to see more extensive background.

After stating the purpose of the research, and having provided some background information, the introduction should then state what the research is going to do to fulfil the purpose. This means that the introduction also contains a statement of objectives, including a discussion of the information needs and of the target population. One way for readers later to judge whether the research was any good is to look at the problem statement, see how well the information addresses that problem, and then see how good the research was at actually getting the information.

The main body of the report should first cover how we did what we said we were going to do. This is the **methodology** section. It should outline how the research was carried out. The critical issue here is how samples were taken, not how we traveled to the library to find secondary data. Managers always want to know who provided information in a survey and how they were chosen to provide it. State, in detail, exactly how someone got into the sample. Do not simply say "respondents were chosen randomly". The term "random" is misused so often that it really has no meaning without some statement of exactly what procedure was used. If it was a random sample, state how the random numbers were generated. If it was a convenience sample, state how the locations were chosen and what procedure was used to approach people at the location.

After telling how the sample was taken (including specifics on time and place), discuss who actually got into the sample, i.e., the demographics. Managers always want to know whom the information actually came from. The discussion should include an analysis of how well the sample matched the target population that was defined above. This will help the marketing manager judge how useful the information really is.

The entire introduction section and most of the methodology section can be written before any of the information gathering has actually been started. In fact, these parts probably should be written at the very beginning of the research process, to force researchers and marketing managers to clearly state what the project is all about and how it will be carried out. When these sections are written, they should usually be condensed into a few pages, unless extensive background is needed. Introduction and methodology are supporting sections, not the main substance. The main purpose of the report is to present the information, not to present what the project was going to do. What it was going to do was settled earlier.

The section on **results** is the main substance of the report. The results section contains a **discussion of the findings**. The first thing to remember is that simply presenting a lot of tables is *not* a discussion. The "analyst" who only presents tables has not really analyzed anything at all. He has simply told the reader "I am too lazy to figure this out. Here are the numbers, you figure it out yourself." The discussion provided must talk about what the numbers *mean:* it must provide an *interpretation* of the numbers. It must point out important patterns in the data, key relationships.

Tables alone do not constitute a research report. They are simply the supporting evidence. Most tables belong in the appendix with the rest of the supporting evidence. Too many tables in the text distract from the flow of the discussion. Readers get lost looking at lots of numbers and lose the logic of the argument. Those tables that are brought into the text should generally be summary tables, or composite tables of information presented in several other tables. They should concisely present the key data that support an important point. Highly detailed tables still belong in the appendix.

If only a few tables should go in the text, which ones should we include? Refer back to the information needs in their order of priority. The most critical information, the most important points, can and usually should be supported directly in the text by a table or figure. If it is not a key point, the table or figure should be left in the appendix. Finally, the table should follow the place in the text which refers to it, so that readers know what it is for by the time they get to it.

Discussion of the results should be self-contained, in the sense that readers would know what was going on even if they had no tables, and even if they had lost the appendix. So the discussion must explain what is in the tables in enough detail to enable the reader to visualize the patterns. Refer to Chapter 8 for some simple examples of discussions that meet this criterion. The reader should only have to turn to a table if he wants a lot of detail on the specific numbers that constitute the pattern.

The discussion should be organized. Generally, a report that simply goes through the questionnaire discussing questions one at a time is not very effective. The individual questions on the questionnaire all address some information need. It may take several questions to answer one thing that the manager wanted to know. The manager is more interested in the information needs at the beginning of the report than in the individual questions on the questionnaire in the appendix. Organize the discussion of results into sections based on topics following the information needs.

Proper organization helps avoid the trap of thinking that only data from the survey can be included in the report. The report addresses topics, not questionnaire items. Remember, the purpose of the project is to provide information on certain topics to the manager. Certainly, the survey itself is not the only possible source of information about those things. Some relevant information may have come from secondary research, from qualitative interviews, from observation, from any of the many methods of getting data in addition to surveys. Any relevant information can be included in the report, provided that the reader is made aware of the source.

The writing must be clear. The objective in writing is effective communication about the information needed by the manager. This requires a writing style that is easy to follow and understand. Readers should be thinking about the issues that are being discussed when they read the report. They should not be distracted from this by having to to think about how to follow the report. Some of the same rules applicable to questionnaire writing are also appropriate in report writing.

Short, simple language is best. Long, complex sentences belong in literature, if anywhere, but certainly not in marketing research reports. Pronouns are generally bad, especially if they appear in a discussion where more than one noun appears. In a report on interviews with wholesalers and retailers, exactly what does it mean to say "They said that they like to use promotions"? Does it mean the wholesalers said that the retailers like promotions or, the retailers said the wholesalers like promotions? Maybe the wholesalers said that they themselves like promotions. The report should be clear.

Technical jargon used just for effect must be avoided, although terms must be used precisely and defined explicitly. In particular, the report is not about statistics, it is about marketing. Statistical jargon has absolutely no place. If it is known with complete certainty that *only* technical people will be reading the report, some technical jargon may facilitate communication. For example, if all the product managers and marketing people are engineers, they will understand engineering terms. But even then, not much engineering jargon should be used if there will also be other readers of the report who are not engineers.

No research is perfect, and for that reason, reports may also include a **limitations** section. This section points out any potential problems with the research. But it is not enough to simply state that there is a (potential) problem. Some analysis must also be presented on how serious the problem is, and how it is likely to affect research findings. For example, non-response is usually an issue in survey research. But the simple fact that some people did not respond may or may not affect results.

For some kinds of research, such as food items, the topic is not a sensitive one, so people do not mind talking about it. In an intercept survey, people who refuse to answer would mostly just be too busy. There may not be any reason to think that busy non-respondents regard soft drinks any differently than less-busy respondents. Non-response, a potential limitation, is not much of a problem when we think about it a little bit. If the research is about convenience food items, though, busy people might well have different views from people who are not so busy. Non-response could bias the results; those who have more favorable attitudes toward convenience foods may be underrepresented.

Inexperienced researchers often think that pointing out problems detracts from the credibility of the report. Managers see the list of problems in the limitations section and decide that they cannot trust the report. This is not true. Sloppy research detracts from credibility, but this has nothing to do with whether the researcher admits that problems exist. When good research admits to certain problems, credibility is enhanced. The research is more trustworthy for clearly pointing out where the reader should be careful, instead of pretending that all is perfect. If the reader discovers a major problem himself, which the report did not point out, *that* destroys credibility.

Conclusions bring together all of the information presented in the report. Conclusion does not mean summary. Most marketing research reports do include a summary, but this section is not the place for this. *The conclusions discuss what all of this information means.* They are opinions based on the results of the research. Data are brought from the report into the conclusions only as supporting evidence in the building of the opinions.

Generally, conclusions should correspond to the research objectives. We wanted to know about attitudes toward computers, now, what do we think we know about attitudes? If we developed formal hypotheses at the beginning stages of the research, here is where the discussion should confirm or disconfirm those hypotheses.

Recommendations are suggestions about what should be done. This is a marketing, and not a research-related section. Recommendations correspond to the marketing problems. The researcher should know a great deal by the end of the project about the marketing environment, and is in a good position to say what actions should be taken. But recommendations must be presented skillfully and subtly. Marketing decisions, after all, are the responsibility of the marketing manager, who may not like to feel that his authority is being challenged.

In any event, everything down to the conclusions should flow from the data and should be beyond challenge, although different people might show the results differently. The recommendations, though, are more idiosyncratic. They represent the best professional judgment of the researcher. The marketing manager may see the same facts and interpret them differently. We are dealing with people not automatons.

APPENDIX AND FRONT MATTER

Following the body of the report comes the *appendix*, which contains important supporting materials for the report. One thing that must appear in it is a copy of the **data collection forms** (questionnaire) that were used if questioning was part of the research. Also, summary statistics of answers should be included which show how people answered each question of a survey questionnaire. Often, the summary statistics can simply be included on the questionnaire itself.

Most **tables and figures** are also included in the appendix. There should be a direct correspondence between what is discussed in the text and what appears among these tables and figures. If the body of the report discusses something, there should be supporting evidence, i.e., a table or figure. If it is not important enough to be discussed in the text, tables and figures about it should not clutter up the appendix. Remember, the function is to provide supporting evidence. Showing that the analyst ran every possible variable in every possible way with every other variable is not what the appendix is for.

We said above that the body of the report should be written so that readers can understand what is going on even if the appendix tables are lost. Similarly, the tables and figures should be clear enough that they can be understood even if the text part of the report is never seen. Each table and figure should have a name which describes what it shows.

Get rid of the uninformative variable names that computers love. Income should be clearly labeled "income", not INC. Attitudes toward Brand A should be so labeled — they should not be labeled ATTA. The analyst knows what all these variable names mean because he has been working at analyzing the data. On the other hand, most readers will not know. Get rid of excessive decimal digits. Usually, two digits are more than sufficient. How much more does the manager really know if he learns that the mean spending per week on soft drinks is HK$43.5375 rather than HK$43.54? This is just false precision anyway, since the sampling error is certainly greater than 0.0075.

With percentages, just an integer will usually do fine (73 percent, not 73.42 percent, or even 73.4 percent), except if we are looking at brand shares, where one decimal is usually desirable. Overall, remember that needless decimals just give a false picture of accuracy. They clutter things up without presenting any useful information.

Detailed calculations about things like sample size, test statistics, and so forth belong in the appendix, not the text. The text is for managers to find out about marketing information. A few of them may want to see all the statistical details; they can look these details up in the appendix. Most managers do not want to see all those quantitative details. They should not be forced to wade through them in the text.

The **bibliography** should be included in the appendix. Some supporting evidence comes from secondary data, not from the survey. Managers may need to know where it comes from so that they can look up more detail. Certainly, the credibility of the report can be enhanced if they know that the researcher's analysis is based on previous work, not just personal guesswork.

The *front matter* to the report should be written after the report itself is finished. The **title page** comes first. It includes a title which concisely describes the subject of the report. It should also include information on who prepared the report, whom they did it for, and when they did it. The names of the authors should appear, along with their affiliation, and the organization which carried out the research. The title page includes the names of the client, both the names of the company and contact person within the company. The date should be listed. Readers later should never have to guess how current or outdated the report is.

The **executive summary** is the summary referred to above. This should be a self-contained mini-report (preferably calling attention to itself by being on a different color paper) covering all of the key points in the larger report. It has all of the sections of the body of the report. The introduction must very briefly state the research problem, summarize information needs, and present the methodology. The results must summarize the key findings of the research. Important conclusions must be presented, and the main recommendations should be given.

All of this must be done in a very few pages. Executive summaries that are more than about two or three pages long reflect sloppy writing and thinking more often than they indicate huge masses of truly crucial information. The summary cannot be shortened by referring to the main report instead of stating what needs to be said. It must be self-contained. Often, only a handful of people most directly involved with the problem will actually read the full report. Other managers who want to know something about the results read the executive summary. Often, the summary is the only part of the report that is even circulated.

The **table of contents** lists the divisions and subdivisions of the report, showing on which page a given division can be found. The purpose of this is to make it easy for a reader to turn directly to the page which discusses a topic of interest to him. Take a look at the page numbers that show up in the table of contents. If several sections all start on the same page, things are divided up too finely. Too much space in the report is devoted to headings, and not enough to discussion. Tables of contents may also include a list of tables and figures which appear in the text, but usually not those which are contained in the appendix.

THE ORAL PRESENTATION

Most marketing research reports also include an oral presentation of the results. This presentation is a kind of spoken executive summary. It covers much the same things. It is typically brief, lasting usually about an hour or less. In that time, probably no more than five minutes should be devoted to a brief statement of the research problem and information needs, a short discussion of methodology, and later, a brief statement touching upon the research limitations. Managers show up to hear the presentation because they want to hear the results, conclusions, and recommendations. These things must fill up most of the time.

One key rule for presentations is to know the audience. This is important even in writing the report itself, but it is even more important here. The presentation must be oriented toward what the audience wants to find out. The researcher must be prepared for the kinds of questions the audience is going to ask when the formal presentation is over.

The oral presentation is self-contained. It should be understandable to the listeners even if they never read the report itself. It should be oriented toward showing how the research objectives were addressed, what the key findings were regarding the information needs, conclusions about how these findings affect marketing, and suggestions about what marketing actions to take. Practice making your presentation. Make sure that the presentation does address what the audience wants to hear about. Make sure that it is not oriented toward a long, boring recitation of hundreds of numbers, which no one wants to hear.

Visual aids should be used effectively. In the planning stage of the project, we thought about "the boards", the set of tables and other illustrations that we would be presenting. The oral presentation presents an opportunity to use them. Generally, those boards can meet most of our visual aids needs. Only a very few key issues will have come up during the research that were not anticipated in planning a project well. The visuals address key issues, and enhance understanding with an easy-to-understand table or figure.

The visuals must not be used to illustrate every minor point that the researcher is going to mention. If there are too many visuals, they go past too quickly for anyone to make sense of them. If the visuals are too complex, people have a difficult time understanding them in the short time they appear. But people will try to make sense of them. They will devote most of their attention to trying to understand all of the data in each briefly appearing visual, and they will not hear much of what the researcher actually says.

Always be prepared for questions after the formal presentation is over. Many questions can be anticipated by knowing the audience. Good presenters have prepared not only the presentation itself, but the answers, perhaps including a visual, to many of the most likely issues to come up in the discussion.

Follow-up is often a critical part of the research presentation, but it is too often neglected because it does not take place until later. Follow-up focuses on two different research direction concerns. Internally, after a project is over and everything has been given and presented to the client, the project should be evaluated. How could problems have been avoided, how could the research have been better, how could the report and the presentation have been more effective?

Externally, the client should be contacted again within a couple of weeks. Sometimes a particular point must be explained in more detail now that managers are actually beginning to use the information. Sometimes clients want a small revision to highlight a critical point. Occasionally they may want a specific section pulled out of the report and written up separately for distribution to relevant personnel. Providing all of these minor things (of course, major additional work would require a new budget) help to develop a lasting relationship with the client. But equally as important is the continued feedback about how the managers are using the research.

PART III

Varieties of Marketing Research

Part III asks: What do marketing researchers actually DO? What are the specific kinds of studies in which all of the concepts or approaches from Part I and all of the skills from Part II actually get used?

They get used in every phase of the marketing process. Part III expressly emphasizes the *marketing decision-making* function that marketing research serves. The names of the studies may vary from company to company, from place to place, and from time to time. But the broad areas we spell out constitute the essence and the bulk of what marketing researchers really do.

These broad research areas are summarized as follows. **Concept and positioning** (Chapter 10) refers to the idea behind the product. The **product itself** (Chapter 11) is what people perceive it to be and how it performs. The **package** plays many roles; it and **product name** (Chapter 12) cannot be readily changed and so must be right the first time. Setting the **price** (Chapter 13) and making sure the **place** (Chapter 14) facilitates the smooth flow of products are critical.

Advertising (Chapter 15) is probably one of the biggest single parts of the whole marketing research world. **"Below-the-line" promotional activities** (Chapter 16) are a huge part of the marketing world and are becoming more important to research. **Market studies** (Chapter 17) seek to broadly define the size, shape, boundaries, and customers of markets. Research plays a key role in the process of developing **new products** (Chapter 18) from conception to testing in the marketplace.

Concept and Positioning Research

Marketing research has an important role throughout all stages of the marketing process, from planning, to implementation of the marketing mix, to control and evaluation of marketing efforts. The very beginning stages, when one is trying to come up with ideas that may work well in the marketplace, may be one of the most difficult parts of the whole process. Research can be critical in this nebulous area of concept development.

THE PRIMACY OF THE IDEA

Today, success in marketing products — whether they are tangible goods or intangible services — depends upon the product idea as much as on the product itself. This idea, this "consumer offer", is what marketers are really asking consumers to react to and buy. It consists of the total package that consumers get, from the basic core benefit, to the actual product, name, logo, package, to intangible "augmentation" aspects such as service, warranty, etc. The glue that holds this bundle together is the overall image of the product.

The core benefit to the customer is at the center of this product idea. People do not spend good money just to acquire physical objects, they pay to obtain benefits. The product image is the exterior which consumers really see. From this exterior, they decide whether the core benefit really fits what they need. The rest of the product is technical detail, constructed to match the product benefit to the consumer's ideal image.

To get the image right, and therefore to get the technical detail right, marketers must think from the consumer's point of view: What does the product do for the consumer — for "me"? What needs does it fill? What dissatisfactions will it help allay? How will it fit into lifestyles? What is special about it? In what ways does it make consumers feel special about themselves?

These questions must almost always be explored if a product is to succe modern world. Nowadays products whose primary (if not total) thrust is what and what they contain seldom perform as well as products whose thrust is al they stand for. The tangibles, physical products, features, ingredients, are all that can usually be quite readily copied. But what they stand for, a clear and relevant image, is very difficult to copy well.

What a product "stands for", its basic idea ("concept"), ultimately decides whether it will last. Marketers who are good at these aspects, who create products with valid concepts, and appealing images, create "brands". It is when a "product" becomes a "brand" that the long-term magic takes over.

Most aspects of a "product", then, are something made and copiable. A "brand" — a product with an idea and personality behind it — is something more. Then the consumer may be able to think: This is something I can be loyal to, something that is "mine" — something that is "me"!

The search for good new ideas can be carried out by the Research and Development (R&D), Marketing Management, or Marketing Research departments. The R&D Department should work on how to make new, different, and better products. The Marketing Management Department should contribute ideas from its knowledge of the market, perhaps from feedback from customers. And the Marketing Research Department, working as always with the Marketing Management Department, should constantly probe for and test the saliency of still other ideas. Good ideas on how to satisfy unfilled consumer needs from the Marketing Management and Marketing Research departments can then be further explored by the R&D Department to determine their technical feasibility.

As this progresses, the Marketing Management and Marketing Research departments should monitor, test, and assess those ideas, as well as make sure they address some consumer need or want, and that they have some core benefit to consumers. This process should also include working alongside the advertising agency crew, the creative team, and the account team, to make sure that the core benefit and the technical product details can be built into a coherent image.

Whether the ideas emerge from the R&D, Marketing Research, Marketing Management departments, or even other sources, it should be apparent that these are in fact ideas in a testing stage. It will take a long time before ideas tested at this stage of the product development process actually give rise to any physical products (or services) which may ultimately be marketed. In fact, the product may never be made at all.

But testing the idea must begin just as soon as there are potentially important ideas to test. This is because — to repeat — it is the idea (and its ultimate transformation into advertising fact and advertising imagery) that will spell the real difference between success and failure in the modern world. And the idea never ceases to be vital: it must be reviewed again and again, even after the product has come to market. It must be reviewed in line with the realities of the world as it stands now, because "now" realities may have changed somewhat from "then" realities.

THE NOTION OF THE "CONCEPT"

Ideas, such as just discussed, are usually referred to as "concepts". They may be "product" concepts, ideas for goods or services. Usually these will be for new goods or services, but may also be for restaged or existing ones. Or they may be "advertising" concepts: ideas for how to present products, the product image. This may mean new campaigns, new ways to say old things, new ways to say new things, or a return to older ways of saying things.

But whatever their focus, these are all still "concepts": "ideas", "notions", "visions", and "dreams". In fact, there is really no definitive agreement about exactly what a concept is. Before we can discuss the nature of concept testing, though, we must try to have a better understanding of the term "concept" itself.

In marketing, a concept may be thought of first of all as an idea that states a benefit or fulfils a need. A simple example might be: a battery-operated electric razor. This electric razor is as good as the best blade shaving system (single, twin, cartridge, whatever) but avoids the well-known messiness of cream and water and can be used anywhere and quickly.

A concept may be thought of as a mental image — something like Paul's notion of "faith": "the reality of things unseen". It is within a person's head, rather than fixed in solid, real terms. It is something like a Platonic Ideal, something like the "Tao" of Taoism: that which is the essence of everything, but which, if expressed, cannot be the "Tao".

And so, too, a concept may be thought of, by extension, as a germ or a nucleus. This core, when given flesh and blood and words and music, will emerge as a final written or pictorial expression that we call an ad or commercial. Consumers will be exposed to this presentation of product image and asked to react to it; i.e., to buy it.

So with all this as background, we summarize our "concept" of what a "concept" is:

- A concept is simply an idea for a product or a service or some advertising. It is a glimmer in someone's mind. It is not written down, or formulated, or thought through yet.

This is a pretty nebulous thing to test. In fact, what we seek to develop and to test might more correctly be called a "concept statement". Other ways of saying pretty much the same thing include the terms a "selling proposition", or an "expression of an offer". Such a statement, proposition, or expression may be defined as a description for a product or service that includes its essence and its benefits.

We never really test a concept then — but rather a *description* of it. It is all right to talk about "concept testing", but only so long as we remember that it is not really the concept we are testing, but its expression, which is in the form of a product (perhaps non-existent) which we describe by its attributes and benefits.

It is not easy to write a good concept statement. If it is under-written and has no "sell" at all, we will not get useful reactions to the idea. If it is over-written, so embedded in ad-talk that the essence is submerged, we will not be able to separate the reactions to the idea from reactions to the ad-talk. Reaching the happy middle-ground between these extremes is difficult, but essential.

USEFULNESS OF CONCEPT TESTING

Some marketers are still wary of concept testing ("How can people react to what just doesn't exist?"). But the fact remains that concept testing is growing in importance. It is a vital first step in the process of developing a new product, product modification, or product line extension. Concept testing can be useful in nearly every situation that requires appraisal of an idea at a stage early enough so that the appraisal can be considered for further marketing action.

To be useful, concept work must be conducted with the same thoughtful, action-oriented approach that is used in more established areas like product testing. Sloppy work here, perhaps even more than in many other areas of marketing research, will render results worthless. But good work can give critical guidance in product development, saving millions of dollars from being wasted.

Concept testing does have its limitations. Several valid questions concerning realism have rightly been raised:

- How realistic is concept testing? Are we just tilting at windmills?
- Why not just put the product on the market and see if anybody buys it? Isn't that the real proof of the pudding?

One problem is that some overenthusiastic proponents seem to claim that concept testing can be the universal solution to all puzzles. It is not, and it is no wonder at all that disillusioned marketers challenge this type of exaggerated claim. Concept testing, if done well, can be useful and even critical in developing marketing strategy in many situations. But, just like other aspects of market research, it offers no guarantees. Good information does not always insure good marketing decisions.

Furthermore, even if concept-testing information is good, it cannot hope to cover all aspects of how people will react to products and marketing campaigns. Concept testing can never tell what the reaction to a product will be once it has been on the market for a while and has been massively advertised and promoted. When our "magic" shaver becomes the norm, there will be different issues, different worries: how to make it smaller, quicker, etc. But these things must come later, not at the concept-testing stage. Therefore, especially for something radically new and different, all that one can hope for is a rather minimal level of comprehension and affirmative feeling.

For now, a minimal level of comprehension will do, but how minimal is minimal? That depends on the combined marketing judgments of the marketer and the researcher. Ideally, judgment can be buttressed by some sort of normative data — some "action standards" — based on reactions to similar new concepts at the same stage of development. This kind of data would be especially useful if it followed through as the new product went into the market place, so that reactions at the concept stage could be compared to actual market performance.

This ideal is certainly possible for a manufacturer or a service organization that believes in continuing research and keeps track of what has happened in the past. Most companies, though, do not have such a continuing record. For them, concept testing must mostly be based on judgment, an educated guess on whether the reaction is satisfactorily high to commit funds for additional testing (product, package, copy, etc).

Most important, even after the clarity of such a concept has been shown, the researcher and marketer must be convinced that a need is being met. Perhaps the need cannot even be articulated yet. But somehow, in some way, marketers must divine that it is there. Often reaction to the new thing being offered (say a horseless carriage in a day of horse carriages) may not be articulated clearly. People may be vague, confused, doubtful about believability, worried about ramifications (say: service, garaging, roads).

Addressing these issues must, of necessity, come later on. Technological and infrastructural change will eventually solve some things. Advertising and promotion can help educate people about how to deal with other things. But in the beginning, there must be some understanding of what is being offered, and there must be some need to be filled. In this sort of case — or their modern equivalents — all one can say is that at least concept testing is the way to begin attacking the problem.

GENERATION OF CONCEPTS

In the course of research involving concepts, three basic issues arise:

- Generation
- Form
- Testing

Concept generation can come from many sources. R&D can generate concepts, as can marketing management, marketing research, and other parts of the organization. So can the customer. Often, concepts from customers are some of the most valuable, because they may be most closely tied from the start to real needs.

How can the researcher utilize consumer research to help generate concepts? First, the general area of company interest must be defined (here, men's shaving products — specifically razors). This is usually not a research matter, but is tied to the company's experience and expertise — the business they are in. Then, probably the most productive way to proceed is via a series of "one-on-ones" (depth interviews), or group sessions, or both. The researcher will use an outline-guide, developed through detailed internal discussions and searches of all sorts. Then the respondents must be encouraged to express themselves in their own language, and, in the case of groups, interact. What is the ritual of shaving? Is the mess really that messy? What really seems to be the essence of people's concerns, if any? Speed, portability, cleanliness, what? The key here is not our ideas, but theirs.

If there are already some ideas about these issues beforehand, they may be presented as individual "bits". Respondents may react to these bits and actually help the marketer and researcher "build" a concept that has already been envisioned. If no ideas have been brought up, we may start virtually from scratch in getting respondents to identify problems and begin thinking of solutions. We hope, and it is usually the case, that the concepts developed for us are grounded in needs that are in turn grounded in problems.

Whether we begin with ideas or hope to develop ideas through interaction with customers, endless patience, skill, and an eye and ear for serendipity are required here. And, of course, time is needed. There is no shortcut to this process of digging out ideas from consumers who may not even know they have the ideas.

FORMS OF CONCEPTS

Words

Concepts may be presented to respondents for their evaluation in the form of statements, or in the form of advertisements (or commercials). If we believe that execution will be the key, then we will make advertisements (or commercials) for products we do not yet have and may never make. We can present these to respondents as real products sold elsewhere. It is important to get them to respond as if to real products and not to concepts.

However, many think that the only acceptable way to test a concept is in the form of a statement, in unemotional, straight-talk language, through words on a card. And indeed, if the concept involves a new development, a new way, a new form, something tangible and readily explicable that is not grounded in execution, then this is a correct first approach.

The concept is first "flattened": shorn of extravagant-claim language. Then it is "sharpened": worked and reworked based on consumers' reactions until it is in its clearest form. We need to make the points that the concept is trying to make clearly understood. Some of the questions to be researched may include:

- Does the concept statement clearly convey the germ of the idea that you wish to convey?
- Is there a clearer way — a more forceful way — to express this idea?
- What is the product like that consumers visualize when they hear the statement?
- Specifically — how "unique" is it? What needs does it fill? How would it be used? What does it do? How does it do it? When would it be used?
- Overall, what are its perceived advantages and disadvantages?
- How believable is the claim made for it?
- How does the proposed idea (as product) fit into the consumer's "lifestyle" and "buying-style"?
- What would a customer have to give up (in whole or part) to buy it? What does the product compete with?
- How much might it cost?
- Where would it be sold?

This "sharpening" process may continue for several sessions or surveys. The process may be likened to a series of successive approximations. It can be a time-consuming process to be sure. But it is absolutely necessary if we are to test the concept finally in its most acceptable form.

The objective of such research is to end up with a statement that tells all about the product as clearly and meaningfully as it can be presented. The statement must convey the product's physical characteristics, sensory associations, and customer benefits. It must reach two levels, both specifically as it relates to this particular product, and more generally in fitting into the inner and outer worlds in which the consumer lives.

At some point during the new product research, usually as early as possible, it is very important to resolve the question of what it is exactly that consumers are valuing. Then we can alter the original product idea so that, if undervalued, we can increase the value that consumers see in the idea. This is a vital step. Unless we know how valuable, at the extreme, a concept can be made to be, there is no way of assessing what criteria the product itself must live up to. For want of a better term, we can call this concept optimization.

The process of concept optimization, the aim of the successive approximations, requires perhaps the greatest skill of any aspect of consumer research. Its success depends on a high degree of interviewing as well as analytical skill. We need to arrive at a final statement that neither overpromises nor underpromises. Instead, it must provide realistic (as well as exciting) expectations. Ultimately, we must be able to meet these expectations (or even surpass them), to sell the product, gain repeat customers, and build a new product success.

Beyond Words

For some propositions, a concept statement in the form of words only may be sufficient before moving on to the next step in the marketing process. However, in some cases the heart of the concept is something complex (needing visuals) or emotional (needing the aura of the advertising message). Then, as noted above, it may well be advisable — indeed, essential — to put the concept into the form of an advertisement or commercial. Such a test may look like an advertisement test, and perhaps it is. (Categories are never as neat as we would like them to be.) Still, it will test for the important issues in concept development: uniqueness, believability, etc. The only difference is that the visuals and such are now made explicit and embedded in the execution.

It can be argued, too, that if the consumer will ultimately see the concept in the form of an ad or commercial, then it is always valid to get the reaction to the proposition in that form. This is true even when the concept is also tested in a "description-only" format. For concept testing in this form to work, the ad or commercial may have to be presented with somewhat less "advertisingese" then it will ultimately have. We do not want the "advertisingese" elements to overwhelm the basic concept message.

This is not a simple area to work out between the marketer and the researcher. But through thought and mutual understanding a workable agreement — such as semi-finished copy — can usually be devised.

TESTING CONCEPTS: PRINCIPLES

In the following sections we shall describe three kinds of quantitative testing situations that researchers encounter. These kinds of quantitative testing would follow the qualitative work already discussed; and they are merely suggestive of the rich range of situations that actually turn up in the field of concept testing. The methods are slightly different in each of the three cases. But the four broad guideposts discussed in this section should guide the researcher's approach in any of the cases.

First, wherever possible, choices and reactions should be made on a "will-they-buy-it" basis. Some form of money value should be involved. Some sort of "put your money where your mouth is" questions need to be made. We can ask respondents to "buy" the product, for example, by sending for it in the mail. We can have them send for a cents-off coupon for it. We can let them choose between our concept, a competitive product, or cash. There are many ways to do this where cash is involved. The key element, though, in all such methods is to get a "hard" response to our "product" by asking the respondent to part with some cash.

Secondly, in testing concepts quantitatively, it is desirable to include one or more control concepts which can serve as a benchmark. A control describes an existing product, usually the leader in the product class. Such a control can be derived by extracting the claims made for the product in its current advertising. This control allows us to compare the new concept with already existing alternatives.

Third, such quantitative testing should be continuing, not a one-shot thing. Over the course of time, this develops norms for various product categories against which to measure new concepts as they are developed. For example, the researcher may find that, on average, 40 percent of all respondents will react favorably to a new concept idea in a given product class. From this, we may be able to say that any new concept should probably score at least 40 percent in order to have any chance of ultimately being a success.

Obviously, the less data we have to establish these norms, the more necessary it is to have control concepts to measure against. It is also obvious that these norms become more meaningful as standards for management decision when they are related to the actual marketplace performance of the product, once it goes on sale. This means that good norms are based on data gathered throughout the new-product introduction process, from concept testing all the way to commercialization.

And fourth, here in the quantitative evaluation stage we should begin to think about segmenting the appeal. To whom does the concept appeal? Can we distinguish different sorts of responses among people who differ on common segmentation variables relating to such things as demographic, geographic, psychographic, behavioral, attitudinal (ideas about brands, categories, and end-benefits) differences?

A relatively small segment of the total audience who react strongly in favor of our product concept statement may well be worth going after, even if nobody else really cares for it very much. It is in the course of quantitative work in this area that we will then develop our estimates about size: how big is each segment in terms of people and sales volume, and how big is the total market.

ONE OR FEW CONCEPTS

The researcher may have one concept which seems viable. After it is now "flattened" and "sharpened" sufficiently, we can move ahead to the next step. Now the thing to do, probably, is to test against concept statements which have been written for the leading brand(s) in the category.

Alternately, there may be several concept statements, some (or all or none) of which may warrant further development. They can all be tested against each other, and then the winner can be tested against a competitor. Or, they could each be tested against the competition.

Suppose it is mainly a problem of positioning a new product which has definite advantages. We will probably want to go with this product, but we just do not know exactly how to present it right now. Suppose we think we really can produce an electric shaver that really shaves as well as a "wet shave". What is the best way to find out if anybody cares?

Two alternative concepts — flattened and sharpened — might be developed, (again based on the qualitative work). These concepts might read as follows:

- This is a new electric razor which gives as good a shave as a blade razor — but without the inconvenience (soap, styptic pencil, towel, etc.).
- This is a new electric razor which gives as good a shave as a straight razor that barbers use — but without the danger of cutting yourself.

The control concept (which is a "concept" for an already existing product) might read:

- This is a new electric razor that gives the smoothest and quickest shave of any electric shaver on the market, thanks to its many-speed action and special trimmers for hard to get at places.

Remember that the purpose of the control concept is to use its scores as a baseline. The new product concept must score at least as well as the control, or the new product would have difficulty competing in the market against existing products. The new product concept should also score up to whatever level the marketing manager's action standards may be set at. Otherwise, actually introducing the product would violate experienced and educated thinking about what is necessary for a successful product.

The actual presentation of the concepts would probably include screening for usage of shaving products. Here, for example, we might want half of our respondents to be electric razor users, half non-users. The researcher would show the first concept and the control to the respondents. They would be asked to discuss the product: for example, how does it compare to what they use now, what is its overall effectiveness, would they purchase it? (Remember, intention-to-purchase information is more valid if they must actually have some commitment.) Then the researcher might get information on what respondents think it would cost, general reactions, products used, etc.

The researcher would then show the second concept statement and the control to a matched sample. Then answers from the two groups can be compared — especially on the more scalable items like the comparison to current product, overall rating, and intention-to-purchase.

MANY CONCEPTS

Sometimes, there is a vast array of concepts, probably all in the same product class, or possibly in a few different product classes. This is often true when brainstorming or other methods have been used to generate a lot of preliminary ideas. We may have done some partial screening already, but are still left with a number of concepts that look good. Then, we need to know how to single out those ideas which seem most worthy of further work.

This time the problem is different. Let's assume that we have had sufficient patience and have tested out many concepts. Some of the ideas have been killed after careful thought. The remaining ideas really look like "go" situations, maybe eight to ten from an initially much larger list. So we have a handful of concepts in good shape now, developed through discussions with respondents in the qualitative phase. Some may even be for the same product.

Now we want to know: which one(s) should we go with? Now we also need numbers, but what numbers? Again, and this time even more clearly, dollars-and-cents numbers are essential. Nothing can conclude research on the possibility of multiple product concepts better than an appraisal of whether anyone would buy these concepts (which eventually become the product) in the marketplace.

One useful method in this kind of situation is the "catalog" approach. The concepts are presented as products in a small catalog, which is mailed to a sample of consumers. The concept (product) statements can contain pictures if necessary. Some form of dollars-and-cents price is put on the "products" in the catalog. Respondents may be asked to "buy" those two or three products in which they are interested (if any), and to indicate which two or three are least attractive.

The catalog might be explained as showing products which are being sold elsewhere and may soon be available in the respondent's area. When asking the respondents to indicate those items they do not like, you might use a pretext such as: "We must cut back on our product line, and we want your input on which products appeal least to you." A few benchmarks could be included in the catalog by giving descriptions of real, existing products. Different versions of the catalog might contain different prices, labels, names, features, or other things we might want to test. All of these aspects could be tested at the same time under carefully controlled conditions. Possible variations on the catalog are endless.

The closer to reality such a catalog becomes, the better research results measure what we really want to measure, which is whether the product would actually sell if it is developed. Better information should lead to better marketing decisions. Ultimately, of course, the concepts correspond to no real products yet, so people who order them must be debriefed. Usually, respondents are provided with an explanation about the nature of the research and with a cash payment for their trouble.

Of course, there are also other ways to approach the problem of testing. Many methods involve requiring from respondents some sort of choice among concepts. One would offer a number of such concepts to respondents — say about eight at a time. (If the number of concepts exceeds about eight, the choice task becomes too complex. Data obtained from forcing respondents to perform overly complex tasks can be of poor quality. With more than about eight concepts, we might use computer-generated rotations of eight at a time, in random combinations and permutations. Any specific respondent would only be offered one version of the choice task.)

Some of the issues to be explored would include relevance, uniqueness, believ-ability, clarity, regular use, etc., plus, finally, a propensity-to-buy measure. Then, the concepts are assayed together, and choices, from first to last, are solicited. Often each concept might be assessed monadically on a 0–100 scale. We also ask the respondents to explain why they gave different concepts their scores. The whole process is based upon the premise that the proffered concepts (products) are all that are available, and that respondents have had to buy just one.

Still other techniques in the concept-testing process might include, for example, tradeoff analysis and conjoint analysis. These are similar notions, and simply require the respondent to give up something, (say durability) to get something else (perhaps light weight). (We cannot build every feature into a product and still keep it within the price range of target customers.) Such techniques, which can be used in both the generation and testing phases, are merely reflections of the ultimate realities of the marketplace in a free-market economy. There is choice: consumers cannot really have everything — at least not all at once.

THE NEXT STEP

Concept testing is not an end in itself. No piece of research should ever be, but especially not concept testing. Once a concept has gone through the research process described here, it can lead us down any of four roads (the last two, of course, can be effected simultaneously).

- Kill the idea.
- Send the idea back to the drawing board. It has merit, but even after all of our testing, we have not yet come up with the right way to handle it.
- Develop the concept into finished form for positioning (below), including, if necessary, copy testing (Chapter 15).

- Make prototype products and packages for further testing (Chapter 11).

Wherever the results of concept testing may lead, it should be apparent that the testing of new-product concepts cannot be a rigid, routinized, process. It requires imagination and flexibility, and considerable personal judgment in direction and interpretation. It also requires the closest possible liaison among the departments for marketing research, R&D, marketing management, and other parts of the organization, and the continuing applications of all the talents available at the advertising agency.

PRODUCT POSITIONING

Once research shows that a concept is viable, then the "theme" must be looked at, to see how it registers in the consumer's head. This theme is product positioning. Positioning has been a flashy notion that has been both worshipped and ridiculed. Neither reaction is justified. Rather, the essence of positioning, and sensible research methods necessary to examine positioning, must be understood.

Positioning is not hard to understand, although achieving good positioning can be quite difficult. Essentially, for each product category we can identify a "map" in the consumer's head. In the center of this "perceptual map" lies the ideal kind of product the consumer would like. Real products are scattered around the map according to how they measure up on the key attributes that define the map for the consumer.

The objective of positioning is to put our brand in the dominant position near the center of this map. Skilled product positioning can even drive all the other brands to the edges of the map, or even off it entirely. We want our brand to be seen as the best, the brightest, the only sensible one. (Who would even want to shave messily again when they could shave cleanly, quickly, and effectively — in a modern rather than a medieval way?)

Research on positioning usually involves presenting information about the key attributes of several brands (including ours). Often the information includes some visual representation for our product (concept), maybe even a finished advertisement along with finished advertisements for existing brands. Rating scales are used to measure the consumer's perception toward the various attributes of each brand, including our (potential) brand. For our shaver, we might include attributes like: modern, clean, economical, reliable, and then draw up a perceptual map. (The Appendix covers some of the methodologies for doing this.)

Remember, in researching positioning at this stage of the product development process, we are still dealing with a concept, even though we may have gone as far as to produce finished advertising. It is easy to vary the attributes of this still imaginary product now, but it will be difficult and expensive to vary attributes once the product is marketed (if it ever is), and images have already been established in consumers' minds. Now, we can even draw up several alternative finished ads, each one emphasizing something different. Only one version would be included in the batch of competing product ads shown to any respondent. Then we could draw up perceptual maps for each of the variant positionings of our product.

This makes it easy to compare how the presentation stressing different things (modern, clean, economical, reliable, etc.) will affect where our product fits into perceptual maps. Which, if any, of the alternative positionings beats the competition? Which competitors specifically does it beat, and which ones has it failed to knock out? The answers to such questions are critical in helping the marketing manager decide how to best present the new product in advertising, and even how to build the very best version of the new product. After all, the "best" version of the product and of the message is crafted to gain wide acceptance in our target market. This is not necessarily exactly the same as "best" in a technical sense.

All the research in this chapter has helped the marketing manager develop viable concepts and identify attractive positioning for (potential) new products. Concepts and positionings that survive this process are now ready to move out of the "twilight zone" of ideas. The next chapter addresses the research we need to do on the actual product itself.

11

The Product Itself

At some point, usually early in the product development process, it is necessary to test the actual product. Product testing research is not the answer to *every* question, but it *is* the answer to many questions. As Posner notes:[1]

> If the question is, I want to diagnose if I have any problems in some of the attributes in my product to give direction to the labs, then maybe traditional product testing is the answer.
>
> If the question is whether I want to see how my product fares versus a previous formula or competition or versus a technical standard, then maybe product testing is the answer.
>
> If the question is who will like the product or how might it initially be used, then maybe product testing is the answer.
>
> If the question is what are some of the interest appeals of my product, then maybe product testing is the answer.

But, as he notes further:

> While traditional tools are adequate for screening out obvious product deficiencies, they generally are not sensitive enough to identify a product which, on the surface, appears acceptable, but which over time might fail because of consumer apathy . . . Products dying [such] a death . . . are usually those with an inadequate level of conceptual appeal . . .

KEY ISSUES IN PRODUCT TESTING

We have noted frequently that the research process involves a lot of interweaving. The various kinds of things that researchers do (Chapters 10–18) can be, and usually should be, done in combination. Of course, the thinking behind the sequence and its follow-up must not be mechanistic, but marketing-driven. In the sequence of research that helps to bring a product to market, concept testing (Chapter 10) is also vital in determining the fate of a product. Concept testing surely should precede advertising testing (Chapter 15), and must be thought of together with product testing, now or later.

And vital too is consideration of *when* product testing should be done in the broad march of marketing development. Surely it should not be done routinely only *after* formulations have been finalized. Just as surely, product testing should not wait until a catastrophe seems imminent before we look at it seriously. Like the best advertising testing, product testing should be done on final products, of course. But it should *also* be conducted on products under development. This is the time when there is opportunity for real use of the data: before minds, deadlines, and budgets have been closed.

> We in market research can help our companies reduce their investments in new product development by using the consumer at a very early stage of work to diagnose the performance of the formulas. A planned testing program can be set up on a small scale basis in which all formulas involved would be our own and we would not be particularly concerned with competitive brands. Often, R&D has several alternatives available at various points in time which they feel could ultimately be the "winning" formula. Market research can help keep the development costs down by conducting product tests at these early stages to determine the potential of these alternatives.
>
> The timing of these tests would be at a point when relatively little R&D expenditures would have taken place. The marketing strategy for this new product possibility would have probably already been decided; the desired product characteristics are therefore already known and consumer testing can take place among the specified market target groups. These formulas can be examined on absolute and relative bases to see if we are on target.
>
> A consumer research screening program like this requires more expenditures but reliable tests can be conducted for very little out-of-pocket money. More importantly, these expenditures are very low compared to the remaining costs for R&D to complete their work, sometimes lower by a ratio of 25 to one. Now isn't it more beneficial to a manufacturer to spend perhaps several thousand dollars in consumer research than to spend 20 or 30 times that amount in R&D costs for a product that won't do what they want it to do?[2]

There is no automatic time, then, to do product testing, and there is no single and only way to do it. Of course, the researcher should try to do product testing the way it has been done before, on previous products or previous versions of the current product. This would allow us to compare results over time. But we should never simply copy the previous methodology at the expense of always looking afresh at what is being done, how it is being done, and whether we are making the best use of product testing. Sometimes, we can come up with better ways of doing things even if they have never been done that way in the past.

Effective product testing always presumes that, in advance, we have done our homework and studied our market in all ways possible. By the time we do product testing, we should already know what our target consumers want (and what they do not want). This gives us the backdrop we need to draw up a meaningful checklist. Reebok did this to develop its tennis shoes, the best selling in the world. Said Reebok's Paul Fireman:

> The key [is] providing a product which [makes] a difference to consumers . . . . We're not just about putting out shoes with our labels [on them] . . . .
>
> We came up with a theory that consumers constantly put up with things they don't like because they don't think they have a choice. Our research indicated [that] people changed their tennis shoe brands a lot, so we asked them to tell us what they don't like.[3]

And from such research emerged a product that has indeed profoundly changed how we live, and, especially, how we play.

Back to Our Computer

For our home computer, we should have gotten the concept straight by now, and have some ideas about what we will want to say and to whom we will want to say it. Now, it is time to test the computer as a product. This is no simple thing. It is not like testing two soaps or two coffees or two anythings.

But test it we must, to find out many things critical to its success in the marketplace. How does it perform compared to expectations? (We will probably have shown a concept or some potential advertising first.) What difficulties did the user have in figuring out how to use it? What did he try to do on the computer that he was not able to do? What delightful surprises and annoying disappointments did he experience? How did *this* computer compare with others he had used before (perhaps at the office)? How would he describe the computer to other people, and what would he tell them about it?

The form of the test could be a version of a standard "home trial". We might give the tester the computer, ask him to use it for some period of time and record his impressions on a form. Then we would go back to collect the form and ask a few more questions. Or, as we have hinted at only half-jokingly, the researcher might try to "live" with the respondent (at least for a time). The researcher would note unobtrusively when and how the computer is used (observation) and be available to answer questions if they arise. We might also provide a tape recorder for the tester to give spontaneous reactions over time, and maybe even install a videotape machine so we can watch him at the computer.

It is art and it is craft again. Again, the key thing to remember is that there is no one set pattern which is right. The methodology can vary. What is important is that the research be in line with clearly established marketing needs and research possibilities.

The Bare Essentials

There are many subtleties in marketing and in researching marketing issues, and sometimes certain subtle issues may escape us despite well-thought-out marketing and research strategies. We may sometimes fail to grasp the full impact our concept makes. We may occasionally fail to understand all of the implications of how people view our advertising. But there is *no* excuse at all for our product failing for the single, simple reason that it did not do what it was supposed to do. Imagine a soap failing in the marketplace because it did not get people clean! Imagine a beer failing because it tasted bad! Imagine a juice product failing because it tasted sour and unnatural!

These are not complicated matters to figure out. Early research (or indeed just common sense) could easily have suggested that these things were unacceptable, and that products would fail because they had these things wrong with them. But these are not simply nonsense examples. All of them have happened, and more. Soaps have failed because people were not happy with how clean they got them. Beers have failed because people thought they tasted bad. Fruit juices have failed because people thought they tasted unnatural.

Simple "blind" testing (see also the section on design of the study below), without any brand identification, could prevent these pointless failures. But sometimes managers are just so sure (so arrogant, actually) that their product has the best ingredients or formulation possible. (But does anybody notice or care that the ingredients are the best possible if the juice tastes bad?) Since the product cannot possibly fail to please, product testing is just skipped, or done very perfunctorily.

Yet blind testing is only a basic first step, not necessarily all that must be done. It can tell us very clearly whether people like the product or not — as simple as all that — and why. But obviously a successful blind test cannot be the only research. For example, if the advertising and positioning will turn people off, then it really does not matter finally whether they like the product or not.

Even more subtle perhaps, and tricky, are cases where knowledge about the product interacts with people's taste, so that results come out opposite when people know about the product from when they do not. For example, people probably will say that they do not like a "bad" taste when asked in a blind taste test. But the bad taste may be acceptable, or actually preferred, as part of a "medicine" positioning. That is, people may well believe that if something tastes good, it cannot be any good as a medicine!

As another example, consider the introduction of the "new" Coca-Cola in the US during the early 1980s. Blind tests *were* done before the product was changed. These tests showed that people liked the taste of the new formulation better than the old. But when the product got to market and people found out that the taste belonged to Coke, it caused an uproar. Many people were outraged that the corporation was tampering with the taste of an American icon.

Again, everything must go together: marketing understanding must complement research design.

> Blind tests are particularly useful in the initial development of new products and throughout the research process in conjunction with nonblind tests (that is, research which reveals product concept as well as manufacturer) . . . [They are] essential to providing clear, unbiased feedback.[4]

The bare essentials never change in product testing: what do people want; did they get it; what "won" (if we are testing one product against another); why; by how much; and among what groups.

"Tension" in Product-Testing Designs

What, then, do we do and how do we do it? The consideration of the overall picture is the most overlooked and yet the most obvious. There is an eternal "tension" between two approaches to product testing. There is a desire, and a need, to test products in the same way time after time so that we are able to compare results based on historical data ("norms"). But it is also critical to keep our minds open to new ideas, variations on old ideas, new possibilities, and new techniques as we proceed from test to test over time.

We should not fail to recognize this "tension". We should not either slavishly follow old designs simply because we have always done things that way in the past. Nor should we forever create new designs simply because they are new. Either extreme can easily lead to failure. This "tension" exists in every sphere of research. But in product testing, because it is seeming so straightforward, it is especially easy to overlook the tension, and lose everything because we are too rigid, or too whimsical, or both.

In terms of actually executing product tests, five major elements must be considered. These are listed below, and then each will be discussed in turn.

- The "lead-up": The ways they judge
- The design of the study
- Questions to ask
- Issues to consider
- Analysis

THE "LEAD-UP": THE WAYS PRODUCTS ARE JUDGED

Different people may judge the same product on the basis of different aspects of it. They have different expectations of what they want from a product and, also, they place widely different relative weights on the various aspects. Usually, there are at least four different ways in which people may regard and judge a product. And people may not even be aware very consciously of how they evaluate products. The ways may change not only from product to product, but also from brand to brand. The elements of judgment interweave and interlock both predictably and unpredictably, since they may be rational or emotional, or both, or sometimes (seemingly) neither. Thus we need to discover through supporting research which of the ways seem to matter in this particular test, for this particular product, for this respondent, now.

The four ways in which people may regard and judged a product can be described as follows:

1. *Physical aspects* of the product include such things as size, shape, color, aroma, taste, and style.
2. *Product-in-action* concerns how the product performs: quickly or slowly, neatly or messily, simply or through complex, complicated procedures.
3. *Consumer end-benefit* can be a perceived effect. For example, does the shampoo make hair more manageable? (Any hair, or just thin hair, or just thick hair?) End-benefit can be something less tangible. Products can provide freedom from drudgery, or they can make consumers feel better about themselves, or maybe give peace of mind.
4. *Image dimensions* may include aspects of: what kinds of people use it, what would *my* using it say about *me*? People often buy products, or particular brands, because they want to be associated with the kind of people who would use that product or brand.

These four ways, and examples, are merely suggestive, of course. But they help underscore the complex nature of the product testing process. These elements should also help underscore the idea that it may not matter if we have a demonstrably better product than our competitors. If nobody notices, or cares, or can tell the difference, we have no product advantage. Or, if they *can* tell the difference, consumers may prefer not only a technically inferior product but also one that really is not even branded out in the marketplace (generics). They may even recognize the clear advantages, but not believe that they are worth the extra cost. There can be all sorts of ways that consumers can baffle us with their preferences.

These issues can, and do, confound rational engineers and dedicated R&D people. But they are puzzles that researchers must seek to interpret and address "objectively" ("without fear or favor"), as noted in Chapter 1. What is vital to understand, then, is that we must have a good grip on how people evaluate our specific product before we attempt to write another mechanical, mindless product-testing questionnaire.

And the nature of the product and the four ways it might be evaluated are not the only essential things we must grasp before we go plunging into the product test itself. We must also come to grips with the target market. Is it, for example, concentrated (one sharply defined target group), or broad (many)?

What has our earlier research disclosed about the segment or segments we want to look at? If it has identified target segments, then we can concentrate on them in our product test. If it has not, then, clearly, finding out who likes us best, and why; and who does not, and why; may well become one of the key objectives of the product test. Then we can determine what marketing implications emerge from all of that.

Once such vital questions have been addressed, then the design of the study and the various elements it encompasses should begin to reveal themselves rapidly and clearly.

STUDY DESIGN: HOW AND WHAT TO COMPARE

"Blind" vs. "Branded"

As already discussed above, one of the key issues in product testing is whether you should test *just* the product ("blind" testing), or the product with identification of its brand and manufacturer ("branded" testing). It follows from the previous discussion in this chapter that blind testing is probably where product testing should begin if we need to see whether a new feature (more this, less that, or something new) is liked absolutely (and perhaps relatively too). As noted, if people simply do not like the taste, the feel, the look, the smell, then it probably does not matter much how well or badly the rest of the marketing mix is executed.

But endless considerations may also enter into product testing. If, say, we want to determine the effect of the brand name, we might want to test two products against each other blind *and* branded. Suppose A beats B in blind testing, but loses in branded testing. Then we have learned that the problem is probably not in product A itself, but in its "image" as projected by its brand name, advertising, etc.

"Product-only" or "Product-plus"

The blind vs. branded problem is part of the larger marketing (not research) issue that always needs to be addressed. What is it that consumers *really* need to know to help them make intelligent decisions in the marketplace? Realities determine the method; not the other way around.

The researcher could, for example, if it were appropriate to the specific case, do product testing by first showing a concept (Chapter 10) for a product (or an advertisement). This could generate ideas about respondents' expectations. Then the actual product test would follow, so that reactions to the product could be compared against the expectations built up by knowledge of the product from the ad or other sources. Quite clearly, the marketer is in an advantageous position if the product exceeded the promises derived from the concept or ad. He would be in a very weak position if the product disappoints peoples' expectations, even if they did happen to rate it somewhat better than competing products.

Of course, to capitalize on the advantage, or correct the weakness, we must recognize exactly how and why the product is better (or worse) than expected. Then we can perhaps build more "sell" into the message, concentrating on what was unexpectedly good. Or we can change the product so that it no longer disappoints. Maybe we would even want to restructure the message to slightly lower expectations, if the product actually beats competition but is just not as good as we promised.

Overall, sometimes products require an explanation of what they are supposed to do, or do for people. Sometimes, it is likely that the first time someone will become aware of products is through an advertisement (which maybe here we could show in concept form), so that it is necessary to see the "message" to judge the product validly. In such cases, a concept and/or advertisement should surely be presented along with the product in the product test. It is, as always, marketing vision and flexibility that will determine the answer to the question (product or product-plus), not rote and rigid formulas.

Order of Presentation

Sometimes we test only one product, sometimes two against each other, or sometimes more than two products. There is enormous heat (and not much light) generated among researchers about what the "right" way is. The answer, of course, is that there is no "right" way at all. There is only the way that will give the most salient answer to *our* problem at *this* time. We need to take into account history, opportunity, and possibility as we decide what is the "best" way. But, to repeat, nothing can substitute for a blend of intelligence and open-mindedness.

Let's look at the three basic approaches to situations where (for the sake of convenience) we're testing two products — and indeed, most of product testing does involve two products.

1. In the *pure monadic* approach, we test only one product at a time and get reactions to it on whatever attributes seem important. We can relate scores, by segments and attributes, to past or concurrent monadic data, including data from a test of the other of the two products. Obviously, also, pure monadic testing can be especially useful when there are three or more products that must be tested at the same time.

    Questions would include asking respondents to compare the product to their current favorite brand or any other standard which might be appropriate, including an "ideal" product. There is great flexibility, as always, in what to do and how to do it.

    "Bench" testing very early in the product development process is typically monadic. In these tests, we want just a quick "feel" of whether the product has any obvious defects. Similarly, at the end of whatever testing we do, we may need to "go back to the drawing board", and test further variations: more of this, or less of that, in different combinations. To establish the level of JND ("just noticeable difference"), we may need to do what seems like an eternity of further sensory evaluation tests.

    We must have patience here, but such patience should pay off if the product testing methodology is sound. Indeed, proponents of monadic testing say it is the *only* way to test. They believe that people simply do not buy something new and then test it in a "paired comparison" way against their current brand. Instead, people try the product, by itself, make up their minds, and that's that. They do not go through a process of buying two products at the same time so that they can explicitly compare them.

2. In *simultaneous paired comparison*, we offer the respondent both products at once. We ask him first to judge each individually, and then the two against each other. This could be, for example, pure orange juice on the one hand, and a synthesized vitamin-enriched flavor-enhanced product on the other. It could be two pieces of *dim sum* (Chinese hors d'oeuvres) of the same type (maybe roast pork dumplings) on the same plate — one might be freshly made and the other frozen and popped out of the toaster-oven or microwave. Or the test might involve using one razor blade on one side of the face, and another blade on the other side.

3. In the *paired monadic* approach (sometimes called "sequential monadic" or "sequential paired comparison"), one product is given to the tester to try, who then fills out a full questionnaire (ratings, rankings, etc., similar to a pure monadic). Then, without telling the tester in advance that it was going to happen, we give the tester a second product to test also. The same questions are answered. And finally, we ask what the preferences are between the products.

    It should be apparent that the first product test here is, in effect, a pure monadic test. It is tested on an absolute basis, with no other product also tested. The second product, though, is likely to be compared to the one that the respondent has just finished testing.

While these three broad types of product tests may seem a bit complicated, they really are not. They are different approaches to the same issue: how good (or bad) is my product on an absolute basis, and in the context of other products. Which approach to use depends on some knowledge of the buying and product choice process. Researchers who favor pure monadic methodology are correct, *sometimes*, in believing that people simply buy one product at a time, and decide whether it is better or worse than products they have used in the past. They probably do not buy many different brands of chocolate bars, then sit down to eat them all at once so that they can compare taste and texture.

Other times, though, this is exactly how people make decisions. They may, for example, go to an audio shop and carefully examine many different brands of stereo, paying attention to sound quality for each one. They may go to a food products trade fair and go around from booth to booth trying samples of different brands of *dim sum*. The point is, then, that the possible methodologies are wide, but the same end is always there: to finally offer the best product we can to whom we think will be most likely to buy it. To best reach that end, it is critical to match the methodology to the buying process.

Tested Against What?

We must frequently test our product against another product, such as we've just described. But what exactly is the "other" product? This is a key issue, and one which is surprisingly often misunderstood.

There is no one "right" way to do it (again), in spite of many companies' policies of automatically doing such testing always one way. There *are* options.

1. *Test against another version of the product.* Suppose for example, we are considering a new flavoring that we think is more pleasing than the current one, or we are looking at potential cost savings by substituting a newer, less expensive, ingredient for what we have now. Then testing against another version of our own product is probably what we want to do. The operational questions are: Can they tell the difference in "blind" tests (see above), and if they can, do they (who?) prefer the old to the new, and why?

   We could well find that each of the new "candidates" has different merits relative to the current product. Then we may need to proceed further with the testing of several new versions. Perhaps several versions will ultimately be marketed under different names to different segments, and featuring different claims in their advertising. Thus, in such a series of tests, where we test current versions against new ones in a series of paired tests, the answers can be consistent or divergent. Any number of marketing possibilities may emerge — provided we keep our minds open.

2. *Test against a leading competitor or competitors.* This is typically done as a blind test. We must be sure that brand names and identification are removed from competitors' products so that they do not offer clues which would invalidate the blind nature of the testing. This sort of testing is particularly useful if we have established one particular point of difference where we think our product is better. Before we eventually battle it out with a competitor in the marketplace, we should make sure that consumers also agree with us that our product is better on that point.

   As in all blind testing, we must be certain that the point of difference is one on which a sensible choice can be made. For example, if we have a new strawberry soda to test, it might not be wise to test it against a leading cola, or even raspberry soda. We run the risk here when we ask for preference that the respondent might be saying to himself: "I like this strawberry soda, but I also like this cola — how in the world can I give a meaningful preference? I mean, I like wine and I like beer too, but don't ask me to test one of each against each other!"

When we get the product to the market place, consumers will go on buying the competitor's cola when they feel like drinking cola, regardless of what the test showed. When they feel like drinking something with a strawberry taste, we don't know in advance what they will buy, our brand or the competitor's, if we did not test our brand against the competitor's strawberry soda.

3. *Test more than two products in one test.* That is, we might want to test A vs. B vs. C, in "round-robin" testing. First, we could do A vs. B, then B vs. C, then C vs. A. While theoretically quite possible, this can lead to accurate, but puzzling, inconsistencies, where, for example, people prefer A to B, they prefer B to C, and they prefer C to A. (This can sometimes happen, because with multiple products, we are usually dealing with multiple segments which prefer different brands. In any pair of the A, B, C tests, some segment will not find its favorite brand available to choose, so that there is some distortion of results.)

It is often better to avoid multi-product tests if possible. Certainly, San Miguel, Carlsberg, and Heineken are all on the market. But usually, fairly well-defined segments are buying most of any particular brand. So it would be more appropriate to test our own new beer against San Miguel in segment A, which mainly prefers San Miguel. Then we would test our beer against Carlsberg in segment B, and so on.

As always, more than one of these, or other variations, can be done. It all depends on what we really want to know.

STUDY DESIGN: WHERE, WHEN, WHO

Delivery of the Products to Respondents

Products can be given to qualified respondents at shopping malls (often called "central locations"). They can then be taken home, with a "callback" in person or by phone, or even with a mail return of the questionnaires. Or testing could be done right at the shopping mall, often in research offices especially set up for product testing. In testing food products, for example, the office may be equipped with ovens where baking could be done right on the spot.

Similarly, the product could be delivered to respondents door-to-door. Or products can be mailed to testers, with mail or phone follow-up. The researcher could ask people to test the product immediately, or at their own convenience. There is a rich range of possibilities, and we will decide on the basis of both infrastructure and intelligence.

As always, it is often important to match the method with the nature of exactly what kind of product we are dealing with, and exactly what we want to know. For example, baking a cake in an oven at the research office may be sufficient to judge how well consumers like it. Such a dessert is likely to be eaten alone, and how it tastes with the vegetables, meat, and noodles in a normal meal might have little relevance. But testing a new sauce to put on vegetables may need to be done at the respondent's own home, during a normal meal. The sauce is not likely to be eaten alone, and how it fits in with the overall meal is very important.

Finally, in product testing we must also remain aware of any *legal* ramifications of testing. What can we send, what can we give, where can we test? What about claims for damage if the product is faulty and causes harm to the respondent? *Nothing* in this area must be overlooked!

Quantity and Time

If, say, we are testing a new shampoo, will one little paper packet be enough? Two? A whole bottle? The answer, of course, lies in experience and foresight. How different is the test product from what the respondent usually uses? The less unfamiliar, the fewer times it may need to be tested, and vice versa. (Indeed, if it is very unfamiliar, we may well leave the telephone number of the research company for the tester to call if there are questions about the product.)

As in all research, budget is an issue here. (What should be spent in light of the benefits from making a right decision, or losses from making a wrong one?) But budget considerations should never be allowed to cut down on the quantity used in product trials if too small an amount will just give an uninformed and terribly misleading result. If we want to market a dandruff shampoo, which takes several weeks to clear up dandruff, then a single use of a single, small packet in a product test will not tell us what we need to know.

The concomitant question which comes up in this example is how long should the test last? Again experience and foresight are important. Normally, we think of a "cycle" of use. For example, a beauty cream might be used one way by women during the week, and another way on weekends. The first way is for business perhaps, the second for social occasions. So we may need to ask for a whole week's usage, probably recorded in a diary (journal) to get reactions as the woman goes along. We probably need both "closed-end" (our questions) and "open-end" (free responses) sorts of answer.

Other considerations affect this too. For example, if the product to be tested is really dramatically new, then there may be a "fad" effect. People might like it or loathe it on first use. This kind of situation clearly calls for extended testing, to see whether the liking lasts after people get used to the product. Unless we are planning to survive on a continuous stream of new, fad products, repurchase will be the key to profitability.

If brand loyalty will be important (and it usually is) once we are in the marketplace, we may also need to see how preferences stand up over time. As part of a design to test a new laundry detergent, for example, we might give one box of the product to testers to try, and then have them call the research company a week later. Respondents might be asked if they finished with the box. (If it was thrown out before it was empty, this alone may tell us all we need to know!) If the respondent liked the detergent, we can send a second box.

Suppose she still likes it when the second box is finished. We could tell her that our allocated budget for this product test is used up, but we would be pleased to send her another box if she would like to buy it. Of course, we would not actually take money, or if we did, we would send it back. (*Never* confuse research with sales.) But asking the respondent to pay the price for the detergent would be one way to judge reactions on a longer-term basis. After all, unless the product is really bad, people might be perfectly willing to use it as long as we keep sending it free. What counts is whether they are willing to buy it.

Where do We Get the Products?

We can get our own products from our factory as they come off the line, or from our R&D division in the case of new products not yet in production. In addition to testing them for quality (and recording their exact specifications), we might also want to do a good time sample, getting representative batches over a period of time.

We must be especially careful about getting competitive products. If we get them without much thought from retailers, we may get old ones, stale ones, products not comparable to our fresh and new ones. We should, rather, go to high-volume wholesalers (in various cities) to get competitive products. Otherwise, we may just be fooling ourselves. We would be testing our "good stuff" against their "not-so-good stuff", and getting invalid results on preference.

On the other hand, sometimes, particularly in economies where traditional retailing is still strong, a lot of products actually do move through low-volume channels, such as small neighborhood or rural retailers. In these channels, they may sit on the shelf for a long time. If these channels are important to our product's distribution, we may even want leave our product sitting around for a long time before the product test, then test it against a competitor's product which has been on the shelves for a long time. People may like ours better fresh, but if it does not stand up as well or as long sitting on retail shelves, they will still buy the competitor's product in those small stores.

Sample

The most important thing about samples in any research is that we get to the right target group. In this case, of course, we're looking for people who are reasonably easy to define, if not necessarily easy to find. This should be based on sound preliminary work, usually quantitative but maybe less formal, that has singled out the target.

Typical target populations might be: "men 35 or more years of age who are former users of our brand"; or "teenagers who do not eat out in fast food restaurants"; or "adults 18–54 who are regular readers of at least two different magazines per month"; or something like that. The more sharply we can define our description of the target group, the more likely we are to develop useful marketing data at the end.

As to sample size (see Chapter 5), the key is to get "enough" people in each cell (say "last-time purchasers of a German-made car") to analyze it properly. The minimum number we would like to analyze in a cell is very fluid: 30, 50, and 100 are numbers often suggested. If we really want to look at one group in detail, we might want to get 100 (or 200, or whatever) people in that group, and analyze them very finely. If they are in our sample in a greater proportion than they are in the population as a whole, we may ultimately need to "weigh" them down when we look at the samples as a whole. For this notion and other statistical ideas, see Chapter 8.

QUESTIONS, ISSUES, AND ANALYSIS

Questions to Ask

Product testing questionnaires tend to be rather straightforward. But the best ones do not just copy what has been asked on other tests. Instead, they try to meld questions from these (for comparative purposes) with questions pointed right at our particular product. Typical things included in these questionnaires are:

- Ratings and/or preferences on given qualities (e.g. sweet, mild, etc.)
- Ratings and/or preferences on the product overall
- Open-ended questions on likes, dislikes, etc.
- Occasions to use
- Likelihood-to-buy

As always, it is the "mechanical" part of the craft (writing the questions) that must be combined with the "humanistic" (insightful) elements. This means knowing what dimensions seem to matter most (touch, taste, smell, sound, whatever), and emphasizing these in the questionnaire. It also means knowing the marketing issues and the marketing realities.

For example, in international marketing it is often necessary by law or custom to include a certain percentage of "local content" (things grown or made in the host country). Suppose that this content has increased steadily over time, maybe from 10 percent to 20 to 30 to 40 percent. Now we want to raise it again: to 50 percent. Each time we want to know if users notice or care.

It is probably wrong (although one might be tempted to do it anyway) to test the 50 percent local-inclusion product against the 10 percent one (the "best"?) as the "standard". Rather, if the 40 percent product is now the one we sell, and people seem to have gotten used to it, then clearly the 50 percent one should be tested against the 40 percent one. A test of 50 vs. 10 percent is not relevant. This is often called the "salami" effect. We are cutting up a large whole (0 to 100 percent). We should remember to test the two adjoining slices against each other, not one slice against some other slice in some arbitrary position on the salami.

Over and over again, there is a need to think before we write. We are not asking a series of bloodless questions, but engaging in a real flesh-and-blood marketing effort. The project must be designed to sell more products, and not simply to gather more numbers.

Issues to Consider

In addition to freshness of products, especially competitors', certain other procedural issues must be considered in doing effective product testing. These include *removal of competitive products* and *rotation of labels*.

If we are doing an especially sensitive test and must concentrate attention on the products to be tested, we might choose to use door-to-door screening with personal placement and callback. Under these circumstances, we may need to ask respondents/ testers to hand over all brands of the product they have in the house. (Maybe we will pay for them, or just promise to return them later.) This technique is sometimes used when we want to be sure that during the test period respondents use only the products that we have given them. A small measure of reality is lost (the tester cannot go back to the regular, favorite product if our test products are truly awful!). But we can perhaps hope to gain fuller cooperation during the test period.

As to rotation of labels, we will always seek to use neutral labels for blind-product testing. If we want to avoid bias, for example, we may code one blind product "X" half the time, and "Y" half the time. If there are any prejudices for or against "Brand X" or "Brand Y" or even against the letters "X" or "Y", the prejudices will be cancelled out. Similarly, in a paired comparison, one product should always be tested first half the time, and second half the time to avoid possible position bias.

Analysis

Analysis of product tests follows some pretty standard approaches. Ratings, rankings, preferences for each product tested and compared are stated on an overall basis, and for each attribute separately. The data should be for the total market and broken down into key segments. Of course, appropriate statistical tests must be performed. We need to be more confident that any differences in rating or ranking we think we see from the data in fact represent real differences in preference.

Preference by attribute should also usually be cross-tabulated by overall preference. Thus we might note, for example, that "79 percent preferred A to B overall on Attribute No. 1, but only 12 percent of those who preferred A to B on this attribute also preferred it overall". From such an obvious analysis, we can begin to deduce which are the attributes whose preferences seem to matter — that is, which preferences correlate to overall choice. They may well be the ones to concentrate on in our marketing effort.

As noted, tests of significance will be conducted to determine levels of statistical reliability, and reference will be made to normative data ("norms"). The latter is especially important (indeed essential) for monadic testing. All along we will look to see where "points of attack" seem to lie. Are there, for example, certain segments who "love" us (say 90 percent preference level), while others are just lukewarm? Such analyses, seeking "gaps" for us to exploit, are a vital part of using the researcher's marketing skills to point out marketing opportunities. Just reporting numbers is a job for low-level technicians, not marketing researchers.

Problems always exist, which gives the researcher a chance to put his "art" (as well as his "craft") to the service of the "business". For example, sometimes we may need to test our product against the competitive product among knowledgeable users of the competing product. It is quite possible that these users, even "blind", will be able to discern their "favorite", and "vote" for it. So what can we do?

Again, if we do enough of these tests, we may be able to establish "norms". We may be able to suggest that, perhaps, a 65 percent to 35 percent "loss" to the competing product among its users is quite probable on average. So if the "loss" in our current test with our current product formulation is "only" 55–45, well, then we may surmise that our product would be reasonably strong in the marketplace, especially when we surround it with the "words and music" of our advertising.

Methods of analysis will vary. Classical ones may be forever viable, but still newer and better ones (utilizing computer technology and business sense) must always be sought out. Suppose, for example, in a rather complex test we show a concept, then an ad, then a package, then give information about price. Finally we show the product itself, to be tested on the spot, or tested elsewhere and data reported to us later.

Suppose the following favorability scores (say, positive intention-to-buy) for this product are recorded at each level:

Concept	17%	
Plus advertisement	23%	(+6%) (adding this element)
Plus pack	26%	(+3%)
Plus price	15%	(−11%)
Plus product	27%	(+12%)

We may well deduce from this test that the advertisement adds a lot to our "simpler" concept (+6%); the pack adds too (+3%); but the price is somehow "wrong" (−11%). And the product itself? Well, it brings us up to the highest score yet . . . it looks like a "winner".

FINAL WORDS

Competition is increasing for marketers everywhere, both from at home and overseas. The pace of technological change and technological possibilities is quickening. Given these dynamics in the market, it is quite obvious that the pace of product testing must increase. It can be both simple and complex, with possibilities for sound statistical work and yet creativity at the same time. All of this is in the most direct and actionable service of business. In a sense, product testing can almost stand as a surrogate for all of marketing research.

The marketing implications mean as much as the research itself. Perhaps more. For example, in a crunch we may need to do a smaller-scale product test compressed in time and size if we have to. It will still be valid, but less pervasive perhaps. It will still be reliable, if somewhat less precise. Still it *can* be done.

Indeed, as suggested before, the Japanese typically do use large numbers of smaller "semi-quantitative" or "touchy-feely" product studies, in which their marketing executives become personally involved. This contrasts with the big quantitative studies perhaps more typical in Western corporations. The Japanese constantly explore and refine rather than do "make-it-or-break-it" studies. Perhaps such an approach is in the nature of Japanese culture: more sensitive to subtleties and more patient than Westerners. Who knows? What we *do* know is that *our* minds should never be closed to other possibilities. The way the Japanese do product testing often works, so we should consider it when appropriate.

In today's global marketing environment, differences in cultures have become a key marketing issue. (Do cross-cultural buying behaviors tend to converge, or diverge, or both?) Marketers may be called upon to find ways to work with headquarters management and local offices around the globe. They all have their own ideas about how issues related to one product might be sorted out for all; what modifications should be carried out on a given product(s); or whether quite different products are needed for different areas.

These issues mean that product testing will not soon lose its fascination and centrality. Rather, product testing will spread its net to explore ever-newer areas, both geographically and conceptually. For many companies, it is just as important to know what consumers in Hong Kong think of the product as it is to know what domestic consumers think. There is also an increasing need to test "service products", which seem more and more to preoccupy us in the marketing world nowadays. Understanding how consumers view bank performance, airline service, or relations with the dentist, can be critical to the success of such service providers.

We must keep open minds on everything here, because it is all too easy to do product testing by rote and mummify it. Product testing must not become sick and arthritic, but must stay healthy and vital, because it is becoming ever more important to modern marketing.

12

Package and Name Research

Marketers do not sell only the product. What they really sell (or try to sell) is an agglomeration of things and ideas. We have called this agglomeration the "consumer offer". It consists of the product itself (the actual formulation), the package it comes in, the name and what it stands for, the price we ask people to pay, the expectations aroused by the advertising, and many more elements.

It is very clear that the package, in an age of quick decisions and self-service, plays a very special, even central role, in the success (or failure) of the total marketing effort. It is the package (with the name on it — we discuss name research later in this chapter) that the consumer really sees first much of the time. In Hong Kong, for example, surveys have shown that up to one-third of consumers first learned of well-known brands of a wide variety of products by seeing them on store shelves. For minor brands, which do little advertising, the proportion can be much higher.

Even when consumers do not see the package first directly, but perhaps do see the advertising first, the advertising has usually tried to implant in consumers' minds what the package looks like. After all, when they get to the store, we want them to recognize the product and choose it at the point of purchase. Certainly, nearly all consumers will have seen the package before trying the actual product itself.

Leo Burnett, the founder of the renowned advertising agency that bears his name, expressed the importance of the package very well.

> [It] is your number one display piece . . . your star salesman. In many cases it is your number one advertising medium, viewed by far more people than the readers of [large circulation magazines] combined. It should have personality, high visibility, and intrigue — and should reveal the drama inherent in the product it contains. . . . It must communicate . . . [it] should tell me what the product is, what it is called, who made it and what it is supposed to do for me, all in one swift glance.[1]

And Louis Cheskin echoes this, going directly to the marketing heart of packaging:

> Marketing people often fail to realize the importance of the package. They attribute failures to a poor product, bad advertising, wrong distribution channels, unenthusiastic salesmen, or tough times for business. They often overlook the real reason for the failure: the package.
>
> A mistake that marketing executives can make is to let a package designer view his package as a work of art. A work of art belongs on a wall, not on a store shelf.
>
> A package that is a work of art is not always effective in selling a product.
>
> A package must be viewed as a symbol. It's a nonsemantic, nonverbal way to communicate. For motivating consumers it's superior to words. People have no defense mechanism against symbols. They don't realize the effect symbols have on them and how the symbols unconsciously influence their behavior.
>
> Shape, color, lettering, and arrangement, or composition, of a package are not mere decorative elements. They communicate to the person looking at them.
>
> Marketing executives and package designers alike usually don't realize that they must think of the package and its make-up in terms of psychology or the behavioral sciences rather than as art.[2]

THE PACKAGE: ITS RESEARCH AND ITS ROLES

It becomes evident that the package stands as a vital factor in marketing success. As such, researchers are frequently called upon to investigate the effectiveness, or lack of effectiveness, of the package. And as in most facets of marketing research, the "form" of the research should follow the "function". What is being tested and what information is needed become the determining factors in research design.

Thus, it is necessary to look in detail at the nine roles we often want the package to play. They are listed below, and then each role is discussed in turn: what it really means in terms of marketing, and what kind of research can be done to shed light on the job it is doing, to see how well or how poorly it is doing it. The nine roles are:

- Aesthetic
- Image communication
- Informative
- Offers extra value
- Protects the product
- In-use by consumers
- Visibility
- Effectiveness at the trade level
- Environmental spokesman

As always, these roles overlap, interweave, interlock, and synergize. And so, while we discuss them one by one below, it should be remembered that any particular package study may include several of these roles. Any specific research project may also overspill the boundaries of package testing and include other elements as well, like concept, product, price, or any combination. Often this blending of topics will test the researcher's understanding of marketing as much as his understanding of the research process itself.

For example, what kind of package form would consumers prefer in milk containers? One recent study[3] found that the main attributes could be reduced to five things: design, sturdiness, nutrition protection, convenience, and weight. These attributes include aspects of at least five roles. Consumers consider the extra value available from package design (many consumers have a wide variety of uses for milk cartons or jugs). They worry about light-degrading nutritional content (product protection), usage of the package (whether it is hard to open or drips), product visibility, and environmental friendliness (convenience vs. recyclability). If the marketer expanded the focus beyond simply the physical form of the package as consumers see it, the other four roles would be involved as well. Even with a package as mundane as milk containers, the marketer must consider a wide variety of roles.

Aesthetic

While the package need not, and probably should not, be a work of art (see above), it still should not be ugly. It is better to be liked than disliked. This does not mean that the "safe way" should always be taken, to imitate other nice, lovable packages. That way, maybe nobody would dislike our package, but neither would our product stand out. It does mean that it is necessary to consider the simple aesthetic judgment of consumers. Rarely are we are seeking to stop people dead in their tracks with something overwhelmingly different and maybe even risk ugliness to "make a statement".

We do not usually want consumers to play design expert, a role we might use them in during product development. But we do need their reactions. We must remember that sometimes people may display some packages at home (see below). We do not want to lose the sale right at the beginning because consumers think the package is too plain or too ugly, and would feel uncomfortable if someone saw the package in their home.

Simple tests that ask whether the package is liked or not will often do here, preferably in a competitive context. Of course, if people answer that they do not like the package, then we need to know why. But a lot of the purely aesthetic issues are best handled even before worrying about like or dislike of a particular package design. Focus groups and other research at the qualitative "touchy-feely" level can often best get at people's aesthetic sense, which may be hard to measure by quantitative methods.

Image Communication

Far more important than the aesthetic quality of the package, perhaps (provided our package meets some minimum aesthetic level), is what the package communicates about what is inside. The package in many ways must communicate everything the marketer wants to say about the product, including its very essence, its basic *theme* (idea, concept) as it is expressed in the advertising and by its very positioning.

> Every package should carry the marketing theme. . . . It should be on the package and in the ads. The brand name alone is too abstract. It is not always effective in holding attention and in maintaining good eye flow. It doesn't contribute enough toward developing a favorable psychological attitude toward the product.
>
> However, to get the theme on the package, you must develop it well in advance of the advertising campaign. You come up with the theme when you develop the package. In fact, you should develop and have evidence that your package is effective before starting your advertising campaign.
>
> Advertising agencies don't warm up to this because it makes them break their job into two parts: (a) creating the theme, and (b) developing the advertising as a whole. This is a two-phase job and the same agency should carry out both phases.[4]

Some of the most important work we do in package testing comes right here. It seeks to answer the question: what does the package convey in terms of image, promise, performance, etc. about what is inside? This notion, often called "image transfer", is often the only package research we need to do. For it is the *significative* role of the package, rather than its more *physical* aspects, that we are after. This is the key area of research.

So how do we do this work? Well, the color, the boldness or timidity of the type, the masculine or feminine slant to the graphics, etc., all give clues to what the package contains. We deliberately "plant" these clues, because (hopefully) from preliminary research we have decided what we want to "be", what we want to "say", and to "whom". It now remains to be seen if we have done it successfully or not.

Essentially, what we do is show the package to the respondent. We might want to inform the respondent that this package is for a product (focus on the product inside!) that is being marketed elsewhere, and that we don't have any of it around right now. Note that this is not a lie or a deception. Rather, it is our way to set the stage for the perception testing we are doing. We want to find out what people *think* is inside (the product) when they look at the outside (the package). We do not want them to answer our questions based on how they view the product itself, so no product should actually be in the test.

Frequently we will show two different versions of a package, and use a battery of image items to elicit the information we want. The items might include many "semantic differential" pairs, with "polar adjectives". We would ask the respondent to give a rating on the scale about the product inside (which to repeat, they do not see, taste, touch, or anything). Questions might look like:

HAS A STRONG TASTE	1	2	3	4	5	HAS A MILD TASTE
HAS A PUNGENT AROMA	1	2	3	4	5	HAS A GENTLE AROMA
FOR YOUNG PEOPLE	1	2	3	4	5	FOR OLDER PEOPLE

It should be noted finally that respondents will answer such questions. One might well ask how they could even hazard a guess as to what is inside without actually knowing what was inside. But they do guess, and for exactly the reasons stated above:

that the package conveys a message about the contents. Our marketing task is to make sure that it conveys the *right* message.

Consider this instance in which research showed how a formerly strong message conveyed by the imagery on a package had become weak — an asset had become a liability.

A few years ago, we were asked to create new packaging for Corona, the leading brand of beer brewed in Puerto Rico. The beer, once a great local favorite, had been losing ground for some time. The questions were: Why? And how could redesign help overcome the problem?

Our predesign research took two forms: Interviews with brewery officials, retailers and bar patrons, and a study in which consumers were asked to rate attributes important in choosing a beer.

True to the crime detection nature of research, no single test provided the answer — only clues. Years ago, the brewery's steel cans had a leakage problem that resulted in product spoilage. The problem had been corrected, but we discovered that local drinkers still associated the brand with flaws and flatness.

In focus groups, we uncovered another perception issue. As Puerto Rico's population grew more cosmopolitan in outlook, and as more U.S. products entered the market, the brand had come to be perceived as second rate.

The once-beloved product symbol — a singing farmer prominent on each can — was now symbolic only of the beer's poor status. Test participants who were shown slides of the brand on the store shelf said they thought it would taste less refreshing than the competitors'.

Yet taste was never actually the issue; the beer rated extremely high in blind tests. People just associated design inadequacies with the idea of inferior flavor.

The collective data gave us our redesign criteria. We needed a prestigious international appearance, which included retiring the farmer, a switch to aluminum cans to allay fears of perceived spoilage, and color and graphics to create a refreshing image in any competitive retail setting.[5]

Informative

The package may also play a role as a source of information. It may give a vital signal (probably the only signal in many cases) to the shopper about what is inside: how many, what color, what shape, what ingredients, and so forth.

We can simply show the package to the respondent and ask what information can be recalled, either with the package still available or not (or even both ways). We would then record the answers for accuracy or lack of accuracy, as well as note how long it took the respondent to answer. Finally, we would note any questions (both solicited by us and offered spontaneously) that the respondent had about the package in terms of the information on it.

All of this is vital if we have or need information on the package that serves to point out a difference we may have, or in other ways helps to spur purchase. Many people use packages to gather information about products. We do not want to lose a sale because they cannot find or do not understand the information they want before committing their money to a product.

Offers Extra Value

What more could the package do? It might, for example, serve as something for the kids to read as it sits on the breakfast table. Such a breakfast cereal package might show the adventures of a comic strip character, or have a puzzle, or whatever. If we show the package to respondents without mentioning this presumed (to us) "extra value" element, we might ask casually in the course of the interview "What, if anything, did you find 'special' about the package?" If there was no unaided mention, we might point the feature out.

Either way, we would eventually ask if they thought it was nice (or maybe not nice; maybe they think kids should not read while they're eating). We would also need to know why it was nice (or not), and maybe what they think should also be on the package.

Sometimes people physically use packages for something, also. For example, they often use paperboard milk cartons for freezing ice, milk jugs for carrying water, and so forth. If they do not think it matters much exactly what kind of package the milk comes in as far as characteristics of the product are concerned, they may choose a package because they have some use for it after the product is gone. Sometimes marketers can even design packages as special premiums which add this type of extra value. For example, jellies and jams occasionally come packaged in a glass instead of a jar.

Protects the Product

Originally, this was what the package was supposed to do, and it is still one of the things that a package must do. Does our package effectively protect our product? Obviously, the first line of research here is in the laboratory, which can test very scientifically how well the package preserves freshness and nutritional value, how well it guards against change of color, form, etc.

The laboratory can certainly measure these points under "laboratory" conditions. What about when the product comes home, and in its package, it is left lying about in the sun? What about other conditions relating to how the product may actually be used in "real life"? Consumers are never very happy to be told that it is really their own fault that the product spoiled, because they did not treat it like we treated it in the laboratory.

To see what kind of a job the package does under those circumstances, we must do an extended in-home test. The actual methodology can vary, as always. It can be a monadic or paired comparison. It might, occasionally, focus on the package itself, or more commonly be disguised as a product test. We know that if people are told that it is a package test, they will be more conscious of the package. They will use it more carefully than they probably would if they were not thinking of it consciously. They will tell us about the package in more detail, considering the issues more carefully, than they normally would. If protection is the issue, we are likely to find out that the package works better when respondents know that protection is the research topic. The answer is always a function of the question.

At the end of the test, we can do one or both of two things. First, in the midst of other product-related issues, we should ask respondents for their appraisal of how fresh the product has been kept and how fresh it is now. The timing of this callback interview is vital since we need to be sure there is still some product left. Second, we could take the product back to the laboratory for scientific analysis. Probably the respondents' perceptions are more critical. Even if the laboratory certifies that the product is still fresh, it is *not* fresh if consumers do not *think* it is fresh.

It is probably also useful here to ask the tester to keep a diary. We would like a record of how the product was used, by whom, when, etc., and — what we really care about but do not want to call undue attention to — where was it kept. It does no good from a marketing standpoint to learn from the scientific lab people that a certain cream retained its pure glistening whiteness for weeks when *they* kept it protected from outside elements. Consumers may keep it on windowsills in the sunlight where it will quickly turn into a yellow goo.

Once we know where the package is used, the marketing people can figure out how to prevent the cream from turning into a yellow goo. Maybe we could educate consumers by improving product *labeling* ("keep out of the sun"). Maybe we could reformulate the product so that it has a longer shelf life even after opening. Maybe we want to change the shape of the package so that it will not fit on window sills. At any rate, to decide what to do, we need information. That is why we test for this package role.

In-use by Consumers

Obviously all kinds of packages may require further thinking if they are to be used conveniently by consumers. A package could turn out to be very clumsy to handle. (Most people did not like glass gallon milk jars; they are very heavy. When something lighter came along, they quickly switched.) A package may be so poorly shaped that consumers hesitate to keep it out. It may require scissors or teeth to open (because marketers did not think to provide a tab to pull), or people cannot find it if it was provided. Some packages do not close securely so that the contents spill out, or get soggy, or get stale.

Packages may be too big, too small, or too awkward to store where you normally store such things. (Imagine a product too big to fit on the refrigerator shelf !) There are plenty of packages with such problems, and they all may require further thinking. If we do not rethink them, some competitor will eventually do so, and we may well watch our sales disappear.

Again, this is usually best evaluated by consumers in a normal in-home extended use test. Again, we would not necessarily focus on the package itself. The package needs to be looked at by the design team, but not only by them, just as scientists are necessary but not sufficient in determining protection roles of the package. Surely design people can handle the package expeditiously, but they are not typical consumers, using it under normal conditions.

Just consider the automobile industry. Experts get in and out of cars and sit in them, all in perfect comfort. The cars are theirs, and they know every detail of what to watch out for, or how to get the little edge for more comfort out of some little detail. Experts are not the normal drivers or passengers, though. Everyday product users may find such things exceedingly clumsy because they use the car in the hurried way that normal people do, not carefully and professionally like the experts do.

The car is a product, of course, but the same thing is true of packages. Normal people must certainly get the product out of the package. They do not know, as the designer does, exactly which piece folded over, which piece folded under, where the spots are that were glued. In other words, experts may well be able to open a package easily, because they know exactly how it was constructed. Consumers do not know that.

Sometimes, consumers must continue to use the package, because the product is stored in it even at home (such as milk, shampoo, over-the-counter medicines, etc.). Consumers may easily be frustrated trying to open the wrong side of the paperboard milk carton, a problem that can be avoided easily by buying the competitor's milk in a plastic jug. Consumers may get mad when they drop the small cap of the shampoo tube and it washes down the drain. They may buy a tube with a rotating nozzle, not a cap. Consumers may not like having to go find their glasses every time they want to take an aspirin, because they cannot see the little arrow on the bottle. They may switch to a brand that comes in foil pouches which can easily be torn open.

Package designers know how to avoid all these little problems and frustrations, because dealing with the package is what they do. They are familiar with it. Designers are important people in package design. But consumers are more important, and we need research to bring them into the design-for-use part of packaging.

Visibility

Can the product be seen in the store as the shopper moves through the aisles of supermarkets containing 20,000 products, probably without a written shopping list? Does it scream "I'M HERE!!!"?

Testing for this can involve making simulated store shelves and letting consumers go through them. Then we ask what brands were noticed. Various configurations of products on such shelves can be made, until we have the ultimate potential visibility. Alternatively, we can make slides of such shelves and use the light-box or tachistoscope (see Chapter 6) to find out how well our package can be seen in a competitive context.

It should be pointed out that while much of this kind of work is done, it is often conducted on an ad hoc basis. This can mean a project specifically tailored to fit a specific need. In practice, though, it often means a study done in panicky reaction to some bad news from the field, like a sudden precipitous sales fall, or the introduction of a spectacular new competitive package.

In reality, such "visibility" work should be ongoing — literally a "program", not just an isolated project. It should be done regularly (say quarterly) to try out new arrangements at the retail level and to test variants the marketing people have worked out and would like to test.

Effectiveness at the Trade Level

Is the package easy for wholesalers and retailers to handle, store, and stack on their shelves? Think about such a novel idea as the package for *L'Eggs*, a brand of pantyhose. The package was shaped like a plastic egg and was stored on freestanding displays in supermarkets. It revolutionized pantyhose marketing. But as times change and as space becomes more precious (manufacturers now typically pay a fee "slotting allowance" to get their products into the store), changes may need to be made. Research needs to be done on an ongoing basis to make sure that real problems aren't happening.

As for L'Eggs, they will now "be sold in a kind of art-school depiction of an egg, a small cardboard box . . . not coincidentally, the new package crams more product into scarce retail space. [The manufacturer] will be able to put 992 L'Eggs packages into the typical supermarket display, 264 more than can fit now".[6]

How do we know what is right for the package in the store? In the course of test market research (Chapter 18) or trade research (Chapter 14), trade views about the package is one of the key things we should be seeking to learn. We must keep in touch with what managers, salesclerks, and customers feel is going on, what problems they are having, and what they would like.

Environmental Spokesman

Sometimes environmental and ecological concerns and the "green" revolution are important to our customers. In some areas and among some segments, for example, returnable glass milk bottles are making a comeback, because they seem more environmentally friendly than paperboard cartons or plastic jugs. The fact that our customers have these concerns makes them important to us. We may need to know whether our package is a good "environmental spokesman" (or "spokespackage") for us.

If it matters, then new, more environmentally friendly, packaging may need to be considered. The researchable issues are obvious, if very difficult to quantify. These issues include the question of whether increased consumer approbation and publicity, perhaps leading to higher sales or to a decline in erosion of sales, offset higher production costs?

The more this matter is handled proactively, and not treated as a nuisance but as an opportunity, then the more intelligent and focused the research can be in this sphere of the packaging dimension. The "green" revolution, while probably overstated as a factor in consumer purchase habits, is important to some consumers. Sometimes, these consumers can make the issue important to wider circles of consumers. And the issue is not going to go away with time. If anything it will get bigger. It is much better to find the opportunities than to leave them to competitors.

As for L'Eggs in the example above, the manufacturer made the change to the modified egg with a package which it said "addresses today's consumer preferences: a package that's more compact, easier to read and uses less packaging material. . . . 90% of consumers, the company noted, recognized the environmental benefits of the new package form".[7]

And as with any change in marketing comes not only opportunities, but problems too. As package reduction goes on, so does research to ensure that consumers do not think they are being "cheated"; that there is something new there that they do not want.

> Eye-tracking [see Chapter 6] has become a popular tool for testing reduced packaging. . . .
>
> Said Elliot Young: "A marketer has to realize that now that they've changed [packaging], the shopper's orientation will change too. . . . In changing a package, you want to hold the equity of current franchise, the current customers. You want them to know it's just a packaging change, that the product is the same."
>
> Eye-tracking records what viewers look at in images projected onto a screen. A light beam bounces off the viewer's eye, letting researchers follow the eye's movement. Viewers look at photos of store shelves and close-up shots of packaging; post-testing interviews let viewers elaborate on their attitudes and perceptions.
>
> If reduced packages don't test well, marketers don't abandon the concept but test different colors, contrasts, type styles and shapes, Mr. Young said.[8]

Timing Packaging Research

Packaging research can be done both before the package is finished or after. As in so many areas of research (notably product and advertising) some of the most valuable things we can do are done in the preliminary stages, when changes can still be made. All we need is patience and will, as we seek especially to look into the image communication dimension.

Qualitative research, especially focus groups, can be invaluable here as different variations are played with. And, if the design consultants can be there to sketch out new ideas on the spot, the results can be especially dramatic. In one case:

> The design consultants were present at the group sessions. They found they were able to use the findings of the report directly without further quantification in their refining of the packaging prototypes shown. They incorporated the elements [uncovered] into the packages that are now on the market.[9]

Groups can play with many things, and in another series of groups these were the kind of elements recommended for consideration:

- Readability — bold-face print, for example.
- A professional or "prescription drug" look (clean, not cluttered) suggesting that a doctor would recommended the product.

- Eye-catching appeal, without being gimmicky.
- Product explanations in laymen's terms.
- A dye cut (or a picture) on the box showing product form.
- Clear identification of the product type and benefits.
- A safety seal and a safety seal notice somewhere on the package, not necessarily the front.
- No need to emphasize the manufacturer's name.

Having obtained this information from the focus groups, new package design could then be tested out:

These elements, along with others, were incorporated into four new package designs. The new designs and the package designs then in use were tested quantitatively.

The significance of the above elements was confirmed in the quantitative phase. They all appear in the packages that are currently on the market.[10]

The possibilities are endless, and the time for package research never ends. For the rewards can be considerable, since indeed

the package functions as the in-store salesperson and spokesperson for the brand. At the exact moment of the purchase decision, the advertisement and any previous trials are only memories, but the package is on hand to make or close the sale.[11]

PRODUCT NAME RESEARCH

Names are at the heart of a brand's personality and are the most potent way to distinguish one product from another, so why are they so often forgettable? One factor is that market research into consumer trends and opinions (themselves formed by current terms of reference) persuades companies that if they want a successful new brand, it should be similar to the most popular brand of the day. Failure of nerve is another factor. By copying existing brands, the new brand can be shown to be not too far wrong, even should it flop![12]

But we do not want the new brand to flop. Therefore, researchers are called in — but not as often as they should be — to see what name looks best for a potential new product or line extension. It is not the aim of such research either to copy existing names or to find "way-out" new ones. It is the aim to find the name that, with the package, conveys the essence of what we want to communicate for our brand. The name must work with the product itself to create a powerful whole, a successful "consumer offer".

Of all the elements of this mix, this "consumer offer", the name is the one that can be changed least readily. Perhaps it cannot be changed at all once it becomes widely accepted. The concept, the formulation, the price, the advertising, even the package, can be changed (and often are) as times and circumstances change. The constant is, or should be, the name. The name, in a sense, conveys the essence of the brand. Perhaps it is the brand: the "promise" that the marketer makes, and the equity.

Researchers are well equipped to study name testing. Questions relating to brand names just need to be asked.

Timing and Process of Name Research

Name research should begin with ideas from everyone in the company, including marketing, R&D, and sales people. In both formal and informal sessions, drawing from all sources in the company and in the outside world, names should be submitted on an ongoing basis, for present and future use. The researcher should organize informal groups of people in the company to "brainstorm" this issue, and nothing should be rejected out of hand.

Similarly, panels of consumers should be gathered together regularly not only to toss around possible new names, but also to constantly explore and reexplore current ones. The object of all of this is to have relevant information in time to do something with the findings. We do not need to get data just to file away because the name was already decided before the research was done.

For example, we should do name research on our home computer while the concepts (Chapter 10) are being tested. We should look at various names, which suggest perhaps fun or seriousness or whatever, and have them ready as the research unfolds. The name is not just a nice "add-on" — it will reflect the essence of what we hope to come up with!

The process of name testing always begins with generation of many names both inside and outside the company. Then the list is narrowed. Then remaining names can be presented for both diagnosis (qualitative orientation) and evaluation (quantitative orientation) in the course of a logically structured sequence.

> First, it is necessary to establish the basis on which names will be developed and later evaluated. Assuming the company has a well planned strategy for the new product or service, a written statement is prepared encompassing the consumer problem or need to be addressed by the entry, and the benefits or advantages of the solution it offers, including salient attributes and characteristics.
>
> Using key dimensions of the concept platform as stimuli, a pool of possible name candidates is generated in company and researcher brainstorming sessions.
>
> Inevitably, the process produces name ideas in great abundance; internal company prescreening is helpful to whittle the list to a manageable number. If necessary, the list can be reduced further by quick, preliminary consumer screening.
>
> The remaining pool of candidates now is ready for consumer scrutiny. But superficial preference/suitability ratings no longer are adequate for making this important decision.
>
> Rather, the most beneficial action is to subject name candidates to tough screening among appropriate consumers.[13]

Nothing is more important in the course of this orderly thinking then to be sure that, whenever possible, the name is presented to the respondent in the form in which consumers will actually see it. It should look exactly like it will be shown on the package, or like it will appear in the sales literature, if it is a service or something else that does not have a package.

Best of all is if the name is actually shown on the package itself, along with the logo that is planned to go with the name. The principle is simple: whenever we can get closer to conditions in the real marketplace we should take the opportunity in research to do so, provided this can be combined with the discipline of organized research flow.

Obviously, if the logo is also to be decided upon, then the test will involve both name and logo:

Name A using logo X
Name A using logo Y
Name A using logo Z
Name B using logo X
etc.

Straightforward analysis (see Chapter 8) can then sort out the separate effects of name and logo.

Elements of the Name

There are seven elements that we need to consider in a good name. The techniques needed to cope with each element will, as always in research, follow from an understanding of what we need to know and what we will do with it. Techniques will flow from the need, not the other way around. The seven elements are:

- Pronounceability
- Memorability
- Denotation
- Connotation
- Uniqueness
- Suitability for other countries
- Legal issues

Pronounceability. The element of pronounceability speaks to the difference between *brand* and *brand name*.

> Branding is simply the identification of a particular product or service. The term "brand" is often confused with terms such as "trademark", "logo", "brand mark", etc. In fact, a brand can be a name, a symbol, a design or any combination that distinguishes a firm's product from its other products or from those of competitors.
>
> Without exception, however, the brand includes a brand name. This may be a single word such as Sellotape or Access, but it usually consists of several words such as Ford Fiesta Ghia or Parkinson-Cowan 5000 Automatic. The brand name itself is utterable, unlike the brand mark, which is not. For example, Lacoste can be spoken, whereas the alligator design cannot.[14]

Indeed, a brand name is utterable and is often uttered, even if the product is usually bought in self-service stores. Thus, it must be easy and comfortable to pronounce. Are the combinations of letters easy to get off the tongue or are they tongue-twisters? Does the name seem too long? For example, "High Mountain Country Green 100's Light Menthols" might be a mouthful if the consumer has to ask for this hypothetical brand of cigarettes.

Marketers may also need to consider any possibility of embarrassment if the customer has to ask for a brand: "Red Stream" might be a very poor name for a feminine sanitary product. "Pocari Sweat" was an unfortunate English name for a popular Japanese sports drink; the "Sweat" has now been dropped outside of Japan.

Stories also abound about names emanating from China that are dubious assets, like "Pansy"-brand men's underwear. As to ease of pronunciation, marketers should remember that many Chinese and Japanese speakers frequently have trouble with the "r" sound, as do Japanese speakers with the "l" sound. Other examples, like the English "th" (as in "the"), the French and Spanish "r", and the German "ch" (as in "ich") could also be cited. Research in this area can be qualitative (e.g., focus groups) or quantitative (with clearly defined methods of assessing responses).

Memorability. This type of research is usually quite straightforward, with cards usually being shown to respondents containing the candidate names (carefully rotated). Then the respondent is asked to state all he can remember on immediate recall, and, perhaps five minutes later (or even the following day), on delayed recall.

Denotation. What, literally, does the name mean? Is it relevant to the product category or not? Why? The fact is that there are many names in the marketing world today that seem unusual: *Camel* for a cigarette; *Apple* for a computer; *Coca*-Cola for a family-oriented drink. These often reside in history: Camel for the Middle Eastern (tobacco) slant; Apple because Apple's John Sculley was a fan of the Beatles, whose record company bore that name;[15] Coca-Cola because the "original formula was believed to contain cocaine".[16] These instances suggest that a good name can be gotten by many means. But they should not suggest that today research should or can be ignored in helping us get not only a good name, but the best name possible.

Connotation. What extended meanings does the name have? What imagery might be in consumers' heads that we may not have thought of? Are there any problems here?

Uniqueness. Does it "stand out from the crowd"? Is it seen to be different, clever, or special, without being quirky? Is it creative without being outlandish? Does it identify THIS BRAND AND NO OTHER, echoing the special nature of this product and perhaps embedding that special nature right in the name?

Suitable for other countries. We have already mentioned Pocari Sweat sport drink and Pansy men's underwear. Such are the issues we need to research for our name if it is to be used across national boundaries. Above all, we want to avoid vulgarity or confusion. We need to think about examples like why Chevrolet's "Nova", or Nestle's "Nescafe" did not do well in Latin America. The former could be misunderstood as *No Va* ("It does not go"), and the latter as *No es Cafe* ("It is not coffee"). Generally today, computer programs are used, covering major (and minor) foreign languages to spot potential problems in using a name overseas.

Finally on this issue, the unique naming problem in Chinese-speaking markets must be mentioned. Chinese countries (China, Taiwan, Hong Kong, Singapore) and Chinese segments in other countries (especially Southeast Asia) are important markets now. They are poised to become even more important as time goes by. Since Chinese is the only language without an alphabet, it is necessary to use Chinese characters (ideograms) that symbolize the brand, and (usually) sound like the name in its original form. Since many characters can be chosen that approximate the sound, it is essential to choose those that mean "good" and "appropriate" things, not silly and negative things. Coca-Cola's characters can roughly be translated "Pleasant Mouth Pleasant Feeling"; Pepsi-Cola's "Hundred Things Pleasant Feeling"; and Marlboro's "Ten Thousand Treasures Road".

Legal issues.   This probably should come first in name research. Any new name must be checked for trademark infringement both at home and abroad. While this is not properly a marketing research function, the researcher still must make sure it is being done as part of the name testing.

Reinforcing Marketing Aims

Overall, name research should be used to find names that underscore our positioning; emphasize our style; fit in with other products or lines our company makes; and highlight benefits. Examples of successful product names include "Sweet & Low" Sugar Substitute (surely one of the best names anyone has ever devised for anything!), and "No More Tears" Baby Shampoo by Johnson & Johnson.

These are marketing aims, and our name research (with its own aims) must fit into the totality of these aims and not dominate them. Rather, name research should blend with other research to produce the best total "consumer offer" possible. Maybe we need to blend it with packaging: could the package benefit, if it is important, possibly be incorporated into the name? The goal is coming up with a name that embodies the total consumer offer, a name that will serve us well for a long time to come!

13

Price Testing

Price is one of the famous four P's of marketing, along with product, place, and promotion. Important questions are always being tossed around by marketers as they seek to get the price "right". These include:

- What happens if I cut my price?
- What happens if I raise my price?
- What should I price my new product at?
- Will changing the brand's image allow me to charge more?
- What will competition do if I change my price?

While these are important marketing questions, the reality is that the fruits of price research are probably more limited than in any of the other major areas of marketing.

> Such factors as new-product introductions, product improvements, advertising campaigns, and changes in product availability can alter brand shares and obscure the effects of pricing from accurate observation.[1]

While academic work on pricing (including whole tomes on the subject) abounds, it is a fact that businesses are highly constrained in how they can set prices. After all, the limits of what it costs to make something (as calculated via cost accounting) set lower limits. The realities of the marketplace (competition, one's own entries, and an estimation of what the future will be like) set upper limits.

The marketer's philosophy and strategy has as much to do with setting a price for a new product, for example, as does any sophisticated numerical work. He may want to "penetrate" a market; get in quickly and deeply, and plan to stay and try to discourage potential competitors by taking a lower margin. Obviously, this strategy requires choosing a lower price. And then, of course, the marketer is certainly constrained later on from raising the price appreciably because of the value-price image that has been created.

On the other hand, the marketer may want to "skim" a market; go in with a high price, seek to become the "gold standard" as it were, and maybe make lot of money and then get out. Just as obviously, this kind of strategy calls for a higher price. Among consumers, this higher price is as likely to be associated with perceived exclusivity as with economics.

The absolute difference between possible lows and highs in pricing is apt to be quite small, and not very researchable. In any event, the research must defer (as in every aspect of marketing, but especially here) to marketing itself. That is, pricing is but one element, deeply embedded in the broader notions of strategy and tactics. It is perhaps unfortunate that the possibility of mathematical sophistication in pricing research has often enchanted researchers into going beyond what is feasible and reasonable from a broader pragmatic marketing perspective.

Such a broader pragmatic marketing perspective might mean cutting prices, even taking temporary losses. The objective may simply be to hold on, until possible new products and a new image can pull the company out of difficulties. As MaGrath noted: "Once a company decides to maintain its share, it usually has to tough it out and often loses money until it can fight back to improve its margins and get its customers back."[2] While mathematical models and analysis can be useful, they cannot help if the factors of the marketplace (where *dis*equilibrium and not equilibrium reigns) are ignored.

Similarly, it can be deceptive to look at just one price. In real markets, different segments suggest a strategy of segmented pricing, with varying product or service for each group and its needs. This is much less tractable mathematically, but probably more realistic. Consider this observation on looking at pricing when selling to an organization:

> As part of a segmented approach to pricing, marketers have to learn to identify the *buying center* of the segment. Within each organization, there is a buying center with multiple players who all care and think about price differently. Therefore, not only should a firm price between market segments differently, but often it should present the price *differently* within the same organization.[3]

So it may well be that much work on pricing should not delve into numbers and theory at all. It may be more critical to get a qualitative appraisal of image and competitive reality, a thorough understanding of our own pricing philosophy, a knowledge of where we stand in the product life cycle. Likewise, but usually absent, it may be more useful to have an in-depth analysis of projections, margins, and prospects.

Much of this involves concentrated thinking and often unpleasant appraisals (and reappraisals) of corporate, divisional, and category and brand goals. And much involves exploration and "feel". Both of these kinds of research take time and offer no "quick fixes" or "magic numbers". Thus, they tend to be unpopular.

And so usually nothing very serious or sensible is done in price testing. The decision is frequently a perplexing and petulant demand from some ego in a seat of power to "price it at that" for no apparent reason. (This is similar to having someone tell us to "call it that" (name testing)). But, as we have shown in Chapter 12, name testing can be done that is sensible and meaningful for marketing. This is also true for price testing.

SURVEY TECHNIQUES

Various survey techniques are available to help us make better decisions on pricing, of course, and we will discuss some of them below. The difficulty is not that they are not sound. Rather, the big problem is that they must always be continuously reevaluated in the light of the realities of the marketplace. These realities include competitive retaliation and consumer fickleness. More than for most other kinds of research, such market dynamics can render pricing research irrelevant in a flash.

Important techniques include:

- Simulation scenarios
- Indifference analysis
- Tradeoff analysis

Simulation Scenarios

This is much less awesome than the name suggests. Here the term simply suggests research that offers price scenarios to consumers, and solicits their responses — what they might do in the marketplace. A question might be something like this:

What brand would you be most likely to buy in each of these situations?

(1)   A at price 1, B at price 2, C at price 3, D at price 4, E at price 5.
(2)   All the above at prices higher by 20 percent, except A, up by 10 percent.
(3)   All the above at prices lower by 5 percent, except A, lower by 10 percent.

The questions continue in this manner for various situations. The respondents answer about the likelihood they will buy for each situation. From such lines of questioning, current and hypothetical market shares can be estimated. Ideas about price elasticity (what might happen to demand if price is changed), and optimum pricing can be studied.

Indifference Analysis

Another approach is to ascertain peoples' perceptions of what prices along a continuum seem "right" for a product. By determining, for example, at what points a product would be considered "too cheap to be good quality" and "too expensive to be good value", we can arrive at a range of suitable (and unsuitable) prices. Perhaps, and probably more importantly, we can even estimate one possible "best" price. An example of this type of case might produce results that look something like Table 13.1.

Table 13.1. Cumulative frequencies for various price levels.

Price	READ UP (a) "Too cheap"	READ DOWN (b) "Too expensive"	(c) (a) – (b) (absolute number)
$ 1	100	0	100
2	100	0	100
3	90	0	90
4	80	0	80
5	60	10	50
6	20	30	10
7	5	50	45
8	0	80	80
9	0	100	100
10	0	100	100
11	0	100	100
12	0	100	100

(a) is the percentage of people who think the product is too cheap to be of good quality at the price. (b) is the percentage who think the product is too expensive to be of good value at the price.

The table can be read: At $7, a total of 5 percent of the respondents think the product is so cheap that it could not be any good. When the price gets down to $6, 20 percent believe this. At $5, 60 percent believe the product is priced too low to possibly be of good quality. By the time we get down to $2 (or less) no one thinks the product can be any good.

The "too expensive" column is read the same way. At $5, 10 percent of respondents think the product is too expensive to be good value. At $6, 30 percent of them think this. At $7, 50 percent think the product is too expensive, etc.

We could graph this, and where the curves cross (here, between $5 and $6) can be thought of as an ideal price: where people are least antagonistic. The point is also sometimes called the point of "indifference". People neither see the product as too cheap nor too expensive.

We once used a simplified version of this method to determine how much to raise parking fees at a university. (Lowering fees was not an option, since the increase was needed to fund parking lot improvements.) Embedded in the questionnaire about parking in general, we asked whether people would continue to park if annual fees were raised X amount. The X differed by increments of $5 on different questionnaires, so that we could compute percentages of people who would stop parking on campus at different levels of price hike. The percentage who would have left was low and fairly steady for all increases up to $40, where it shot up dramatically. The physical plant was able to implement a $35 increase in parking fees while losing very few patrons.

Obviously, there are many variations of this technique. Exactly how to use it depends on factors relating to marketing realities, and not just statistical procedure and analysis.

Tradeoff Analysis

A third way to do price testing by surveys is called "tradeoff" (or conjoint) analysis. With this method:

Customers are shown sets of hypothetical products that vary on such factors as performance, safety, consistency, convenience, and price.

The hypothetical products are selected and configured based on experimental design theory. Customers are asked to evaluate the options; the utilities for different product features as well as price can be derived from the evaluations.[4]

Appraisal

These three techniques, which are merely representative of many that may be used, can provide clues as to price ranges. But by calling attention to pricing, and by placing price in a non-contextual situation, they risk artificial, rather than market-based appraisals.

But some type of price question can nonetheless be a useful part of the overall picture of what our price should be. Again, though, it only will be useful if we understand price in general, and these results in particular, as part of the whole puzzle. Such techniques can rarely give a final, definitive answer. As noted, the real marketplace is too fluid for this work to be definitive. But it can be helpful.

STORE PANELS

To supplement our knowledge from surveys (above), and to build upon those findings, we may also do testing in stores. If, for example, we wish now to test the price of a new product at levels A, B, and C, this is one way we can do it. In such a quantitative, non-question-asking study, we would find (here) three matched panels of stores, either in one city or in three different, matched markets. The panels would be matched as best as possible geographically, socioeconomically, by purchase habits, by brand shares, etc.

In one panel, the product is sold at price A, in the second at price B, and in the third at price C. Then we rotate (see schematic below) and count how many have been sold in each panel. Since we know how much we make as net profit at each level, *total* profit at each level can readily be calculated. This simple test can offer additional clues.

The test might look like this:

	Panel I	Panel II	Panel III
First week	Price A	Price B	Price C
Second week	Price B	Price C	Price A
Third week	Price C	Price A	Price B

This will be recognized as an experiment. As in all experiments, we must be careful to get it right. For example, we must be careful to note what competitive activity went on in each panel, especially competitive price deals. While this is "scientific", we obviously cannot shut out our competitors, who may notice our new product even if they do not know it is being price-tested.

This is not a "laboratory". It is the real world of the market place, so we cannot control everything that we should control if we want to be quite sure that any differences we see are certainly due to price. Sometimes, there may be appropriate statistical methods we can use to "correct" for uncontrollable variables. Sometimes we just have to recognize that we must accept some uncertainty because of our inability to control everything. And certainly we must insist on "de-aggregative" data, that is, we must look not only at the panels in total, but each of the stores individually, to sort out "outliers" and "aberrations".

14

Place

In terms of importance to the marketing mix, "place" is certainly impossible to ignore. But place is probably the least researched of the traditional four marketing P's, which also include product (Chapter 11), price (Chapter 13), and promotion (Chapters 15, 16). While place is the focus of many courses in the academic curriculum (usually called "Channels of Distribution" or "Channel Management"), little serious marketing research (other than repetitive counting) is done on this issue.

This is especially strange and sad, because there has been a major change in marketing in recent times. There has been an enormous shift in power in the marketing chain from marketer (manufacturer) to retailer. Nowadays, marketers typically must pay fees ("slotting allowances") to retailers to get their goods onto the retailers' shelves at all.

Moreover, marketers everywhere are seeking to establish ongoing relationships with major (and sometimes also minor) players in the distribution system, such as wholesalers, chains, large independents, etc. The marketers want to underscore, as well as to pay lip service to, the reality that these players are, in fact, their first "customers". Understanding their needs can help pave the way to better sales success by the retailer to the ultimate consumer.

By better understanding their needs, all will benefit. Thus, it should be obvious that there is a need to do many things in research to ensure that our products get to the "place" we want them to get to (so that the ultimate consumer can buy them there). Clearly, we also need to seriously measure what happens once the product gets on the shelf.

This suggests two broad lines of attack in the realm of "place" research: trade awareness and acceptance studies, and sales research at the retail level. These will be discussed in turn below. These two ideas are obviously not exhaustive, and should suggest many other ways in which we can get valuable data at the trade level to help understand our business better and to plan for the future.

TRADE AWARENESS AND ACCEPTANCE

This is a real headache. The Research Department is frequently aware of the need for such research. As part of its charter to "drive the research function" itself, as well as to respond to requests from others, the Research Department may suggest various projects in this area. These may include such issues as:

- Does the trade (wholesalers, retailers others) believe that our sales reps are doing the job they should? This job would include providing good "deals" whenever they are available. It would also include being a real "partner": keeping the trade player informed of what is going on with his own company and the industry in general; a kind of Who's Who and What's New?
- What kind of "deals" would most benefit the trade (those "first customers" of ours: those wholesalers, retailers, and others). We routinely offer special things like our prepackaged "setsells" ("three-for-the-price-of-two", "take-ones" for contests, etc.) without ever asking the players about what they and their customers (the ultimate consumers) really want.

We do, of course, use research frequently to prepare sales pitches to players like chain buying committees. We can encourage them to carry our products when we provide evidence that they have done well in test markets and can help the chain to make a lot of money. But what do we do to involve the players? What do we do to proactively find out what they would like to know, and get their views on what they think about us in general?

The response from management whenever such studies are suggested is often all too predictable. What they say all too often is: "We don't need such studies. Our sales reps are there all the time, talking to their contacts in the chains and everywhere. Our sales reps know what the trade wants, and you can bet the trade will tell us if they're not getting it."

While our sales reps are obviously outgoing, friendly, spirited, skillful, and motivated, they are not necessarily especially self-critical. Indeed, self-criticism is frequently a hazard to success for them. Can they really elicit "objective" (Chapter 1) responses from the players? Even if they do, will they really relay those objective responses to top management if they feel their jobs would be on the line if they did so? What if the objective response from the wholesaler is that the company is doing a terrible job?

Of course, we should encourage information flow through sales channels. But we must also recognize that we will never get a complete picture relying only on this channel. It is much better to do such studies on a professional basis, using professional interviewers, so that the sponsor of the study remains anonymous.

Such studies are typically done using semi-structured questionnaires, and involve attitudes about all the companies in the field — us and our competitors. These studies are usually inaugurated by a letter indicating that someone will call for an appointment, are followed up by a call, and are best done in person. The interviewer should be given all the information needed on the background of the industry (names of the firms in it, trade terminology, etc.) to enable him to be knowledgeable as well as professional. Often, the senior members of the market research team should also do some of the interviews, to make sure that they really have the flavor of what people are saying.

The line of questioning will vary widely from survey to survey and from person to person. We may ask different things, obviously, of top chain buyers than of salespeople in stores, because they have different levels of responsibility and have expertise in different areas. The top buyer certainly knows much more about chain policy in cooperating with promotions or negotiating on prices. On the other hand, the salesclerk on the floor undoubtedly can tell us much more about how consumers react to our marketing efforts.

Usually, though, questions will includes at least some of these items:

- Advertising awareness.
- Reactions to advertising.
- Awareness of consumer and trade promotions.
- Reactions to consumer and trade promotions.
- Awareness of sales reps and their performance in handling routine matter, deals, "trade talk", etc. (But note that the names of sales reps, if they come up, must never be reported back to management!)
- What the players would like to see from companies, but do not see.
- What they do not like to see from companies, but do see.
- Other issues as they may emerge.

The last item, other issues, is critical for maintaining flexibility. Sometimes important things come up that we would never have anticipated. For example, Coca-Cola installed vending machines in Paris, on streets near to many cafes and restaurants which were big purchasers of Coke. The matter was never discussed with these retailers, who were very upset by the idea. Many switched to Pepsi-Cola, and eventually, Coke had to remove the vending machines. We would not have wanted our interviewer to ignore this issue just because we did not think to include it in the list of question topics when we designed the research.

The specific positions or people in companies in the distribution chain will often be designated by the client, and other times set by the researcher. But the names of further players should be elicited by the interviewer, and they should be interviewed too. (This is often referred to as a "snowball" or "self-generating" sample.) Information from channel members is much more valuable when it comes from several sources, each with differing views because they are dealing with issues at different levels and from different angles.

Why should channel members participate? What is in it for them? Usually, channel members are just as much in need of information as the client marketer. We can offer as an incentive the highlights of the study (with the client's permission, of course). It should be broadly disguised (so as not to reveal specific companies or people). But even disguised, it can indicate things the channel is doing well and things that are being done poorly, areas where consumers are satisfied and areas where they are not.

SALES RESEARCH AT THE RETAIL LEVEL

Audits

The need to know what is going on at the trade level, specifically at the retail level, has never been greater. This is particularly true because of the increasing power of retailers to "call the tune": to take what they want, to keep what they want, to throw out what they do not want.

Retail "audits" (such as those conducted by the A.C. Nielsen Company) have long been a part of the research function. They produce information on sales, shares, distribution (in-stock, out-of-stock, facings, promotional activity, etc.). Although a company can do audits for just itself on an ad hoc basis, frequently audits (like Nielsen's) are done on a "syndicated" basis, with many clients contributing to the cost, and sharing all of the data.

Researchers typically have not paid a lot of attention to this area of research, because, like interviews with players (above), it is not big, complicated, or glamorous. After all, audit figures on sales are derived from a simple enough formula:

Sales = Opening Inventory (beginning of sales period)

+

Store Purchases (during the sales period)

–

Closing Inventory (end of the sales period)

Neither researchers nor clients typically concern themselves with how these studies are executed. (Many never even go into the field with the auditors!) Yet when problems arise, like share figures that do not look right, researchers are forced to show concern. "Did the auditors find *all* the inventory, both on the shelves and in the storerooms?" "What kind of inventory was being counted anyway: just the shelves or back-room stock too?" "And what did the term 'out-of-stock' mean: just on the shelves, or anywhere in the store?"

These and other loud and nasty questions frequently upset the researcher because audits are usually regarded as a "mechanical" function conducted by "somebody else". But in truth, they should always remain the responsibility of the researcher. And whether custom-made or ongoing, questions need to be constantly asked about audits, such as:

- Is the sample of stores really representative of the market we are looking at today? (What about shifts in purchase patterns?)
- If we are going into a new market overseas, are we looking at it with a fresh eye, or are we just replicating what we do at home? For example, an audit in a developing country should not include only department stores and grocery stores. A lot of product may move through all sorts of permanent and semi-permanent fixed stalls or kiosks, as well as street-sellers and hawkers of all kinds. Many retail settings may be impossible to define without going out to the "field" and making observations, putting aside comfortable home-country categories.
- Is promotional material (the full range: consumer price promotions, banners, shelf talkers, etc.) adequately described by brand, with photographs?

Today, auditors tend to have an easier task than before. They tend to use hand-held computers into which inventory data is entered in precise detail, and which can be downloaded easily into the central computer system. And today stores' purchases are usually available in the form of scanner data. (Previously, printed forms were used to count inventory, and one had to use stores' actual purchase invoices.)

So there is more opportunity than ever to report data in meaningful detail (not in voluminous confusion) to produce summaries that are compact, coherent, cohesive, and comprehensive. The data can be on a virtually on-line real-time basis to meaningfully help marketing decision-makers and marketing decision-making.

Scanners

Today, enormous volumes of retail information are available through the use of scanners. These are machines that pass over the "bar codes" (like UPC) which now appear on most items in the consumer package goods area. The scanner records the item, price, and time of purchase. Such data can allow us (for example) to keep track of sales on couponed or special-priced items on a day-to-day (even hour-to-hour) basis.

We can use the incredibly accurate retail sales information in this area to make vital marketing decisions. For example, scanner data can help us decide which newspapers are best to advertise in. (We can vary the papers we use on some random basis, and track sales.) We can decide what other kinds of in-store merchandising best supplement our promotions, and how to time promotional support.

These data come from the trade level, right at the "place" where the customer meets the product, and buys (or does not buy) what we are trying to sell. They are invaluable, and eventually more and more marketers will recognize this. Productive (rather than merely mindless and mechanistic) use of scanner data will play an increasingly important role in shaping marketing decisions as time goes by.[1]

Marketing managers who share full details of their marketing plans with their researchers will benefit most. To take full advantage of scanner data possibilities, researchers must be able to play upon this gold mine of data, exploring possibilities and fruitfulness.

Other Means

Obviously, audits and scanner data may not always be available. Under certain circumstances, competitors may agree to provide shipment data to a trade association, which then gives it to members. This, too, may be a way to follow sales and market share trends by brand, packaging, etc., providing we do *not* automatically accept any such data at face value. We are better off if we can also assess it for validity by comparing it to numbers that we already know from our own audit or scanner work.

Finally, in developing countries none of these means may be available. In some such countries, no merchants or companies may be willing to give anything to anybody for any money. They may fear — often with good reason from past history — that the government is behind requests for information, waiting to grab more taxes as soon as they find out exactly how much product is being sold. In some cultures, business people believe that any information can be used against them by competitors, so they do not give any information.

It often takes great skill and persuasiveness, and considerable confidence building to get any cooperation whatsoever in such situations. But it usually can be done, especially by enlisting the services of local researchers well versed in the local language and the local culture.

Even governments can help. For example, maybe the researcher can get them (sometimes for a fee) to provide information on how many tax stamps they sell to each company in an industry: this may give a good clue to brand share. Sometimes governments even routinely collect retail sales information. The Hong Kong government, for example, periodically publishes a retail survey. Such published data are sometimes too general to be useful, but one may find more detail in the unpublished data, which may be available for purchase from the agency which conducted the survey.

Anything is possible. We just have to attempt to do it.

15

Promotion: Advertising

Among the four P's — product, price, place, and promotion — promotion is undoubtedly the most glamorous to most people. But promotion is also the one that can most clearly differentiate one brand (or "consumer offer") from another. More specifically, it is to one part of promotion that these observations apply: advertising.

Promotion consists of two main parts. One is *advertising* (or "media advertising"), which consists essentially of print or electronic messages in the traditional media (newspapers, magazines, radio, television, outdoor, etc.). It now also includes many newer media and ways of conveying messages. Direct mail could be included here, plus telephone marketing, plus commercials as part of video cassettes, plus who knows what in the future? These are all paid announcements by identifiable sponsors. We call them *above-the-line* in industry jargon.

The other part is *below-the-line*, or "collateral" activities.[1] In this chapter we will discuss what researchers do to test the above-the-line part, media advertising. In the next chapter, we will discuss research on the below-the-line part.

Of course, above- and below-the-line activities are often (even usually) mutually supporting, part of a single campaign. Research, at its best and most professional, will try to tie both of these elements together, whenever possible, so as to produce a picture that is more like a "whole". This might be called "through-the-line" — a seamless activity that ties the two parts together and relates them to the totality of the marketing mix.

THE TRIUMPHS AND FAILURES OF ADVERTISING RESEARCH

Advertising research probably is the most frequently done of all research, and that part to which the lion's share of the budget goes. This makes sense, since so much of what we learn about product, place, price, positioning, the needs and wants of the market, must ultimately be summed up in the marketer's advertising. This is how he communicates it all to an audience he has hopefully accurately defined, and whose responses are now what matters.

What does *not* matter are the awards that the commercial may have won, or the pride that the CEO can express to other CEOs (on the golf course of his country club) about the cleverness of his agency's work. The *triumph* of advertising research is that some researchers have gone beyond such shallow considerations. They have taken seriously the complex nature of assessing advertising effectiveness, and have devised ways to try to measure it sensitively, reliably, validly, thoughtfully, and usefully.

The *failure* of advertising research is that it is beset with systems and rigidities. Too often researchers and research companies have an attitude that goes something like this: "We have a technique to measure your advertising; let's hope that your problem fits our technique." Many researchers fall easily into this trap of accepting systems and thoughtless repetitiveness. (Maybe they want to get normative data, which is fine, but not at the expense of constant rethinking.)

Too often the researcher is brought in to test things after a final advertisement or commercial has already been produced and no changes are going to be made. Too often, many marketing managers and advertising agency people just do not believe research results if they do not confirm personal prejudices. They do not trust any of it no matter how good it is, even if they have been drawn into the research early in the process. They will not accept that the judgment of anybody outside the industry could be as good as the judgment of the highly-paid creators of the advertising. (Even, or maybe especially, what consumers say is mistrusted. After all, what could the layman who knows nothing about advertising possibly tell us about how to make an advertisement?)

Still, advertising research can be helpful, even highly useful if done right and paid attention to. Doing it is both an exciting and satisfying part of the researcher's life, where business, art, science, integration of intelligence, and craft all come into play.

There are five issues that we will deal with in relation to this subject. They are:

- What can we learn?
- When should we do it?
- What are the obstacles?
- How do we do it?
- What key considerations must we always keep in mind?

WHAT CAN WE LEARN?

Many techniques concentrate on one or another aspect of what we can learn from advertising testing. This is all right if we know what we want to learn; if we have set objectives; if, in fact, we have thought about this matter at all.

A good way to think about it is to examine the phases that we believe people go through in making a marketing decision. That is, we want to see how attitudes are formed. (Note that the sequence below applies largely to products that "matter", that we do have to think about.) On these "high interest" products, the sequence probably is something like See-Learn-Do: attitude-formation precedes purchase. For "low interest" matters (like chewing gum, perhaps) the sequence might run See-Do-Learn: attitude-formation follows purchase.

But the fact that the sequence may differ for different products should not divert us from the fact that there is a sequence. We need to understand the sequence for our brand at this time among relevant consumers before we begin to do advertising research. The understanding, and not some rigid guideline, will determine what we do in our advertising testing.

There are ten stages (or states) in the process, which we can call the "attitude chain". In the course of the stages, advertising is first comprehended, ultimately a sale is made, and then matters beyond-the-sale arise. Of course, these stages over-lap. But it is useful to look at each stage in turn, because each suggests what we can test for. Later in this chapter, we will suggest what can be done in each stage. So here, in sequence, is what we want from the audience as it is exposed to our advertising.

- **Awareness.** To know our brand exists: its name, its promise, and maybe much more.
- **Liking.** To react with pleasure (or without displeasure) to what we are saying. Certainly some very effective advertising can be heartily disliked and not turn people off. It can create some uncommon remembering (next step) that, in the course of disliking, can still make our brand stand out enough from the crowd so that people try it. But the product itself had better be very different and very good. In general, we cannot count on disliked advertising working well.
- **Remembering.** To retain what they "learned" from the advertising: name, promise, etc., long enough to keep our brand in their "evoked set" in the market place. That is, ours should be a brand people would at least consider buying, if they do not actually buy it now. Remembering can also take the form of "recognition". Perhaps people are not able to recall our brand from memory, but they do "recognize" it (call it up from below the conscious level perhaps) when a stimulus (like a package on the store shelf) "echoes" the advertising.
- **Perception.** To create a "picture" of our brand in their mind combining "fact" and "image", a picture in line with how we are trying to "position" our brand.
- **Understanding.** To comprehend what we're trying to say.
- **Belief.** To accept the fact that what we claim can in fact be done: "try us and see!" Sometimes people can even scoff at what we claim, really believe that it is probably not true, as long as that small seed of possibility is planted. "But if it were true, then . . . well . . . I'd sure try it. Maybe I should try it."
- **Involvement.** To make them care. We do not want people to think: "Your technology or image-making is great, but it isn't unique and/or it has nothing to do with me." We want them to see how it relates to their needs, or wants, or fantasies.
- **Persuasion.** To convince people that this is so, and "move" them closer to buying the brand. By whatever means (entertaining, informing, scaring, educating, etc.), we need to get them to the point of making a decision in the marketplace in our favor.

- **Purchase**. To actually get them to buy it.
- **Post-purchase reassurance**. To "cement the bond" between customer and the product, reinforcing their decision by convincing them that they made the right choice. Now that they are more aware than ever of the product category and all its advertising, we need to reassure them, through advertising, that our product was indeed the best, is the best, and will remain the best — for them!

It will be obvious that any one piece of advertising (or campaign) may be asking the audience to do one or more of the above, may be trying to produce one or more of these states.

All the while, of course, we must never forget that what we really care about is whether the advertising helped produce sales. Unfortunately, except for retail or coupon advertisements, measuring the impact of advertising directly is very rarely possible. There are too many intervening variables in the long time it takes to build up to most sales. And so in advertising research, it is usually necessary to measure some or all the intervening stages we have just described to get a "surrogate" measure of success. It is up to the researcher to ask which stages it is necessary and possible to measure in each case, so as to find the right road to travel.

And thinking about what we can learn, we can look at advertising in yet another way, centering now on a marketing focus. Broadly speaking, we can seek to:

- **Remind**, or carry on a campaign, possibly with a longstanding message or image, which says, in essence: "We're big, we're important, we're spending money to remind you of how good we are, and so you can believe we're good. Otherwise, we wouldn't be spending this money; be reassured you're right to use our brand."
- **Create an image or belief**, which is very important in positioning new products.
- **Change in image or belief**, which is very important in repositioning old products, and in luring people away from competitors.
- **Bring news** of a new product, perhaps.
- **Offer something**, e.g., a coupon, a deal, a give-away, etc.

Each advertisement or commercial, then, has a definite aim, and the researcher must insist on knowing what this aim is before beginning the research. If no one can tell us the aim, if we cannot figure it out (even from a statement of the copy platform), and if it does not seem like there is an aim at all, then we should hesitate to start the research. (The marketer should be thinking about whether the advertising should even be running.) While the researcher is constantly pressured to "do something" (usually to follow what has been done before), it is stupid to "do something" without knowing "why".

In other words, we need to know what we are supposed to measure before we start trying to measure it. What, really, is the advertising seeking to do, and, in seeking to do that, how will it help to move the marketing process along? We need to measure what it is trying to influence. This orientation is probably what we really mean by the "scientific spirit" of inquiry. It is certainly what we mean by saying that research must serve marketing, and not just gather numbers for their own sake.

WHEN SHOULD WE DO IT?

If we can't figure out *why* it should be done (above), then maybe the answer to *when* is never. Maybe it should not be done at all. But once we are tuned into the marketing process, and the marketing needs and decisions are being addressed, the basic answer to when we should do it is AS EARLY AS POSSIBLE.

It may well be that the most propitious time is in the very early "rough" stages of development, even in the half-world between Concept (Chapter 10) and Advertising proper. Using cheap studio-made commercials with amateurs as actors for early evaluation, or animatics (sequentially exposed line drawings), or such things, we may be able to spot flaws early, AND REMEDY THEM. Taking action is what it's all about really.

The argument is often made that without the final music, the final special effects, the real actors, etc., nothing useful can be learned. If the commercial is supposed to be a misty, atmospheric, artsy-fartsy kind of thing, this may sometimes be valid. Then, everything must come together to produce the whole, and studying some of the parts individually may not tell us much.

Otherwise, the argument against early testing can be deceptive and self-serving, reflecting a lack of concern for the budget. (Maybe managers operate like: "I'd really like to take a trip to Tahiti to shoot the commercial. I certainly do not want to learn anything beforehand that would cause us to cancel it.") The researcher must know about the commercial, its real aims and real forms, and about the dynamics of support for it in the marketing team, unpopular as that may make him.

The truth is that the earlier the researcher is called in, before huge quantities of time, money, and reputation have been irrevocably invested, the more useful advertising research (or any research) will be. The researcher can probably only get in early if he has the ear and confidence of the marketing manager and the advertising manager. These are precious things to have; they must be earned; and they are probably the most valuable tools in the researcher's tool-box.

This early-stage work should also be repetitive, even compulsively so. It should seek to "diagnose" rather than "evaluate": to see what is right, what is wrong, why they are right or wrong, what can be fixed and what cannot, what will be kept and what discarded. This is not a matter of "all-or-nothing". A first phase of research may detect some problems. We adjust the advertising and do a second round to see how well we have fixed things. A third, fourth, or even more rounds may be necessary to fix it if it can be fixed.

Clearly, this is what we call "pretesting" advertising: making it as good as we know how. The focuses of such pretesting become awareness (which is also researched in the course of market studies (Chapter 17) for broader campaign recall), remembering (in a real situation, in the midst of competitive clutter), purchase, and post-purchase reassurance.

WHAT ARE THE OBSTACLES?

If we know so much about advertising testing, why does it so often fail us? There are many obstacles to good advertising testing. Five critical ones will be highlighted here.

"Theme" vs. "Execution"

"Theme" research deals with the basis of why people will react or not; it largely deals with getting the idea (concept) right. "Execution" deals with how we do it: the words and music that make the idea come alive. While "theme" and "execution" deal with each other, they do occupy different realms of activity. We really should not test the "execution" till we get the "theme" right. We must understand the difference between the two.

Again, we can summarize the two types of research as follows:

- Theme research ("strategic alternatives") focuses on what we are offering.
- Execution research ("copy testing") focuses on how we tell people about it.

Lavidge focuses on the former quite insightfully:

> Planning any strategic advertising research should begin by asking the purpose of the advertising. Are we trying to introduce the product or service? Are we trying to make people aware of it and impart information about it, the cognitive factors? Are we trying to instill favorable attitudes, imagery, or associations with it, the affective elements? Are we trying to get potential customers to develop and act on positive purchase intentions, the cognitive factors? Or is the purpose of the advertising to do all of these?
>
> At whom should the advertising be aimed? What kinds of people are they? What are their demographic and psychographic characteristics? What kind of values do they have? What kind of attitudes do they have? What are their wants and needs? What are the product (or service) benefits that are most important to those people? What are their motivations? What are the most meaningful appeals to them for the product type with which we are concerned? On what bases do they differentiate between brands? Where do we get the answers to these questions? ...
>
> The most valuable strategic advertising research may be the research that helps answer such fundamental questions. Such research may not be, and frequently is not, labeled nor thought of as "advertising research." It certainly is not likely to involve any of the commonly used standardized advertising research procedures.[2]

Lack of Objectives

We have already stressed the necessity of understanding what an ad or commercial is supposed to do before we seek to measure its effectiveness. Otherwise, what criteria can we possibly use in assessing whether it is good or bad? Looking at *campaign* measurements, Brady noted:

> Without preestablished goals, an otherwise well-structured evaluation process can degenerate into a simplistic posterior analysis, where "goals of hindsight", set in the context of post-survey results, become meaningless expedients....
>
> If... marketing management's basic goal is to increase brand name recall, the ad manager must translate that conceptual goal into an operational one.
>
> Realistically, he must determine what he believes his campaign expenditure is capable of buying him: a 5% increase in brand name recall? A 10% increase?[3]

Rigid Systems

As noted, rigid thinking tends to make us do testing according to established techniques, whether or not the techniques are suitable to our problem. Rigid people try to force us into their favored techniques. Sometimes, the established or favored technique is appropriate. Then, we should use it. Often it is not, and we should not use it. Unfortunately, researchers frequently do this silly thing anyway (using inappropriate techniques), because they do not know what the problem is.

Indifference and Lack of Communication

We can cut down on these problems if we invite marketing managers and agency creatives to take part in early-stage advertisement testing. We want them to see real people — real consumers. Neither marketing managers nor agency creatives are likely to ever see real consumers in the course of most of their work. And then we need to communicate advertising research findings to them in a way they can best grasp. Listen to what Gregory Rathjen, a director of Account Planning and Research, has to say:

> It ought to be the job of researchers and planners to present information about the target consumer so that it is meaningful to creatives, who are the people who need it most.
>
> Unfortunately, too much consumer information is presented in terms of statistics, facts and numbers. That's great for account planners and marketers, who are pretty analytical, linear thinkers. But it isn't all that helpful for creatives, who think visually, spatially, intuitively, conceptually....
>
> The key is to humanize and personalize the research. Category Dynamics breaks the information about the target audience into six components: needs and desires, decision-making process, brand images, product expectations, current mind-set and desired mindset.
>
> Each of those components is then presented via graphics, on a board or in slides as a series of consumer comments expressed in the first person.
>
> For example, some of the needs/desires of customers of Henderson client Milliken Visa (a producer of napkins and linens for upscale restaurants) were presented this way: "Everything in my restaurant has to be just right" and "My clientele expects the best."[4]

Impatience and "Magic Numbers"

Many marketing managers really seem to be after an answer expressed by one "magic number" ("the commercial scored a 76.9"), and hope that this will end the research on the matter. Out of frustration, lack of thinking, or just habit, that magic number is all too often exactly what they get from researchers. It should be clear that one such number, without reference to diagnostic details or reference to objectives, is likely to be a very phony solution. Research should build on itself, not come to an end suddenly with one test of one commercial one time.

One number may be all right if we are studying, for example, one in a series of advertisements tested for recall over time, and reference is made to a vast and valid storehouse of norms. But for testing of a new advertisement, commercial, or campaign, where data should be related back not only to other numbers, but to the whole fabric of the marketing effort, one member just won't work. The researcher should never give in and pretend that the one number managers may want is all that they need to know.

HOW DO WE DO IT?

Battles and Paths

Advertising research sometimes seems like the talking dog. The striking thing is not that he talks so poorly, but that he talks at all. With the obstacles noted above, and the reluctance of researchers to exchange fads for common sense, it is often surprising there is any useful advertising research at all.

Battles rage. Is it the broad measure of awareness that matters in the long-run, or is it recall (perhaps the most graspable of notions) that matters? Or maybe persuasion is most important, or . . . ? There are endless battles of this sort, but there is really no need for conflict. How *can* there be just one way? The goals of different advertising differ, so what matters and what should be measured must change to fit the situation.

Consider the various things we may want the advertising to do (see above). And consider also that we may not even know what we want it to do. Finally, consider below just a few of the many executional devices that are used to try to get across whatever we may want to get across. Surely each path (and combinations of paths) will suggest a research approach of its own. Common devices (paths) include:

- **Slice-of-life**. Ordinary people recognize some problem; our brand appears and we say it can solve the problem. The people appear again and tell us that the brand has indeed solved the problem, and tell us also how it did this. Often, the issue of credibility is as important as recall. We want people to think: "Those people are like me, and they have the same kind of problem. Maybe the product will work for me, too!" Without credibility, recall does not matter.
- **Comparison**. Our brand vs. theirs. We can compare sharply, naming the competing brand and showing exactly why our brand is better. Or, the comparison can be fuzzy,

against a general "Brand X" or the "world of competitors". One thing we must measure, especially in sharp comparisons, is recall and impressions of the competing brand.

Consumers might gain a favorable impression of our brand, but an even more favorable one of theirs. (Because people do not always pay much attention to what is said. They simply hear the brand names in the background, to reinforce awareness.) We do not want our advertising building their sales.

- **Pack-as-hero.** Perhaps we present a new package: graphics, logo, opening, size, etc. Or maybe we need a major effort to get a current package emblazoned in the minds of the audience. Either way, we want it to "trigger" a reaction, a recall, at the point of purchase: "Yes, that's the package I saw in the advertising!"

  For low-involvement products, visual recall of the package can be much more important than copy recall. Since people do not think much about the characteristics of potato chips, it does not matter much whether they remember exactly what we said about our potato chips. But they must immediately recognize our package when they walk down the store aisle to get some potato chips.

- **Image.** Misty, atmospheric, maybe; or bright and clear. But no concrete message or information is being presented. So asking for "copy-point recall" in such a case is useless, regardless of the fact that it is often done in research. The message is not in the copy, but in the overall intuitive impression that viewers get.

  Consumers get impressions from images that McDonald's is fun for kids; good fun for the family; inexpensive; fast; clean; safe; part of the way we live today. Or Coca-Cola: the spirit of America for the young at heart all around the world. Or Marlboro: Marlboro Country (symbolized by the Cowboy, "The Marlboro Man") is the place to experience the spirit of freedom and adventure, where there are no geographical limits, just limits of the mind. Asking consumers to recall copy from mainstream McDonald's, Coke, or Marlboro advertising will not tell us anything about whether they are getting the message.

- **Simple demonstration.** This kind of advertising is often used if we need to show consumers how the product works. We may need to demonstrate if the product is complex or obscure, and consumers might not know how it works or what it is for. We might also want to demonstrate that our brand of a product they are familiar with works much better than other brands. (Maybe comparison is also used.) Here, we do need to measure exactly what people learned from the advertising, but what they learn may be in the visual presentation, not the copy.

- **Testimonial.** Use of important or famous people is supposed to lend credibility to advertising claims, enhance certain images we may be trying to project, or simply grab people's attention because they know the celebrity. Exactly what we need to measure depends on which among these and other reasons was the reason we have for using testimonial advertising. For example, when we use Michael Jackson to enhance Pepsi's image, we should do image research. When we use the Surgeon General of the United States to lend credibility to a message, we should measure message recall and credibility. And so forth.

- **Borrowed interest.** Something else: a festival or an event or such is the centerpiece, and the product sell (usually on the "soft" rather than "hard" side) is built around that. Often, we are just projecting a kind of image; we want people to subconsciously think: "When I am doing this, this product fits in well." (San Miguel, a beer, fits in well at sporting events.)

- **News.** A new product; a sale; a deadline; an offer; etc. Here, the key object is presenting some piece of information, so measuring how well people received the message is important.

TO WAR

We do advertising research with enormous forces, enormous budgets, and enormous fanfare, something like the "pomp and circumstance" of war itself. We need to look back on the ten things we ask of advertising (above) and see what approaches each suggests. Then, we need to look even further back, and think about what we know about the consumer and the buying situation. Appropriate research approaches are indeed needed in this never-ending war to test advertising well. For the war produces many casualties, only some of whom (the misunderstood thoughtful few) we need bother to mourn.

Awareness

In large-scale ad hoc or periodic tracking studies, or even in some limited small-scale ones, we ask at the start of a sequence something like: "When you think of (PRODUCT CATEGORY), what brand comes to mind first? What other brands have you heard of?" For those not mentioned, but on our list, ask: "Have you ever heard of (BRAND A)? how about (BRAND B)? and (BRAND C)? etc."

The first way of asking, without mentioning any specific brand, gives us brand awareness, *unaided*, including first mention, or "top-of-mind" awareness. But the second way of asking, where we specify brand A and the other brands, tells us *aided* awareness. These various brand awareness measures provide clues to the ultimate ability of the advertising to register the brand name on the mind. Often, we need both unaided and aided awareness of each brand of interest, since true awareness may actually lie somewhere between the levels.

But clearly, whether aided or unaided awareness tells us what we need to know depends on the specific buying situation. If consumers make up a specific shopping list before they go to the store, and stick to it while shopping, we would surely strive for high levels of unaided awareness. P&G wants Pringles to go onto the list when the shopper plans to buy potato chips. But where shopping is somewhat less planned, and the brand choice is made at the retail shelf, high aided awareness may be sufficient, even if unaided awareness is low. Once the consumer sees the packages, they will think: "Oh, yes, I remember this brand."

We can ask a similar series of awareness questions for the advertising itself, something like: "When you think about advertising for (PRODUCT CATEGORY), which brand's advertising comes to mind first? Which others? How about (BRAND A)? etc." Obviously, we can go deeper and seek awareness of slogans, spokesmen, action in the advertising, etc., depending on what aspect we need to know about. As always, we should ask only for what we need, and can use, and not for everything about the advertising. The more we ask for unimportant things, the less likely we are to get useful answers to those (usually limited) areas which are really vital for us.

Liking

For years, the "persuasion vs. recall" argument [see above] dominated [thinking in the research profession about advertising research]. But in a study released last year, the Advertising Research Foundation found that overall reaction to a commercial, or whether a viewer liked the spot, did better at predicting an ad's success than any of the other seven measures tested.

The study caused quite an uproar in the research industry. Russell Haley, who presented the results at an ARF workshop last summer, said that's because "no one had included [likability] in their standard battery of tests." Most of them had relied primarily on persuasion and recall, the other top two contenders in the study.[5]

Common sense had always suggested to many researchers that it was better, in general, to be liked than not. But before, no "liking" scale was well known, well tried, with proof that the results were useful. We have already mentioned that the industry can be maddeningly rigid at times. It was not used, so it should not be used, even though everyone vaguely felt that liking was important. Finally, someone broke through the rigidity and found that liking was, indeed, important.

Now that liking has "come out of the closet", we need not hesitate to delve into this element anymore. We can ask questions such as: "Some people like certain ads and commercials, while others do not. For each of the following, please tell me whether you like it a lot, like it a little, dislike it a little, or dislike it a lot?" After they answer each scale, we can ask "Why?"

Like all such sequences, liking questions will be varied to fit the methodology and the need. For example, they could be part of a broad survey such as a market study, which includes other topics such as questions on awareness. Or, consumers could answer liking questions in response to a direct exposure of advertising as a stimulus.

Remembering

One example of such testing might be giving a magazine to people, and having them take it home, on the pretext that we want their opinions about the articles. Then we call them back on the phone, usually the next day, hence "Day-After Recall" (or "DAR"). We ask (usually aided) for what they recalled about each advertisement in the magazine. Similar work can be done for television. We could go down a whole list of programs (from the TV listings, maybe) and try to elicit recall for the commercials on them. Or we could call people, and, having assured ourselves that they had the television on when a specific commercial appeared, ask recall questions about that commercial.

In a controlled situation, we can show advertisements either by themselves (so called "portfolio" tests), or embedded in editorial matter, or commercials alone or embedded in program matter. After exposure we ask respondents what advertisements or commercials they can recall. The variations are endless.

But the objectives are the same: Does it stick in the mind? Moreover, *what* sticks? Is it the trivial details of the presentation, or the core message of the product? Typical questions are: "What did it say?" "What did it show?" "What was it trying to get across?" etc.

An alternative, or sometimes complementary, method is *recognition* testing. Here we show an advertisement, commercial, etc., but cut out the brand name, and then ask what the brand name is. In theory, since people do not usually pay much conscious attention to names in most advertising (unless they have sought out the advertising), what matters is whether the name has stayed in their subconscious. We try to check this by asking them to play back the name when presented with the "clue", the advertising stimulus with the name excised. What has stuck in the corner of their mind? In practice, this might be one way to check on whether comparative advertising is building our brand or our competitor's.

Perception

After exposure to an advertisement or commercial, or on a general survey without specific exposure, we may ask respondents a series of questions on the image of the brand. Some of our image items may be oriented toward the brand itself (e.g., mildness, safety, uniqueness, etc.), and others to users of the brand (e.g., young, modern, "a brand for me", etc.). We can include questions of "pure fact", the "cognitive" element of perception (what I know for a fact — or think I know!).

Images can be derived from both advertising and use, if the respondent has actually used the product. And image can differ, depending on how people developed it. By including questions on use, we can examine whether images do, in fact, differ depending on whether people know of the product only from advertising, or from actual experience with it. (If our image strategy and execution are sound, there should be no differences. People should retain the same image when they are using the product that we told them the product had. But, of course, marketing is not always done perfectly.)

An abstract, isolated image does not tell us much, so we usually compare the image that is generated of our product to some other image. There are many ways to compare image data. For example, we can compare our brand's image against the respondent's "ideal" brand. We can compare it against our own ideal, what we would like to be seen as. We can see how our current image has changed (or not changed) relative to what it was in the past, when we were running different advertising with a different theme. We can compare against competitors' brand profiles now and in the past. All these ways help us measure what "positioning" we have established in people's minds: what our advertising is planting or misplanting.

Understanding, Belief, and Involvement

Understanding research is simple. In testing understanding, we expose respondents to advertising (hopefully in the pretesting stage) and then perhaps re-expose them to it (refocus the exposure). Responses can be unaided, after taking back an advertisement or shutting off the commercial ("What did this ad say?"). Responses can be aided ("You will notice that this ad says '(WHATEVER)'; what do you think they are trying to tell you by that?"). We can do both in sequence, first unaided, then aided, perhaps with a rerun of the commercial.

This is so simple, but it is often not done, even when consumer understanding is vital. If consumers do not understand advertising, even after obsessive "refocusing" in a research setting, are they likely to understand it if we go ahead and run it anyway? Testing understanding may, simply, be too simple to be fashionable among many weighty researchers. Yet it may be the most valuable of all advertising research. At least, such research is easy to grasp, because it is so simple. The importance of research methods which even marketing managers easily grasp should not be underestimated.

Belief is simple too, and is again too often undervalued, even when we are making a claim about the brand. Do viewers (or readers) believe the claim? Do they, perhaps, doubt it, but are willing to try the brand to see for themselves? Do they prefer trying it through a sample, rather than buying it themselves, so that they do not have to run the financial risk or psychological risk (of being laughed at by friends or relatives for being so gullible)? Ask them.

Do people care about what the advertising is saying, even if they believe it? This is the *involvement* dimension, again often undervalued because it, too, is so simple. We must look for clues here about how well our brand's advertising fits into the lifestyle, rituals, and aspirations of the respondent. We need to ask questions that tell us whether the consumer feels that "this ad is talking to me! I should pay attention. It is relevant". If, instead, we find out that they are thinking more like "this doesn't have anything to do with me. I don't need to pay attention", then we need to be very careful about further development of the advertising.

Persuasion

This measures the so-called "conative" ("likely-to-buy") dimension. This kind of research is very popular in the advertising research world. Measuring the likely-to-buy dimension is quite valid, so long as the advertising being measured directly seeks, in fact, to change likelihood-to-buy. But some advertising is some kind of image-oriented, misty, poetic, opaque, artsy-fartsy, self-indulgent advertising, or even seeks only to reinforce long-established images. This kind of advertising is not really trying to influence people's likelihood-to-buy directly, and therefore, measuring the likely-to-buy dimension does not yield anything useful.

The techniques for this kind of research are varied, but they mostly follow a simple pre-post (before-after) pattern. That is, we get information about images, cognitive material, likelihood-to-buy, etc., from respondents. Then we expose them to the advertising, and then we ask them the same questions again. Differences between the "pre" and the "post" figures are considered to be the "attitude-shift" ("persuasion") effect of the advertising.

We must be wary here of thinking we have really shifted attitudes if in fact the attitudes are deep-seated and go to the level of values or other deep-seated "core" beliefs. Has our advertising really touched such nerves? We must be very self-critical and avoid self-deception as we tackle this issue, and be very sure we know what we have affected and accomplished in a meaningful marketing way.

Purchase

Of course, as we have said, purchase is what we really care about. As we also noted, directly measuring the sales impact of advertising is very difficult except in certain specific situations. If we do coupon advertising, we can find out directly whether it led to purchase by counting those who send in the coupon and later buy. When consumers must order through the mail in response to a direct mail campaign, a mail order is certainly a direct response to the direct mail advertising. Sometimes retail advertising may be structured so that sales impact can be directly measured (e.g., advertising for "one-day-only!" sales).

Otherwise, when we do not have situations similar to these, direct measurement of the sales impact is very difficult. There are too many factors clouding the picture, like timing, competitive response, and endless unmeasureables ("noise"). Then, we have to get all the "intervening" variable measurements discussed above to help guide us.

Today, with "single source" research, we can come closer to directly measuring the sales effect of exposure to media. In essence, we recruit a panel of consumers, and use scanners in stores and in homes to record all their purchases. We also record their television viewing, and magazine and newspaper reading. A.C. Nielsen Co. is one of the suppliers of such integrated services. In seeking to directly relate viewing to buying, that company

> is filling an acknowledged gap in its single-source research services by including tracking of print media.
>
> The Nielsen Magazine Measurement Service is being phased in as an adjunct of the Scan Track National Electronic Household Panel.
>
> The panel's 18,000 households nationally use handheld bar-code scanners to record all purchases, including prices and whether each item was on sale. That information is then correlated with TV viewing patterns measured by people meters.
>
> Those same scanners will be used now to record the magazines and weekday and weekend newspapers read by each adult household member. Each periodical will have a coded card panel members scan when the periodical has been read by a household member. Information is transmitted weekly over phone lines to Nielsen.

"The notion of single-source research has been to capture all media influences and purchases. In practice, that has focused on TV. . . [but] now we're following that single-source concept and pursuing [print media influences] more vigorously with a consistent measurement approach."

Tracking exposure to print media will improve Scan Track's picture of causal influences on purchase patterns and provide an additional tool for brand managers and media buyers.[6]

But *tool* is what single-source research is, not a panacea, an answer for everything. And like any tool, it must be constantly rethought and reconfigured to meet changing needs and possibilities. As noted above, Nielsen has added magazines and newspapers to its service. It has also gotten away from the notion of recording panelists' purchases in stores (using bar code scanner data recorded by salesclerks), and is moving towards collecting all such data in the home, by using the "wand" to be "waved" over bar-coded purchases.

We may well ask whether "single-source" research, combining media usage and buying, and loaded into computer databases, will eventually obviate the need for all the other kinds of things we do in advertising research: recall, comprehension, persuasion, etc. Churchill has considered this question:

Clearly, one of the primary causes for anxiety about the health of custom marketing research is the impact of single source data systems and related syndicated scanner-based services. There are certainly other problems unrelated to technological developments, but undoubtedly the conventional survey research business has already undergone some displacement by single source data services. The question on everyone's mind seems to be, "Is there a role for attitude and survey research in the post-scanner-data world?"

The sky is not falling. Ad hoc survey research is still valued and relied upon as much as ever. It remains the major concern of corporate research directors and the area of research activity that demands the major share of their resources and staff recruitment effort. Moreover, the collective expectation of these people is that custom research will continue to occupy a position of high priority in terms of corporate investment, and will continue to be a tool that contributes mightily to marketing strategy and planning. . . .

[Some research directors] made the plausible argument that single source systems frequently do not provide confident answers to "why" some observable market phenomenon is occurring. Their internal clients — brand managers and agency partners — need to know the "whys" in order to perform their roles. Or, as one of the research directors put it, "Scanners do a good job of looking into people's wallets, but they're not very good for looking into their heads and hearts."

Another research director described scanner-based data systems as largely evaluative, whereas conventional survey research tends to be developmental and diagnostic. Marketing managers need both.[7]

Post-Purchase Reassurance

It is not enough to get people to buy. We want repeat purchases. Or at least we need to keep our brand high up in the "evoked set" — those brands or companies consumers would consider the next time they are in the market. We may wish to put such "reassurance" advertising right in the product itself ("Congratulations! You have just bought the best there is . . . we hope you enjoy it and buy it again whenever you are in the market").

If we can get a list of our users, we can do periodic telephone follow-up surveys. (Increasingly often, we collect data on users through coupon offers, so that we gradually build up a database on current and past users.) Of course, we must divorce the questions from any tie-in with coupons or any specific brand. The survey sponsor must be anonymous or results will be biased. So the consumer knows nothing about "follow-up". To them, it is just another survey, in which we ask what they are buying or using now, what their "evoked set" is, whether they remember the "reassurance" advertising, etc.

Marketers also know that something called "cognitive dissonance" exists. After people buy something (especially a major purchase of goods or services), they become more aware than ever of competitive advertising, since they are now involved with the product. They can well begin to doubt the wisdom of their purchase. We must monitor this carefully.

This post-purchase phase is the last step in the purchase process, *not* the purchase itself. We must be prepared to offer feedback to management about all phases of the purchase process. Furthermore, the whole process itself is not really a linear chain, but a feedback loop. Post-purchase experience with the product feeds back into other stages, affecting awareness, liking, image, and so on. We need to constantly review what consumers think about everything as they gain more experience with our product. This constant review helps us gain an ever sharper picture, partly because they have increasingly sharp pictures of how they view the brand.

KEY CONSIDERATIONS IN ADVERTISING RESEARCH

In advertising research, which some would argue is perhaps the most complex part of marketing research, we must forever be aware of (and beware of) fads, fancies, systems, and the self-interest involved in selling such fads, fancies, and systems. The possibilities are vast. We must always seek to combine the best and the most appropriate possibilities in clear-headed analysis and consistency. Old methods (fads, fancies, systems) may well work best, or may well not work, depending on the situation. New methods constantly arise from new technology. Because of ever-changing promotional strategy and execution, new needs constantly come up requiring new methods, adaptation of old methods, or new ways of looking at old methods.

Advertising research can be product-centered (as in image-battery work), or advertising-centered (as in research on remembering, understanding, and believing). It can measure one ad (or commercial or whatever) or a whole campaign. It can look at our own advertising only, or evaluate how we stand relative to the competition. Advertising research can be "natural" (on-air, in-magazine) or "controlled" (leaning toward the experiment side). It can be "diagnostic" ("fix it if possible") or "evaluative" ("keep it or kill it"). It may cover one medium (maybe print) or cross media (comparing magazines to television). It may use generic techniques (suitable for any medium) or techniques suitable to one medium only.

Finally, when we do advertising research we must accept the fact that the purchase process chain (really a feedback loop) is long, from awareness to post-purchase reassurance. Each step offers different challenges and has different focuses, from recall to understanding to persuasion and all the other elements cited in this chapter. Some parts of the research can be combined, and multiple measures used. Some parts must be explored alone. Some can (and must) be done repeatedly, while some can only be done once (like on-air Day-After Recall (DAR) testing).

A willingness to be flexible, imaginative, strong, and useful must be the advertising researcher's basic creed as he works with marketing managers and advertising agencies. Only arrogant stubbornness is unacceptable.

16

Promotion: "Below-the-Line" Activities

If advertising research (Chapter 15) is the biggest part of the whole marketing research world, then the testing of everything else in the promotion mix, the "below-the-line" part, is probably the smallest. Surely it is one of the most overlooked, along with "place" research (Chapter 14). Because of its visibility and glamour, advertising research is loved by researchers for its excitement and their ability to make their mark at it. Testing of "below-the-line" (BTL) activities is at best ignored.

This is both strange and unfortunate, since the scope of BTL activities in marketing is enormous, and growing. According to Donnelley Marketing's Annual Survey of Promotional Practices, as a percentage of total US promotional expenditures in 1991, for example, media advertising ("above-the-line") accounted for only 25 percent of expenditures. The balance was divided between trade promotions (50 percent) and consumer promotions (25 percent).[1] As Anthony O'Reilly, Chairman-CEO of H.J. Heinz Co. noted: "Because two-thirds of all food buying decisions are made in the store, we stress deals, allowances, and trade promotions that strengthen our presence at that critical point of sale."[2]

The scope of BTL activities is enormous, as the list below (not exhaustive, surely) may suggest. The first group is aimed at consumers, and it is these (and similar things) that are often collectively termed "sales promotion":

- Consumer deals: Money-off coupons, gifts-with-purchase, etc.
- In-store consumer activities: Merchandising, point-of-sale material (also called POP: point-of-purchase), banners, special displays, etc.
- Contests
- Sweepstakes
- Sampling

Secondly, there are BTL programs aimed at the trade. These include:

- "Free goods", allowances, deals, cooperative advertising, slotting allowances, etc. All of these are aimed at the trade, as part of a trade "push" strategy to complement a consumer "pull" strategy.

Other BTL activities include:

- Public relations: The ongoing program to create and maintain a good image of the company, to deflect bad news, and plan for crisis control. This realm of corporate communications is so complex and addresses so many of the firm's divergent publics (customers, employees, etc.) that it would better be called Publics Relations.
- Publicity: Notices in media that often look like articles, etc., but are really "planted" there as news (to increase source credibility), but definitely don't look like advertisements.
- Event marketing: Special "events" promoted by (and perhaps even created by) the marketer.
- Sponsorships.
- Corporate graphics.
- Trade shows and exhibitions.
- Seminars.
- Direct marketing.

BTL AND RESEARCH

Two Sides

It is beyond the scope of this chapter to explore each of these areas of BTL activities in detail. But it should be obvious that many of them essentially complement the basic function of media advertising ("above-the-line"), supporting efforts to build the brand's name, image, and equity. Indirect BTL appeals to "BUY" include public relations, publicity, event marketing, sponsorships, corporate graphics, trade shows and exhibitions, and seminars. Research here is quite clear: the marketer needs to know about awareness and effect. But although the key issues are clear, the direction of the research is not always apparent. There is often a lack of clarity about the target group, when the research should be done, and, indeed, *if* it should be done at all.

Other activities essentially do not subtly suggest that we "buy". Rather, they scream out: "BUY NOW!" These activities include trade programs, consumer deals, contests, sweepstakes, sampling, and, of course, the most direct solicitation of all to "BUY NOW": direct marketing. In this group of activities, "counting" (company sales, audits, scanners, etc.) is quite possible, and often valuable in measuring impact. "Counting" should be used together with surveys (involving contests, sweepstakes, sampling, etc.), to see which consumers are exposed, possibly compare them with non-exposed consumers, and to discover what effect, if any, the activity had.

Why Not Research?

It is obvious that a vast amount of valuable marketing information can be derived from research into BTL activities. So why is there so little BTL research? The answer is three-fold.

First, in the old days, BTL was often considered "throw-away" stuff. Marketers did BTL with whatever budget was left over after the "important" activities of media advertising had been carried out. Yet, while BTL is now actually the *dominant* part of the promotion mix, old habits are hard to break. There is little interest here on the part of marketing managers, little glamour, little glory. It is all very easy to pass it all by, when so many other more fun things are around. If that is how marketing managers feel, it is not surprising that few marketing researchers take a strong interest in BTL research. They do not see how they can be a hero by doing this kind of work. Unfortunately, they are usually right. They cannot become heroes by focusing on BTL.

Second, researchers who would like to do BTL research find it very difficult to do so. There is little history of how it has been done, few precedents to guide us, so often research must come up with new approaches or new ways to apply old approaches. Of course, there is nothing wrong with that, and we should always consider whether new ways might work better in any research. Nevertheless, we have already noted that marketing research can at times be maddeningly conservative and tied to the tried and true. Obstacles to developing the new areas of BTL research seem to abound: getting names, getting accurate information from brand managers on what was and is being done, etc.[3]

Third, and worst of all, marketers often genuinely do not *want* to know about the effect of BTL. Many of the elements in the BTL arsenal are frequently whimsical (to help get the CEO onto the Board of Directors of the local Symphony Orchestra, maybe); egoistic extensions of the CEO's fancies (like sponsoring soccer or skydiving); or somehow socially motivated, but only vaguely connected with the business and its interests. It is not surprising that nobody wants to research this to see if it has any value to the company. There could be big trouble if we found out that it does not, in fact, have any impact on sales, or awareness, or image, or anything else. Rational appeals by the researcher in attempts to do anything in this area are apt to be met by silence or scorn.

Yet in spite of the reluctance of many marketers to seriously assess the effects of BTL activities of all sorts, useful research has been done, and much more can be done. From a marketing standpoint, here is what Blattberg[4] reported that BTL research has discovered:

- Promotions explain a significant percentage of sales volume to the consumer. In high volume categories of consumer nondurable goods, 30 to 70 percent of a brand's volume (to the consumer) is sold on promotion. A higher percentage of durable goods volume is sold on promotion.
- Promotions appear to be the single most effective marketing device for increasing *short-run* volume.
- Consumers stockpile and accelerate their purchases when a deal is offered.
- Retailers forward buy and divert products when trade deals are offered.

Some of the questions he says still need to be addressed are:[5]

- Do consumers develop expectations about when promotions will be run and therefore wait for deals? That possibility particularly affects durable goods manufacturers and retailers.

- How do coupons work? Are they simply offering discounts to current buyers, do they attract switchers, and do they attract new customers?
- What percentage of the population prefers promotions and what percentage prefers everyday low pricing? What do those percentages imply about the long-run viability of promotions?

EXAMPLES OF BTL RESEARCH

In spite of the reluctance to conduct BTL research, some work nonetheless has been done. We can briefly examine several examples of what has been done, and suggest what more could be done.

Consumer-Oriented Sales Promotion

In-store sales data, via audits or scanners, can be done to see what's going on. The effects of deals, whether advertised in media or just in the store, or both, can now be readily assessed on a day-by-day (even hour-by-hour) basis to help marketing target them more effectively. Overall, one recent study examined the

> effects of sales promotion on brand switching in 10 product categories: alcoholic beverages, automobiles, batteries, coffee, floor coverings, motor oil, personal appliances, pet food, shampoo, and toothpaste.
>
> In five of those categories — batteries, coffee, personal appliances, shampoo, and toothpaste — the survey found that promotions can persuade a majority of consumers to try a different brand.
>
> Promotions are more effective in persuading consumers to change the brands of products they feed to their pets or use in their cars.
>
> The study also found that the likelihood of a consumer switching brands because of a promotion decreased with age. In eight of the 10 categories, respondents of ages 18–34 typically showed a 10 percent greater likelihood to switch brands than the 35 to 54 year olds, and a 20–30 percent greater likelihood than those respondents age 55 and over.[6]

Couponing offers particularly rich possibilities for research, since it is possible to get names and brand usage data. The marketing objective of much couponing, as well as of sampling, is to entice competitive brand users to switch to *our* brand. We need to see if this switching, in fact, happens, rather than use of coupons by people who already buy our brand. (Reaching only our own customers merely lets them have for less what they would buy at the regular price, anyway.)

Survey data suggest, for example, that brands with high market shares do not attract a lot of competitive brand users because most consumers who use other brands have already tried the leading brand at one time or another. Other data suggest that food categories attract more users of competing brands than non-food categories.[7]

Note that these data on food categories echo the results cited above, which included coffee as a particularly promising product category in which to gain new triers through consumer promotions. It is precisely this building up of ideas from survey to survey that makes it necessary not only to do thoughtful research, but also to conceive of research as a "program", not just a series of isolated studies.

All sorts of analyses on the effectiveness of promotions can be undertaken, including memorability, perceptions of uniqueness, and how they stand out in general from the whole huge agglomeration of such promotions in the marketplace. Above all, perhaps, we need to constantly try to measure whether the money we spend is a good investment. Despite the fact that BTL research is far less common than advertising research, it is really more feasible to measure the sales impact for sales promotion than for media advertising. So much of advertising is devoted to building images and longer-term effects — "buy sometime" — that measuring the impact at a specific "now" is difficult. Much sales promotion is oriented toward "buy now", so measuring the impact at a specific "now" can be easier.

So a simple measurement of sales promotion payout can be easily contemplated. For example, in a sampling effort, we could keep track of the names of those who participated (received a sample) and contact them to answer our survey. Basic calculations might look like this:

Cost of samples (10,000 @ $10)	$100,000 (a)
Converts (people who now use the brand	
regularly but who did not use it regularly before they got the sample)	200 (b)
Value of each convert (net contribution to margin per year)	$170 (c)
Total value of converts per year (b × c)	$34,000 (d)
PAYOUT PERIOD (a/d)	2.9 years

To make these calculations, we need questions to measure brand switching and brand loyalty (i.e., to calculate the number 200). We also need a measure of purchase frequency (to calculate the value $170). Of course, we must be sure that the questions do *not* reveal that the survey is really about our sampling and our brand. If respondents know the survey sponsor, some might think "I didn't like the sample. I am not really going to buy the product. But I don't want these people to feel bad. They have gone to a lot of trouble, giving me a sample, so I will say I plan to buy it in the future".

Calculations like those above should be neither overly complicated nor too simplistic. There must be goodwill to search the financial records, or better yet, there should be agreement *in advance* to keep close track of financial performance (here, costs of $10,000). Then, some sort of measure (questions) can be devised so that we can make the other calculations. Even imperfect measures will be better than nothing. Once we have figured out the questions for calculating impact, we can figure out the other questions needed for other analysis. Maybe we would want to see such things as whether previous exposure to our or competing promotions influences the impact, or whether different segments of the market respond differently.

Trade Deals

Conceptually, measuring the impact of trade deals is no different from measuring how consumer promotions work. Careful monitoring of trade deals must include keeping track of incremental sales to the trade (the difference between what is normally sold and what was sold during the trade promotion). The impact on profitability can easily be computed. This analysis should be complemented by ongoing interviewing of key people in the distribution chain, as noted in Chapter 14. We need to keep our finger on the pulse of what our channel members want, *not* what we want to give them.

Indirect Appeals

Recall that many BTL activities, such as public relations, publicity, event marketing, sponsorships, and corporate graphics, make essentially subtle, indirect appeals to buy. Each of these BTL activities should be undertaken with specific goals in mind, otherwise, there is really nothing to measure. (If we have no goal, nothing we want to achieve, there is no real need to see if we have achieved it.) These goals can be associated with any of the phases of a company's marketing planning: the corporate mission (to be reassessed perhaps); the scenarios managers envision, how they might react to some, and act proactively in anticipating others; marketing strategies; and marketing tactics.

Much of the time, though, unfortunately, there are no goals, just egos and fuzziness. Then we have to assume goals anyway, if someone wants the research done anyway. We can measure awareness (did anybody notice?), assuming that one purpose of the activity was to get people to notice our company. We can measure reaction (did anybody care?), assuming that we were trying to get people involved in thinking about our products. We can measure usage, assuming that the purpose was to increase sales. In other words, there are things we can do to carry out research, but we still need to work with goals, even if management has none.

But if there *are* goals and there *is* a will, then these highly notional, fragile, and volatile elements can be measured quite effectively, to provide useful input for better-informed marketing decisions. The impact of public relations, for example, can surely be usefully researched. Much more can be learned than by just counting the number of clippings in the press our public relations campaign generated. Goal-oriented public relations must be trying to achieve more (and more concrete) things than just "keeping our name in front of the public". Rather, public relations can be a vital part of an integrated BTL mix, helping to build favorable images, generate interest in our products, and so forth.

Once clear, explicit goals are stated, it is easy to tie measurements to them. One government agency (the Connecticut Department of Transportation, ConnDOT) provides a good example of using public relations well and measuring it seriously. In developing the public relations campaign, they began by using quantitative research, which included five focus groups of single-occupancy vehicle (SOV) commuters, car/vanpoolers, bus and train riders, and business, community, and transportation officials, followed by a telephone survey of 800 commuters.

From this research they were able to learn that most commuters:[8]

- Drove alone more than 80 percent of the time.
- Felt ConnDOT should lead ride-sharing efforts, but should not be the sole source of help and information.
- Preferred hearing about specific ride-sharing incentives and disincentives rather than generalities. Messages should be positive, light.
- Felt the best benefits of ride sharing were that it saved money and wear and tear on cars, and that it made commuting easier, less stressful, and more fun.
- Were interested in employer-based ride-sharing programs.
- Said major obstacles to ride sharing included convenience of driving their own cars, stable gasoline prices, widely available free parking.

With this information in mind, ConnDOT decided to develop the program theme, logo and jungle to address commuters' preference for a state-led, positive program. ConnDOT also set goals on the basis of this research: to begin to raise the commuting public's awareness of ride sharing and to start making ride sharing a top-of-mind issue. Recognizing the complexity of the issue and the many ride-sharing obstacles outside its control, it set the following objectives:[9]

- Raise awareness among 25 percent of commuters of ride-sharing and public transit opportunities.
- Heighten awareness among at least 10 percent of commuters of the negative aspects of riding alone.
- Achieve public recognition among 10 percent of commuters of the campaign message.

The program was then implemented, and the effectiveness of the program was assessed. ConnDOT selected media targets and public relations activities based on the demographics and interests of commuters that the research had identified as associated with people most likely to share rides. After nine months of program activities, ConnDOT sampled 400 commuters in the three targeted counties. This follow-up research showed that:[10]

- 39 percent said they heard more about carpools, vanpools, or public transportation opportunities than a year ago.
- 34 percent said news about the advantages of riding together increased or greatly increased.
- 18 percent said news about the disadvantages of driving alone to work increased or greatly increased.
- 14 percent recalled the campaign theme.

The tracking research also identified issues and commuter hot buttons that would become important in ConnDot's subsequent program activities.

It is also desirable to research our participation in trade shows and our performance in seminars. Questionnaires may be handed out to participants with a self-addressed, stamped envelope. No effort should be made to identify the sponsor of the survey — indeed every effort should be made to *disguise* it. Alternatively, interviewers can be stationed right at the site. Questions should center on what the attendees liked best and least, why, and open-ended remarks they may wish to make.

Direct Marketing

For this vital tool, research is readily available, more easily indeed than for anything else. We know what we spent, how much spending works out to per inquiry, and how many inquiries ultimately lead to a sale. We can use "split samples" to compare one approach to another, and we can compare everything to previous efforts of a similar nature. With the name, address, and phone number of the buyer, we can readily conduct follow-up research (always divorcing it from any mention whatever of the direct marketing program) to determine repurchase, attitudes towards the product, needs and wants, etc. Data can easily be cross-tabulated by demographics, psychographics, etc.

17

The Market Study

The *market study*, is the "crown jewel" of quantitative research. It sets out to deter-mine size and shape: what the boundaries are right now, and how they might be reshaped, expanded, or both. The market study seeks to take a snapshot of what is out there in the market *now*. And, in the course of repeating it, market studies show what is happening again, at a later time. Marketers can compare, contrast, analyze, and then act upon the trends they see emerging: the snapshot becomes a moving picture.

Through this ongoing process, market studies seek to examine the present, understand the past, and predict the future. Past, present, and future, of course, all interweave. So, too, do the two major areas of marketing that research continually seeks to cast light on: the "market" (the consumer) and the "product" (the marketer). It is the "matching" of these two upon which marketing success rests, and which this type of research seeks to uncover.

The market study recognizes that we and our competitors have our "consumer offers" out there for people to accept — or reject. To discover exactly whose consumer offer they are likely to accept or reject when faced with a choice, market studies must set out clearly defined and implementable objectives. With these objectives, market studies boldly explore what the world (the market) thinks, what it does, and who, specifically, thinks and does what. There is no room for timidly reining in our study because we are not sure we will like what we find out.

Specifically, what market studies most often cover can be broadly classified into two main areas: consumer (market) segmentation based on demographics, psycho-graphics, end-benefits, or some other segmentation variable; and product differenti-ation. Each type of focus leads to clues to strategic and tactical marketing action.

Haley has pointed out that there can be confusion over the two notions:

Market segmentation is customer oriented. It attempts to identify customer subgroups of the market as they currently exist. The presumption is that once such segments have been identified and understood, it is possible to focus marketing activities on them in such a way as to achieve relatively deep penetration of segments and, at the same time, to make it uneconomic and otherwise difficult for competitors to mount effective counterattacks.

Product differentiation, on the other hand, is product oriented. It concerns the identification of subgroups of competing products. Once this has been accomplished, attempts can be made to favorably differentiate the brand of interest from its principal competitors. The presumption is that some restructuring of the market is possible — that an unspecified consumer target will perceive the product, in its new and differentiated position, to be superior to alternative choices and therefore will try it.[1]

Both market segmentation and product differentiation are vital, integral parts of the successful marketing study, as well as of marketing itself. They must be sewn together seamlessly in the study and become its foundation stone.

THE SETTING OF THE MARKET STUDY
The Urgent Note

Often, usually when management is worried, some question comes down from above, like: "Why aren't we doing better?" As long as sales and profits are good, these guys think it perfectly fine to ignore the fact that we do not really know anything about our markets, about our customers. But when sales and profits start falling, even most managers realize that ignorance is not bliss. They can no longer ignore the fact that they do not know why. This sort of thing may well set off the market study. So a market study may be commissioned to answer questions such as:[2]

- What is the real brand franchise situation and what is the most realistic prognosis for its future?
- Are the brand's difficulties only temporary or is it in big trouble?
- Is the deterioration a function of current economic conditions? Have our competitors suddenly gotten better and started making some smart moves? Are there specific problems with our own marketing: deficiencies in our product, pricing, distribution, or promotional campaign?
- Is the market itself changing, due to changing lifestyles, changing values, or other broad marketplace forces? This, too, can shift demand within the product category.

For the market study to move ahead with good prospects of furnishing useful and usable information, it must focus on objectives rather than recriminations, and management's panic must yield to order. If it can do this, a market study can be extraordinarily productive.

Using the "backward" approach of Chapter 4, it is time to think about what management really needs and what it is really saying to us. The standard course of action involves looking at the end first and then using the "rewind" button. Where do we start? We will probably start with secondary ("desk") research and explore all the various "Answers Without Questions" possibilities mentioned in Chapter 6. We need to understand more about the problem at hand. Once we have understood as much as we can, we will probably be ready to proceed ahead to quantitative work.

Most important of all, to make the market study (or any research) meaningful, there must be a commitment to use the findings, in ways that are predictable. One should also understand that sometimes it is even better to use findings in unpredictable ways; i.e., we (and marketing managers) need flexibility if we find things we did not expect. Because, once we reach the end of the study:

> [We] . . . have an idea of who [our] consumers are, who they are not and what [our] and [our] competition's strengths and weaknesses are. [We] are ready to put together either a short or longer term plan of action to take both [our] consumers and [our] competition by surprise.
>
> The tactical strategy now is speed, for as Sun Tze (the author of a classic Chinese text on warfare) wrote: "When the thunder clap comes there is no time to cover the ears." We are frequently competing with companies who reach similar strategic decisions and the person who wins the battle is the one who gets there first.
>
> We all see the same information about the marketplace and can obtain the same information about competitors and consumers. The key is to come up with the unexpected and undiscovered and incorporate this into our strategic plans. Don't be satisfied with a cursory view of the available facts. Dig deeper and discover what lies beneath the surface. Then challenge your organization to come up with daring and exciting new ways to exploit these finding.[3]

The research department should push, with all the vision and firepower it can command, to see that such a commitment has been made to boldly use the new knowledge. We are committing much in time, money, and professional skills. We may be deciding the long-term (surely the near-term) course of the company's marketing efforts. We are about to do a Market Study.

The Proactive Move

If we are lucky, marketing management understands and values the role of research even when there is no apparent trouble on the horizon. Marketing is supposed to be market oriented, after all, and to be market oriented, we need to know about the market. Some marketing managers *do* understand this, and the market study fits right in with how these marketers do things.

Suppose our work with product R&D is moving along well, and we have learned what technology is available and what we can probably make. We know something about what concepts offer potential (from Chapter 10). But for whom? And how many of them? Exactly what product configuration will really suit them best? How will it fit into their lifestyles? What will they have to give up?

We are in a marketing-oriented company now, so we want to know all these things *before* we move too far toward product launch, not later on when we need to figure out why we are in trouble.

Some of these things are the stuff of the New Product Study (Chapter 18). But the market study goes beyond that. It looks not only at this specific opportunity, but also puts on our futurist's hat. We try to see beyond the boundary of this specific product, so that when tomorrow comes, we will be there to greet it. We want our products to be instrumental in making that tomorrow what it will be.

The Tracking Study

The setting is different again. In this situation, management has resolved that they want to know what is happening in the market on an ongoing and timely basis. We are neither looking for a special opportunity at a specific time, nor reacting in excessive haste, if not panic. Rather, tracking studies seek to keep tabs on the market in an orderly, systematic, way. This provides insights for marketing management on where we have been, where we are, and where we are going — the only three questions, in fact, that marketing managers ever need to get answers to, because they encompass everything we might need to know.

This study can be done as we wish, "tracking" the market as a hunter tracks his prey (our "prey" is consumers, whom we need to capture not by stealth or force, but by making sure they get what they want). It can be done periodically, maybe annually or quarterly, but during the same month each time, to remove problems of seasonality. It can be done continually, collating data for a report whenever it seems right. Or, it can done at special times, maybe after something has happened in the market, like a new campaign that we should be measuring to see if anything is happening.

Tracking studies can be done in personal interviews (essential, of course, if we have to present stimuli like ads or packages); by mail; or by telephone. They can sometimes be done using quota samples entirely or in part. Perhaps we would want to oversample to make sure we get enough people who use a certain brand. But most tracking studies are more likely to use a probability sample, often on a household basis, with random selection of respondents within. Since the studies are done many times, our numbers must be comparable to each other within the limits set by sampling variation.

Tracking studies can be done using exactly the same questions each time the study is done again. Or, we can continuously revise the questionnaire, deleting some questions as they no longer provide useful information and adding questions as new issues come up. The market, after all, changes, and we do not need to continue asking about typewriter usage if all our customers have switched to word processors.

In short, market studies can encompass almost any aspect of research we have discussed in this book. There are no hard and fast rules except concern and usefulness, which we have assured before we start. And so we do a market study.

POSSIBILITIES OF THE MARKET STUDY

The possibilities for what we can cover in a market study are diverse, and the real issue is usually not what to include, but what to leave out. We must determine what is relevant now and potentially useful up ahead, rather than ask about everything that everybody may have a passing interest in at this time. Similarly, the real technical concern is usually not what statistical techniques to use to analyze the data, but what *not* to use. We must apply those techniques that will enlighten and not merely bedazzle. Nothing should ever be reduced to mere formula, even in a market tracking study where we may have asked the question many times before.

This is especially true when we venture out into international research, where conditions may not be as they are at home. For example, in the lands of Eastern Europe, once communist-dominated, and now "hot spots" for growth, the researcher will have to take into account the following challenges:

Market research in the [former] Soviet Union can be different compared to research in most Western countries, and it presents some unique challenges. . . .

Communications and travel are difficult, productivity is low, and the market research industry is not at all developed.

Such problems are not especially new for international researchers, but there's one characteristic of the Soviet economy that most of us have never dealt with: widespread product shortages. . . .

Researchers must consider the reality of Soviet life when designing, carrying out, and interpreting surveys conducted in the Soviet Union.

Because of the product shortages, many questions that might be asked in Western industrialized countries (or even most of the Third World) make no sense in the Soviet Union. For example, though a number of domestic and foreign brands of toothpaste are sold in the Soviet Union, measurement of market share for a particular brand is an iffy proposition.

There are many questions about purchase behavior that we all routinely ask consumers. For example, we ask them what brand was bought last and what brand is bought most often.

These questions seem harmless enough, but they are often misleading in the context of product shortages.

The brand purchased is more of an indication of availability than preference. Brands in the market change from month to month due solely to availability, and measurements at two different points in time, even if only a matter of one or two months, can often produce vastly different pictures of the market.

Asking consumers what brand is preferred or asking them to rate different brands according to specific characteristics may give answers that could lead the researcher in the wrong direction in two different ways.

First, shortages limit consumers' experience with various brands, and unfamiliarity could result in a low rating because the consumer prefers only the one he or she knows about.

Second, it's possible that foreign brands will be overrated in comparison to domestic brands. This is due to the common assumption that foreign brands are superior in quality to those manufactured domestically, even if respondents have never tried the foreign brand.

The concept of a brand name simply does not have the same meaning to the Soviet consumer as to the Westerner. There is little in the way of brand image as we know it, because consumers are generally not exposed to brand advertising. Also, a single local Soviet factory will churn out a vast amount of a product with multiple brand names. Brand names, thus, have little meaning to the average Soviet consumer. The country of origin, however, does have meaning.

We also routinely ask consumers when they last bought a particular product, how many packages were bought that last time, and what size of pack was bought. Again, Soviet shopping practices will produce some very unusual results when viewed in the context of normal market conditions.[4]

For China, where there are many mutually unintelligible major dialects plus a "national" language (though only one written language unifying over 1.1 billion people), other research issues arise.

> It is essential that interviewers speak the local dialect and carry the accent of the city to win the people's confidence. . . .
>
> To conduct market research in China, it is important to bear in mind that you are collecting data in a country that is accustomed to closing its door to the rest of the world for a long time.
>
> The line between information and intelligence is not clearly drawn in China. You must remember that it is a society that has just recently opened its door to outsiders.
>
> Some people are not quite willing to provide information, especially to foreigners. China does not want to show too much of itself to the world.
>
> A few do's and don'ts are critical to carrying out market research in China:
> - Obviously, you must avoid asking politically sensitive questions or questions that may be considered a challenge to government policy.
> - You should allow plenty of time for the necessary liaison work with the appropriate government authorities. . . .[5]

Market studies need not cover just one country. Indeed, with the development of economic trading blocs (the Single European Market, the North American Free Trade Association, emerging Asia-Pacific trading blocs), cross-national research has already become more common. Writing about pan-European brands, Lannon notes:

> . . . the structures of the major markets are increasingly comparable. . . Aging populations, declining youth populations, rising divorce and remarriage rates, smaller households and so forth are features of all markets with comparable levels of affluence.
>
> . . . social trends also cross borders . . . green awareness, interest in health and fitness, home centeredness, creative use of leisure time, (and) female careerism . . . are showing up in the main markets . . .
>
> . . . successes (have occurred where) there are target groups that cross borders . . . the young . . . the rich . . . the business community. All of these groups have been "global" for some time.[6]

In a world where the market study may be as narrow as a single city, or as broad as the whole world, the premium more and more is on "think" and not on "thing".

ORGANIZATION OF THE MARKET STUDY

The organization of the questionnaire for the market study is quite free, but often the sections appear in an order we call "ABC":

A is for *Awareness*, followed by *Attitude*. What do people know (cognition) or think they know (image), to form perception. What are their opinions about key things (importance of various elements to choice, ratings and rankings of brands, satisfactions and dissatisfactions, etc.).

B is for *Behavior* (purchasing, usage, etc.).

C is for *Characteristics* (demographics and psychographics).

The order is, of course, suggestive rather than definitive, but the flow is logical: What is the horizon of consciousness (awareness)? What do respondents think about it all (attitude)? How do they act in the world (behavior)? And what are they (characteristics)?

In the best market studies, these and other elements will interweave, threads from one logically derive from somewhere and lead somewhere else. They will interlock, so that they hold together in a cohesive way. They will synergize, so that the whole is a powerful instrument, drawing on the parts and, in the end, being more than just a simple addition of numerous questions.

Finally, the study should deal with every part of the company's planning process. At least it should examine every part before we finalize the study, to see what needs to be researched out in the market. Do we need to study the corporate mission, the very reason for being? This would involve measuring the company's image, perhaps, in addition to the image of its brands. We must decide if we need to research scenarios, (management's alternative visions for the future); or corporate strategies; or tactics. Of course, most marketing studies also cover aspects of the four P's (product, price, place, promotion). Other parts of the "micromarketing" mix, controllable things, are also researched — like other P's: positioning, packaging, personality, premise, promise, proposition. Macromarketing C's, the "uncontrollables", are researched, like competition, change, culture, etc. So are the M's, executional elements like media, money, message, and all the rest.

ELEMENTS OF THE MARKET STUDY

Awareness

Measuring awareness can involve asking respondents a whole host of things. Many of the questions simply seek to find out if people have heard of products. We ask which brands they can name unaided. We are often particularly interested in "top-of-mind" awareness, the brand named first, which is usually (but not necessarily) their own brand. We ask which other brands they can recall aided. We want to know what new products they remember seeing.

We are also interested in whether people are getting information about brands from advertising. We ask which brands they have seen advertising for. We want to know where and when they saw it. We are usually especially interested in seeing how much attention people pay to advertising for new products. For all advertising, we also want to know how much information people get from it. We ask about what the advertising said and showed.

Similarly, we often want to know about promotions. What brands do people remember promotions for? Do they recall promotions for new products? And, of course, for brand, advertising, and promotions, we always should find out what people think of them. High awareness is no good if everyone knows about the product, but they all think it is terrible; or everyone saw the advertising but it turned them all against buying the brand.

Attitude

Measuring attitudes in market studies is no different from measuring them in other studies. We need to know what the most important product attributes are for respondents. We want to know what their "ideal" brand would look like. Key criteria and ideal brands can change as lifestyles and values change.

We ask about how each brand rates on key attributes. These should include physical attributes such as taste, aroma, or packaging, as well as image items like perception of users, suitability "for me", etc. The list should be derived from previous work, both qualitative and quantitative. It should include a wide variety of items that have been shown to impact on choice. Such a list can be a centerpiece of a factor analysis to uncover which of them go together to form a single construct.

For example, for shampoo, the list of attributes might include:

- Acts fast
- Doesn't hurt eyes
- Easy to use in the shower
- Easy to use in the bathtub
- Can be used by the whole family
- Good value
- Helps relieve itchiness
- Keeps hair clean
- Fights dandruff

- Gentle to hair
- Keeps hair soft
- Makes hair shiny
- Conditions as well as shampoos
- Not greasy
- Modern way to keep hair nice
- Smells nice
- Can comb hair easily after using it

We would need to know whether respondents believe that there are real differences among brands. Also, whether they believe that there *could* be real differences among brands. If there are or could be differences, on which attributes? We sometimes need to learn what people think are the specific similarities and differences among brands. We could have them sort cards containing brand names into piles of brands that are "like each other", and tell why they are alike.

We would ask about what people like and dislike in general about brands in the product category and about specific key brands. That is, we want to know brand satisfactions, and, even more important, their dissatisfactions. What would they like to see in the market that is not there now? Which brand do they think they would buy next? Why? Which others *might* they buy? Which brands would they *not* consider buying and why?

Behavior

We may never know everything about "why", even after extensive analysis of material such as just suggested. But it is vital to know all the "what's". We may choose to go with the flow or we may decide that the time is right to buck a trend, but, whatever we decide, we must know what is actually going on!

Typical things we might cover in the study include finding out about brand usage. We can ask about the respondent's current brand, and how long it has been used. This is psychologically what people think of as their favorite brand. Actual practice may (or may not always) be the same, so we have to check sometimes. We can ask what the last brand purchased was. One way to start learning about brand loyalty is to find out how many of the last ten (or some other number) purchases were brands A, B, C, etc. We can also ask what brand they plan to purchase next time.

We can also learn something about the depth of brand loyalty by finding out what respondents would do if their own brand was not available where they usually buy it. Would they wait until it was in stock again? Would they go to another store to look for it? Would they buy another type or size of the same brand? If they do these things, they are pretty loyal. Would they buy a different brand entirely? This would indicate that the brand "loyalty" is really just habit.

We may need to get an idea about brand switching. We might ask questions about the previous brand they used. We would want to know how long they used that brand. We would certainly need to find out why they switched from the previous brand to the current one. We must get information on *both* what they *like* more about the *current brand*; *and* what they did *not like* as much about the *previous brand*.

How did they learn about the new brand or come to try the new brand or even other brands not their own? Was their old brand out-of-stock? Did they respond to some special offer or promotion and decided they liked the new one better? Did they get a free sample? Maybe friends or relatives had the brand and they tried it while with them.

Purchase patterns are important. We may need to know how often people buy the product, as well as how much of it they buy at a time. Where do they buy it? Who actually buys it and who made the decision on which brand? We would want to know about the likelihood that respondents would buy at a special price. This might also be related to how often, how much, and where they buy.

We want to know about people involved in product purchase and usage. Is the user the same person as the purchaser? If not, who does the purchase? Who decides on what brand, the user or the purchaser? It does not help much to advertise to husbands if the wife makes all the decisions about what car to buy.

Demographics

Demographics should be asked for selectively, based on what we have learned from preliminary work. Some demographics are relevant, some are not. There are endless demographics, but about the only time we might need lots of demographics is in segmentation studies, not usually in market studies. Demographics can be looked at one at a time, and also in meaningful combinations, such as age within sex by education. Typical items that may be relevant for specific studies include standards on individuals and/or families such as:

- Age
- Sex
- Education
- Occupation
- Income (personal)
- Income (family)
- Marital status
- Number in family (and age, sex, etc., for each)
- Dwelling unit (house or apartment; rent or own; etc.)
- Geographical location (city, suburb, rural, etc.)

Typically, we may want to know about other things, such as life-cycle stage. But some of the more complex concepts we attach to people can often more easily be estimated by putting together basic demographic information. The items above, for example, can tell us most of what we need to know about life-cycle stage, which has a lot to do with spending patterns. People who are unmarried, newly married, married with young children, and people at each stage of life have different concerns, such as concerns about raising living standards now, or saving and investing for a more secure future. They have different levels of affluence: as careers are starting, are well established, or are over.

Socioeconomic status is another of these more complex concepts. It is also often tricky to measure. The interviewer's decision about which socioeconomic category to put a respondent in can be much influenced by perception. It is better to have objective standards to determine socioeconomic status. But if we do have objective standards, we can measure the standards directly, and just compute status. For example, we might compute socioeconomic status from some equation including income, education, and occupation.

Increasingly in multi-ethnic and multi-cultural societies, and in international marketing, we need to know things like race, ethnicity (e.g., Hispanic, Bengali, Malay), or languages (spoken at home, at work, etc.). These give us clues to underlying cultures, which can differ widely in spending and product usage patterns.

We also often want to measure personal characteristics which would be related to product use. For example, research on our shampoo might include questions about scalp type (oily, normal, dry), hair problems (such as brittleness, split ends), etc.

Finally, another common type of information that is often considered demographic is about media habits. We need to know what the respondent sees, hears, reads, etc. For our home computer, a key item in any market study would be where people got information about computers. In the US, for example, there is a wide range of computer-oriented magazines covering both business and general areas. Just a few examples include *PC Magazine, PC Computing, PC Week, MacWeek, MacUser, PC Sources*, and *Computer Shopper*. We would want to know which of these kinds of magazines, if any, are received by subscription, are bought at newsstands, and so forth.

Psychographics

Psychographics provides us with a picture of the make-up of the inner person. It can often be the ultimate factor in segmenting the market for such products as clothing, furniture, cigarettes, alcoholic beverages, and even such services as vacations. No doubt too, psychographics also affect brand choice for things that have an outwardly more rational face, like automobiles, and . . . home computers! Typically we explore such dimensions as:

- *Activities.* Work, sports (as observer and player), social events, entertainment (movies, plays, media, VCRs), hobbies, shopping, community involvement, eating and drinking, etc. The role of ritual. What do people do and what don't they do?
- *Aspirations.* For themselves and their families. Things like money, travel, security, food, drink, possessions. Peer-groups and reference-groups.
- *Interests.* Family, home, job, recreation, food, fashion, health, achievement, politics, issues (such as the "green" revolution).
- *Opinions.* About themselves, life, social and political issues, economics, education, sex, religion, brands, categories.
- *Values.* "Core" beliefs like love, family, friends, success, hedonism, modesty, etc.
- *Lifestyle.* A broad term encompassing many of the above elements of thinking and doing. Often we put labels on lifestyle groups like Yuppies (Young Urban Upwardly-mobile Professionals), Dinks (Double Income No Kids), and Glams (Good-looking, Affluent, Aging, Matrons).

Obviously, these six dimensions overlap and interweave, but we must delve into them to sort out our thinking on what is going on in the minds of consumers out there. Questions we ask may be tailor-made for our study, or we can use established systems like VALS. Tailor-made questions can be constructed that pinpoint our specific situation and our specific needs; established systems offer simplicity of execution.

ANALYSIS

Methods of analysis will vary widely. A classic start is to run a factor analysis on attitudinal statements, and reduce a big list of statements (say 50 or more) to a few "core" dimensions which incorporate basic ideas that people have. (Factor analysis is covered in the Appendix. To those not familiar with it, it is simply a method for seeing what variables (statements) seem to be measuring the same underlying construct, that is, have high intercorrelation.)

For example, take the following three statements from a hypothetical study on baby care products. We may have asked mothers to agree or disagree with the following statements:

- "I'm more comfortable using even a simple product if my doctor recommends it."
- "I'm concerned that my baby is developing at a normal pace."
- "I'm very concerned about all the contagious diseases that seem to be going around these days."

We may find a very high intercorrelation among responses to these three items. That is, mothers who agree very strongly with one tend to agree very strongly with the other two also. We may then eventually decide that these three statements (plus others in the survey along the same lines which also correlate with these) constitute one underlying construct, or factor. We might choose to call this factor "Health Concern".

Then, in addition to this factor analysis, we seek to find groups of people (here, mothers) whose responses to all our items seem to follow the same pattern: high on the same things, low on another set of items, middle on another. We group the people with similar patterns of answers into clusters (cluster analysis). We can give the clusters names too. One group might become "Worried Mothers"; another "Laid-back Mothers".

For each cluster, then, we show their scores ("factor loadings" — see appendix) on each factor, which suggest the end-benefits (one form of segmentation) that these groups of mothers want from baby care products. Profiles of the groups can be constructed from demographics, psychographics, behavior, attitudes towards every key brand, media habits, etc. We then have a full picture of who they are, how many they are, how to reach them, and what to say to them.

This comprehensive picture of the consumers in our market is only available through quantitative research, and specifically, through a comprehensive market study.

Many other analyses can also be done (some of which are also discussed in more detail in the Appendix). A few common methods employed in market studies include:

- **Discriminant analysis.** This deals with the characteristics that most clearly distinguish users of one brand from users of other brands.
- **AID** (Automatic Interaction Detector). This groups users automatically by the most unique ways they hold together — for example, it might show that for our brand the target is "first-time mothers in low-income households".
- **Conjoint** ("Tradeoff"). Here we look for what people want, and what they would give up to get it.
- **Perceptual mapping.** How our brand is perceived in two or more dimensions. (It is probably best to take two key dimensions at a time. While three dimensional plots are available, they usually test the goodwill of the brand manager beyond reason. N-dimensional plots (going off into hyperspace) are best reserved for internal Research Department discussion, not for presentation to anyone.)

Of course, simple analysis ("unidimensional" rather then "multidimensional") can also be used. It should be used if what we need to show does not require complex, multi-variable methods. Often, data presented in simple cross-tabulations (maybe behavior by age) can provide as much valuable insight as advanced techniques. We need to think things out in advance, though. What are the variables that are likely to be most relevant in helping us discover who wants what? Which variables will help us determine whether the brand is seen in different ways (factor analysis) by different groups (cluster analysis) to such an extent that different advertising may be required for different groups? What new product possibilities suggest themselves? What competitive "levers" have we found? Whose eyes have been opened in the company? To what? What burning questions have been answered? What established answers have been questioned?

There is no magic to this, except to make sure that key ideas have been put into the questionnaire. Our "dialogue" (interaction) with the consumer must stand a good chance of producing sweet, rather than bitter, fruit. After all, once again, it's GIGO: Garbage In, Garbage Out! We do not want that!

18

New Products and Test Marketing

Marketing research on new products is, in reality, a summing-up of all the things that we have discussed in Chapters 10–17. We thus already have the framework for intelligent exploration of anything "new" that comes before us. We can envision the new product, dissect it, assemble, assess, and reassemble it. The new product and attitudes toward it can be measured and counted, in whatever ways we want. We decide on whether to go with it, expand it, or ultimately, even decide to put it to sleep peacefully. All these decisions can be made on the basis of our examination into the contribution the new product is likely to make to our profits, to building our marketing skills, and to helping us learn about the market.

WHY NEW PRODUCTS FAIL

But if we can know all this (and we really can, and often do, execute the things described in Chapters 10–17), why is the failure rate on new products so horrendous? And horrendous it is, as 80 to 90 percent (or more) of all new products that ultimately reach the market fail. The answer is essentially four-fold, and for each of the four problems, marketing research can — to a greater or lesser extent — help to cut down on the fatalities.

Egos and Fears

The development of new products, and the research that attends it, is too often guided by violent instincts that eagerly suppress (or at best ignore and pervert) any data that does not help move the new product process forward. No matter how feeble research shows the new product to be, unspoken egos and unexpressed fears often find a way to keep it moving ahead into full national (and even international) distribution.

It happens again and again. A company gets hungrier for a new product which is a winner. As the months pass, the lab director realizes he better come up with a moneymaker, or he won't stay on the payroll. In trying a new toothpaste mix, he discovers that you can blow bubbles with it. This could be a winner with the kids who won't brush their teeth because they can now have fun blowing bubbles while they brush their teeth.[1]

The marketing process — especially in new product development — often *seems* to be guided by reason and information derived from awesome Marketing and Management Intelligence Systems (MIS). In reality, it is driven more by raw emotion and power-grabbing, no matter how destructive this may be to the company in the long run. But, in the long run we are all dead (as Keynes said). It is the short-run in which the egoists must play out their double game of seeming rationality but real selfishness. Research cannot change this, but it can try to put forward its reasoned case.

The Young Tigers

Typically, it is the brand manager who is the adversary. Such people are usually young, aggressive, stealthy, wary, solitary, protean, and plastic. Their only aim is to get "their" new product to the market, so they can command the salary that comes from overseeing a large marketing budget, and the power that comes from that line on their resume: "Went national with product X at a budget of Y".

These are the "Young Tigers". In pursuing their goals, they will make everything look right in the research findings including things that look very sour indeed. The new product must move ahead. Even if it fails, that important line on the resume will be there, and no worry, they will find a way to explain away the failure when they apply for the next, bigger job. Perhaps research did not inform them well enough!

This state of affairs is allowed to exist because secretly top management often shares the voracity of the Young Tigers. It all too eagerly gives into their too rosy versions and visions of what the numbers mean. While the marketing researcher may also secretly share the appetites of the Young Tigers, it is nonetheless clear that the researcher must fight them if they seek to bend the numbers.

It is up to the researcher how far he wishes to carry his fight for objectivity and reason. The penalty for fighting and losing could be getting eaten for lunch. And the benefits of winning may be slim. It is, after all, difficult to quantify just how much was saved by following what research has learned, and modifying the product launch, or even killing it. If we don't do it, how can we know how bad it would have been?

What's "New"?

The two problems above — egos in general, and the Young Tiger Syndrome in particular — are "people" problems that the researcher must try to work with as best he can. Although they are not, strictly speaking, "research" problems they nonetheless become the researcher's problems. It is the "art" part of his repertoire that will come into play most here.

More directly, the researcher needs to work with the "new" issue if research is to play a role in new product success rather than new product failure. Simply put, the researcher must determine what the marketer means by "new". Is it "new" to the product line; "new" to the company; "new" to the industry (a slight advance)? Or is it *really* "new": a genuine innovation that addresses wants, needs, life styles, in a way that has not been done by anybody before?

There are, of course, few of these truly "new" kinds of things: the automobile, the radio, television, VCR, when they were first introduced. All the hoopla and excitement reserved for genuine advances should not be expected of a simple addition to our own product line. More likely, the "new" product is simply a parity product that we hope will sell big by association with its family name (heritage) in the promotion program.

Scores in preliminary research indicating how excited consumers are about new products should indeed be modest. They must be examined in detail for areas of leverage, if there is any leverage. On the other hand, for the big "discontinuous" advances (automobile, radio, VCR) we should expect bigger scores. At the same time, genuinely new products also require greater "leaps of faith" to gain acceptance. (What will it replace?; how will it fit into my rituals?; what further avenues will it open?) People may be excited and intrigued, but they may not be sure exactly how truly new products will fit into their lives.

Thus, the researcher must fully understand what is (and is not) "new" in the new product. He must devise inventive ways to look at the issue squarely on its own terms, while seeking consistency with past data for better interpretability. We cannot fit all new product research into a mold of repetitive mindless testing via a "new product testing machine". That would often provide data without information, because "new" can be many things, not all of which will fit the "new product testing machine".

A Pattern

Most of all, new product research fails because it is usually jagged and fragmented. To avoid this, the researcher must keep a firm hold on the process, worked out in advance with the marketing manager. Whether or not put into the form of flowcharts with arrows and time spans, a master plan should be laid out so that each element (concept, product, name, logo, package, price, etc.) is reviewed through every phase. This structure helps ensure that minds are kept open all the way along, even at the stage when the market is tested (if things get that far). Structure lends support to sensible (rather than ego-driven) decisions on whether to go, abort, revise, or whatever.

Providing a structure, a coherent procedure, is simple and logical, as will be discussed below.

SEQUENCE IN PRODUCING A NEW PRODUCT

Generation of Ideas

Perhaps the most important step that marketing research can oversee is the first step: generation of ideas to be tested. As noted over and over in this book, successful marketing research will lead to successful marketing only when the twin forces of the marketing process are coordinated. That is, we must follow what the market needs and wants, and we must also stay within our technological capabilities.

Thus, the job of marketing research is both to constantly keep tabs on the market, and also to see what, indeed, the changing technology is. In reality, it is probably the marketing manager, rather than the scientist, who should be the conduit for information flow to the researcher, if only because the scientist even today, is apt to be hermetic, reclusive, and arcane. As Gruber notes: "Products are not merely assembled pieces of hardware; the hardware is conceived to satisfy needs, and the knowledge of these needs must come from the marketing people."[2]

But tapping the marketing manager and scientist is not enough. It is necessary for the researcher to reach for everybody in the process of idea generation. And everybody means *everybody*. It means the marketing people, who should be (but not always are) the wellspring of knowledge about the market. It means those scientists who will talk if coaxed and cajoled, and convinced that we do want to hear what they have to say. It means production people. It means the advertising agency (who can come up with ideas for "advertisability" that may shape our whole course of thinking). It means the financial people, whose dour views on what is possible may send us into furies, but also give a more realistic appraisal of where we may really be able to go. Of course, it means "the market": consumers, whose voices must be heard as they suggest ideas and respond to our ideas.

We have repeatedly discussed that role of early consumer work in all aspects of research: to find gaps, dissatisfactions, longings, etc. Through secondary and primary research we need to explore concepts, positioning, and the whole chain. It is only necessary here to redirect attention to research's role in working not only with "the market", but inside the company too: building bridges and building trust to build successful new products.

Screening of Ideas

Screening involves sorting out the ideas generated in the process above. It involves *screening in* ideas that seem to have even a germ of viability in them. It requires *screening out* ideas that seem to be leading nowhere. (But we do not forget them forever: revitalization for other projects should always remain a possibility. Market conditions may change and make viable something that has no chance now.) Screening includes patching together parts of ideas from here and pieces of ideas from there to interweave into a whole which can then be explored.

Screening requires an open mind (not the same as a gullible mind). It also needs determination and ability to see what *is not* even more then what *is*. Truly "new" concepts cannot come from plodding thought mired in the "is".

Evaluation of New Product

All of the things that researchers do (Chapters 10–17) are brought together here. Each part is taken singly, then in combination, and finally as a whole to determine what needs are being met, of what groups, and how many there are likely to be (volume projections). It is here that those last fine-tunings are made in the new- product development process. And it is from here that we move into test marketing.

TEST MARKETING

Test marketing is the last step in the new-product research process. Here we see how the new product does on real shelves, in real stores, with real people who have been exposed to real promotion, who decide to buy or not to buy. If everything has been done right up to now, only test marketing remains. And if agreements are firm within the company, the decision to let the product live or die should now be a relatively rational one. After all, we have set up objectives, timetables, and all that. Now, recognizing consumer sovereignty, we wait to see what will happen. Research's most vital role here, perhaps, is to see that sense continues to prevail, and feedback from the market is fed back into our thinking concerning the next marketing move.

In setting up the test market, and in working out the readings from it, perhaps three phases should be emphasized:

- Getting the test market
- Using the test market
- Losing the test market

Getting It

The objective of test marketing overall is to go in and see what happens when we finally offer our new product. We want to be able to read sales, market shares, and more, and then make a prediction of what might happen if we went national. Obviously, we look for a market that is reasonably typical of the whole. We can define the whole any way we like, so long as it is relevant to the product, of course. This can be in terms of demographics, media availability, retail chain domination, company share performance, etc. Every case will be different, but the goal — to predict the whole from the part — remains unvarying.

And we also want a market that gets most or all of the media we put into it. Little or nothing from the media effort should spill out of the test market area. And certainly, there should not be spill-in from other areas. In short, good test markets should be relatively isolated.

It is at this point that some marketers may consider simulation in place of a test market. Simulations are possible. But this alternative requires a vast amount of prior knowledge, firm action standards, and faith in computer projections. Many simulations are done, but few of them really contain the depth of a real market. Therefore many still feel that only by real people being exposed to real products can we really know how a product is going to perform.

Using It

Selecting a test market, then, will come from an analysis of what we want and what we know. Rationality should prevail. Implementing a test market should also be a clear-headed thing. Suppose we need to know whether the trade will accept the new product or not, even before consumers get a crack at it. Then we can set up a natural test: our people can attempt to sell it, and deal with all the issues of providing a persuasive story to the chain's buying committee, working out slotting allowances, etc. Or, we can adopt the opposite approach — a "controlled" test — with hand-picked stores that we can work with intensively, since we have paid for their cooperation.

Either way, the work in test marketing will further involve seeing where the product sits on the shelf, what is around it, whether it stacks well, etc. And the major reading will be sales and share figures, either through traditional auditing, scanning, or whatever we want to do.

All the time we will also be looking desperately for competitive reaction. Have competitors stepped up advertising and in-store promotions? Are they changing prices in the marketplace to defeat us? Certainly no simulation can be very useful if we do not attempt to assay the effects of competitive reaction. Surely in an actual test market, this phase of the work is all the richer because we are not hypothesizing about it. We are actually following what the others are doing.

And, of course, all these measures will need to be supplemented by consumer-tracking studies, covering many of the issues discussed in Chapter 17, such as purchase, repurchase, previous regular brand, likes, dislikes, and so forth. Obviously, we need to know not only how much we have sold, but who we sold it to, and what they think of it.

Losing It

Once a decision has already been made to go ahead with a new product introduction, should we drop the test market? Probably not. Surely we may want to add many new wrinkles later on, fool around with new packaging and pricing, and even line extensions. By keeping the test market, we may be able to gain useful information about reactions many buying-cycles down the line. We can also continue adjusting our marketing, remain proactive, and force the competition to forever react.

Problems

Researchers must try to set up test markets that can be in some way replicated on a large scale when we do go national, if that happens. But, in relation to this task self-deceptions abound. Since careers are at stake, wishes often substitute for facts. Typically, test markets tend to be full of enthusiasm, carrying forth the Young Tiger's determination that the new product *will* go national regardless of its inherent merits. In addition to the Young Tiger's aims,

> men in the sales division . . . are determined that the new bubbly toothpaste shall not fail in [the] test market for lack of stocking stores. So three men out of a nationwide sales force of a dozen are sent to the test city to insure retailers have [the product] on their shelves. . . . [But] when going nationwide, the company will have to rely on telephone and direct mail trade effort. *The test market is not a genuine experimental test.*[3] [Emphasis added]

Neither is the ad agency going to let the product fail in the test market if it can help it. It has its own Young Tigers who want the account on *their* resumes.

> Extra effort is made to get prime spots and extra news coverage . . . about the new miracle toothpaste. . . . The result is an intensive level of promotion which could never be sustained nationwide.[4]

FARMERS AND COMPUTERS

Ideas about successful new-product marketing and research apply, of course, far beyond the borders of classical consumer-package goods. For example, new agricultural technology must be "sold" to traditional farmers in the Sudan. The problems and opportunities offer striking parallels to selling shampoos or computers in developed countries in terms of what should be done and how we should measure it. One of the important things in Sudan is to find the innovators and see what they are doing and thinking as a measure of new product success down the line.

> In a broad sense the target for an agricultural development program is the whole category of subsistence farmers. However, because of resistance to change among such farmers, the problem becomes one of identifying those particular farmers most likely to adopt innovations . . . There is considerable overlap between these innovators and people considered to be opinion leaders within communities. [They are] the people other community members look to for guidance in their own adoption decisions.[5]

These insights into the new product task and research's role (here locating the innovators) underscore our notion of learning from life, then transferring practice back to theory, and then back again into all our worlds of decision making.

And what, finally, what about our home computer? Can marketing research succeed in grasping what is really going on? Other than use as a modern typewriter and convenient video game arcade, are there no other startling breakthroughs that would make marketers' dreams come true? Or is just too much trouble to do more, even with a mouse and with Windows? What if there were easy voice commands to everything, and no mouse or keyboard, and what if opinion leaders were able to speak on our behalf: that you had to have one of our machines, or else . . . ?

All of this is for research to find out. The product of all of this research — insightful and constantly unfolding — is success. And that is one idea that is definitely *not* new.

PART IV

Observations and Speculations

What marketing research can do and why we ask it to do those things are discussed in Chapter 19. A firm commitment to using technology is suggested, but not at the expense of a firm orientation to marketing usefulness. Always the goal remains to obtain better information for better marketing.

19

Looking Into, Looking Out, Looking Ahead

To look into the marketing research business today is to see shining possibilities. The very essence of a free market economy is what research is really all about. For choice, caring, innovation, listening to the consumer, and molding our programs around what consumers want, working to blend the imperatives of technological change with the ever-changing needs of the market are indeed what research is really all about.

We take research for granted, but we should not. It is something special, something to drive the marketing engine: really invisible but really essential. Listen to what a young man working in the media in the former Soviet Union said about America:

> There is something convincingly powerful about a nation that can afford to have media so numerous as to satisfy the needs of every "target audience" as the selling of products prompts what seems to be an unceasing nationwide consumer research [effort] to learn people's likes and dislikes . . . something that socialism in the Soviet Union . . . failed to accomplish.[1]

Research can do an astonishing amount with its evolving technology. Computers have software that lets us do cluster, factor, discriminant, and tradeoff work that used to be a struggle. Software now makes table transformations and perceptual mapping a treat rather than a treatment. And scanner technology can give us a sales picture minute-by-minute. We can relate sales to advertising exposure and promotional efforts — on-line, real-time. This ability is eminently usable and necessary for things like mammoth new-product decisions.

Evolving marketing research has given us the ability to do world-wide research as our products and services — like Coca-Cola, McDonald's, Sony, and Benetton — become "global" brands, rather than "national" ones that happen to be also marketed overseas. Global research is being further strengthened by an evolving sense of and respect for different cultures and systems. Research has helped foster the necessary broad (if often imprecise) understanding of the need to think globally but act locally (and also act globally but think locally at times).

And so research can serve as well in helping to make better immediate decisions (tactics) and setting long-term roads to follow (strategy). Research can look into not only our own company, but into competition and broad social changes as well. In short, research, with its generalists, specialists, humanists, technicians, visionaries, and executors, can do it all. It can produce results that impact meaningfully on marketing decisions in reports, presentations, charts, print-outs, and just plain sensible marketing-oriented talk that is:

- Clear (simple but not simplistic or simple-minded)
- Concise
- Comprehensive
- Coherent
- Cohesive
- Concrete
- Cogent
- Creative

We might also add "calculated" to this list. Research is not calculated in the sense of "here are my lovely mathematical and statistical 'calculations'", though research may contain some of that. Instead, it offers information and implications that are truly "calculated": well thought out, measured, and focused on who should use it, why, when, and even whether it should be used. Research in a calculated manner goes back to absorb what was learned to start new projects on a still higher base of understanding.

ENCHANTMENT AND DISENCHANTMENT

Watch out for poor research. We have been talking about good research — well thought out and well executed. Not all research is. Research can become enchanted with its technology, even bewitched by it, and use its computers to provide data without information. It can try to force marketing problems into its research methodologies and solution systems. It can abandon common sense (which is not so common, anyway), and produce results that are stunning in their silliness and uselessness. Any of these things can happen, especially if the "backward" approach of Chapter 4 is ignored.

Look Back in Satisfaction

Up ahead, we might envision perhaps further dramatic breakthroughs in input technology: respondents punching into a keyboard, with their answers being instantly transmitted to computer control central in the researcher's office. Maybe with every 100 interviews, we could immediately generate cross-tabs, cluster analysis, or perceptual maps. And when the pattern has stabilized (after 200, 300, or 400 interviews), the research could be terminated and a report given to the client within minutes.

This is already well within the bounds of the possible in a world where we have so much technical know-how already. We have packages that can help us code open-end questions or even what is said in focus group discussions by seeking out "key words". We have programs that help us in questionnaire construction by sorting out the logic of skip-patterns. We have computerized statistical methodology that do all manner of simple and complex things like correlations, regressions, and tests of significance.

Indeed the future is sunny technologically: we can take it wherever we want it (and us) to go. We may not be so confident, however, about people. Pigheadedness on the part of marketing managers and marketing researchers is a human condition that only the building of trust can help resolve. And trust in a field as volatile as marketing (and especially its advertising subset) is not easy to come by. For the researcher to be seen as a man of confidence rather than a confidence man in the mind of the marketer is a goal not likely to be fully achieved ever.

But try we must, as we must try to accept the fact that, machines or not, research is a staff function: a "service": people doing things for people. Indeed, in speaking of his coding supervisor, a research company owner once said: "The most significant variable around here is Sally!" And Sally, and all the rest of us, too, need to understand that information is always what we are seeking, information derived from data and leading to decisions.

"In the last three years," noted Clayson, "there have been at least thirteen marketing research texts published, six of which do not even mention the word 'information' in their indexes. [What is information? . . . It] is communicated knowledge. It changes the state of knowledge of the person who receives it . . . [and] in marketing research the purpose of information is to facilitate decision making through the appropriate change in knowledge of key decision makers."[2]

Research must see itself now and in the future as such an agent of change and not as just a source of numbers. If it can really deliver the goods, it will never have to look back in anger. Rather, it can go to work figuring out how to successfully market our home computer. Or bravely say: "No way", and stick to its guns!

Appendix A

Selected Advanced
Data-Analysis Techniques

Chapter 8 illustrated how to interpret and write about data using basic techniques. A great many practical marketing research studies do not really need much more statistical sophistication than those basic techniques to do a very good job of telling managers what they want to know. Far too often, the complex methodology used by researchers is not really necessary. Poor analysts sometimes think they can cover up the fact that they have nothing much to say by dressing things up in complex methodologies, but sophisticated trivia is still trivia.

The more complex the methodology, the less likely it is that users of the marketing research report will easily understand it. Therefore, the only time when it is permissible to use any of these methods is when the basic techniques cannot show what the manager needs to know. Whenever possible, simple, understandable methods should be used. When that is not possible, one of the methods here or other more complex methods may be appropriate. But always make sure that the true reason for using them is to show something that cannot be shown in a more simple manner.

REGRESSION

One of the most common advanced techniques is regression. Typically, it is used to measure how a (ratio) dependent variable is influenced by a (ratio) independent variable (or variables). For example, we may want to measure how sports drink spending depends on spending on participation in sports activities. (Of course, the analyst must not abandon common sense. People probably spend on the drinks because they are active in the sporting event, not because they spend money to participate in it. The spending on sporting events is simply a way to measure participation in activities.)

Once the relationship has been modeled, regression can also be used for prediction. If we know that teenagers in a neighborhood spend an average of $378 a year on sporting events, we can use the model to predict average spending on sports drinks. Sometimes this is critical, for example, in choosing which market segment to focus on and which to ignore.

Several requirements must be met to use regression. Both the dependent and the independent variables must be ratio or interval data. The relationship between the dependent and the independent variables must be linear, i.e., a straight line must give a good approximation of what the data look like. The spread of the data from the "best" straight line must be similar for the range of the data being modeled. Figure A.1 illustrates that these conditions are met by the data for sports drink spending and sporting event spending.

The equation for a simple regression model is a simple straight line equation: $y = ax + b$. (Simple means that we have only a single independent variable, x, in the equation. It does not imply that the mathematics are necessarily simple.) Here, y, the "dependent" variable, is sports drink spending, which is in dollars, ratio data. "Dependent" here means that this is the variable we want to predict, or see how it is influenced by other variables. The "independent" variable, spending on sporting events, is x, and is also ratio dollars. "Independent" variables are the ones doing the influencing.

One thing to keep straight is that the "dependent" and "independent" terminology do not, in the strict sense, imply anything about causation. Regression can be used in either descriptive or causal research designs. But the use of regression or any other technique does not in itself show causality. Only a causal research design (Chapter 5) can provide strong evidence of causality.

The coefficients a and b in the straight line equation are the slope and the intercept of the straight line, respectively. But of course, there are an infinite number of straight lines that we could draw through the data, each differing slightly in either slope, intercept, or both. The problem is to find the "best" line, the one that fits the data most closely.

Visualize a line that follows the trend of the data in Figure A.1. Most of the actual data points do not lie exactly on the line, but are above or below it. The vertical difference between the data point and the line is the "error" for a particular observation. The "best" line will be one that minimizes the total amount of error. But we cannot simply add up all the errors for some specific straight line. The positive errors (when the data point lies above the line) will tend to cancel out the negative errors (when the data point lies below the line). The sum will be close to zero for many different lines. The regression model finds the "best" line by choosing the slope and intercept so that the sum of *squared* errors is minimized.

Table A.1 illustrates typical output from a regression run on the sports drink spending and sporting event spending. The first thing to look for in evaluating regression output is the F-statistic. This tells whether there is anything to evaluate in the first place, i.e., whether the model is any good in explaining sports drink spending. Recall the statistical tests of Chapter 8. This one works the same way. If the model explains absolutely nothing, the F-statistic will be zero. Because of sampling error,

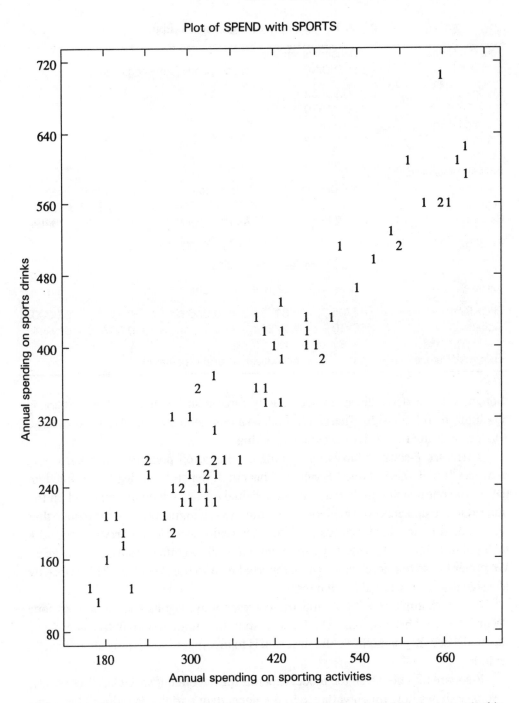

Plot of SPEND with SPORTS

1 indicates only one data point, 2 indicates that two data points fall in the same place. A 25 percent sample of the data was used to make the plot.

Figure A.1.   Example of a straight line relationship between two ratio data variables.

Table A.1.   Example of regression output.

Equation Number 1	Dependent variable
	SPENDING annual spending on sports drinks

Multiple R	0.95692
R-square	0.91570
Adjusted R-square	0.91535
Standard error	43.32418

Analysis of variance

	DF	Sum of squares	Mean square
Regression	1	4791556.39011	4791556.39011
Residual	235	441091.39048	1876.98464

$F = 2552.79467$ Signif $F = 0.0000$

Variables in the equation

Variable	B	SE B	Beta	t	Sig t
SPORTS	0.87705	0.01736	0.95692	50.525	0.0000
(constant)	4.85210	7.27374		0.667	0.5054

End Block Number	1	All requested variables entered.

though, we are never likely to see exactly zero in any sample, even if there is absolutely no relationship. Therefore, small F values mean the model is no good, large F values indicate that it does explain something.

There are F-statistic tables for looking up the cutoff point (the decision value) between "small" and "large" F values. This cutoff depends on degrees of freedom (DF) of the regression equation and of the residual (error), which are reported on the output. It also depends on confidence level, the risk the manager is willing to take that we decide the model is worth using when it is really worthless. Carrying around F tables all the time and trying to figure them out is all too much trouble, in our view. We prefer to use the significance value reported next to the F-statistic. This is exactly like significance discussed in Chapter 8.

In our example, $F = 2552$, and the corresponding significance is zero to four decimal places. This F is "big", i.e., it shows that the equation does fit the data. Since the model does say something, the next step is to investigate something about exactly what it says.

R-square tells how well the model explains the dependent variable. (Technically, R-square shows how much variance in the dependent variable is reduced by calculating deviation from the regression line instead of from the simple mean of the dependent variable.) It is a measure of the strength of the relationship. If there is no relationship and the model explains nothing, R-square would be zero, or something close to zero (because of sampling error). In this case, about 91 percent of the variation in sports drink spending can be "explained" by the independent variable — spending on sports events.

R-square is also a measure of *managerial* significance. Knowing about 91 percent of what is going on is pretty good. This equation can be quite useful in planning marketing of the sporting drink. It shows pretty clearly that a strong relationship exists between spending on the drink and participation in sporting events.

So, since it can be useful, continue analyzing it by checking whether the parameters (a and b) are significantly different from zero. For this, t-tests are used (recall Chapter 8), and they show that a is significant, while b is not (significance of $t = 0.00$ and 0.50, respectively). We cannot say that b is anything different than zero, so the line crosses the y axis at zero. This means that when spending on the events is zero, so is spending on the drinks. The slope is something different than zero, and the best estimate at its value is 0.87. The equation looks like this:

spending $= 0.87 \times$ sports $+ 0$.

The a value shows the nature of the relationship between the dependent and independent variables. In this case, for every dollar spent on activities, people in the sample spend about 87 cents on soft drinks. For prediction, the manager might look at that neighborhood where teenagers spent US\$378 on average for sporting events, and "predict" that they would spend about US\$331 on drinks ($0.87705 \times 378 = 331.52$; always round off for reporting *after* calculations).

The standard error of the regression is used for constructing confidence intervals around predictions such as this one. Chapter 5 shows how confidence intervals are constructed. Technically, when they are calculated for regression predictions, an adjustment must be made depending on how far a point is from the middle of the data used to compute the regression line. In practice, except for very sensitive and/or precise work, there is no real need to complicate things with the adjustment. For a 90 percent confidence level, we would say that predicted spending is about 331 ± 70 ($\pm 1.645 \times$ SE).

If R-square were very small, the equation would be almost worthless to the manager, because not knowing most of what is happening in the market means that the manager does not really know much at all. Table A.2 shows an example where the equation is statistically significant (significance of F is 0.0005). This means, again, that this model is showing some relationship between spending and income. But the model only explains about 5 percent of the total variation in spending (R-square $= 0.05$). Ninety-five percent is not explained, so this model does not really tell the manager much of anything. We would probably not want to bother using this model.

For the sake of illustration, though, we will analyze Table A.2 further. It shows a negative relation between spending and income (a is significant and is equal to -0.002). This shows the need to consider one further thing in analyzing regression models. Do the parameters make sense? This parameter says that as income

Table A.2.   Example of regression with small *R*-square.

Equation Number 1	Dependent variable				
	SPENDING	annual spending on sports drinks			

Multiple R	0.22524				
R-square	0.05073				
Adjusted R-square	0.04670				
Standard error	145.38533				

Analysis of variance

	DF	Sum of squares		Mean square	
Regression	1	265477.36561		265477.36561	
Residual	235	4967170.41499		21136.89538	

F = 12.55990   Signif *F* = 0.0005

Variables in the equation

Variable	B	SE B	Beta	t	Sig t
INCOME	– 1.94320E – 03	5.48307E – 04	– 0.22524	– 3.544	0.0005
(constant)	390.50130	16.22629		24.066	0.0000

End Block Number	1	All requested variables entered.			

increases, spending declines. Common sense says this cannot be true. Of course, common sense is wrong sometimes. On the other hand, it is often right. Whenever something goes against common sense, it should always be investigated further. Is something wrong with the model, something left out, something specified wrong? Or maybe we really do not know as much about the situation as we thought we did, i.e., common sense does not work because we have incomplete or incorrect information. Either way, we should find out.

The two regression models shown here for illustration are both simple regressions, which means that they contain only one independent variable. Regressions can contain more than one independent variable. The relationships cannot be visualized graphically anymore, but the interpretation remains similar whether there is one or many slope coefficients in the equation.

ANALYSIS OF VARIANCE

Regression models use a ratio data dependent variable, and also ratio data independent variables. If the variables in the relationships we wish to look at have these characteristics, the researcher can use regression. When the independent variables are categorical, but the dependent one is ratio or interval, a different method is required. (There are special modifications of regression that allow the use of categorical data. Those methods are beyond the scope of this book.) Analysis of variance (ANOVA) models are based on analyzing variation of the ratio dependent variable around means. As such, it is a more sophisticated and more general technique for measuring differences in means, which we did with t-tests in Chapter 8.

For example, recall the soft drink data in Chapter 8. Several examples looked at spending by some category, such as job category. But t-tests could only test the difference between two means at a time. It took lots of t-tests to thoroughly check all differences. ANOVA can test differences among two or more means, i.e., among many categories, to see whether the means across categories are all the same or not.

The simplest ANOVA is one-way analysis of variance, which means that only a single independent variable is used. The basic model says that there is some overall mean for the dependent variable. Individual observations differ from this overall mean because they belong to some category which has a higher or lower mean than the overall. The level of the dependent variable can be predicted by taking the overall mean and adding (or subtracting) the difference due to the category. The prediction may not be exact, because each observation still has some individual variation, i.e., the error.

ANOVA works by looking at the variation. Variation within a category around the category mean (within group variation) is error in the model. It is what the model cannot explain. Variation of the categories around an overall mean (between group variation) is the part that the model does explain. Table A.3 provides an example, using the same data that were used in Chapter 8 for illustration. Knowing that someone is in a white collar job, for example, will tell the researcher something about that person's soft drink spending. A general spending level can be predicted. This is the model part. The prediction will not be exact, because individual white collar workers may spend more or less than the average white collar worker.

On the output, we want to see whether knowing what job people have actually does tell us anything about their spending. If the job has absolutely nothing to do with spending, the means of the different jobs will be the same, i.e., there will be no variation among the jobs. Between group variation will be small compared to variation within the jobs. The F-statistic will be small. If job does have something to do with spending, the means of the jobs will vary, and the F-statistic will be large. The F-statistic for between groups in Table A.3 ($F = 165$) is large, as can be seen by looking at the probability of F (i.e., the significance).

All this one-way ANOVA has told us so far is that job does indeed have something to do with spending; the means are not all the same. Which means differ from which other ones? The multiple range test provides that information. It simultaneously tests difference in each pair of means. Here, the results show that mean spending among blue collar workers is significantly different from spending by any of the other three jobs. But none of the other jobs differ significantly from each other. The results still do not say anything about actual spending levels by job. To see that, we would have to look at the actual means for each job, which we did in Chapter 8.

Table A.3.   Example of one-way ANOVA.

| Variable | SPENDING | annual spending on soft drinks, US$ |
| by variable | JOB | job classification |

Analysis of variance

Source	DF	Sum of squares	Mean squares	F ratio	F probability
Between groups	3	3560139.341	1186713.114	165.3230	0.0000
Within groups	233	1672508.439	7178.1478		
Total	236	5232647.781			

Multiple range test
Tukey-HSD procedure
(*) Denotes pairs of
   groups significantly
   different at the
   0.050 level

Mean	Group	w h i t e c o	u n s k i l l e	u p p e r m g	b l u e c o l
256.7258	white collar				
257.1111	unskilled				
266.4222	upper management				
522.0526	blue collar	*	*	*	

ANOVA can have more than one independent categorical variable, just like regression. We could analyze means of spending by job, by education, and by income category, as shown in Table A.4. Each of the three different independent variables is called a main "effect", and the first thing to look at is whether any of these main effects is statistically significant. This is the same type of question as before: does job matter for spending, does education matter for spending, does income matter. In this example, they all do matter (at a 90 percent confidence level). Check the *F*-statistics.

This means that someone's spending can be found by taking the overall mean, and adding or subtracting something depending on what combination of categories (job, college, income category) the person is in. The multiple classification analysis shows how much the something to be added or subtracted is. Take a white collar worker who has not gone to college and who has an income of US$20,000 to 30,000. That person is likely to spend US$343 (grand mean) – US$54 (difference for job) + US$20 (difference for education) – US$21 (difference for income). This works out to US$288.

Table A.4. Example of ANOVA with several independent variables.

	SPENDING	annual spending on soft drinks, US$			
by	JOB	job classification			
	COLLEGE	college education			
	INCAT	income categories			

Source of variation	Sum of squares	DF	Mean square	F	Signif of F
Main Effects	3832222.714	10	383222.271	61.844	0.000
JOB	795716.321	3	265238.774	42.804	0.000
COLLEGE	236422.643	1	236422.643	38.154	0.000
INCAT	74922.627	6	12487.104	2.015	0.065
Explained	3832222.714	10	383222.271	61.844	0.000
Residual	1400425.067	226	6196.571		
Total	5232647.781	236	22172.236		

237 cases were processed.
    0 cases (0.0 PCT) were missing.

Due to empty cells or a singular matrix,
higher order interactions have been suppressed.

MULTIPLE CLASSIFICATION ANALYSIS
Grand Mean = 343.738

			Unadjusted		Adjusted for Independents	
Variable + Category		N	Deviation	Eta	Deviation	Beta
JOB						
1	upper mgmt	45	− 77.32		− 134.73	
2	white collar	62	− 87.01		− 54.08	
3	blue collar	76	178.31		228.72	
4	unskilled	54	− 86.63		− 147.54	
				0.82		1.08
COLLEGE						
0	no college	181	28.28		20.79	
1	college	56	− 91.42		− 67.19	
				0.34		0.25
INCAT						
1	0–10000	53	− 84.63		43.79	
2	10000–20000	72	161.89		− 65.99	
3	20000–30000	61	− 53.10		− 21.98	
4	30000–40000	9	− 92.52		16.53	
5	40000–50000	11	− 91.10		46.84	
6	50000–60000	16	− 60.68		86.26	
7	above 60000	15	− 75.07		115.12	
				0.72		0.39
Multiple R-squared						0.732
Multiple R						0.856

Note that we used the "Adjusted for Independents Deviation" column to figure this. This column gives results for one variable after controlling for the influence of other variables in the equation. This is necessary because the "independent" variables may not be independent of each other. For example, it is more likely that people in top management positions make more money than other people. The difference we figure for top management people will be influenced by the difference for high income. The "adjusted" differences take this influence out.

The β values in that column are sometimes used to judge the relative importance of each effect in the model. Job, with a large β value, has more influence on spending than education or income. The R-square is interpreted as in a regression model. It is a measure of the proportion of variance in the dependent variable (spending) that the model explains. In this case, about 73 percent of spending can be explained by the ANOVA model.

There is also a fairly commonly used modification of ANOVA which allows one of the independent variables to be interval or ratio data. Analysis of covariance (ANCOVA) analyzes means of different categories while controlling for the influence of the ratio-independent variable. In the previous example, income categories were used in the model, since ANOVA requires categorical independent variables. ANCOVA can use ratio-data income. It does this essentially by performing lots of little regressions of the ratio-data dependent variable on each group of data defined by combinations of the categorical data. Then for white collar people with no college education, there will be a small regression of spending on income. There is another regression for upper management people with no college education, and so forth.

Its interpretation is also similar: first the significance must be checked to make sure that the main effect variables really have some influence on spending. In Table A.5 job, education, and (ratio data) income all do. To predict spending for a white collar worker with no college education who makes about US$26,500, take the grand mean, add the job and the education impact ($343 - 77 + 22$). Then compute and add the income impact just like in a regression equation ($0.004 \times 26,500 = 106$). This kind of person could be expected to spend about US$395.

This example contains an interaction, an important issue in ANOVA that did not appear in the previous example. An interaction is some impact due to the particular combination of categories that is in addition to any impact from each individual category. Maybe the particular combination of college education with white collar work depresses spending even more than could be expected from the lower spending among white collar workers alone, or among educated people alone. In other words, college-educated white collar workers may spend even less than $343 - 77 - 72 + 106$.

Interactions are nasty things, because they make things difficult to interpret. If there is an interaction between job and education, we cannot talk about jobs alone, and education alone. We cannot generalize about white collar workers, then blue collar workers, then generalize about people who have no college education. We have to talk about white collar workers with college education, then white collar workers without college education, then blue collar workers with college education, and so on. Fortunately, the interaction here is not significant (significance of $F = 0.439$), so we can ignore it.

Technically, any independent variable can interact with any other independent variable. ANOVA and ANCOVA usually report only interactions among categorical

Table A.5. Example of analysis of covariance.

	SPENDING	annual spending on soft drinks, US$
by	JOB	job classification
	COLLEGE	college education
with	INCOME	annual income in US$

Source of variation	Sum of squares	DF	Mean square	F	Signif of F
Main Effects	3834288.307	5	766857.661	126.526	0.000
JOB	3196364.188	3	1065454.729	175.792	0.000
COLLEGE	265167.789	1	265167.789	43.751	0.000
INCOME (Covar)	76988.220	1	76988.220	12.702	0.000
2-way interactions	16479.041	3	5493.014	0.906	0.439
JOB COLLEGE	16479.041	3	5493.014	0.906	0.439
Explained	3850767.348	8	481345.919	79.418	0.000
Residual	1381880.432	228	6060.879		
Total	5232647.781	236	22172.236		

Covariate	Raw regression coefficient
INCOME	0.004

237 cases were processed.
  0 cases (0.0 PCT) were missing.

MULTIPLE CLASSIFICATION ANALYSIS
Grand Mean = 343.738

Variable + Category	N	Unadjusted Deviation	Eta	Adjusted for Independents + Covariates Deviation	Beta
JOB					
1 upper mgmt	45	-77.32		-180.73	
2 white collar	62	-87.01		-77.30	
3 blue collar	76	178.31		197.71	
4 unskilled	54	-86.63		-38.90	
			0.82		0.97
COLLEGE					
0 no college	181	28.28		22.41	
1 college	56	-91.42		-72.43	
			0.34		0.27
Multiple R-squared					0.733
Multiple R					0.856

variables. Table A.4 did not report any interactions because the interactions could not be estimated. The table implicit in that example (JOB × COLLEGE × INCAT) had too many cells (4 × 2 × 7 = 56). With so many cells, there was too little data in most cells to measure anything about the interactions.

Multivariate analysis of variance (MANOVA) and covariance (MANCOVA) do the same thing in principle as ANOVA and ANCOVA, except that instead of one dependent variable, there can be more than one. Then, the statistical test is not measuring whether means of the dependent variable differ across categories. Instead, it measures whether the *vector* of means for the set of dependent variables is different across different categories. Table A.6 shows a MANCOVA output, testing whether the set of means for soft drink spending and for beer spending differ across categories of job and education. Income is a covariate. Hotelling's T is the most commonly used statistic to test jointly across both dependent variables whether an effect has an impact.

Table A.6.   Example of MANOVA.

EFFECT .. WITHIN CELLS Regression
Multivariate tests of significance (S = 1, M = 0, N = 112 1/2)

Test Name	Value	Approx. F	Hypoth. DF	Error DF	Sig. of T
Hotellings	0.05858	6.64844	2.00	227.00	0.002

Regression analysis for WITHIN CELLS error term
Dependent variable .. SPENDSOFT spending on soft drinks, US$

COVARIATE	B	Beta	Std. Err.	t-value	Sig. of t
INCOME	0.00386	0.20867	0.001	3.222	0.001

Regression analysis for WITHIN CELLS error term (CONT.)
Dependent variable .. SPENDBEER spending on beer, US$

COVARIATE	B	Beta	Std. Err.	t-Value	Sig. of t
INCOME	0.00302	0.13398	0.001	2.042	0.042

EFFECT .. COLLEGE
Multivariate tests of significance (S = 1, M = 0, N = 112 1/2)

Test Name	Value	Approx. F	Hypoth. DF	Error	DF Sig. of T
Hotellings	0.10581	12.00973	2.00	227.00	0.000

EFFECT .. JOB
Multivariate tests of significance (S = 2, M = 0, N = 112 1/2)

Test Name	Value	Approx. F	Hypoth. DF	Error DF	Sig. of T
Hotellings	1.05042	39.56569	6.00	452.00	0.000

EFFECT .. JOB BY COLLEGE
Multivariate tests of significance (S = 2, M = 0, N = 112 1/2)

Test Name	Value	Approx. F	Hypoth. DF	Error DF	Sig. of T
Hotellings	0.01771	0.66726	6.00	452.00	0.676

Here, income does have an impact on the vector containing the mean spending on soft drinks and the mean spending on beer (sig. of T = 0.002). Its regression coefficient for soft drink spending is 0.00386, and for beer spending 0.00302. College education and job level also both influence joint spending on soft drinks and on beer. The interaction has no impact (sig. of T = 0.676).

FACTOR ANALYSIS

In factor analysis, there are no dependent or independent variables. Instead, factor analysis is a method that can be used to analyze interdependence among a set of variables. Variables are measures of some underlying concept or dimension, and sometimes there are many measures for one concept. By examining how variables depend on each other (interdependence), one can determine which variables measure the same thing and which ones measure something different.

There are several reasons why this might be necessary. Sometimes the researcher simply wants to identify underlying dimensions that are relevant to consumers. For example, we may be interested in the concepts of prestige, economy, or convenience in automobile ownership. A questionnaire can have many questions all addressing some aspect of these three dimensions. Suppose one question asked about driving down to the mass transit station to avoid waiting for a shuttle bus. Another might ask about perceptions toward struggling through crowds on the train. If the answers to these two questions vary together, i.e., when one answer is "strongly agree", so is the other, and when one is "disagree", so is the other, they are probably measuring the same underlying dimension, which we might call convenience.

Another use of factor analysis is to determine which variable can represent underlying dimensions. By seeing which sets of variables associate with each other, we can identify a few variables that represent the underlying dimensions well. The next time we do research, we can just ask one or two questions about convenience, not ten or twelve, and we will be sure that the two we do use are good at representing convenience.

We may want to take the whole set of variables, with all the information contained in the set, and reduce it to a smaller set of variables which embody all of the variables representing the dimension. This is not quite the same thing as picking out the one or two which represent a concept. Here, a part of each of the old variables remains in the new variable.

Factors are built by taking linear combinations of the variables, so that factor 1 (the first dimension) looks like:

$$F1 = aQ1 + bQ2 + cQ3 + \ldots$$

for as many variables as are used. The second factor has a similar equation, and so forth. As many factors can be built as there are variables in the analysis. Conceptually, each equation is handled much like regression, so that the coefficients $(a, b, c, \ldots)$ are figured out for each factor. A large coefficient (a high factor loading) would indicate that the variable has a big influence on the factor, while small coefficients mean not much influence. Typically, most of the influence from the variables is concentrated in only a few factors, and the rest are all discarded.

In other words, the factor which we might name convenience is a combination of all of those ten to twelve questions on convenience, as well as of any other questions that go into the analysis. Even little pieces of the prestige questions go into building the convenience factor, and little pieces of the convenience questions go into building the prestige factor. Of course, the convenience questions make big contributions to the convenience factor, but only small contributions to the prestige factor. Most of the variation in the original variables can be accounted for with only a few factors.

An example of the use of factor analysis mainly to discover underlying dimensions appears in Table A.7. The data come from an investigation of how Hong Kong consumers use country-of-origin information in evaluating beer. We believed that

Table A.7. Factor loadings of six beer choice criteria by occupational group.

Rotated factor matrix: Professional/Upper management			Variance accounted for by 3 factors
Cbrand	0.90275	−0.02886	−0.14801
Bname	0.54949	−0.11218	0.40819
			71.0%
Image	−0.21859	0.90406	−0.07831
Taste	0.13762	0.78708	0.45356
Price	−0.08200	0.05797	0.85380
Cprod	0.09157	0.12885	0.68036
Rotated factor matrix: White collar/Clerical			
Cbrand	0.71129	0.56783	0.03607
Bname	−0.84617	0.07937	0.05017
			69.6%
Price	0.07334	−0.89976	−0.04937
Cprod	0.17864	0.47099	0.60567
Image	0.47077	−0.06730	0.50512
Taste	0.15789	−0.01817	−0.82281
Rotated factor matrix: Blue collar			
Cbrand	0.66251	0.01849	0.49621
Image	0.63631	0.06652	−0.07112
Price	−0.74596	−0.01770	0.17199	65.2%
Bname	0.01370	0.82058	−0.09752
Taste	0.07584	0.82497	0.05383
Cprod	−0.16394	−0.04388	0.90650
Rotated factor matrix: Students			
Cbrand	0.77520	0.02650	0.08095
Image	0.73195	−0.02728	−0.20061
			72.6%
Taste	0.16173	0.86369	−0.07139
Bname	−0.49911	0.72395	0.06984
Cprod	0.07322	0.16314	0.89589
Price	0.28200	0.37456	−0.74848

Taste = taste of the beer   Image = image of the beer
Cbrand = country of brand   Price = price
Bname = brand name   Cprod = country of production

different segments use country-of-origin differently, quite apart from how important country-of-origin is to them. We needed data to show whether we were correct or not.

How people use a particular criterion in product evaluation can be measured by seeing how it varies with variables measuring some important dimensions. For example, if people think country-of-origin tells them something about price, it should show response patterns similar to those for price questions. If country-of-origin is used to tell something about quality, it should vary with the quality questions.

Six criteria variables were used. Two of them were country-of-origin measures: the country of the brand, and the country of production. The others were brand name, image, taste, and price. The figure shows factor loadings for three factors which account for most of the total variance. For professional respondents, for example, three factors account for 71 percent of all the information contained in the original six variables.

Among professional people and students, country of production loads with price (the highest factor scores for these two criteria are on the same factor). These people use this information to tell them something about price. But among white collar workers, country of production loads with image and taste. For blue collar workers, country of production does not load with anything; it apparently does not convey any information about any beer choice criteria to these people.

DISCRIMINANT ANALYSIS

Conceptually, discriminant analysis is similar to regression and ANOVA. The equations assume a dependent variable, which is some linear function of one or more independent variables. But discriminant analysis should be used when the dependent variable is categorical and the independent variables are interval/ratio data. In other words, the equation is used to predict group membership, whether the dependent variable falls into one or the other of the categories it is made up of.

To do this, discriminant analysis must estimate the coefficients of the linear function (or functions; there is one less function than number of groups). The value of the equation is computed for each observation, and averaged across all observations belonging to each category to get group means. When we have a new observation for which the values of the independent variables are known, we can compute a value, called the discriminant score, for the dependent variable in the equation. If it falls closer to the mean of category one, we could predict that the new observation would belong to category one. If the score was closer to the mean for category two, we would predict it to belong to that category, and so forth.

Let's look at a simple example from the data on use of country-of-origin information in evaluating beer. Suppose we wanted to find out whether the fact that people think imported or domestic beer is higher quality was a function of how important they think image and country-of-origin information is. Quality choice is categorical in the information it provides – either the beer is imported or not.

Image, country of the brand, and country of production are interval data, since they come from a seven point scale ranging from "very important" to "not important at all".

The results are shown in Table A.8. The statistical significance of the model is determined by a measure called Wilks' Lambda, which is checked with a chi-square test. This particular model is not significant at the 90 percent confidence level we have been using. The canonical correlation (0.29) can also be squared to determine the amount of variance in the dependent variable that is explained by

Table A.8.   Example of discriminant analysis.

Dependent: Preference (import/domestic)

Canonical discriminant functions

Fcn	Eigen-value	Pct of var	Cum pct	Canonical corr	After fcn	Wilks' Lambda	Chi square	DF	Sig
				:	0	0.9159	5.578	3	0.1341
1*	0.0918	100.00	100.00	0.2900 :					

* marks the 1 canonical discriminant function
  remaining in the analysis.

Standardized canonical discriminant function coefficients

	FUNC 1
CBRAND	– 0.36051
CPROD	0.95178
IMAGE	0.54336

Structure matrix:

Pooled-within-groups correlations between discriminating variables and canonical discriminant functions (variables ordered by size of correlation within function)

	FUNC 1
CPROD	0.79385
IMAGE	0.46509
CBRAND	0.02300

Canonical discriminant functions evaluated at group means (group centroids)

Group	FUNC 1
1	– 0.49241
2	0.18088

Classification Results

Actual group	No. of cases	Predicted group membership 1	2
Group 1	18	11	7
		61.1%	38.9%
Group 2	49	15	34
		30.6%	69.4%

Percent of "grouped" cases correctly classified: 67.16%

the model. Here, it is only 8.4 percent, not much. So we would not expect this particular discriminant function to be very good at discriminating between which beer people think is higher quality. So in practice, we might not want to use it and would instead look for a better set of variables to predict what people think about imported vs. domestic beer.

However, for the sake of illustration, we continue our analysis of the model. The standardized discriminant function coefficients are the coefficients listed next. They are used to compute discriminant scores of each observation. Discriminant scores cannot be computed directly, but use standardized data, i.e., z-scores. If we have a new observation, we must compute how many standard deviations the value of each independent variable (CBRAND, CPROD, IMAGE) is from the mean of that independent variable.

Then we use these standardized values to compute a discriminant score for the new observation. If the new discriminant score is closer to the group mean for local beer (-0.49), we would predict that the person thinks local beer is better. If the person's discriminant score is closer to the group mean for imported beer (0.18), we predict the person would think imported beer is higher quality. The exact cutoff value between the two group means for domestic and imported beer used to determine what "closer" actually means would depend on the sample sizes of each type of preference in the original analysis.

The correlations between discriminating variables and the discriminant function is a measure of how useful the variable is in discriminating what people think about local or imported beer. The importance they attach to CPROD (country of production) apparently plays a large part in the choice. How important they think CBRAND (country of the brand) is, apparently plays a very small part. (It has a correlation of only 0.02.) If we want to refine the model, we might want to get rid of CBRAND and look at some other variables.

With regression, we talked about R-square as a kind of measure of *managerial* (as opposed to statistical) significance. In discriminant analysis, the managerial measure is found in the classification table. This table shows how many of the observations are actually assigned to the correct group (local vs. import preference). In this case, the discriminant function correctly predicts about 60 percent of people who think local beer is better. It correctly classifies 69 percent of those who think imported beer is higher quality.

Just by flipping a coin, we would expect to get about half of each group correct, since there are two groups, so this function is a little bit better than just flipping a coin. (Formally, we would have to adjust the coin flip probability to account for different sizes of the groups if we wanted to be statistically correct.) On the other hand, if we made absolutely no attempt to discriminate at all, and arbitrarily assumed that everyone thinks imported beer is better, we would be correct 73 percent of the time on this sample.

CLUSTER ANALYSIS

Cluster analysis is actually the name given to a set of techniques whose main purpose is to group observations into categories based on their similarity across some set of criterion variables. (Note: this is not the same as factor analysis, which groups variables, not observations.) In marketing research, some form of cluster analysis might be used for segmentation. In the beer example we have been looking at, we could try to group people into segments according to how important they think various beer choice criteria are.

Cluster analysis does not really have dependent or independent variables. We simply specify a set of variables that are the basis for grouping. Generally, there is no restriction on the type of data in the variable, categorical or interval/ratio, though the application of cluster analysis becomes more complex when a mixture of data types is used. Then, the analyst must specify the method by which observations are determined to be similar to one another, and the method of building clustering. Sometimes, even the number of clusters wanted must be specified. Discussion of all of these methods is beyond the scope of this book, but simply be aware that results can differ depending on which methods are used.

In our opinion, interpretation of cluster analysis is much more *art* than most other statistical techniques discussed here. Getting a meaningful interpretation of results requires both a good understanding of the statistical/mathematical properties of the methods used in the specific clustering, and a good understanding of the market. To show how difficult this might be, refer to Figure A.2, which shows a dendogram resulting from one type of hierarchical clustering. The scale across the top is the distance (in the metric space defined by the criterion variables) at which observations are assigned to clusters. The vertical axis is simply a list of each observation, for example, the 117th respondent, the 129th, the 4th, and so on.

The set of respondents from 117 to 51 are all quite similar to each other in the importance they assign to the set of beer choice criteria. The set of respondents from 70 to 42 are similar to each other. Three other sets are also defined by very close similarity in the part of the dendogram shown here (69–39; 76–37; 128–7). There are also many other sets, since this dendogram of all the observations in the data set was several pages long.

But now the analyst must decide whether he wants lots of little clusters, and whether the differences between any two of these little clusters is meaningful. Sets 1 and 2 are similar to each other a little bit farther away in the metric space, as are sets 4 and 5. The lone exception (respondent 54) is similar to the people in set 3. Then, groups 3, 4, and 5 combine a little further away, and so forth. At a larger distance (less similarity) all of the groups on this page combine with groups on another page. How close do things have to be to be regarded as similar, and how far apart must they be to be regarded as different enough to treat as different segments?

Though there are some statistical attempts to answer these questions, they do not seem entirely convincing. Anyway, we think that the question of how many clusters

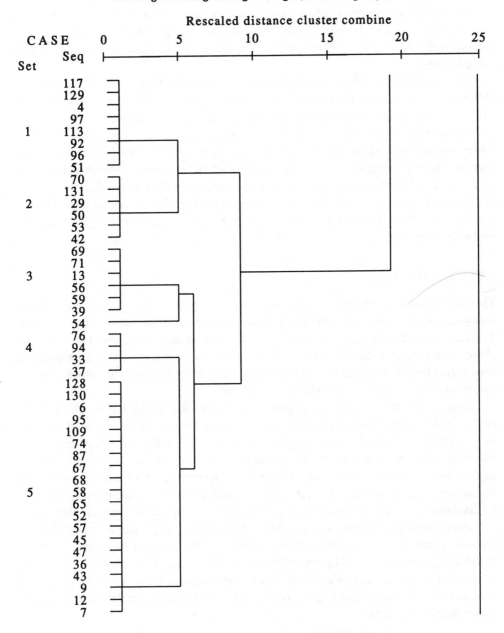

Figure A.2.   Example of a cluster analysis dendrogram.

are used is really a managerial issue. Twenty little clusters in a sample of several hundred respondents (defining clusters at the closest distance) would not be very useful for most application. On the other hand, a niche marketer may be looking for that little segment that is quite different from the mass of people. Defining only two clusters based on the last combination at a very great distance might not be very useful, either, if one of those two clusters is also made up of two groups of people who are not really very similar. Experience is the main way to learn about dealing with these issues.

Once clusters are defined, so that we have segments of people who think similarly about beer choice criteria, then we may be able to associate demographic character-istic with each cluster so that people in it can be more easily targeted.

Since there is so much *art* in this technique, it is even more important than with most other techniques to have a way to check the results. One common way is to keep a "holdout" sample, i.e., do not use some of the data in the analysis. Then, the analysis can be performed again on the other part of the data to see if similar results are obtained. If we can easily identify the same number of clusters and these clusters associate similarly with the demographic variables, then the analyst's choices were probably good ones.

OTHER METHODS

The methods discussed above (regression, ANOVA, factor, discriminant, and cluster analysis) are all a level of complexity above simple statistics such as basic means, frequencies, and cross-tabs. They are fairly common in marketing research where the clients (external or within the company) are relatively experienced at using marketing research. There are still more techniques that generally require even more sophisti-cation in proper application and managerial use.

Some of these techniques we have touched on, like conjoint (tradeoff) analysis and AID (Automatic Interaction Detector). These and other advanced statistical tech-niques all have their place, so long as they are truly used to increase our under-standing of the marketing situation, and not simply to show that we know how to do high-powered number-crunching. Generally, successful use of such sophisticated techniques requires considerable statistical knowledge by the marketing manager. If he does not understand the technique, he will not trust it and will not use the results.

All of these techniques are available in software packages these days. Subject to the researcher being able to explain them well, and the manager being able to under-stand them, they should all be part of the researcher's tool-box, what we have called in Chapter 2 the researcher's "craft". Our best friend in these heady realms is the statistician . . . but only if he is also a real researcher: a searcher after answers and not just a number-cruncher!

Appendix B

Selected Statistical Tables

The following statistical tables were reproduced or modified from Richard A. Johnson and Dean W. Wichern, *Applied Multivariate Statistical Analysis*, Third Edition, © 1992, pp. 629–35. Reproduced by permission of Prentice Hall, Englewood Cliffs, NJ.

Table B.1. Standard normal probabilities

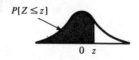

$P[Z \le z]$

z	.00	.01	.02	.03	.04	.05	.06	.07	.08	.09
.0	.5000	.5040	.5080	.5120	.5160	.5199	.5239	.5279	.5319	.5359
.1	.5398	.5438	.5478	.5517	.5557	.5596	.5636	.5675	.5714	.5753
.2	.5793	.5832	.5871	.5910	.5948	.5987	.6026	.6064	.6103	.6141
.3	.6179	.6217	.6255	.6293	.6331	.6368	.6406	.6443	.6480	.6517
.4	.6554	.6591	.6628	.6664	.6700	.6736	.6772	.6808	.6844	.6879
.5	.6915	.6950	.6985	.7019	.7054	.7088	.7123	.7157	.7190	.7224
.6	.7257	.7291	.7324	.7357	.7389	.7422	.7454	.7486	.7517	.7549
.7	.7580	.7611	.7642	.7673	.7703	.7734	.7764	.7794	.7823	.7852
.8	.7881	.7910	.7939	.7967	.7995	.8023	.8051	.8078	.8106	.8133
.9	.8159	.8186	.8212	.8238	.8264	.8289	.8315	.8340	.8365	.8389
1.0	.8413	.8438	.8461	.8485	.8508	.8531	.8554	.8577	.8599	.8621
1.1	.8643	.8665	.8686	.8708	.8729	.8749	.8770	.8790	.8810	.8830
1.2	.8849	.8869	.8888	.8907	.8925	.8944	.8962	.8980	.8997	.9015
1.3	.9032	.9049	.9066	.9082	.9099	.9115	.9131	.9147	.9162	.9177
1.4	.9192	.9207	.9222	.9236	.9251	.9265	.9279	.9292	.9306	.9319
1.5	.9332	.9345	.9357	.9370	.9382	.9394	.9406	.9418	.9429	.9441
1.6	.9452	.9463	.9474	.9484	.9495	.9505	.9515	.9525	.9535	.9545
1.7	.9554	.9564	.9573	.9582	.9591	.9599	.9608	.9616	.9625	.9633
1.8	.9641	.9649	.9656	.9664	.9671	.9678	.9686	.9693	.9699	.9706
1.9	.9713	.9719	.9726	.9732	.9738	.9744	.9750	.9756	.9761	.9767
2.0	.9772	.9778	.9783	.9788	.9793	.9798	.9803	.9808	.9812	.9817
2.1	.9821	.9826	.9830	.9834	.9838	.9842	.9846	.9850	.9854	.9857
2.2	.9861	.9864	.9868	.9871	.9875	.9878	.9881	.9884	.9887	.9890
2.3	.9893	.9896	.9898	.9901	.9904	.9906	.9909	.9911	.9913	.9916
2.4	.9918	.9920	.9922	.9925	.9927	.9929	.9931	.9932	.9934	.9936
2.5	.9938	.9940	.9941	.9943	.9945	.9946	.9948	.9949	.9951	.9952
2.6	.9953	.9955	.9956	.9957	.9959	.9960	.9961	.9962	.9963	.9964
2.7	.9965	.9966	.9967	.9968	.9969	.9970	.9971	.9972	.9973	.9974
2.8	.9974	.9975	.9976	.9977	.9977	.9978	.9979	.9979	.9980	.9981
2.9	.9981	.9982	.9982	.9983	.9984	.9984	.9985	.9985	.9986	.9986
3.0	.9987	.9987	.9987	.9988	.9988	.9989	.9989	.9989	.9990	.9990
3.1	.9990	.9991	.9991	.9991	.9992	.9992	.9992	.9992	.9993	.9993
3.2	.9993	.9993	.9994	.9994	.9994	.9994	.9994	.9995	.9995	.9995
3.3	.9995	.9995	.9995	.9996	.9996	.9996	.9996	.9996	.9996	.9997
3.4	.9997	.9997	.9997	.9997	.9997	.9997	.9997	.9997	.9997	.9998
3.5	.9998	.9998	.9998	.9998	.9998	.9998	.9998	.9998	.9998	.9998

Table B.2.   Student's *t*-distribution critical points

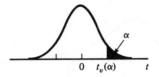

d.f.		α				
ν	one-tailed	.100	.050	.025	.010	.005
	two-tailed	.200	.100	.050	.020	.010
1		3.078	6.314	12.706	31.821	63.657
2		1.886	2.920	4.303	6.965	9.925
3		1.638	2.353	3.182	4.541	5.841
4		1.533	2.132	2.776	3.747	4.604
5		1.476	2.015	2.571	3.365	4.032
6		1.440	1.943	2.447	3.143	3.707
7		1.415	1.895	2.365	2.998	3.499
8		1.397	1.860	2.306	2.896	3.355
9		1.383	1.833	2.262	2.821	3.250
10		1.372	1.812	2.228	2.764	3.169
11		1.363	1.796	2.201	2.718	3.106
12		1.356	1.782	2.179	2.681	3.055
13		1.350	1.771	2.160	2.650	3.012
14		1.345	1.761	2.145	2.624	2.977
15		1.341	1.753	2.131	2.602	2.947
16		1.337	1.746	2.120	2.583	2.921
17		1.333	1.740	2.110	2.567	2.898
18		1.330	1.734	2.101	2.552	2.878
19		1.328	1.729	2.093	2.539	2.861
20		1.325	1.725	2.086	2.528	2.845
21		1.323	1.721	2.080	2.518	2.831
22		1.321	1.717	2.074	2.508	2.819
23		1.319	1.714	2.069	2.500	2.807
24		1.318	1.711	2.064	2.492	2.797
25		1.316	1.708	2.060	2.485	2.787
26		1.315	1.706	2.056	2.479	2.779
27		1.314	1.703	2.052	2.473	2.771
28		1.313	1.701	2.048	2.467	2.763
29		1.311	1.699	2.045	2.462	2.756
30		1.310	1.697	2.042	2.457	2.750
40		1.303	1.684	2.021	2.423	2.704
60		1.296	1.671	2.000	2.390	2.660
120		1.289	1.658	1.980	2.358	2.617
∞		1.282	1.645	1.960	2.326	2.576

Table B.3. χ^2 critical points

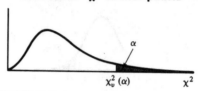

$\chi_v^2 (\alpha)$ χ^2

d.f. v	α								
	.990	.950	.900	.500	.100	.050	.025	.010	.005
1	.0002	.004	.02	.45	2.71	3.84	5.02	6.63	7.88
2	.02	.10	.21	1.39	4.61	5.99	7.38	9.21	10.60
3	.11	.35	.58	2.37	6.25	7.81	9.35	11.34	12.84
4	.30	.71	1.06	3.36	7.78	9.49	11.14	13.28	14.86
5	.55	1.15	1.61	4.35	9.24	11.07	12.83	15.09	16.75
6	.87	1.64	2.20	5.35	10.64	12.59	14.45	16.81	18.55
7	1.24	2.17	2.83	6.35	12.02	14.07	16.01	18.48	20.28
8	1.65	2.73	3.49	7.34	13.36	15.51	17.53	20.09	21.95
9	2.09	3.33	4.17	8.34	14.68	16.92	19.02	21.67	23.59
10	2.56	3.94	4.87	9.34	15.99	18.31	20.48	23.21	25.19
11	3.05	4.57	5.58	10.34	17.28	19.68	21.92	24.72	26.76
12	3.57	5.23	6.30	11.34	18.55	21.03	23.34	26.22	28.30
13	4.11	5.89	7.04	12.34	19.81	22.36	24.74	27.69	29.82
14	4.66	6.57	7.79	13.34	21.06	23.68	26.12	29.14	31.32
15	5.23	7.26	8.55	14.34	22.31	25.00	27.49	30.58	32.80
16	5.81	7.96	9.31	15.34	23.54	26.30	28.85	32.00	34.27
17	6.41	8.67	10.09	16.34	24.77	27.59	30.19	33.41	35.72
18	7.01	9.39	10.86	17.34	25.99	28.87	31.53	34.81	37.16
19	7.63	10.12	11.65	18.34	27.20	30.14	32.85	36.19	38.58
20	8.26	10.85	12.44	19.34	28.41	31.41	34.17	37.57	40.00
21	8.90	11.59	13.24	20.34	29.62	32.67	35.48	38.93	41.40
22	9.54	12.34	14.04	21.34	30.81	33.92	36.78	40.29	42.80
23	10.20	13.09	14.85	22.34	32.01	35.17	38.08	41.64	44.18
24	10.86	13.85	15.66	23.34	33.20	36.42	39.36	42.98	45.56
25	11.52	14.61	16.47	24.34	34.38	37.65	40.65	44.31	46.93
26	12.20	15.38	17.29	25.34	35.56	38.89	41.92	45.64	48.29
27	12.88	16.15	18.11	26.34	36.74	40.11	43.19	46.96	49.64
28	13.56	16.93	18.94	27.34	37.92	41.34	44.46	48.28	50.99
29	14.26	17.71	19.77	28.34	39.09	42.56	45.72	49.59	52.34
30	14.95	18.49	20.60	29.34	40.26	43.77	46.98	50.89	53.67
40	22.16	26.51	29.05	39.34	51.81	55.76	59.34	63.69	66.77
50	29.71	34.76	37.69	49.33	63.17	67.50	71.42	76.15	79.49
60	37.48	43.19	46.46	59.33	74.40	79.08	83.30	88.38	91.95
70	45.44	51.74	55.33	69.33	85.53	90.53	95.02	100.43	104.21
80	53.54	60.39	64.28	79.33	96.58	101.88	106.63	112.33	116.32
90	61.75	69.13	73.29	89.33	107.57	113.15	118.14	124.12	128.30
100	70.06	77.93	82.36	99.33	118.50	124.34	129.56	135.81	140.17

Table B.4. *F*-distribution critical points ($\alpha = .10$)

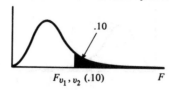

$F_{v_1, v_2} (.10)$ F

v_2 \ v_1	1	2	3	4	5	6	7	8	9	10	12	15	20	25	30	40	60
1	39.86	49.50	53.59	55.83	57.24	58.20	58.91	59.44	59.86	60.19	60.71	61.22	61.74	62.05	62.26	62.53	62.79
2	8.53	9.00	9.16	9.24	9.29	9.33	9.35	9.37	9.38	9.39	9.41	9.42	9.44	9.45	9.46	9.47	9.47
3	5.54	5.46	5.39	5.34	5.31	5.28	5.27	5.25	5.24	5.23	5.22	5.20	5.18	5.17	5.17	5.16	5.15
4	4.54	4.32	4.19	4.11	4.05	4.01	3.98	3.95	3.94	3.92	3.90	3.87	3.84	3.83	3.82	3.80	3.79
5	4.06	3.78	3.62	3.52	3.45	3.40	3.37	3.34	3.32	3.30	3.27	3.24	3.21	3.19	3.17	3.16	3.14
6	3.78	3.46	3.29	3.18	3.11	3.05	3.01	2.98	2.96	2.94	2.90	2.87	2.84	2.81	2.80	2.78	2.76
7	3.59	3.26	3.07	2.96	2.88	2.83	2.78	2.75	2.72	2.70	2.67	2.63	2.59	2.57	2.56	2.54	2.51
8	3.46	3.11	2.92	2.81	2.73	2.67	2.62	2.59	2.56	2.54	2.50	2.46	2.42	2.40	2.38	2.36	2.34
9	3.36	3.01	2.81	2.69	2.61	2.55	2.51	2.47	2.44	2.42	2.38	2.34	2.30	2.27	2.25	2.23	2.21
10	3.29	2.92	2.73	2.61	2.52	2.46	2.41	2.38	2.35	2.32	2.28	2.24	2.20	2.17	2.16	2.13	2.11
11	3.23	2.86	2.66	2.54	2.45	2.39	2.34	2.30	2.27	2.25	2.21	2.17	2.12	2.10	2.08	2.05	2.03
12	3.18	2.81	2.61	2.48	2.39	2.33	2.28	2.24	2.21	2.19	2.15	2.10	2.06	2.03	2.01	1.99	1.96
13	3.14	2.76	2.56	2.43	2.35	2.28	2.23	2.20	2.16	2.14	2.10	2.05	2.01	1.98	1.96	1.93	1.90
14	3.10	2.73	2.52	2.39	2.31	2.24	2.19	2.15	2.12	2.10	2.05	2.01	1.96	1.93	1.91	1.89	1.86
15	3.07	2.70	2.49	2.36	2.27	2.21	2.16	2.12	2.09	2.06	2.02	1.97	1.92	1.89	1.87	1.85	1.82
16	3.05	2.67	2.46	2.33	2.24	2.18	2.13	2.09	2.06	2.03	1.99	1.94	1.89	1.86	1.84	1.81	1.78
17	3.03	2.64	2.44	2.31	2.22	2.15	2.10	2.06	2.03	2.00	1.96	1.91	1.86	1.83	1.81	1.78	1.75
18	3.01	2.62	2.42	2.29	2.20	2.13	2.08	2.04	2.00	1.98	1.93	1.89	1.84	1.80	1.78	1.75	1.72
19	2.99	2.61	2.40	2.27	2.18	2.11	2.06	2.02	1.98	1.96	1.91	1.86	1.81	1.78	1.76	1.73	1.70
20	2.97	2.59	2.38	2.25	2.16	2.09	2.04	2.00	1.96	1.94	1.89	1.84	1.79	1.76	1.74	1.71	1.68
21	2.96	2.57	2.36	2.23	2.14	2.08	2.02	1.98	1.95	1.92	1.87	1.83	1.78	1.74	1.72	1.69	1.66
22	2.95	2.56	2.35	2.22	2.13	2.06	2.01	1.97	1.93	1.90	1.86	1.81	1.76	1.73	1.70	1.67	1.64
23	2.94	2.55	2.34	2.21	2.11	2.05	1.99	1.95	1.92	1.89	1.84	1.80	1.74	1.71	1.69	1.66	1.62
24	2.93	2.54	2.33	2.19	2.10	2.04	1.98	1.94	1.91	1.88	1.83	1.78	1.73	1.70	1.67	1.64	1.61
25	2.92	2.53	2.32	2.18	2.09	2.02	1.97	1.93	1.89	1.87	1.82	1.77	1.72	1.68	1.66	1.63	1.59
26	2.91	2.52	2.31	2.17	2.08	2.01	1.96	1.92	1.88	1.86	1.81	1.76	1.71	1.67	1.65	1.61	1.58
27	2.90	2.51	2.30	2.17	2.07	2.00	1.95	1.91	1.87	1.85	1.80	1.75	1.70	1.66	1.64	1.60	1.57
28	2.89	2.50	2.29	2.16	2.06	2.00	1.94	1.90	1.87	1.84	1.79	1.74	1.69	1.65	1.63	1.59	1.56
29	2.89	2.50	2.28	2.15	2.06	1.99	1.93	1.89	1.86	1.83	1.78	1.73	1.68	1.64	1.62	1.58	1.55
30	2.88	2.49	2.28	2.14	2.05	1.98	1.93	1.88	1.85	1.82	1.77	1.72	1.67	1.63	1.61	1.57	1.54
40	2.84	2.44	2.23	2.09	2.00	1.93	1.87	1.83	1.79	1.76	1.71	1.66	1.61	1.57	1.54	1.51	1.47
60	2.79	2.39	2.18	2.04	1.95	1.87	1.82	1.77	1.74	1.71	1.66	1.60	1.54	1.50	1.48	1.44	1.40
120	2.75	2.35	2.13	1.99	1.90	1.82	1.77	1.72	1.68	1.65	1.60	1.55	1.48	1.45	1.41	1.37	1.32
∞	2.71	2.30	2.08	1.94	1.85	1.77	1.72	1.67	1.63	1.60	1.55	1.49	1.42	1.38	1.34	1.30	1.24

Table B.5. *F*-distribution critical points (α = .05)

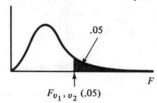

F_{v_1, v_2} (.05)

v_2 \ v_1	1	2	3	4	5	6	7	8	9	10	12	15	20	25	30	40	60
1	161.5	199.5	215.7	224.6	230.2	234.0	236.8	238.9	240.5	241.9	243.9	246.0	248.0	249.3	250.1	252.1	252.2
2	18.51	19.00	19.16	19.25	19.30	19.33	19.35	19.37	19.38	19.40	19.41	19.43	19.45	19.46	19.46	19.47	19.48
3	10.13	9.55	9.28	9.12	9.01	8.94	8.89	8.85	8.81	8.79	8.74	8.70	8.66	8.63	8.62	8.59	8.57
4	7.71	6.94	6.59	6.39	6.26	6.16	6.09	6.04	6.00	5.96	5.91	5.86	5.80	5.77	5.75	5.72	5.69
5	6.61	5.79	5.41	5.19	5.05	4.95	4.88	4.82	4.77	4.74	4.68	4.62	4.56	4.52	4.50	4.46	4.43
6	5.99	5.14	4.76	4.53	4.39	4.28	4.21	4.15	4.10	4.06	4.00	3.94	3.87	3.83	3.81	3.77	3.74
7	5.59	4.74	4.35	4.12	3.97	3.87	3.79	3.73	3.68	3.64	3.57	3.51	3.44	3.40	3.38	3.34	3.30
8	5.32	4.46	4.07	3.84	3.69	3.58	3.50	3.44	3.39	3.35	3.28	3.22	3.15	3.11	3.08	3.04	3.01
9	5.12	4.26	3.86	3.63	3.48	3.37	3.29	3.23	3.18	3.14	3.07	3.01	2.94	2.89	2.86	2.83	2.79
10	4.96	4.10	3.71	3.48	3.33	3.22	3.14	3.07	3.02	2.98	2.91	2.85	2.77	2.73	2.70	2.66	2.62
11	4.84	3.98	3.59	3.36	3.20	3.09	3.01	2.95	2.90	2.85	2.79	2.72	2.65	2.60	2.57	2.53	2.49
12	4.75	3.89	3.49	3.26	3.11	3.00	2.91	2.85	2.80	2.75	2.69	2.62	2.54	2.50	2.47	2.43	2.38
13	4.67	3.81	3.41	3.18	3.03	2.92	2.83	2.77	2.71	2.67	2.60	2.53	2.46	2.41	2.38	2.34	2.30
14	4.60	3.74	3.34	3.11	2.96	2.85	2.76	2.70	2.65	2.60	2.53	2.46	2.39	2.34	2.31	2.27	2.22
15	4.54	3.68	3.29	3.06	2.90	2.79	2.71	2.64	2.59	2.54	2.48	2.40	2.33	2.28	2.25	2.20	2.16
16	4.49	3.63	3.24	3.01	2.85	2.74	2.66	2.59	2.54	2.49	2.42	2.35	2.28	2.23	2.19	2.15	2.11
17	4.45	3.59	3.20	2.96	2.81	2.70	2.61	2.55	2.49	2.45	2.38	2.31	2.23	2.18	2.15	2.10	2.06
18	4.41	3.55	3.16	2.93	2.77	2.66	2.58	2.51	2.46	2.41	2.34	2.27	2.19	2.14	2.11	2.06	2.02
19	4.38	3.52	3.13	2.90	2.74	2.63	2.54	2.48	2.42	2.38	2.31	2.23	2.16	2.11	2.07	2.03	1.98
20	4.35	3.49	3.10	2.87	2.71	2.60	2.51	2.45	2.39	2.35	2.28	2.20	2.12	2.07	2.04	1.99	1.95
21	4.32	3.47	3.07	2.84	2.68	2.57	2.49	2.42	2.37	2.32	2.25	2.18	2.10	2.05	2.01	1.96	1.92
22	4.30	3.44	3.05	2.82	2.66	2.55	2.46	2.40	2.34	2.30	2.23	2.15	2.07	2.02	1.98	1.94	1.89
23	4.28	3.42	3.03	2.80	2.64	2.53	2.44	2.37	2.32	2.27	2.20	2.13	2.05	2.00	1.96	1.91	1.86
24	4.26	3.40	3.01	2.78	2.62	2.51	2.42	2.36	2.30	2.25	2.18	2.11	2.03	1.97	1.94	1.89	1.84
25	4.24	3.39	2.99	2.76	2.60	2.49	2.40	2.34	2.28	2.24	2.16	2.09	2.01	1.96	1.92	1.87	1.82
26	4.23	3.37	2.98	2.74	2.59	2.47	2.39	2.32	2.27	2.22	2.15	2.07	1.99	1.94	1.90	1.85	1.80
27	4.21	3.35	2.96	2.73	2.57	2.46	2.37	2.31	2.25	2.20	2.13	2.06	1.97	1.92	1.88	1.84	1.79
28	4.20	3.34	2.95	2.71	2.56	2.45	2.36	2.29	2.24	2.19	2.12	2.04	1.96	1.91	1.87	1.82	1.77
29	4.18	3.33	2.93	2.70	2.55	2.43	2.35	2.28	2.22	2.18	2.10	2.03	1.94	1.89	1.85	1.81	1.75
30	4.17	3.32	2.92	2.69	2.53	2.42	2.33	2.27	2.21	2.16	2.09	2.01	1.93	1.88	1.84	1.79	1.74
40	4.08	3.23	2.84	2.61	2.45	2.34	2.25	2.18	2.12	2.08	2.00	1.92	1.84	1.78	1.74	1.69	1.64
60	4.00	3.15	2.76	2.53	2.37	2.25	2.17	2.10	2.04	1.99	1.92	1.84	1.75	1.69	1.65	1.59	1.53
120	3.92	3.07	2.68	2.45	2.29	2.18	2.09	2.02	1.96	1.91	1.83	1.75	1.66	1.60	1.55	1.50	1.43
∞	3.84	3.00	2.61	2.37	2.21	2.10	2.01	1.94	1.88	1.83	1.75	1.67	1.57	1.51	1.46	1.39	1.32

Notes and References

Preface

1. Neil Bruce Holbert: "Research: The Ways of Academe and Business", *Business Horizons*, February, 1976, p. 36.

Chapter 1

1. "New Marketing Research Definition Approved", *Marketing News*, January 2, 1987, p. 1.

Chapter 2

1. Jack Honomichl (in *Marketing News*, May 27, 1991, p. H1) gives a figure of US$3.1 billion, while ESOMAR (see note 2) gives US$2.4 billion.
2. Data derived from Jan Oostveen and Joost Wouters: "The ESOMAR Annual Market Study: The State of the Art of Marketing Research", *Marketing and Research Today*, November, 1991, p. 214. In addition to the source in note 1, see also data on US spending for marketing research in *Advertising Age*, May 27, 1991, Section H; and for Asian markets, see Karen Winton: "Regional Research Strikes it Rich", *Asian Advertising and Marketing*, March, 1991, p. 35 ff.

   Asian spending is still low by European standards. For example, 1990 estimates for Hong Kong and China combined are US$17 million, and South Korea showed an estimated US$15 million for 1990 (Source: Dr. Peter Weldon of Survey Research Group Ltd.). Each of these is less than marketing research spending for Portugal (US$20 million), a country still on the fringe of European development. But East and Southeast Asia (excluding Japan, but including South Korea, Hong Kong, China, Taiwan, Singapore, Malaysia, Philippines, Thailand, and Indonesia) show good growth potential for marketing research. Weldon estimates the total market at US$73 million for 1990, US$88 million for 1991, and US$106 million for 1992, a gain of 45 percent between 1990 and 1992.
3. "Towards a New Sampling System in Malaysia" (p. 7), and "The 'Bird of Paradise' Market Monitor" (p. 8), both in *Research News*, Frank Small & Associates, January, 1987.
4. "Koreans Consider China Opportunities" (p. 4), and "Saving Lives in Indonesia" (p. 2), both in *SRG News*, Survey Research Group, May, 1991.

5. Karen Winton: "Regional Research Strikes it Rich", *Asian Advertising and Marketing*, March, 1991, p. 37.

6. Benjamin Gilad: "U.S. Intelligence System: Model for Corporate Chiefs?", *Journal of Business Strategy*, May–June, 1991, p. 20.

7. Laurie Ashcraft: "The Evolving Marketing Research Industry", *Marketing Research*, June, 1991, p. 23.

8. Calvin L. Hodock: "The Decline and Fall of Marketing Research in Corporate America", *Marketing Research*, June, 1991, p. 12 ff.

9. Vivian L. Gernand: "Fantasies for Sale: Marketing Products that Do Not Yet Exist", *Journal of Business and Industrial Marketing*, Summer–Fall, 1991, pp. 32, 34.

Chapter 3: Bibliographical references

Susan P. Douglas and C. Samuel Craig: *International Marketing Research*, Englewood Cliffs, NJ: Prentice-Hall, 1983.

Herbert Jacob: *Using Published Data: Errors and Remedies*, Beverly Hills, CA: Sage Publications, 1984.

David W Stewart: *Secondary Research: Information Sources and Methods*, Beverly Hills, CA: Sage Publications, 1984.

Chapter 5: Bibliographical references

Pamela L. Alreck and Robert B. Settle: *The Survey Research Handbook*, Homewood, IL: Richard D. Irwin, Inc., 1985.

Floyd J. Fowler Jr.: *Survey Research Methods*, Revised Edition (Applied Social Research Methods Series, Vol. 1), Beverly Hills, CA: Sage Publications, 1988.

Paul J. Lavrakas: *Telephone Survey Methods: Sampling, Selection, and Supervision* (Applied Social Research Methods Series, Vol. 7), Beverly Hills, CA: Sage Publications, 1987.

Chapter 6

1. Earl Naumann and Douglas J. Lincoln: "Non-tariff Barriers and Entry Strategy Alternatives: Strategic Marketing Implications", *Journal of Small Business Management*, April, 1991, p. 68.

2. Tim Powell: "Despite Myths, Secondary Research is a Valuable Tool", *Marketing News*, September 2, 1991, p. 28.

3. Mary Goodyear: "Research is a Question of Method," *Asian Advertising and Marketing*, November, 1989, p. 54.

4. Daniel T. Seymour: "Seeing is Believing with Systematic Observation", *Marketing News*, August 28, 1987, p 36.

5. Brian Dumaine: "Corporate Spies Snoop to Conquer", *Fortune*, November 7, 1988, p. 66.

Chapter 11

1. Fred Posner: "If Product Testing's the Answer, then What's the Question" paper presented at the American Marketing Association New York Chapter Conference on "Product Testing — Today and Tomorrow", January 20, 1972.

2. Jack M. Ross: "Parameters of Product Testing", paper presented at the Columbia

University Graduate School of Business Executive Development Program in Market Research, December 4, 1973.

3. Jane Hutchison: "Aerobics Craze Key to Reebok Success" *South China Morning Post*, Hong Kong, November 17, 1991, p. M13.

4. Margaret R. Roller: "Blind Testing Has its Merits", *Marketing News*, September 3, 1990, p. 4.

Chapter 12

1. Leo Burnett: "Leo Burnett Tells What Makes a Package Sell", *Package Engineering: Marketing Edition*, April, 1971, p. 16a.

2. Louis Cheskin: "Your Package: Marketing Success or Disaster?", *Package Engineering: Marketing Edition*, April, 1971, p. 16.

3. Mark Speece and Douglas L. MacLachlan: "Measurement of Milk Container Preferences", *Journal of International Food and Agribusiness Marketing*, Vol. 3, No. 1, 1991, pp. 43–64.

4. Cheskin, p. 16g.

5. John Lister: "That Delicate Concept of Nuance", *Advertising Age*, September 29, 1986, p. 40.

6. *New York Times*, July 10, 1991, p. D1.

7. *Advertising Age*, July 15, 1991, p. 16.

8. Laura Loro: "More Testing of Less", *Advertising Age*, July 8, 1991, p. 24.

9. Sid Shapiro: "Focus Groups: The First Step in Package Design", *Marketing News*, September 3, 1990, p. 17.

10. *Ibid.*

11. Jonathan B. Asher: "Packing: The Interactive Fifth 'P' of Marketing", *Marketing Review*, January, 1985, p. 21.

12. Jeremy Golden: "What's in a Name", *Asian Advertising and Marketing*, September, 1987, p. 10.

13. Helen M. Katze: "Get Tough When Choosing a Name for Your Product", *Marketing News*, November 7, 1986, p. 26.

14. David Shipley, Graham J. Hooley, and Simon Wallace: "The Brand Name Development Process", *International Journal of Advertising*, Vol. 7, 1988, p. 253. This is a remarkably complete article, with both conceptual and applied elements, focusing on the notion of name research in the UK.

15. Leon Richardson: "Make a Name for Yourself", *Asian Business*, July, 1988, p. 42.

16. *Ibid.*

Chapter 13

1. John Morton and Melanie E. Rys: "Traditional Pricing Research Falls Short", *Marketing News*, January 2, 1987, p. 19.

2. Allan J. MaGrath: "Ten Timeless Truths About Pricing", *Journal of Business and Industrial Marketing*, Vol. 6, Nos. 3–4, Summer/Fall, 1991, p. 16.

3. *Ibid.*, p. 18.

4. See note 1.

Chapter 14

1. Scanners have become the subject of a substantial body of literature, much of it technical and transitory. Two especially worthwhile articles are Michael J. Wolfe: " '90s Will See 'Great Leap Forward' in Sales Tracking", *Marketing News*, September 3, 1990, p. 2; and Howard Schlossberg: "IRI, Nielsen, Slug It Out in 'Scanning Wars' ", *Marketing News*, September 2, 1991, p. 1.

Chapter 15

1. The terminology can be confusing. The broad activity is "promotion" — literally "moving forward" — with a capital "P". It is one of the four *P*'s often alluded to. The "below-the-line" part (the "line" is essentially a carry-over from accounting practice) was originally called "collateral" ("on the side") because it was once relatively minor and was paid for out of money left over when we finished with our advertising expenses. "Below-the-line" activities are sometimes collectively called "promotion" (or "sales promotion"), with a small "p". For our purposes, we conceive of "below-the-line" as a conglomerate of specifically "sales promotion" activities (couponing, sampling, etc.) plus such things as public relations, publicity, sponsorships, event marketing, etc. See also Chapter 16.

2. Robert J. Lavidge: "Seven Tested Ways to Abuse and Misuse Strategic Advertising Research", *Marketing Research*, March, 1990, p. 41.

3. Kirk Brady: "How to Design Effective Advertising Impact Studies", *Marketing News*, January 2, 1987, p. 52.

4. Scott Hume: "Shop Humanizes Research", *Advertising Age*, August 13, 1990, p. 50. (The article quotes Mr. Rathjen and deals with a technique called Category Dynamics, developed by Henderson Advertising of Greenville, South Carolina.)

5. Cyndee Miller: "Researchers Balk at Testing Rough Ads for 'Likability' ", *Marketing News*, September 2, 1991, p. 2. The article also contains a valuable discussion of using "rough" forms of advertising in pretesting.

6. Scott Hume: "Nielsen Adds Print", *Advertising Age*, May 20, 1991, p. 42.

7. Verne B. Churchill: "The Role of Ad Hoc Survey Research in a Single Source World", *Marketing Research*, December, 1990, p. 22.

Chapter 16

1. Figures come from Donnelley Marketing's Annual Survey of Promotional Practices, as reported in Scott Hume: "Trade Promos Devour Half of All Marketing Dollars", *Advertising Age*, April 13, 1992, p. 3.

2. Judann Dagnoli: "Heinz Marketing Gets $100 Million Boost", *Advertising Age*, September 18, 1991, p. 7.

3. See, for example, Marti J. Rhea and Tom K. Massey: "Sales Promotion Ripe for Research", *Marketing News*, September 12, 1986, p. 26. In this piece, the authors describe the difficulties they encountered in trying to get information from sales promotion agencies on the effectiveness of sales promotion. They note that these agencies often proved secretive, defensive, and reluctant to share data.

4. Robert C. Blattberg: "Behavioral Research in the 1990's", *Marketing Research*, September, 1991, p. 16. The article is invaluable as a source of ideas for what has been done and still needs to be done in many behavioral areas, such as modelling, segmentation, positioning, new products, advertising, etc., as well as promotions. In its discussion of promotion

specifically (as part of an extensive bibliography) are cited two important works: Blattberg and Neslin's book *Sales Promotions* (Englewood Cliffs, NJ: Prentice Hall, 1990), and Neslin and Shoemaker's article, "An Alternative Explanation for Lower Purchase Rates After Promotion Purchases", *Journal of Marketing Research*, May, 1989, pp. 205–13.

5. Blattberg, p. 17.

6. Anonymous: "Study: Some Promotions Change Consumer Behavior", *Marketing News*, October 5, 1990, p. 12.

7. Steve Kingsbury: "Study Provides Overview of Who's Redeeming Coupons — and Why", *Marketing News*, January 2, 1987, p. 56.

8. Jeffrey S. close and Don Goncalves: "Market Research Assures Measurable PR Results", *Marketing News*, September 3, 1990, p. 49.

9. *Ibid.*, p. 53.

10. *Ibid.*

Chapter 17

1. Russell J. Haley: "Benefit Segmentation: 20 Years Later", *Journal of Consumer Marketing*, January, 1982; p. 5.

2. These causes of trouble are detailed in Theodore Karger: "Diagnostic Research Can Provide Treatment for Old, Ailing Brands", *Marketing News*, September, 1986, p. 18.

3. William A. Jolly: "Research the Key Weapon in Marketing Wars", *Asian Advertising and Marketing*, February, 1989, p. 42.

4. Jerry Stafford and Neil Upmeyer: "Product Shortages Hamper Research in Soviet Union", *Marketing News*, September 3, 1990, p. 6.

5. Jerry Stafford and Louis Tong: "Vast China Market Just Waiting to be Researched", *Marketing News*, September 12, 1986, p. 1.

6. Judie Lannon: "Developing Brand Strategies Across Borders", *Marketing and Research Today*, August, 1991, p. 161.

Chapter 18

1. Purnell H. Benson: "Pitfalls in New Product Research", *Marketing Review*, January, 1974, p. 11.

2. Alfred Gruber: "The Marketing Manager's Guide to New Product Invention", American Management Association, AMACOM, 1977, p. 6.

3. Benson, p. 12.

4. *Ibid.*

5. Mark Speece: "Marketing Management for Agricultural Innovation: Observations from Kordofan, Sudan", in *Proceedings of the Third International Conference on Marketing and Development*, New Delhi, January, 1991; Calcutta: Indian Institute of Management, pp. 290–5.

Chapter 19

1. Fyodor Nosov: "New Russian Icons", *Advertising Age*, March 2, 1992, p. 16.

2. Dennis E. Clayson: "The Product of Research is Information", *Marketing Educator*, Fall, 1989, p. 5.

INDEX

THE AUTHORS

Neil Bruce Holbert, PhD, is Senior Lecturer in Marketing at the Chinese University of Hong Kong. He previously has had extensive teaching experience in New York City as an adjunct at Columbia University, New York University, Fordham University, Pace University, and Queens College. He has also taught at David Syme School of Business in Melbourne, Australia. Dr. Holbert's business experience also spans many decades, and includes time at Metropolitan Life, Forbes, Chesebrough-Pond's, Grey Advertising, and Philip Morris. His AB and MBA are from Columbia University, and his PhD is from New York University. His books, monographs, and articles span the fields of marketing research, marketing strategy, and marketing planning.

Mark W. Speece, PhD, is a consultant with EastGate International and marketing director at Hong Kong Wells, a Chinese trading and manufacturing company. He has taught international marketing, marketing research, and statistical methodology for a decade at Central Washington University, the University of Alaska Fairbanks, and the Chinese University of Hong Kong before returning to the business world. Dr. Speece has also lived and worked in Europe and the Middle East. His BA is from the University of Nebraska, MA and PhD in Middle East Geography from the University of Arizona, and PhD in Marketing from the University of Washington. His numerous publications have focused especially on the fields of international marketing, agricultural and food products marketing, and the role of marketing in economic development.